Gaston Gallimard

Pierre Assouline

GASTON GALLIMARD

A Half-Century of
French Publishing

TRANSLATED BY HAROLD J. SALEMSON

A Helen and Kurt Wolff Book

Harcourt Brace Jovanovich, Publishers

San Diego   New York   London

Approximately a hundred pages have been cut from the original French edition in this translation.

Printed in the United States of America

Library of Congress Cataloging-in-Publication Data
Assouline, Pierre.
Gaston Gallimard: a half-century of French publishing.
Translation of: Gaston Gallimard.
"A Helen and Kurt Wolff book."
Bibliography: p.
Includes index.
1. Gallimard, Gaston, 1881–1975. 2. Publishers and publishing—France—Biography. 3. Publishers and publishing—France—History—20th century. 4. French literature—Publishing—History—20th century.
5. France—Intellectual life—20th century. I. Title.
Z305.G3A8713 1987   070.5′092′4 [B]   87-202
ISBN 0-15-134293-8

Designed by G. B. D. Smith

ISBN 0-15-134293-8

First United States edition

A B C D E

For Angela

Contents

Illustrations

Gaston with Paul Léautaud
Gaston with Marcel Jouhandeau
Gaston, Claude, and Christian Gallimard
Gaston in his later years

Foreword

———

Why Gallimard? Because he was unique and exceptional.

Certainly there were other great publishers who were not insignificant. But of all those who began their careers in the first decade of this century, he was the only one who, as his life drew to an end, could thumb through his company's thick catalogue and say: French literature, *c'est moi*.

He authored no book, yet his name appeared on all of them. His oeuvre runs to millions of volumes, the tone and color of which can be unmistakably recognized in the library of any well-read Frenchman of the twentieth century. Gaston Gallimard devoted his life to betting on the posterity of young unknown authors. From the very beginning, he wanted durability to be his trademark. As a young publisher, he preferred to sacrifice easy, immediate profits and instead take under his wing manuscripts the audience for which might not extend beyond a narrow intellectual élite. But after a few years of practical experience, the amateur that he had once been quickly realized that publishing was above all a business. The nonchalant aesthete, the devotee of concerts and dances, then turned into a formidable businessman, a shrewd bargainer, a determined persuader.

Not that he became overnight a model administrator and unerring discoverer of talent. But having been grazed by defeat, he learned the lessons of that temporary setback, and surrounded himself, first of all, with people of quality who, each in his own way and all together—through their competence, their perseverance, and their way with people—would construct the literary pantheon bearing the name of Gaston Gallimard.

He never stopped trying to bring together under his imprint the very best of French and foreign literatures. Every time he became aware of an error in judgment or a serious oversight, he tried to do the impossible—to get back authors who had strayed to other publishers, convinced as he was that outside the House of Gallimard there were no writers worthy of the name. To achieve his ends, the man whom everyone called Gaston would stop at nothing. He would use charm and wit, kindness and attention, to be sure, but more often, if people and events demanded it, intransigence, prevarication, and even double dealing. The business of ideas, however attractive, was nonetheless a business. Whenever necessary, Gaston Gallimard made that apparent to his various rivals—but with infinite tact, class, diplomacy, and that lordly manner of his that made all the difference in the world.

To try to assure the durability of his works, he published specialized magazines and popular weeklies, brought out books totally opposed to his own tastes and basic intentions, spurned the first World War, and learned to live with the second.

The results of this amazing adventure are to be found on miles of shelves throughout the bookstores of France, and in the best of libraries from Tokyo to Texas. Yet in our dictionaries there is not one biographical entry about this man who made it possible for so many others to express and communicate their ideas. What ingratitude!

A few writers—the Goncourt brothers, Paul Léautaud, Louis Guilloux, André Beucler—have brought Gaston Gallimard alive in their diaries or memoirs. But it is probably in the romans à clé that we get the best picture of him, whether he is portrayed as Gaillard in Francis Jourdain's *Sans remords ni rancune* (Without Remorse or Rancor), Brouillard in André Beucler's *La Fleur qui chante* (The Singing Flower), or Georges Bourguignon in Jacques Rivière's *Aimée*.

The fact that these authors used such literary stratagems indicates how little Gaston Gallimard wished to have people talk about him, at least in his lifetime. He always refused to write his memoirs, despite the most urgent requests of his associates, friends, and peers.

He refused out of respect for real writers, out of bashfulness, or from lack of self-confidence. But mostly, out of honesty: remembering, he would have had too much to tell, and some of the truths would have tarnished the fame of many authors, the prestige of the House of Gallimard, and Gaston himself.

When he died shortly before his ninety-fifth birthday, he carried his secrets with him. This biography, the first to deal with its impressive and largely unknown subject, is also a monograph on half a century of French publishing. In following the steps of Gaston Gallimard, we necessarily encounter his peers—Bernard Grasset, Robert Denoël, René Julliard, and so many others who left their mark on the field.

Strangely, French publishers have brought out few books dealing with themselves. Even worse, they often discourage researchers by not giving them access to the files of their firms, thus perpetuating a tradition of secrecy that is in no way mythical. The exceptions can be counted on the fingers of one hand, and even they deal only with periods long gone.

To reassemble the fascinating jigsaw of Gaston Gallimard's life, I drew on many sources: hundreds of books, unpublished files, private correspondences, the columns of contemporary newspapers, and the witnesses themselves. The result of this research does not claim to achieve historical objectivity, but rather to have intellectual honesty toward a single goal—to answer the question: how does one become Gaston Gallimard?

"Gentlemen, out of respect for the discretion and modesty of M. Gaston Gallimard, no comment will be made here upon his death, which occurred on December 25, 1975, except to designate someone to chair this meeting and proceed to name a new president and chief executive officer."

It is 3:00 P.M. on Rue Sébastien-Bottin, in Paris. Behind the windows of the impressive town house unostentatiously marked with the *NRF* logo, several men have gathered, on this January 15, 1976, around a table in the room where the company's board meetings are generally held. It is their first meeting since the death of the founding father twenty-one days earlier.

The board members look solemn. They are sad. They have been affected by the shock. Even though Gaston Gallimard had not run his company for years, even though he had turned the reins of power over to his son Claude, he had nonetheless put in an appearance every day at the offices of the company he had created. With Gaston gone, a page had been turned once and for all in the history of publishing.

After the concert of public tributes that followed the announcement of his death, no one was more aware of this than the members of this board: Claude Gallimard, Gaston's son; Robert Gallimard, Gaston's nephew; Bernard Huguenin; Paul-Marc Schlumberger; and the two delegates of the workers' committee, Ambroise-Victor Pujebet and Guy Germain. One man was conspicuous by his absence: Emmanuel Couvreux, Gaston's oldest friend, administrator and financier of the Société Gallimard from the very beginning. He was ill. On January 13 he had sent the board a letter of apology: "My health will not allow me to take part in the meeting of our board at which the new head of our company is to be named, following the disappearance of my great old friend Gaston Gallimard. With much emotion, I approve in advance the board's choice of his son Claude, who is well equipped to maintain the traditions that have become associated with our company. I deeply regret not being able to be among you to join in your exceptional decision."

After this message was read, Claude Gallimard pointed out that the maintenance of traditions, to which Emmanuel Couvreux alluded, was also mentioned in a letter his father left before his death. These few lines constitute a sort of moral testament in which Gaston Gallimard asks his successors to follow the editorial policy of the company's founders, in other words, "to seek out new talents, which entails the publication of many manuscripts of doubtful commercial possibilities. Thus the vocation of the company is to establish and increase a literary backlist and not pursue overnight profits from commercial successes that have no sequel. It also requires that the shareholders have a great deal more patience."

Since the mission now given him could be carried out only in this way, Claude Gallimard asked all his associates to give him their approval. The board's vote was unanimous. At 4:30 P.M. the new president adjourned the meeting.

His was a weighty inheritance. Gaston Gallimard had spent more than half a century building it up.

1

His Father

———

1881-1900

"Coachman, to the City Hall of the Ninth Arrondissement!"

Three men have left their mutual home, a moneyed bourgeois private residence at 79 Rue Saint-Lazare, just opposite the Church of the Trinity, to take a hansom cab over to Rue Drouot and there officially declare to the clerk in charge the birth on January 18, 1881, of a baby with the given names of Gaston Sébastien.

"Who is the father?"

"I am. Paul Sébastien Gallimard, thirty-one years of age, architect. The mother is my wife, Lucie Gallimard, née Duché, twenty-two years of age, housewife. And these are the godfathers: my father Sébastien Gustave Gallimard, fifty-nine, investor, and my brother-in-law, Gabriel Duché, thirty, businessman. The child was born two days ago at nine-thirty in the morning."

For Paul Gallimard, the birth of his first son was no doubt the most important event of the budding year. He was a strange man. There was nothing of the fop about him, but he was well turned-out, his elegance discreet and becoming. He was appealing, with a fine intelligence, and attractive. His name in itself was significant, for in Old French it meant writing desk or inkwell. This patronym—so well suited to the newborn Gaston, when one knows how he entered into posterity—was Burgundian in origin. Yet for a long time it was believed that Gaston Gallimard came from Auvergne. That was because, apart from his reputed miserliness, a quality attributed to Auvergnats, the real fortune in the family came from the maternal side, from the Duchés.

Lucie Duché's grandfather, a boilermaker named Chabrier, started his fortune by inventing and marketing the "protective nipple," to be used by nursing women. After this, he left his town of Thiers, in the Puy-de-Dôme, to go to Paris. Being exceptionally ingenious and imaginative, he rapidly climbed the social ladder during the reign of King Louis-Philippe, the Bourgeois King—(1830–48), the so-called July Monarchy that in the eyes of some was the best of all republics. Arriving a few years before the golden age of urbanization encouraged by Baron Haussmann, Chabrier went into the lighting business and was commissioned to install lamp posts on the principal streets of Paris and to provide oil for their lights. When these were replaced by gaslight, his fortune was already made. He promptly invested it in villas, land, buildings, and theaters. At his death, his heirs were professional rentiers, living off their investments, and knew already that their children would do the same.

Before Lucie was thirty years old, the Goncourts were to describe her in their *Diary* as a "brunette with soft black eyes, eyes that sometimes question you as do the eyes of sphinx-women," but also as a woman "so hysterical that taking a ride in a carriage with her makes sensible people exclaim, 'Coachman, stop! Let me out!'"

She was friendly with painters and also with writers. She would be familiar with the friends of her son Gaston, enjoy their company on weekends or during vacations at the family mansion at Bénerville, appropriately named "Villa Lucie," and entertain them at dinner in Paris on Rue Saint-Lazare, where they were always welcome at the family table. When they wrote to Gaston, many of them never failed to ask about his mother. Léon-Paul Fargue would later even dedicate to her his famous book *Le Piéton de Paris* (The Walker in Paris).

As for Paul Gallimard, he was a character in every sense of the word. Very much at home in society, faithful to his own idea of himself, he took no pride in the money he had inherited, but rather in the extent of his culture, the infallibility of his taste, and his reputation for artistic flair. Born at Suresnes in 1850, he had had an easy adolescence and a carefree youth. As an adult he still did not work, but lived off the income his mother supplied him, spending most of his time in the company of impecunious artists. In the Gallimard family, whose men had traditionally been merchants, lawyers, or stockbrokers, such independence set him apart; his milieu, while not Protestant, nevertheless conceived of salvation as coming from the work ethic.

He liked to loaf, live, read, go to art shows, and devote his days and evenings to the pleasures of the eyes and the senses. But not in the same way as his wife. Whereas Lucie discreetly tried her hand at painting, displaying very dependable taste in the shadow of Auguste Renoir, Paul would think nothing of retouching a detail in a painting by Claude Monet that he had just bought.

After finishing his secondary education at the Lycée Condorcet, dabbling a bit in a musical career, and serving as private secretary to the Duc de Morny, he enrolled at the Ecole des Beaux-Arts, where he studied painting with Barillot and architecture with Daumet. Having put in time at these famous studios, he later felt no compunction in describing himself on many official occasions as an architect. It did strike him as unseemly, given his youth, to say that he lived off his income. Feeling cramped by his surroundings, his family, and its society, he chose to travel—not to run away from France but to strengthen his artistic taste. He visited the best libraries and richest museums in the world, in order to measure his intelligence against that of the aesthetes of Europe and the Americas. During one long stay in Argentina, he even drew up a *Catalogue Raisonné of the Works of Art Constituting the Museum of Buenos Aires.*

Courtesy incarnate, Paul Gallimard could also be hateful. His misanthropy was tempered only by the subtlety and elegance of his witticisms. Curious about everything, his aim in life was never to be bored. Since his fortune covered his needs, he could devote himself entirely to the play of ideas, to the enrichment of his mind. The life of Paul Gallimard was the ideal of any enthusiastic dilettante. He was, moreover, a collector, which let him give a coherent form to his passions and tastes by organizing them. Even as an adolescent he collected fine books, remarkable first editions, and rare bindings. This taste of the bibliophile was never to leave him, and the treasures of his library were for a long time his greatest pride. They even surprised the Goncourt brothers, who had seen many other libraries. In 1889, telling of a dinner at Asnières at the home of the illustrator Raffaeli, they noted in their *Journal*:

> In this idiotic world of bibliophiles, in this world of servants of old printed matter, this Gallimard is really a revolutionary, going so far as to spend 3,000 francs, like some superintendent of finance under the ancien régime, to treat himself to a de luxe edition of a modern book, and a book such as *Germinie Lacerteux*.

Revolutionary, indeed! Paul Gallimard had ordered and supervised the production of this de luxe edition of the Goncourt brothers' novel, specifying that only three copies be printed: the first for himself, the second for Edmond de Goncourt, and the third for Gustave Geffroy, who had written a preface dealing with the place of women in the Goncourts' work. The copy that went to the Goncourts turned out to be even more valuable; they decided to have Eugène Carrière do an oil portrait of them in it. Paul Gallimard was bested in his own field—that of rareness and quality.

In 1904 he had the publisher Floury bring out, at his expense, a magnificent quarto volume of *Constantin Guys, l'historien du Second Empire* (Constantin Guys, Historian of the Second Empire) by Gustave Geffroy, with woodcuts by Tony and Jacques Beltrand from Guys's watercolors and drawings. Copy No. 1, the only one on

Japan paper with the full set of illustrations and twelve original drawings, at the time cost 2,000 francs.

This enthusiastic amateur, who could afford all his fancies, did
not hesitate to take up the pen himself. In 1910, at the request of the
Mercure de France publishers, he wrote a very erudite preface for
an anthology of the verse of John Keats. And in 1928, shortly before
his death, he published—under the Gallimard imprint, naturally—
Les Etreintes du passé (Embraces of the Past), a novel in the form of
a dialogue divided into a prologue and five days, taking place in
Dalmatia in 1847. But it was arguably through close association with
the painters of his time that Paul Gallimard came truly into his own.

An habitué of the galleries in the neighborhood of the Madeleine,
Durand-Ruel, Georges Petit, and Bernheim, he had been trained in
a good school by his father Gustave who, around 1860, was already
deeply interested in the Barbizon painters.[1] Paul met Pissarro at the
home of the dealer Alphonse Portier, who sold him several of his
canvases. He got into the habit of visiting Monet at Giverny and
observing the master at work for hours on end, before buying some
of his works. But Auguste Renoir was the one with whom he was
the most intimate. Between 1891 and 1895 the two men spent two
successive summers at the Gallimard mansion at Bénerville, where
young Gaston, aged twelve, leisurely observed the white-bearded
gentleman daubing at his canvas, when the boy was not indeed posing
for him, along with his younger brothers, Jacques and Raymond.

Renoir and Paul Gallimard traveled together to Spain, Great Brit-
ain, and Holland. The painter often advised the collector, leading him
to buy a Goya, for example, which took its place on the walls of 79
Rue Saint-Lazare, alongside a Fragonard, an El Greco, nine Corots,
seven Delacroix, eight Daumiers, as well as works by Boudin,
Manet, Courbet, Monet, Degas, Mary Cassatt, Toulouse-Lautrec,
Sisley, Cézanne, and Carrière, many of which had been acquired
in 1892 and 1893 and covered all the wall space of the apartment.

It was an impressive little private museum; when the Gallimard
collection was sold, it would be dispersed throughout the world to

enrich some of the most prestigious collections. Paul Gallimard, as commissioner of the Centennial Exposition of 1900 and organizer of some of the exhibits at the Salon d'Automne, was in 1903 one of the two collectors who, according to the painter himself, owned the largest number of Renoir canvases. The other was probably his friend Maurice Gangnat, who had bought 180 of them.[2]

Unfortunately for art, toward the end of the century the patron gradually began to lose interest in what had been his devouring passion. He turned his well-known taste in another direction—society women, demimondaines, cocottes, and actresses. His old friend, the architect and art critic Frantz Jourdain, who had been his intimate for half a century, thought the reason for this was "a fit of pique resulting from the ingratitude he found in the art and literary people to whom he had been generous," as reported in the Goncourts' *Journal*. The Goncourts themselves noted the change in "this man who had lived only for books, then for paintings, and now spent all his evenings at the Variétés, a flower in his lapel, among the party girls from his building. He had turned into a complete roué. He declared aloud that artists, once his sole companions, were melancholy, sad, and bothersome beings who had nothing but darkness to offer, while he now wanted to be surrounded by gaiety and joy."

Paul Gallimard a roué? That refined aesthete losing himself in vulgarity? His friends found it hard to believe: their dear dilettante was gradually slipping away from them. Soon he invested in several theaters (the Variétés, the Ambigu-Comique); set up several lady friends in sumptuous surroundings; entertained at his table the frivolous and brilliant personalities of the flighty Boulevard theater world,* instead of the painters and poets so recently present there; separated unofficially from his wife; and took up residence in a town house on Rue de Clichy, not far from the Casino de Paris. Regularly, each month, one or two of the paintings were removed from the family home to be hung in Paul Gallimard's new house. Those around him

---

*The Boulevard theaters of Paris are the French equivalent of Broadway.—TRANS.

understood the break to be final when the walls at Rue Saint-Lazare really began to show the empty spaces.

From that time on, Gaston developed a distrust of his father. The shy and slightly prudish adolescent, rather awkward in his ways and full of admiration for his father's facility and ease, could not forgive him for having made formal, in the eyes of all, his rejection of his wife, the mother Gaston adored. It is not innocently that in one roman à clé (Jacques Rivière's *Aimée*) Georges Bourguignon, one of the leading characters, says: " 'For my part, you know . . . I never had the slightest respect for my father. As far back as I can remember, as small as I can make myself in my imagination, I never find anything in my heart for him but contempt.' "

Beneath the crushing personality of his father, Gaston for a long time had feelings for him that were every bit as contradictory as the character of Paul Gallimard himself. Much later, dining with friends, Gaston described his father as "an absolute unbounded egotist who loved no one, not his wife or children, not his friends or mistresses," but who was given to the most unexpected affections. He went on to tell how his father, seeing a man throw a live kitten down a sewer, bribed the authorities to fish the kitten out and took it home with him, where he kept it for several years, treating it as if it were a king and he its abject slave.[3]

Such was the man in whose shadow young Gaston grew up. He did not just inherit his paintings: some of his father's ways would later surface in his own attitudes toward women, the theater, money, the arts, and life. Artists might call this mimesis; psychoanalysts, father rejection; and physicians, the laws of heredity. As if it mattered. But right there in the biography of his father is one of the keys to the complex character that Gaston would become.

1889: Gaston is eight. It is an understatement to say that his life gravitates around the Church of the Trinity. In the morning, when the governess opens his bedroom windows, the church is the first thing he sees. The sound of its bells is henceforth a constant background noise, as is the bustle of this handsome upper-middle-class street, then largely filled with pedestrians, gentlemen in fine hats and ladies in crinolines, disturbed in their walks only by horses, carriages, and coaches.

When not playing in Trinity Square, Gaston also walks there with his brothers and the servants. That year, the new Saint-Lazare railway station has just opened its doors for the World's Fair. On the same street and for the same occasion, construction has been completed on the Hôtel Terminus, connected to the station by a walkway, and boasting a magnificent reading lobby sought out by tourists as much as by people of the neighborhood.

General Boulanger is triumphally elected to Parliament in Paris after having been acclaimed in many provinces. His name is linked to a political crisis bigger than the movement he inspired, and the near-dictatorial "good general" succeeds mainly in radicalizing the general public, impelling it toward either socialism or nationalism. Paris feels it was lucky to pull through the crisis, but in the provinces the movement has fostered a strong antiparliamentary feeling.

Had it not been for the news vendors yelling in the streets, Rue Saint-Lazare would have seemed unaware of this political agitation. The suburbs indeed were agitated, but they were far away. The people around here mainly rush to get seats for the shows at the La Bodinière theater; they reserve tables well in advance at the Trap restaurant, where Emile Zola holds literary dinners with his Naturalist school, or at another restaurant, the Paillard, which would soon supplant the famous Café Anglais as a place for suppers and assignations. One must be seen at them, as one must go to the Café Napolitain for ices with the pick of newspaper people and writers who are soon to abandon the Café Riche, which has lost its tone.

That is what young Gaston can see, when not watching the people coming out of the Théâtre Mogador, right at the corner of "his" street and Rue de la Chaussée d'Antin. Often he spends long periods looking out the windows at the behest of a family friend, the painter Eugène Carrière, who shows him how to sketch passersby quickly with a few brush strokes. Sometimes Gaston and his brothers sit as models for Carrière after lunch when, to their great delight, he agrees to do some sketching. One of his most famous paintings shows the three little Gallimards looking at a picture book. Gaston at the time is a dreamy, reserved boy; the presence of women both causes him to blush and fills him with joy. At fourteen he spends hours at the window, dreaming that he sees the horses of a carriage bolt and run away, and that he rushes out in time to grab the reins and halt them, and be affectionately thanked by the beautiful lady passenger.[4]

His mother found that in this respect he was truly Paul's son, when one day she took him to the horse races at Longchamp. Standing in the enclosure conversing with an elegant young woman, she suddenly felt her little boy, his hair still curled, wearing short pants and a sailor's blouse, let go of her hand and take her friend's, which he rapturously petted, murmuring, "Pretty lady! Pretty lady!"[5]

From that day on, Lucie Gallimard was sure her son would be a womanizer. And she would be proved right. To be fair, the small circle within which he was raised was predominantly matriarchal. His grandfather was never a man to impose his tastes on others. His father was less and less to be seen. The whole family building on Rue Saint-Lazare was in female hands. On the second floor—the choice one in this period before elevators—lived Gaston's paternal grandmother; on the third, her daughter-in-law Lucie Gallimard, Gaston's mother; and above them, the Duché cousins.

Mme. Gustave—as the family friends called her, identifying her by her husband's given name—had become a pure flower of the bourgeois upper crust. "The total absence of originality was the one original thing about this good lady, who had no problems or axes to grind," wrote a friend more than half a century later, describing the whole family at length under the transparent pseudonym of the Gaillards.[6] According to him, Mme. Gustave's sole concern was money; it was her only standard by which to measure success, human qualities, or culture. She frequently referred to "my world," "my society," "my property," "my birds," unable to see beyond the strict limits of her own circle, her community, and the dogmas she had embraced for all time. Nothing nor anyone could shake her convictions, and certainly not the course of history.

For months on end, every Monday evening at her home, at the

big dinner that brought together all the old moneychangers, lawyers, and fiduciaries of the Gallimard family, in whose footsteps her son Paul had refused to follow, Mme. Gustave would state before sitting down, "There will be no mention of the Dreyfus Affair."[7] Naturally, that was the main subject of conversation. By dessert the discussion had begun taking a violent turn, albeit only verbally.

On weekends and during vacations, the tone was different because of the difference in setting. It inspired more serenity in discussions, placing people and events slightly apart from time, within a snug, calm atmosphere in which the air was suddenly breathable, and worries and obligations of city life seemed suspended. Such was life at Bénerville. For years, Gaston would have a deep feeling for this place at the shore between Houlgate and Deauville.

Gaston often made good use of rainy days there to delve into the summer library his father had assembled with great good taste. Sunday mornings, ritually, Paul Gallimard had all the horses in the stable harnessed up, to take the family and their guests to Mass at Trouville. The younger members, having gone the mile or so that separated the manor gate from the highway, walked the rest of the way on foot. Others took the Decauville, the little railroad that the children enjoyed so much, or else the family omnibus driven by their coachman. And traditionally, at the same exact minute every Sunday, Mme. Gustave would stop the convoy so she could pay a visit to Dérubé, the famous Trouville grocer.

Only Paul Gallimard and Frantz Jourdain skipped the obligation of Mass, which they considered less an act of devotion than a matter of "being seen." They preferred to sit and talk over cigars, reminiscing about their student days at the Beaux-Arts or commenting on what they had read in the latest issue of *Le Temps*, the semiofficial newspaper of the Third Republic, which boasted of having Sainte-Beuve and Anatole France on its staff.

After the traditional Sunday luncheon, everyone played croquet. The game quickly became an obligation just like Mass, but for different reasons: past master in the handling of the mallet, Paul Gallimard ran the game like a diabolical autocrat, taking pleasure in inventing complicated rules and giving himself handicaps of all sorts, the better to humiliate his opponents by a victory that was anything but modest.[8] This was why Gaston enjoyed croquet far less than hunting in Sologne with his uncle Maurice Gangnat, who let him and his younger brother Raymond carry the cartridges and guns. There, in the woods and forests, he was able to dream. His uncle forgave him if he did not concentrate. But not his father, who never missed a chance to make fun of his absentmindedness, in croquet as in everyday life.

He was so absentminded that he forgot that everyone was obliged to assume a pose; so he adopted none. To say that he just let life take its course meant that he did without hairshirt or halo. He did not wish to be admired. Those who put nothing above the will to power take such an attitude to be a baneful sign of weakness. As for me, I see in it a noble modesty, the proof of one's authenticity and intelligence, when it is more than miserable make-believe. There was nothing affected about Gaston; the simultaneously naive and percipient child lived on in him as an adolescent who was still shy and not yet aware of his seductive powers. Even those who wrote him off as irresolute could not completely escape that power. . . . Gaston charmed by making no effort to charm: while seductive, there was nothing of the seducer about him, and one needed fear no trap from him. One spontaneously wanted to like him and could not resist the feeling.

But that did not mean that young Gaston was defenseless; quite the contrary. He had an intense inner life. He put all the power of his inertia in the service of a determined will to independence. That was what lay behind all his demands: never to feel himself the slave of anyone.

Though indolent, he was elusive. Very friendly, but not demonstrative, never distant but often absentminded. It was very hard to see in his beautiful eyes the moment at which the interest he took in you began to disappear or change, the point at which he no longer heard you, or whether what you had said to him had not shunted him to some secret siding, or sent him off *into the beyond*, as the poets of the day as well as railroad employees put it.[9]

Having a nature inclined to nonchalance but not to indifference (he was much too sensitive for that), Gaston got his first taste of the world at the lycée, a society without women, family, or painters. It was another world that he suddenly discovered in 1891, entering the sixth form,* a five-minute walk from his home. Students were still called to the classroom not with a whistle but with the roll of a drum. The recess courtyard was not a very appealing playground, but the peristyle of the building had a classical look not unattractive to the adolescent. And his lycée, Condorcet, which enjoyed a fine reputation and enrolled boys from the best families, is generally remembered by its alumni as a haven of peace and freedom, especially as compared to some of the stricter and more austere establishments over on the Left Bank. Gaston spent all his school years there, until 1898, and formed lasting friendships. The poet Stéphane Mallarmé taught literature there from 1871 on, and during Gaston's time M. Jalliffier, a famous textbook author, introduced the pupils to history, while Paul and Adolphe Ruzé, masters at arms, taught them to handle the fencing foil like true noblemen.

During his seven years at the Lycée Condorcet, Gaston regularly crossed paths with youths of his generation who would later make names for themselves in a variety of fields: André Citroën, Jacques Copeau, André Maginot, and Louis Farigoule (later known as Jules Romains). Several had been there a few years ahead of him—Marcel Proust, Robert de Flers, Henri Bernstein, André Tardieu—and others would follow him on the same old wooden benches—Emile Henriot, Jean Cocteau, and Henri Torrès, among others.

In the third form, Gaston noticed a tall, somewhat heavy lad, a bit awkward, lazy, and absentminded, who seemed interested only in French and history. He took a liking to him, soon occupied a

*Roughly equivalent to sixth grade.—TRANS.

neighboring seat in class, and tried desperately to come to his assistance during oral quizzes in Greek and Latin, when his friend Roger would stand dramatically mute and be raked over the coals by the teacher: "Monsieur Martin du Gard, the only remarkable thing about you seems to be your neckties!"[10] In these incidents of embarrassment and class merriment, a strong, solid friendship developed between them that would go on for decades.

1896: two years after the sentencing of Captain Dreyfus, and two years before the appearance of Zola's *J'accuse*. Gaston was "for Dreyfus, like all the other young men,"[11] at a time when two Frances came face to face in the streets, around the family dinner table, in newspapers and cafés. This was one of the main subjects of conversation for Gaston and his friends when they got together, in the Passage du Havre after school, among well-to-do youths all formed in the same mold. They tried to outdo one another in the daring of their behavior and opinions, whether about the Dreyfus Affair, the rise of the Socialists in the municipal elections, or that memorable scandal created at the Théâtre de l'Œuvre by the first performance of Alfred Jarry's outrageous farce, *Ubu roi*.

That year, in the greatest secrecy, Gaston tried his hand at writing a book, a dream he had had for a long time, without daring to take it too seriously. It was titled *Diogène* (Diogenes), but was not the story of the famous Greek sage who, when Alexander asked him what he could do for him, replied, "Just step out of my sunlight." His Diogenes was merely a man who was against civilization. Gaston got some ten pages written, then gave it up. That was the end of his literary ambitions.[12]

His teachers, however, encouraged him. In 1897–98, the year he was to take the baccalauréat exam, Gaston was much appreciated by his philosophy instructor, Pierre Janet. For the first trimester, Janet gave him the very high mark of 17 out of 20 with the comment, "much good will and effort, seems to know how to succeed"— which is not without piquancy, when one knows what the publisher's career was to be; and in the second trimester, 16 out of 20 with the notation, "good work and some progress, needing a little more effort to stay up among the first,"[13] which was much better than some of his classmates.

But Gaston preferred not to heed the advice of his philosophy instructor. He did not continue his studies, but followed his natural penchant for indolence, letting himself be carried along by events, quite determined to subordinate everything to his personal satisfaction, the pleasures of the flesh and the spirit.

2

A Young Publisher

1900-1914

"What do I like best? Vacation!"

Gaston Gallimard was always frank about things. At twenty, all he cared about was leisure, idleness, luxury, women, and friends. He made no bones about it. After all, his father had lived that way for years. Why not he? His schedule is indicative of the life he arranged for himself. Mornings he lingered in bed, making notes after an attentive reading of the newspapers and magazines. He borrowed ideas here and there, a phrase that appealed to him, a useful address.

Mainly addresses. In his small circle of dandies, one could not shop just anywhere, so Gaston devoted extreme care to his choice of clothes and accessories. His shirts came from Charvet, his hats from Gélot or Delion, his knobbed canes from Antoine, and without ever leaving Faubourg Saint-Honoré, he ordered his suits from the finest custom tailors. He was elegant in his walk, his attitudes, his gestures. He went in for quality, but with discretion. He abhorred bad taste and exhibitionism and affected the ease of the aesthete as opposed to the stiffness of phony nobility, forever keeping his hands in the pockets of his jacket, until he twisted it all out of shape.

Afternoons he walked in the Bois de Boulogne among elegant ladies with their parasols, when not spending hours in search of some elusive book in the bookdealers' stalls on the quays. At times he dropped in on one of the many literary salons of Paris. Often he would stop at the Café Weber on his way to the theater, his favorite entertainment. In order not to go back home to Rue Saint-Lazare to change into a tuxedo, Gaston acquired the habit of always wearing a very simple navy-blue suit with a matching bow tie, making it into a uniform he would wear all his life.

When not at the theater, he would attend a concert or a dance. But his evening always ended at one of three great restaurants— Maxim's, Larue, or the Pré-Catelan—which he fancied for their fame, the quality of their service and food, and the women to be met there. The timid young man had grown bolder. He still blushed when a female presence affected him, but he had gained assurance, grasping that his very embarrassment could also be part of his charm.

Gone were the days when, at seventeen, he paced back and forth several times a day before the windows of Antoinette, a lawyer's daughter who lived at her parents' on Rue Pierre I de Serbie, without daring to go any further. When Antoinette came to the parties given by his mother on Rue Saint-Lazare, Gaston could not bear to see her dancing in someone else's arms. Rather than trying to stop her, as his pride told him to, he would run to the servants' quarters to hide his head in a basket of dirty clothes, so no one could read the jealousy on his face. He went out with her for several years and even thought of marrying her, until his mother talked him out of it, arguing that he was too ordinary and she richer than he. Gaston would then try to forget Antoinette by playing up to an equally young and attractive demimondaine, Fernande Dulac. He paid her a devoted but distant court, never daring to make an overture since she always had an escort, whether in a restaurant or at the opera. One evening, to attract her attention, he got the notion of filling the lady's carriage with hundreds of flowers, which he did with the complicity of the coachman. He then hid in the shadows just in time to see the young woman's surprise and hear her effusively thank her escort of the evening.[1]

Soon Gaston was past twenty-five. He had learned how to go about things, even though that somewhat bruised his inner nature, his reserve mixed with embarrassment, modesty, and pride.

> He accepted from women whatever they might give him that was exquisite, but very firmly rejected anything painful, or even just tiresome, that they might try to include in the bargain. . . . He liked women, but intelligently and without fearing them. To him, they were the source of a whole category of very specific delights. He turned to them, for the needs of his body as well as his heart, with greediness and competence. . . . He made practical use of their charms without danger to himself.[2]

Gaston by then was ready to do anything to keep his freedom, that wild spirit of independence which led him to flee from family or social gatherings without anyone or anything being able to stop him. He wanted above all to pursue his own ends, even if most of his activity reflected only idleness and weariness. People might take him or leave him, but in no way could they change him or make him go against his will. In that case he would simply slip away, not being the kind of man to carry the woes of the world on his shoulders.

> To him suffering was only an unfortunate accident to avoid at all costs. He knew nothing of sin. His only morality was to remain as close to himself, as much like his first-blush impulses as he possibly could. He detested anything that might give his soul a different twist than the one it naturally had. In all things, he stayed with what he had first felt, and was careful not to let that feeling be contaminated by any consideration of duty or decency.[3]

For the first time, Gaston departed from his position as a dilettante rentier, a devotee of the arts and women. The work he took on was not very taxing: he became secretary to a member of the Chamber of Deputies, at a time when any personage in the swim simply had to have a secretary. He saw to it that his employer's correspondence was kept up to date—a light task that he quickly tired of and left for a much more fascinating secretaryship, that of Robert Pellevé de la Motte-Ango, Marquis de Flers, much better known to the devotees of Boulevard comedies as Robert de Flers.

Flers was a popular dramatist at the turn of the century. He had started out in journalism and literature at the behest of the playwright Victorien Sardou, contributing articles to the leading royalist newspapers. But only when he began collaborating with Gaston Arman de Caillavet did he achieve real success. The plays the two men wrote together, satires about women writers, pompous academicians, and the world of politics, played to full houses at the Variétés, the Gaîté, the Nouveautés, until that famous October 1, 1917, when for the first time Flers and Caillavet were accepted into the Comédie-Française repertoire.

In this atmosphere of comedies, operettas, and musical comedies that were regularly hits, Gaston for the first time tried his hand at work. He took care of the many tasks and unavoidable duties that a much-sought-after Parisian personality was subject to. More and more often, Robert de Flers had him cover the rehearsals of the leading plays and bring him news and comments. Little by little, he delegated authority to his secretary, who was soon writing his articles for him. Gaston took a liking to the game and began to contribute news notes and short commentaries to the same daily paper, under the pseudonym "Un strapontin" (Aisle Seat). Sometimes, when *Le Figaro* rejected his copy, he submitted it to *Le Journal amusant*, a slightly risqué old magazine founded in 1848 that was fast losing its popularity; there his signature was "Le Moucheur de chandelles" (Candle-snuffer).

It had been a good idea for Gaston to accept the job with Robert de Flers. Not only was it enjoyable work, but it gave him a chance to meet on a daily basis the few dozen personalities who made and unmade Parisian reputations in the salons, at dinners, or at gala shows. Yet, curiously, it was not through this avenue that, sometime in 1907 or 1908, he had the meeting which was to make such a lasting impression upon him.

While spending a summer vacation at Bénerville, Gaston went for the day to Blonville to see Robert Gangnat, the representative of the Dramatists' Society. While there, he saw approaching in the distance, on the road from Villers, a young man of incongruous but charming mien, in clothes misbuttoned and too tight. The young man wore a long velvet-lined cape, a high stiff collar, a straw hat much the worse for wear, slouching too far down his forehead, and patent-leather shoes covered with dust. Gangnat introduced them:

"Gaston Gallimard, meet Marcel Proust."

It was the first time Gaston heard the man's name. But he was immediately struck by the extreme warmth of his eyes, his carefree, easy manner; he felt that being so attired, in such heat and so much sun, was not without elegance and even grace.

The stranger told them in well-chosen words of his walk over, covering the ten miles from Cabourg to Blonville, and was about to go on to something else, when he remembered, "I came over to invite you to dinner tonight at the Grand Hôtel." Gaston was dying to be included in the invitation, but did not dare suggest it. Proust sensed it well enough, though, and "did not fail to do so with such delicate politeness and insistence that it did not even surprise me, though coming from a man older than I."[4]

Young Gallimard looked forward to this dinner with impatience he could barely contain. At the time, Proust was not yet Proust; he was only himself. At the Grand Hôtel that evening, he welcomed his guests "with a courtesy I thought no longer existed. As we were the first, he gave us the names of all those expected and described each. He especially spoke of the Marquis de N., who was to join us, a funny old character, ruined, abandoned, and ill, floating around like some relic of a shipwreck at this huge hotel."

At dinner they discussed travel. When the name of Constantinople came up, Proust recited from memory a page out of Pierre Loti describing it. When it came time to say goodnight, Gaston expressed his amazement at this ability. Proust, amused, whispered to him, "Study the railway schedules—that's much better," and began reeling off place-names to him.[5]

That first meeting was to remain engraved in Gaston's memory. No one ever had to ask him twice to tell about it. But at the time, so early in the century, it was the man himself who made such an impression on him, not the writer—at least not yet.

On the table in his bedroom, books piled up, with some stray issues of *Le Figaro*. But it was mainly in the reading of "little magazines" that he found delight. Since 1880 there had been so many of them. "Rough drafts of the literature of tomorrow," to use the felicitous phrase of Léon-Paul Fargue, they were the best place where the young avant-garde, often highly gifted, could publish its first efforts, before they went out of existence after a few issues. But some of them went on to be successful: *La Revue de Paris*, taken over by the Calmann-Lévy publishing house; the magazine *Le Mercure de France*, in which Alfred Vallette published the early works of Remy de Gourmont, Jules Renard, and Alfred Jarry; and *La Revue blanche*, which, according to the wishes of the Natanson brothers who financed it, meant to be the rallying place for all divergent tendencies.

At the end of 1908 a small group of writers, some of whom were contributing to these magazines, decided to publish their own review. They sought out the help, advice, and experience of the critic Eugène Montfort, who was already publishing a periodical called *Les Marges*. He was the one who baptized the newly conceived magazine *La Nouvelle Revue Française*, more easily referred to by its initials as the *NRF*. But when the first issue finally came out on November 15, the young men were disappointed and outraged because Montfort had also "loaned" them, against their desire, a few articles by friends of his, two of which were especially exasperating: one (much too laudatory) on Gabriele d'Annunzio, and the other (much too critical) on Stéphane Mallarmé.

They immediately decided to cut themselves loose and continue their venture without the "good offices" of anyone else. Montfort, in a lordly gesture, let them keep the title.[6] The "six characters in search of a magazine"[7] then met in an apartment on Rue d'Assas, across from the Luxembourg Gardens, in the home of one of them, Jean Schlumberger, a discreet, rigorous, modest aesthete who came from an old Protestant bourgeois family. The family, originally Alsatian and well-established in industry, prided itself on having the historian and onetime premier and minister of education François Guizot in its family tree.

Schlum, as he was known to his friends, the youngest of the group (born in 1877), and Jacques Copeau had also been students at the Lycée Condorcet at the same time, but Copeau had begun very early to devote himself to literature and especially the theater, while organizing art exhibits and selling paintings at the Georges Petit modern art gallery. André Ruyters came from a totally different background. He was a Belgian with a passion for English literature who had already tried his hand at a little magazine, *Antée*, in Brussels. Currently he was employed in Paris at the Banque de l'Indochine. Henri Vangeon and Marcel Drouin both preferred pseudonyms for their literary work: the former called himself Henri Ghéon and the latter, Michel Arnauld. Ghéon, a physician and writer as stagestruck as Copeau, had not yet lapsed into mysticism. Michel Arnauld, who came from Lorraine, had been a classmate of Charles Péguy at the prestigious Ecole Normale Supérieure and was now teaching philosophy at the Lycée Henri IV. His brother-in-law, André Gide (born in 1869), was the oldest of the lot.

While Gide was unquestionably the dominant personality of their group, each of them had his say. Discussion was free and easy. No rank, no precedence, no organization chart. Schlumberger designed the *NRF* logo that adorned the cover, and the fountain that appeared as a watermark in the special bond paper.[8] Ruyters took charge of finding a printer. He had already had a book published by a master printer in Bruges, Edouard Verbeke, whose shop went by the English name of The St. Catherine Press Ltd. They all thought his presswork and typography most impressive, and his prices reasonable. Gide not only made sure the table of contents looked impressive—he also wrapped and tied the bundles of magazines.

In February 1909 the second "first issue" of the *NRF* appeared: after the false start with Eugène Montfort, this was the real thing. Perhaps they were still at the amateur-artisan stage, since the typographers in the Bruges printshop let a number of typos get by, nor had all the promised contributions arrived on time, but it was an independent magazine and expressed what its founders wanted it to be. It contained some "Considerations" by Jean Schlumberger and an "Image of Greece" by Michel Arnauld, while Gide contributed the first part of *La Porte étroite (Strait Is the Gate)*,* as well as a note in which he polished off the impudent pup who dared attack Mallarmé in the earlier first issue.

Issue by issue the magazine refined its intentions and made its tastes and goals more specific. The six founding fathers fancied art for art's sake, had nothing but contempt for petty judgments and flattery. Wanting to remain pure, they turned up their noses at advertising. Finicky about the high quality of the texts they published, at each meeting they read aloud the more significant contributions and criticized them sharply, determined not to pander to public taste and thus slip into facileness. What did it matter if the rigor of their moral, intellectual, and aesthetic principles limited the size of their audience? They were not out for profit, especially since several of them came from well-to-do bourgeois circles. They could afford to be demanding.

Jean Giraudoux, Paul Claudel, Jacques Rivière, Francis Jammes, Emile Verhaeren—those were some of the contributors to the young magazine whose impact, prestige, and influence bore no relationship to its small circulation. Wishing to induce André Suarès to contribute,

---

*If a work has been translated into English, that published title is given in italics (as here); if the work has not been published in English, a literal translation is given in roman type.—PUBLISHER

in 1912 Jacques Copeau wrote him a letter that fairly well summed up the *NRF* spirit:

> The *NRF* kowtows to no patrons. It prides itself on its independence. Its task is to say what it considers right, or what it is fearsome to think about our times, and against them. I expect we will close our pages only to mediocrity, dryness, and political bad faith, or just plain politics. . . . So please, dear André Suarès, don't wait for the first freshness of the leaves to fade, before coming to have a seat in my garden? Au revoir, and a handshake to you.[9]

December 1910: the *Nouvelle Revue Française* was publishing issue no. 24, the table of contents as strong as ever. The circulation had grown, the variety of contributors as well. The magazine, improved in quality as well as size, became more daring and commissioned more and more special articles and comments. Inevitably, financial and management problems arose. Business matters had been left in the hands of a left-wing publisher, Marcel Rivière, who had an office on Rue Jacob. Schlumberger and Gide regularly had to make up the deficits. Instead of pulling in their sails, the little group of founding fathers decided instead to go forward and fulfill a dream they had had from the start: to extend the success of the magazine by starting a publishing house. The idea took root in their minds despite the obvious increase in financial burdens. So they set out to find themselves a *rara avis*: an ideal manager. How to describe him? He must be

> well enough off to contribute capital and disinterested enough not to expect any short-term profit; experienced enough to know how to run a business, but devoted enough to literature to put quality above profitability; competent enough to command respect, yet flexible enough to carry out the directives of the group, that is to say, of André Gide.[10]

Could such a person exist? The name of Gaston Gallimard came up. Jacques Copeau knew him to be the son of the famous art collector. Gide knew him a bit, for Gaston had called on him and sent him some admiring letters. Jean Schlumberger had heard his brother Maurice, the future banker, say good things about him. Henri Franck, a poet and former Ecole Normale student, had become a friend of his since they met at the home of the poet Anna de Noailles. Pierre de Lanux, who had been acting more or less as managing editor of the magazine, was friendly with him, despite a seven-year age difference. He knew that Gaston was ready to stop wasting his time and that he would enjoy being closer to the *NRF* group, whose purity and authenticity he admired, these qualities being absent from the circles he had frequented. Once already, during the summer at Pontigny, on a long walk through the fields with Gide and Schlumberger, Pierre de Lanux had spoken at length about Gaston's personality, his good qualities, and the devotion he could bring to the management and administration of the magazine, as well as the future publishing house. Gaston appeared to be just what they were looking for. Yet there was an obstacle: he lived on Rue Saint-Lazare—an absolute no-no. No one living on the Right Bank could have the *NRF* turn of mind; one had to live on the Left Bank.

This major failing of his, however, was made up for by his overall qualities, which on the whole corresponded well to the outline the group had set up. The most important thing was that "at age twenty-five, while without any specialized training, he had that flair which allows one not to be mistaken about the quality of a work and to go straight to the best, not on the basis of any reasoned-out principles but through acquisitiveness."[11]

Gaston had just been made a publisher.

In the France of 1911, the literary and publishing landscape was rather strange. Most houses lived off the titles of the previous century. The great publisher-booksellers were Ambroise Firmin-Didot, Louis Hachette, Gervais Charpentier, Henri Plon, Paul-Auguste Poulet-Malassis, Ernest Flammarion, Jules Hetzel, Calmann-Lévy, Emile-Paul, and Arthème Fayard. Albin Michel was still looked on as a newcomer. Alfred Vallette, who started the Mercure de France in

1889, had won wide prestige. He had turned his young firm into the citadel of the Symbolist movement; had himself written a couple of novels, *La Vierge* (The Virgin) and *A l'écart* (To the Side); wrote the drama reviews in the excellent magazine that bore the same name as his firm; and was the publisher of Gide, Claudel, Maeterlinck, Francis Jammes, Henri de Régnier, and Jean Moréas. Vallette was certainly the publisher who most impressed Gaston Gallimard, as he did another newcomer in the field, a young man of his own generation, Bernard Grasset.

The latter had a bit of a headstart on Gaston. In 1909 he had already signed forty-eight contracts with authors, of which, to be sure, thirty-five were vanity deals in which the writer underwrote part of the costs.[12] Grasset liked such deals: the risks being shared, commercial flops were easier to bear. For the publisher, that is. In 1911, four years after starting his firm, Grasset was already publishing Jean Giraudoux and François Mauriac. He was about to publish a book by Alphonse de Chateaubriant, which would win him his first Goncourt Prize. He was publishing the works of Charles Péguy, and had just signed a contract with André Sauvignon that would bring him his second Goncourt. His firm had begun to take shape; he was launched but not yet well known.

Grasset was still very modest and regularly went for on-site training to Péguy who, since the turn of the century, had been publishing, within a stone's throw of the Sorbonne, a magazine that was half periodical and half book: *Les Cahiers de la Quinzaine* (Fortnightly Chapbooks). The originality of Péguy's publication was due not only to the quality of the material he published and its often polemical tone. The *Cahiers* depended on monthly subsidies, some regular and some occasional, which conferred on those who made them no authority whatsoever in the editing or running of the publication. And when the writer-publisher's financial problems loomed too large, he would float a loan and call upon his friend Bernard Lazare to collect the money. All that Péguy asked of his readers was that they read his *Cahiers* regularly for two years before pledging support.[13] For Péguy considered subscribing to be a duty. A satisfied reader owed it to him. This peculiarity was so famous within the profession that it gave rise to a much-repeated quip: "For one subscription, he'll give you *le salut militaire* [a military salute]. For two, he'll give you *le salut éternel* [eternal salvation]."[14]

Vallette, Péguy, Grasset—there were not many such publishers in 1911 ready to break with tradition in the literary field as well as in their professional business practices. At the end of the nineteenth century, Emile Zola was one of the best-sellers. Guy de Maupassant attracted attention by the fact that in six months of 1883 his *Une vie* (*A Life*) sold some 25,000 copies, and Ernest Renan sold 60,000 copies of his *Vie de Jésus* (*Life of Jesus*) in a bare five months. But these were the remarkable exceptions that proved the rule: a "good" novel could not break the barrier of 2,000 copies.

Publishing a book in those days consisted of having it printed; placing an advertisement in the old *Journal des libraires* (Booksellers' Journal); sending autographed copies to a few important figures in the press, politics, and even literature; and then sitting back and waiting for orders. The reputation of a novel was created mainly in the literary salons, those held by Geneviève Strauss or the Comtesse Greffulhe, Madame Bibesco or the Comtesse de FitzJames, places where, like as not, one would bump into Marcel Proust between his bouts of asthma. People met there to gossip, recite poems, spar with one another, be introduced, and be seen. Such was the business of literature.

Setting up in his bedroom on Rue Saint-Lazare as if in an office, the floors piled high with books, newspapers, and magazines, Gaston improvised his new profession. For the time being, his publishing house, the publishing "bureau" as Gide called it, had only a desk— not even a room—in the Rue Jacob offices of Marcel Rivière, a publisher of books on political economy. Wanting to spread out, the NRF group quickly found a small, empty dry-cleaning shop close by. That was something, at least an address, 1 Rue Saint-Benoit, even though Gaston continued to correspond on paper with his Rue Saint-Lazare letterhead.

He was by now thirty and faced with a question: what is a publisher? His model was Alfred Vallette of the Mercure de France. He had seen him at work: up at four in the morning and finished by about nine. After that, Vallette had a full schedule all day, seeing authors and printers. He had neither phone nor typewriter, but carbon paper and a hand press.[15] So Gaston understood that, in getting into this unfamiliar venture he was giving up the easy life. No longer would he be free to dawdle at expositions or in cafés, to go applaud Diaghilev's Ballets Russes and then celebrate their triumphs at Misia Sert's with the literary, artistic, and political Tout-Paris. But there was one consolation: three of his friends who were "well-to-do bohemians" were in on the deal. He would be working with them.

Jacques Rivière from Bordeaux, five years younger than Gallimard, was introduced to the NRF by Gide after failing to graduate from the Ecole Normale Supérieure. He was now managing editor of the magazine, and in his articles and notes represented the tendency toward "pure literature," whereas someone like Schlumberger was more inclined to introduce politics into the magazine. Rivière shared with Gaston his passion for literature and painting, and they were very close friends.

Valery Larbaud, a native of Vichy exactly Gaston's age, was a completely different type. Whereas Rivière had to break completely with his upper bourgeoisie background to give himself over body and soul to literature, Larbaud was deeply rooted within his own. After studying at the Collège Sainte-Barbe, at Fontenay-aux-Roses, "an old prep school more cosmopolitan than a world's fair," he traveled all over Europe. At an early age he inherited a fortune from his father, a pharmacist who had had the good idea of capitalizing on the thermal springs at Saint-Yorre. Fluent in Spanish and English, Larbaud spent his days discovering foreign writers, translating them, and getting them published. To him, literature was a game, not a profession—one of the many things he had in common with Gaston, along with his bon vivant side and his penchant for women.

The third member of this little group was the oldest but also the wildest. Léon-Paul Fargue was an attractive and eccentric personality, a poet who wanted to please and amuse. But although erudite, cultivated, and brilliant, he was hopelessly undisciplined. He would crisscross Paris on foot or by taxi, dropping in on this friend, that friend, going to magazine offices, cafés, or literary salons to drink and chat. This great idler was incorrigible: always late, always somewhere else, he could not organize his ideas or, as a result, his work. His father, an engineer, was famous in the small world of Saint-Germain-des-Prés for having decorated the Brasserie Lipp with ceramics and mosaics. Léon-Paul Fargue, for his part, would have liked to be famous for his poetry, but he never took the trouble to make it known. So much so that Larbaud once said of him, "Fargue is the only obstacle to publishing his works. A very unusual case."

Rivière, Fargue, Larbaud: three sincere friends, three valuable assets for the magazine. But Gaston did not depend on them for launching himself in business. Even if, at the start, the idea was only to set up a branch of the magazine, publishing required financial means. At the *NRF* this had come mainly from the "two Protestants," Gide and Schlumberger. So it was only natural that, according to a contract signed in May 1911, Gaston became a partner with those two, each of the three investing 20,000 francs.[16] But rather than go to his father, with whom he was not on good terms and to whom he did not want to be indebted, Gaston turned to his uncle Duché for a loan.

As the company's manager, Gaston was the one responsible in the eyes of the authors, since his two partners, Gide and Schlumberger, acted mainly as moral support and *NRF* ambassadors. Of the three, from the outset Gaston alone was the publisher. Following the example of his model, Vallette, he did not intend to wait for magazine contributors to come to him with "a long hundred-and-fifty-page piece." He preferred to seek out, principally in magazines and newspapers, writers who might fit in with the aims of the group. As early as January 1911 he started taking yearly subscriptions to even obscure magazines like *L'Effort*, and wrote to its editor Jean-Richard Bloch that he was interested in what Bloch was doing.[17] To maintain the widest possible field of activity, he even kept an eye on the provincial dailies. After reading the *Propos* of a man named Chartier—who had yet to adopt the pen name of Alain—in *La Dépêche de Rouen*, Gaston wrote him on the off chance that he might be willing to have a book published by the *Nouvelle Revue Française*. To his great surprise, he got a reply from the moralist that read: "Dear Sir, I was very appreciative of your letter. However, what I have written does not belong to me, so do with it what you wish, but above all no royalties!"[18]

All writers, alas, were not so easy to please as Emile-Auguste Chartier. Gaston found this out quickly enough. His first such experience was with the *NRF* authors.

On June 16, 1911, the *Bibliographie de la France*, the official journal of publishers and booksellers, carried an announcement of the *NRF* publications. It covered three books, the first put out by the young firm: Paul Claudel's *L'Otage (The Hostage)*, a three-act play soon to be considered one of the jewels of French tragedy; Charles-Louis Philippe's *La Mère et l'enfant* (Mother and Child), the author's memories of his childhood and youth; and André Gide's *Isabelle*, a short, offhand, fast-paced tale. When the first copies came to his desk, Gaston, nervous, called Gide. Gide hefted them, riffled through them, looked them over carefully, then gave a start: some pages of his *Isabelle* had twenty-seven lines, others only twenty-six; moreover, there were typos and mistakes. Gaston tried to calm the author by explaining that the printers in Bruges were Flemings and thus not masters of the French language.

To no avail—Gide was furious. He dragged Gaston to the *NRF* warehouse on Rue Bonaparte, where the two of them, at his insistence, tore up every last copy of the book. Gaston did as he was told; he did not even have the presence of mind to save a few. Gide, who was shrewder, slipped aside half a dozen or so for himself: later he would get a very high price for the copies of this original edition, as rare as they come. For the son of a famed bibliophile, Gaston had not proved true to the family instinct.[19]

With this small gaffe, for which he was less responsible than his printer, Gaston learned that, in the eyes of the author, the publisher is the one accountable for mistakes, the one to blame, a stand-in for all those whose collaborative efforts contribute to getting the book out and into bookstores. But on the whole, Gide's wrath notwithstanding, Gaston was not unhappy: the standard accepted price— 3 francs 50 centimes—had been retained for Claudel's play; the alfa paper it was printed on looked good and would not soon turn yellow; and in the copies of the deluxe edition, the fountain designed by Schlumberger stood out well in the watermark. The typography was good and carefully done: the master printer of Bruges deserved his reputation, having used Cheltenham and Old Style typefaces, rather rare in French publishing. He even created a new character specially for the book, as Paul Claudel requested, since he could not bear to have the name of his heroine, Sygne de Coûfontaine, printed without a circumflex on the *u*. Gaston was quick to learn that these idiosyncrasies, these authors' manias were the daily lot of publishers. The great Flaubert himself often pestered his publisher, Michel Lévy. "The circumflex accent on Salammbô has no sweep; nothing could be less Punic. I demand a broader one," he had written Lévy in 1862.[20]

With his best friends, too, Gaston had this trouble. Fargue, for example, was the most impossible of authors, bad enough to drive even Gide and Larbaud to despair. He kept postponing his deadlines, so that every announcement of publication was wrong by the time it appeared. "Spare yourself the bother of getting a daily letter from me and send me your corrected proofs. No way out of it, you will get printed," Gaston wrote him at the end of 1911. Three months later, he thought he had finally carried the day. Léon-Paul's poems were finally "off the press," as the saying goes. Barring some extraordinary event, they were about to appear. And then that event did happen: Fargue, since at the *NRF* they pulled their hair out when he asked for some new emendation, went directly to Bruges and asked Edouard Verbeke to start the print run all over again. The numerous three dots of elision strewn throughout his text absolutely had to be replaced by a new invention of his own: two dots of elision! The others, he said, looked to him "like so many peas that get lost while being shucked."

Despite these technical problems foreshadowing many more difficult ones to come, Gaston found time to devote himself to literature, not only as a publisher but as an "adapter." As his friend Pierre de Lanux,[21] who had been replaced on the editorial staff of the *NRF* because of absentmindedness, a lack of a sense of order and organization, Gaston was passionately fond of the works of the great German dramatist Friedrich Hebbel (1813–63). During the winter of 1910 he undertook the translation into French of the first of his tragedies, *Judith*, because of its eminently German character and its solid structure. In point of fact, the two young men, having only high-school German at their command, merely "abstracted" a translation that they then had revised by two German scholars, Félix Bertraux and Marcel Drouin, before writing a short biobibliographical note to go with it. The book, appearing in 1911, allowed them to be among the first of their company's authors by way of Hebbel, since his book carried the credit, "translated from the German by Gaston Gallimard and Pierre de Lanux."

The work brought them no money, of course, but gave them a certain prestige and flattered their pride. Jean-Richard Bloch, having noted the appearance of their *Judith*, asked them to write a study for his magazine on the works of Hebbel, all of which the two adapters planned to "translate" little by little.[22]

But for the moment—and a good while to come—most of Gaston's energy went into writing letters. Keeping up a regular, abundant, and diversified correspondence took the better part of his mornings. These letters of his to authors, many of whom he had never seen, were so many bottles tossed in the sea. Some answered, others did not. There is a knack to writing to a stranger so as to make your request stand out from others, or to woo him away from a publishing house he is used to and comfortable with. There is an art to starting and carrying on a correspondence between a young thirty-year-old publisher and writers and poets some of whom already have a name. Little by little, the tone and style of Gaston's letters improved in subtlety, shrewdness, and intelligence. Only his fine handwriting in black ink did not change.

By agreement with Schlumberger and Gide, on October 13, 1911, on poor paper with the Rue Saint-Lazare letterhead, he wrote to Jean-Richard Bloch about two of his stories that had appeared in the magazine:

> Would you be inclined to give these two stories to the Editions de la Nouvelle Revue Française? Could you, at your convenience, add enough to them to make a volume? If my proposal interests you, as soon as I have in hand the full text of the book, I will establish the costs with the printer and on that basis write you what royalties we could pay. You may not be aware that our firm is in no way commercial and that all we aim to do is publish fine books! Please forgive my writing you on these business matters.[23]

An agreement was signed between the author and the publisher at the end of the year, and in 1912 Bloch's first book appeared, under a sober cream-colored cover framed with narrow red and black lines, titled *Lévy, premier livre de contes* (Lévy, A First Book of Stories).

In his earliest letters to authors, Gaston was often technical, going more into the printing process than into conceptions of literature. He kept his personal ideas for the brief notices he wrote for the magazine, when a book, play, or art exhibit met with his favor. The first of these dealt with the publication by the Editions de La Dépêche de Rouen of *Cent un propos d'Alain* (One Hundred and One Remarks by Alain):

> He does not philosophize, does not prophesy. He is a powerful awakener. He jabs us from the right, from the left, to make us raise our heads and look out beyond what we are accustomed to. He thinks out-

of-doors. To him the world is indeed concrete, and he leads us to touch the stars with our fingers. A healthy breath enlivens his discourse. . . . A great pagan, cynical, ascetic, greedy, he gives us the theme for our morning prayers. And these few lines, so powerfully light, are the end result of the richest culture, the most independent reading, a time-tested science, the most exacting analysis of oneself.[24]

Gaston's style is often brief, condensed, percussive, yet charged with emotion. He chooses his words carefully, avoiding overwriting and digressions. Two months later he gave another review to the magazine, this time about an exhibition of drawings, etchings, and lithographs by Frank Brangwyn at the Galerie Durand-Ruel:

There would seem to be nothing to say about so successful an oeuvre. Not that admiration precludes comment. But if the artist has said it all, expressing himself fully through the resources of his art alone, then no transposition is possible, nor any interpretation. All that is required is our sensibility; the miracle of our assent is brought about by the most subtle suggestion. . . .

After looking at all that lacework of scaffoldings, those columns of smoke rising to the heavens to support the architecture of the clouds, those blurred masses of rain, those cargoes, beams, legs of power, pylons, those dirtinesses, those lights that flash out like a cry, the whole gehenna of cities, the soot and smoke, it pleases me to stop before this road in Picardy so soberly pathetic, before this tender landscape of Assisi, in which there is at last some air to breathe! Brangwyn is a great traveler.[25]

But these comments have to do with subjects that do not directly concern him. In midsummer 1912, after seeing an exhibit of Renoir portraits at the Galerie Durand-Ruel, Gaston published an article that any psychoanalyst would relish dissecting—in the context of the biography of Paul Gallimard. There can be no doubt that in Gaston's mind Renoir and his work merged with the image of the friend of the family, the constant visitor at Bénerville, his father's traveling companion.

It would be unfair to judge Renoir *on the basis* of his portraits: there are stumbling-blocks there for this painter who never went looking for difficulties. But it is good to judge him *in relation* to his portraits and to see in them the elements of his talent.

Gaston admires Renoir, to be sure, but never without reservations. The least compliment is always accompanied by a criticism. The enthusiasm is never complete, but always embarrassed:

> In love only with colors, he sought no other forms in which to inscribe his emotion, or rather his greed, than those he found ready-made; so he sometimes approaches banality or ridicule and has no roots in either his own time or the past, although he shows some kinship to the painters of the eighteenth century. . . . Stupid, blue, lifeless eyes, which we know so well, like two bluebells on mother-of-pearl cheeks, disconcert and soften us. We are disarmed. We are ashamed. In front of his canvases I never feel uneasiness: everything in them is brought to light, because what sings in them is the most spontaneous confiding of himself, and this is fully realized. . . . He [Renoir] is the gift itself, but nothing more.

The critic further points out that this painter was not a supreme creator and that his work would be stronger and assured of more lasting appreciation if those around him made use of more discrimination, admitting that the great master's works were of uneven quality. These strictures take on their full meaning when we realize that "those around him" was aimed particularly at the Gallimard family; that Durand-Ruel, the owner of the gallery, was a friend of Paul Gallimard, who lent the gallery a large number of the exhibited paintings, as did Maurice Gangnat, who was related to the Gallimards by way of the Duchés; and that among the portraits was very likely the one done by Renoir of Lucie Gallimard, Gaston's mother.

In the opinion of this amazingly "involved" young critic, the oeuvre of Auguste Renoir would be more accomplished if, for example, the *Portrait of Mme. J. Bernheim and Her Son* was left out, and one concentrated on *La Loge*, "that image of so fine a luster, so proper a lushness, so exuberant an emotion, that in its presence one can no longer consider schools, periods, or originality. It goes beyond all personality. It is the precise and necessary 'anonymous' master-piece."[26] Shortly after this article appeared, Paul Gallimard got rid of a large part of his collection. Gaston, who was present at the sale, found it a "very moving" moment.[27]

1912 was an important date in the life of Gaston, and not only because the great masters' paintings among which he had grown up were dispersed. His friend Henri Franck had just died at the age of twenty-four. Deeply shaken by the suddenness of this loss, he made it a point of honor to hasten the publication of Franck's book, *La Danse devant l'arche* (The Dance before the Ark), which had a preface by Anna de Noailles and was equally hailed by such opposing figures as Maurice Barrès and Charles Péguy.

After the publication of *Eloges* by the poet Saint-Léger—later known as Saint-John Perse—the slim catalogue of the *NRF* publishing bureau improved considerably in quality and quantity. Jacques Copeau let it publish his stage adaptation of Dostoyevski's *The Brothers Karamazov*, Jacques Rivière some *Etudes* (Studies), Paul Claudel *L'Annonce faite à Marie* (*The Tidings Brought to Mary*), Charles-Louis Philippe his *Lettres de jeunesse* (Youthful Letters), and Gide *Le Retour de l'enfant prodigue* (*The Return of the Prodigal*).

The *NRF* founding fathers were already thinking of expanding the magazine and the publishing bureau. They began by leaving their cramped space on Rue Saint-Benoit to move a bit farther off in the neighborhood to 35 Rue Madame. They were to stay there until 1921. At the same time, they were also thinking of increasing the magazine's distribution abroad, especially in England and the United States. An American newspaperman named Sanborn, a friend of theirs who often took part in the *NRF* meetings, helped by getting them the addresses of New York intellectuals and the location of a London bookseller who would stock and distribute it; beyond that, he urged them to join in the lecture circuit of the Alliances Françaises abroad.

But at the end of 1912 Gaston had other things on his mind: he was in love. With two women. Torn between them, he even considered "disappearing." Finally he confided in a friend, sending a long letter from Bénerville to Jacques Rivière, asking his advice.[28] Rivière replied:

> I am wholeheartedly with you and you can count on me. . . . It seems to me that you are meant for a more diversified life than you have led so far. You have the necessary strength and that kind of gravity (in the sense of weightiness) that carries others along.[29]

On December 17 Gaston Gallimard and Yvonne Redelsperger were formally married at the city hall of the Sixteenth Arrondissement. Two days before, in a great hurry, he had dashed off a note to his friend Jacques Copeau: "You will not hold it against me, I guess, if I am not at Rue Madame during the day on Tuesday. I am getting married."[30]

A few weeks later came his thirty-second birthday. He had by now doubly foresworn his cherished freedom, by entering into a literary/business partnership and by getting married. But that did not change his ways. Pierre de Lanux saw him as a man capable of well-thought-out daring in his actions but prudent in his words— one who always worked things out so that he was in the right. Gaston appeared to him as a calculator, a sharp strategist, and a skillful diplomat knowing how to navigate and how to dissemble, capable of much love and just as much nastiness, generous in both senses of the word, full of humor, and preferring always to convince and persuade rather than to impose his will through authority.

Rivière gave a more sharply defined psychological portrait.[31] Like Lanux, he was struck by the fact that Gaston never did or felt anything by halves. He did not let himself be perturbed in his reasoning or in his affection by conflicting ideas that might alter his decision. Rivière was convinced that in Gaston's mind there was room for only pleasure or pain, that Gaston recognized no shadings between the two, avoiding uncertain or difficult things: deprivations, sacrifices, and so on. Unable to act otherwise than by instinct, he was a man who disregarded the social conventions and established rules. For above all he was a man who allowed anything, questioning neither others nor himself.

At the beginning of 1913, the first trip the new Mme. Gallimard took with her husband was not just "alone together." Gaston's mother and Fargue went along with them to Montana-Vermala, Switzerland, to a snow-ringed chalet with three servants and a piano to help them forget a country they disliked. But Gaston's thoughts were elsewhere.

For the past three months, he had often been away from Paris. First, he had had to take his mother to Switzerland before going to inspect printshops in various parts of France as well as visiting future authors who did not all live in Paris. The mail, though forwarded to him, sometimes complained of his unavailability. Marcel Proust in particular wrote him twice the preceding November to request his advice and an interview of ten minutes, no more. His health kept him locked in his bedroom, and he asked Gaston to come see him at his apartment on Boulevard Haussmann.

Proust was asking Gaston to publish two manuscripts of 550 pages each—pages, he specified, of thirty-five lines with forty-five characters to the line. "I would like not to be read exclusively by rich people or bibliophiles," Proust wrote. "And I don't want my entire work to cost the buyer more than seven francs, even if to do this I should have to foot more of the cost; it's a question of reaching people."[32] He also asked him for some technical details, especially how long it took to get a book out. The writer attached a great deal of importance to these details, even stating that, if Gaston did not answer his questions, he would not withdraw his manuscripts from Fasquelle, a publisher he regretted having gone to on the advice and recommendation of Calmette, the editor of Le Figaro.

Apparently, Gaston had already become a remarkable letter writer, for after receiving his answer, Proust wrote: "You found the simplest and most effective words to dissipate the slight mental malaise I felt, and for that I sincerely thank you."[33] But Gaston did not seem fully to comprehend the size of Proust's book: he offered to pick it up at Boulevard Haussmann in person.

Proust had confidence in this young publisher whom he knew only slightly, but who in his eyes represented the *NRF*, a way of writing and thinking that totally appealed to him. Referring to the second part of his manuscript, he took Gaston into his confidence: Read it, but don't mention the names or the subject, because it is rather shocking—it might create a scandal even before publication. In it there is a Baron de Charlus, a "virile pederast," a new type of character, in that Charlus will have nothing to do with effeminate men. "You may think that the metaphysical and moral viewpoint is predominant throughout the work. But in the end this old gentleman will be shown picking up a janitor and keeping a male pianist. I prefer to let you know in advance about anything that might put you off."[34]

Proust would seem to have been sincerely won over by the publisher since, a few days earlier, he had written to Jacques Copeau:

> To be published by the Nouvelle Revue Française is even more attractive to me since you told me that my reader and publisher would be M. Gallimard. I met him once and have so fond a memory of him, that for me who am sick, and whom business contacts frighten to begin with, it all becomes simple and delightful.[35]

Finally Proust had two big manuscripts delivered to Gaston's office, entitled *A la recherche du temps perdu (Remembrance of Things Past)* and *Le Temps retrouvé (The Past Recaptured)*. They were given out to be read, and at the traditional Thursday meeting at Schlumberger's on Rue d'Assas, after the group had been through the agenda, Proust's name was brought up.

"So how about those manuscripts Gallimard brought in?"

"They're full of duchesses, not at all our style. Besides, the thing is dedicated to Calmette, the editor of *Le Figaro.*"

Gide was supposed to have said that. Gaston took the manuscripts and returned them to Proust. Convinced of the value of his work, the writer then decided on a course that at the time had nothing dishonorable about it: vanity publication. René Blum, his friend since they first met at the Bibescos' at the turn of the century, had spoken to him of a young publisher, Bernard Grasset, who in a short time readily signed a contract for this very heavy manuscript which he had not even read,[36] the financial burden of which was to be carried much more by Proust than by the publisher himself.

At the end of 1913, *Du côté de chez Swann (Swann's Way)* came out, as the first volume of a series to be entitled *Remembrance of Things Past*. The reviews, on the whole, were good; the most amazing was written by Henri Ghéon in the *NRF* for January 1914. He recommended to Rivière that he too ought to read the book, and Rivière in turn urged Gide to "reread" it, as he might have dismissed it too lightly.

Gaston and Rivière talked about it at length and agreed that their firm had been guilty of a real blunder. "This is madness," they concluded. "It's a capital work, much better than what our friends are writing!"[37]

Gide himself agreed with them and his mea culpa took the form of a letter to Proust: "turning down this book will remain the *NRF*'s most serious mistake and (since I am ashamed to say I was in large part responsible for it) one of the most painful regrets and remorses of my life."[38] In the *NRF* headquarters on Rue Madame, they tried to figure out how such a mistake could have been made. They came up with excuses: Proust's manuscript was too long, too disorderly, indecipherable because of all the insertions, deletions, and incomprehensible signs. Riffling through the repulsive packet of sheets, Gide had been bored by the endless description of a dinner at the home of some snobs, and was revolted by expressions such as "a head that lets the vertebrae shine through." And Schlumberger recalled that the author wanted it published in toto, without cuts, something unheard of in their company, where a book ran an average of 230 pages. The financial outlay would have been too great, too risky for so young a company.

The harm had been done, but perhaps it was not too late: Gaston would go into action. He went to see Proust, to explain to him how the whole thing had been handled and to apologize.

"Since you are under contract to Grasset, perhaps we can publish something else of yours, say, your articles from *Le Figaro*, which we could collect into a volume," he suggested.

"That doesn't interest me," Proust replied. "Only one thing interests me, and that is my work, *Things Past*."

"Well, I'd be happy to publish it right away."

"But it has to be taken as a whole. I can't give you the sequel unless you publish the first part."

"But Grasset has that under contract!"

"It doesn't belong to him. I paid to have him publish it. You can buy it back. I will write Grasset to tell him to give it to you."[39]

The Proust deal was the first real attempt Gaston made to lure an author away from a fellow publisher. He was treading on thin ice here, and the only thing he had in his favor in 1913 and 1914, his only trump card, was an intangible: the *NRF* image.

Henceforth it was no longer just a question of asking Larbaud to get Fargue to return his corrected proofs on time. Gaston had to avoid errors and seek out new talent, young authors who would live up to the promise of their first books.

In this he was helped by the influence and friendships of the *NRF* people, especially Gide and Rivière. Not wanting to importune Paul Valéry by approaching him directly for a book, Gaston asked Gide to act as intermediary until he was able to overcome his innate shyness and approach the poet himself.[40] And he asked Rivière to be his spokesman with Paul Claudel:

> When you write Claudel, tell him you've taken it on yourself to write him, because I don't dare to act too much the *publisher* with him, to ask for new manuscripts, and so on. Otherwise, he may wonder why I did not write to him myself.[41]

How could one judge the future of a book? By flair, of course, but what else? With hindsight it was easy to make judgments. That same year, 1913, Rivière slammed the *NRF* door on a young man of his social circle, his generation, and his own part of the country, who was very much attracted by the company's spirit and had had only one previous book published by Grasset, *L'Enfant chargé de chaînes* (The Young Man in Chains). Who could know at the time that he would turn out to be François Mauriac?[42]

Paris, June 1913: Gaston was in a taxi on the way to his office. Suddenly, on Rue Halévy, just behind the Opéra, he spotted a figure that looked familiar, ordered the driver to stop, jumped out, and called to him. It was his old classmate, Roger Martin du Gard. They had hardly seen each other since the Lycée Condorcet. It is understatement to say they were happy to renew "the confident and affectionate intimacy of the old days."[43] Now they met again and could revive their adolescent memories: Martin du Gard had not forgotten the rare books Gaston used to "borrow" from his father's library so his friend could see them, or their mutual devotion to the theater, contemporary literature, and their "true friendship based on their many similarities of mind, character, and tastes."

Though they had not seen each other since their student days, Martin du Gard had been following Gaston's career. And providentially Martin du Gard just then was having a problem with his publisher, Grasset. Having had an earlier book published by Grasset's firm, he had promised him his next novel; but after reading the manuscript of *Jean Barois*, the publisher turned it down and criticized it so mercilessly that the author felt discouraged.

Spontaneously, Gaston offered to have his friend's manuscript read at the *NRF*. It was delivered the next day, and Gaston turned it over to Schlumberger, who took it to the country with him. But without waiting for an opinion, on the basis of a few pages published in the magazine *L'Effort*, Gaston wrote Martin du Gard on June 25:

It says the things that we have been thinking and wanting to say. . . . My wish would be to publish it, not just out of friendship but because it is good, solid, long, and goes in a direction I like. If, however, I am obliged to give you a negative reply, don't let it create any doubts in you. There are three of us who have to pass on it.[44]

Shortly thereafter, Schlumberger expressed his enthusiasm for it and sent the manuscript to Gide, who wired Gaston: ONE OF MOST RE-MARKABLE MANUSCRIPTS TO BE PUBLISHED WITHOUT HESITATION STOP BRINGING IT BACK PERSONALLY IN A FEW DAYS.[45]

Having received these two favorable reactions, Gaston took *Jean Barois* to Bénerville, to read "purely for my own pleasure," and let his friend know the deal should be considered settled. His book would be published by *Les Editions de la NRF*, in spite of a few small problems that Gallimard now had to overcome, even though he was dealing with a friend.

However, I now have the thankless businessman's job. You know that our books, printed on real laid esparto paper in Bruges, are not cheap to produce. Will you hold it against me if I can't give you the royalties that Grasset did? And if I send you an agreement just like the ones I have signed with Copeau, Rivière, Vildrac, Bloch, etc., in other words, 30 centimes on each of the first thousand copies, 40 centimes on the second thousand, etc. Answer me without reservations. No point in mentioning Gide, who doesn't take any royalties at all. As soon as we are in agreement, I'll send you a fine contract and we will decide about the typeface.[46]

On his return from Bénerville, Gaston found on his desk a letter from Martin du Gard, who was happy that they had all accepted his book, but wondered how he should handle Grasset. He wanted Gaston's informed advice as both friend and publisher. It was here that Gallimard first displayed his gifts as an artful negotiator. On July 9 he instructed Martin du Gard on the art and manner of getting out of a delicate ethical and material situation:

Here in essence is what I would write Grasset, requesting a formal acknowledgment of your letter: "Since you consider my book a failure, since you leave the decision to me, and after careful consideration I can see neither addition nor cut to be made and do not intend to make any, I believe it better that we leave it at that. So let us just tear up our contract, etc."

Let me know what Grasset answers. It would not be bad for you to get on your high horse and reaffirm the high quality of your book, if only to irritate him some more so he will be glad to be rid of you. And above all, not a word about your plan to turn the book over to us![47]

Martin du Gard followed the advice and on July 10 asked Grasset to release him from his contract. Two days later the publisher agreed, and it was only in mid-August that Grasset would hear, incidentally, that the *NRF* was publishing *Jean Barois*. He was losing an author whose avowed ambition was nothing less than to win the Goncourt Prize. The scion of a family of magistrates and moneychangers with deep roots in the Bourbonnais in Central France, and in the Beauvaisis north of Paris, the writer desperately craved that award so as to free himself from a family environment that had never accepted his devoting himself exclusively to literature after the appearance of his first book *Devenir* (Becoming); his being satisfied with the relatively modest amount of money to be earned in that profession; or his being a Dreyfusard and a freethinker. In his eyes only the Goncourt, awarded as a sign of official recognition, a sort of consecration, would allow him to make honorable amends to his relatives and be rehabilitated.[48]

So he had put the very best of himself into *Jean Barois*, getting away to write without disturbance in the country, south of Paris in the Cher. His novel was new for the period in that it was written like a shooting script, mainly in scenes with dialogue. In it Martin du Gard showed, through the personality and experiences of the eponymic hero, "the psychological course of a soul which, formed by the beliefs of his childhood, then having developed freely and forsaken all faith, returns at the end of his life to the consoling expectations of his youth" (as he wrote in a preface he never used).

The publication of this book was important in Gaston's career for several reasons. Paradoxically, it was with a friend that he was to have his first contractual problem. On November 15—months after Martin du Gard had selected the typeface for his book out of Verbeke's catalogue, and the book was printed and prepared for sale, and a few copies had been hurriedly paperbound so that the members of the Goncourt jury might receive them in time—Gaston finally sent Martin du Gard a sheet of paper filled on both sides with the clauses of the contract that was to bind them. He himself, after consulting a lawyer, had sketched out the main lines.

Article I: M. Roger Martin du Gard grants to Gaston Gallimard, who accepts it, the exclusive right to print and publish, this being understood in terms of both present and future laws governing literary property, a work entitled *Jean Barois*, of which he is the author.

Article II. The volume will be made up in 16mo elephant format, to be sold at 3 francs 50 per copy.

Article III. As the price of this cession, M. Gaston Gallimard will pay Roger Martin du Gard, it being understood that he will be paid nothing for the 10% spoilage customary in the book trade:

—the sum of_____ centimes per copy on the first thousand

—the sum of 30 centimes per copy on the second thousand

—the sum of 40 centimes per copy from the third to the fifth thousand inclusive

—the sum of 50 centimes per copy from the sixth to the tenth thousand inclusive

—the sum of 60 centimes per copy beginning with the thirteenth thousand and indefinitely.

This price will be payable, insofar as the amounts relating to the first thousand are concerned, one half when the first 500 copies are put on sale and the other half when the other 500 are put on sale, and for the following thousands, when each printing is put on sale. The size of each printing will be determined by Gaston Gallimard and indicated on the cover in whatever number of editions he sees fit.

Article IV. One hundred dedication copies will be furnished to the author.

Article V. The parties are formally forbidden, except by mutual agreement, to incorporate all or part of the work covered by the present contract into any new work.

Article VI. The authorization to publish a full or partial illustrated edition, to be sold at a price higher than that of the Company's edition, may be given by mutual consent of the parties at any time whatever, and on the proceeds of such an operation, 20% will be paid to the Company.

Article VII. The authorization to reproduce in France or abroad in newspapers, journals, magazines, etc., either in the French language or in a foreign language, or to publish as a book abroad in any manner whatever either the French text or a translation thereof, must be obtained from the two consenting parties. Proceeds from such operations will be apportioned half to M. Roger Martin du Gard, half to the Company.

Article VIII. Six months after the said work goes out of print, this contract will be automatically canceled if the Company refuses to order a further printing.

Article IX. Roger Martin du Gard gives Gaston Gallimard the right to publish his next three books under the conditions detailed above. Failing to make use of such right within three months of the date when each of these works is submitted to him, Gaston Gallimard will forfeit the right to publish the work so presented to him.[49]

Martin du Gard was disappointed. Even desperate. He wanted to write to Gaston, but labored as never before at his desk, tearing up one draft after another. He turned the contract around every which way, but could not bring himself to sign it. Since Gaston had been his friend before being his publisher, he wrote him just what he felt. He even confessed that, had he been aware of the terms of the contract in July, he would have rejected it in spite of the bonds between them and the attraction he admittedly felt for the *NRF.*

He simply could not accept Articles I and IX. As for Article VII, he said he just could not understand it. Reading and rereading the notarized contract form, he could not help remembering, bitterly, the advice his friend Gaston had given regarding Grasset when they ran into each other again the previous June: "above all, don't give him any share of possible translations: keep all that for yourself!"

More and more perplexed, Martin du Gard then considered the huge gap between his friend's advice and his publisher's offer. He wanted to make Articles I and VII more advantageous to himself and drop Article IX outright. Even though he felt at home at the *NRF*, he could not accept the idea that he would be legally bound for three books—some ten years' work—to one publisher. It seemed inconceivable to him. It was a matter of principle, even though he fully expected to have his next books published by the *NRF*. Nothing guaranteed that Gaston would long remain in charge of the publishing firm: "The day when the one in charge might be someone like Grasset, I especially would not want the police to be able to force me to give him the fruits of my labors."[50]

A tacit understanding, fine, but never a legal contract. Above all, as a writer he wanted to be a free man. The two friends were equally upset that this stupid piece of paper, which could not be eliminated, should cast a shadow on their relations. So as not to let the matter fester, Gaston immediately answered Martin du Gard in a long, reassuring, dedramatizing letter. He let him know that he would be on his side, before getting to the heart of the matter:

> As far as Article IX is concerned, there is no difficulty, it was just an oversight on my part. Of course we will drop it, and on this point we are in total agreement. . . . Doesn't it seem legitimate to you that a publisher who gives an author his start, not being assured of recouping his investment, should at least have the future before him, and that he benefit to a certain degree from the launching he had some part in? Otherwise all the burden would be on the publisher, who might see the author, once successful, leave him for some bigger company.[51]

Gaston's arguments about the translations convinced Martin du Gard, but not the ones on literary ownership: "Today, at thirty, I can't face giving up the ownership of this book forever," he wrote back. "I have to have an escape hatch, a way to get my property back someday, if forced by unforeseen circumstances." Martin du Gard went on to cite what he considered the most telling of cases: an author and a publisher who, twenty years before, at the height of the Dreyfus Affair, were bound to each other by contract even though they were on opposite sides of the barricade. "I am really not a man who can bind himself by such irrevocable commitments!" he concluded, suggesting a different contract wording that would allow the author to take back his property after fifteen years, subject to his making up any deficit.[52]

Jean Barois was in the bookstores by the end of 1913. It failed to win the Goncourt, but for the first time a book published by the *NRF* met with a fair amount of commercial success. This was very good news for Gaston, the more so since, shortly before, he had taken on new responsibilities, over and above being in charge of the *NRF* publishing house.

The feckless dilettante had become unrecognizable: the businessman was now also the managing director of a theater.

The theater was a fundamental element in the makeup of Gaston Gallimard. The geometrical locus of all his passions, it attracted him even more than publishing, and he was never to hide the fact, on many occasions during his life, that he would have liked to make it his career. Even more than the book trade, it offered everything he loved: literature (in the plays), the interplay of people with one another and with the audience (acting), painting (sets), display (costumes), social mingling (intermissions), competition with his father (who had owned the Ambigu-Comique and the Variétés), and nostalgia for his professional beginnings (as secretary to Robert de Flers).

When, in 1913, the *NRF* people considered launching a theater, Gaston had innumerable reasons to be enthusiastic about it. The soul of the undertaking was his friend Copeau, who wanted to react against the ugliness, superficiality, and mediocrity of the contemporary stage. Strict as a Puritan, an enemy of fads, Copeau wanted above all to honor the play itself and the actors, rather than the sets and decorations, things that distracted the audience from the essentials. At thirty-four, this founding father of the *NRF* magazine could no longer be satisfied with expressing himself only as a critic. But to open a theater, even with "unbelievable disdain for profit,"[53] required an auditorium and some financing.

Charles Dullin, a friend of the group who at the time gave readings from the poets at the Lapin Agile cabaret in Montmartre, was looking for an unused theater, on the Left Bank naturally, and came across the Athénée Saint-Germain, on Rue du Vieux-Colombier, belonging to a M. Saint-Père. A lease was signed with the owner and it was renamed the Théâtre du Vieux-Colombier. A company was set up, with Gaston as managing director. It was capitalized at 200,000 francs, split into 200 shares. Gaston, Schlumberger, and Charles Pacquement, a broker, art collector, and above all fellow alumnus of the Lycée Condorcet, were the first and major shareholders. A loan was floated through the Banque franco-américaine in Place Vendôme, to attract other investors. Gaston and Schlumberger tried to find them without delay among their own contacts. They approached the Princesse Bibesco, the Comtesse de Noailles, Marcel Proust, and Emile Mayrisch, and scurried around through fashionable literary Paris, so as to be able to present the lawyers with a bank statement showing that at least a quarter of the value of the shares had been subscribed. The Princesse de Polignac's refusal discouraged them for a time, making them feel they would get more rejections than they anticipated from their society contacts. But they did not give up, and made their pitch wherever they could.[54]

At the beginning of October a yellow poster appeared on walls on the Left Bank. Gaston had asked a printer named Marcel Picard, whom he found in the Faubourg Saint-Martin, to give him a playbill that would attract attention and no one could ignore. In this, it was a success:

"Théâtre du Vieux-Colombier"

APPEAL

—*to youth*, to react against all the cowardices of the commercial theater and defend the freest and most sincere manifestations of a new form of dramatic art

—*to the literate public*, to keep up the cult of classical masterpieces, French and foreign, which will be the backbone of our repertoire

—*to all*, so as to support an undertaking that will establish itself through its inexpensive tickets, the variety of its productions, and the quality of their performances and staging,

The Management

OPENING: OCTOBER 15.

On October 6 the Théâtre du Vieux-Colombier was jumping. The first performance was almost at hand. The rehearsals took place in the midst of debris and ladders, while in the auditorium, on stage, and in the wings everyone pitched in. On one corner of a table Léon-Paul Fargue copied addresses and stuffed envelopes, while Francis Jourdain painted backdrops and Gaston Gallimard swept up.[55]

On opening day Gaston spent the afternoon at the theater. Not satisfied with a mere managerial capacity, he made himself useful. He had accepted the job, but only for the first year. Martin du Gard, who was to meet him there, had trouble finding him. He expected to see him sitting at a big manager's desk, in quiet seclusion befitting his new position. So he was quite surprised to find him trying to keep warm at a folding table in a vestibule full of mirrors, yellow moldings, and drafts. Gaston led him to the orchestra seats so he could watch the dress rehearsal. Martin du Gard immediately recognized a bony, nimble character who was in constant motion, with a balding forehead, a long nose, and a pipe always in his mouth: Copeau.

"That's Blanche Albane over there," Gaston whispered to him, "the wife of Georges Duhamel, you know, the author of that play at the Odéon, *Dans l'ombre des statues* [*In the Shadow of Statues*]. And that's our stage manager, Copeau's right-hand man, a fellow named Louis Jouvet."[56]

The opening finally took place on October 23. All the friends of the *NRF* were there, which was to be expected, but also Tout-Paris, which was much more important. The columnists were quick to note the presence of Arthur Meyer, editor of the newspaper *Le Gaulois*; the politician and sometime cabinet minister Joseph Paul-Boncour; Misia Edwards, later more famous as Misia Sert; the permanent secretary for foreign affairs, Philippe Berthelot; the writer Elémir Bourges; Paul Fort, the "Prince of Poets"; and the Lithuanian-French poet, O.-W. de L. Milosz. They were giving *A Woman Killed by Kindness*, an English play by Thomas Heywood, adapted by Jacques Copeau, and Molière's *L'Amour médecin (Love's the Best Doctor)*, with the same cast in both: Copeau, Dullin, Jouvet, Blanche Albane, Suzanne Bing.

It was a hit. Jean de Pierrefeu, in *La Liberté*, seems best to have caught the spirit of the evening:

> After the lavishness and sensuality of the Boulevard theater, the dry-bread diet to which M. Jacques Copeau subjected us, for the good of our health, seemed very comforting to me. I had the feeling I was entering a poets' cloister. But rest assured, it's a charming cloister, without hairshirts, and with the smartest gowns in Paris and the highest society.[57]

The theater was on its way. It was to revolutionize the French stage.

When he was not busy keeping charts of the business end—on the left the play dates, on the right the titles of the plays, and in the middle the numbers of tickets sold and the total receipts—Gaston held open house for his friends in his office, most often to hear the reading of a poem by Paul Valéry or some piece by André Gide. One December evening, in Copeau's dressing room, there was a reading of Martin du Gard's play *Le Testament du père Leleu* (Old

Man Leleu's Will). Copeau, draped on a couch, was smoking his pipe; Gaston was sitting on the desk in back; Dullin, visibly delighted, was expressing his enthusiasm with mimicry. When Martin du Gard finished reading, Gaston looked around the group "with his good affectionate look," while Copeau finally exclaimed: "But that's good, very good. Good old Gard! It's right on the button. It's good classic theater. It's new and it's classical. We have to put it on, eh, Dullin, don't we have to put it on?"[58] Dullin would be featured in this peasant farce for twenty-six performances.

Shortly after that meeting, Copeau, looking for an actress to play Lechy in Claudel's *L'Echange* (The Exchange), put an ad in the theatrical paper *Comoedia* and for several mornings thereafter auditioned "the proletariat of the theater." Exhausted and discouraged by so much mediocrity, he was taken aback by a tall, slim woman, attractively built, who selected for her audition a scene from the old chestnut *Patrie*, by Victorien Sardou. She did not read it very well but she had a strong human touch, in the view of the Master, who was impressed by that. The fire, youth, ardor, and enthusiasm of the fledgling actress overcame his reservations. He read her some of the Claudel. Wide-eyed, the young woman immediately changed her tone and assured him, "That's meant for me—it's just the sort of thing I can do!"

Copeau was taken more by the personality than by the acting of Valentine Tessier, but this was how she became a part of the Vieux-Colombier company, and consequently a part of the life of Gaston Gallimard, with whom she would have a long-lasting liaison.

It was 1914, and murder was the front-page story of all the newspapers. Mme. Joseph Caillaux, wife of the finance minister and one-time premier, killed the editor of *Le Figaro*, Gaston Calmette, in his office because of his campaign against her husband. At Sarajevo Archduke Franz Ferdinand, heir to the Austrian throne, was assassinated. But the two crimes did not have equal repercussions.

Gide, who was about to publish *Les Caves du Vatican (Lafcadio's Adventures)*, wanted to straighten things out at the publishing house.

While complimenting Gaston on the way he kept the accounts, he wondered whether it was not proving too much for him, being worried that the *NRF*, in its dash and enthusiasm, had not assumed excessive burdens by going into both publishing and the theater. Go forward, to be sure, he thought, but not too fast: the momentum must not be broken, but it must be kept under control. Translated into non-Gidian terms, that meant he was trying to get rid of Gaston, whom he did not like. He had even found a replacement for him, Paul Grosfils, the man who had started the Presses Sainte-Catherine in Bruges and just happened to be available. Gide did his best to get Grosfils into the magazine and the publishing house, but to no avail. Gaston caught on quickly. This brought to a head a malaise festering for months on end. Gaston was discouraged: he had come into the *NRF* out of idealism, to devote himself to an irreproachable under-taking, and now he was considered a mere office manager by writers whose sole concern was money. He was just their errand boy. This attempt to sidetrack him stopped when a formal editorial board was set up, including the six founding members as well as Gallimard, Jean-Gustave Tronche, and Rivière. Henceforth Gaston too would have a word to say about submitted manuscripts. Rivière tried to bring him even closer to the literary side of the *NRF* by running several signed articles of his in the magazine. In this way, Gaston headed off Gide's nominee.[59]

So Gide tried another tack: he put forward a member of the clan. In a letter to Gaston, he wondered whether André Ruyters, one of the founding fathers of the magazine, who after all was good at figures, might not be very helpful to the company, if not to Gaston personally. For some time, Gide had not been equaling Gaston and Schlumberger on the financing front; they had invested more than he had. Schlumberger did suggest to Gide that he put up his royalties, present and future, in order to balance their shares. But Gide, dis-trustful, said he first wanted to study the figures for the last business period and then, since he could make neither head nor tail of them, empowered their mutual friend Ruyters to be his representative in the owning triumvirate.[60]

Then July 1914 came to its close. Gaston was vacationing at Martin du Gard's place, in the calm of the Verger d'Augy. Once a day, at 4:30 in the afternoon, the two friends returned to reality. Along the side of the highway, they went to await the mailman who brought the Paris papers. These were no longer filled with alarmist rumors but with news of grave events: the unions were demonstrating against war, Austria-Hungary had declared war on Serbia, President Poincaré and Premier Viviani were rushing home from Russia, where mobilization was the order of the day, and Jean Jaurès, the popular leader of the French Socialists, had been assassinated.

On August 1, when general mobilization was decreed in France, Gaston left his friend's place. Two days later he was with his family at Bénerville, when he learned that Germany had declared war on France.

3

World War I

1914~1918

War.

In a few days, French troops had lost the border battles. They beat a retreat as General Gallieni organized the defense of Paris with whatever means were at hand. The silences of the general staff, conflicting reports, and alarmist rumors panicked half a million Parisians who in one week fled the city toward the South. As Allies and Germans both burrowed into their trenches, the front became stabilized from Belfort to Nieuport, and the strategists on both sides started reinventing their profession by improvisation.

Gaston Gallimard was against war, resolutely. Not for political or humanitarian reasons: he did not even consider turning into a conscientious objector. Later he would love to tell how he had proudly donned the slacker's garb so as to avoid paying the blood tax demanded by the armaments dealers and their political stooges.[1] "Please understand that I am not a hero! I am a coward!" he would often repeat, long after the war was over, portraying himself as a herald of antiheroism. Heroism struck him as the supreme folly; all things considered, he would rather be a live coward than a dead hero. Sly, self-indulgent, cynical, he would try every ruse to keep out of service—simulated madness, escape through open windows, illness to the point of death, the testimony of his relatives' medical connections. Once exempted, he took pride in his victory, delighted, despite the censure of the majority, that he would not be machine-gunned in the chest because of other people's political ideas. And he did not want to hear about nationalism! "What most disgusts me," he would later say, "are the ones who did everything to avoid the war—as I did—but became superpatriots afterward!"[2]

But for him the years 1914–18 would be no less intense on the moral, professional, intellectual, and even emotional levels, for since early 1914 he was the father of a little boy, Claude.

In the fall of 1914 the Gallimard family was staying at Vannes, on the Gulf of Morbihan in southern Brittany, at a home of some Duché cousins. Gaston had worked out a whole strategy to foil the *marolles*. (In the vocabulary of his friends, this term, the name of a cheese with a smell so strong as to suggest cadavers, meant military service.) First, with a 2,000-franc bribe, he got someone to stamp "deceased" on his records at the local city hall.[3] Then, just in case that should be discovered, he actually made himself sick—to the point that everyone, including his family and best friends, really thought he was at death's door, as can be seen from his correspondence with Jacques Copeau, Jacques Rivière, Roger Martin du Gard, and Jean Schlumberger. He took no food, drank nothing, remained bedridden, let his beard grow to accentuate his emaciation, shivered before visitors, and spoke with mounting difficulty, making a visible effort to get words out.

In short, the business manager of the Théâtre du Vieux-Colombier was proving to himself that he too might have trod the boards. This required no little cynicism, for at the time a great many war wounded, real ones, were coming through this very city of

Vannes, on their way from the front, and the sight of their agony gave the city an eerie atmosphere.

His doctor diagnosed appendicitis attacks and liver problems. After two and a half months of his "diet," Gaston had to be transported to Paris, on a stretcher by ambulance, for an emergency consultation with an eminent surgeon, Dr. Gosset. He had lost about sixty pounds. On the advice of the military medical examiners, he was declared unfit for service.

At last! He had done what he set out to do. He then kept a promise to himself: he had his hair cut and his beard shaved off, then went to Maxim's all by himself to have an unforgettable dinner. So unforgettable that, when he left the famous restaurant on Rue Royale, he threw up in the Place de la Concorde. Feeling ill, he gave a fleeting thought to spending the night at the nearby Automobile-Club de France, but mustered enough strength to hail a taxi and have himself taken to Rue Saint-Lazare. And so to the sickbed, but this time not intentionally.[4]

After two weeks of recuperation, he tried gradually to readjust to his professional life. But what was to be done? Most of the *NRF* contributors were scattered all over France, whether free or in the service. Some were prisoners of war or missing in action—no one knew for sure. Letters from officers in the same outfit as Alain-Fournier, whose *Le Grand Meaulnes (The Wanderer)* had been published by the firm in 1913, told of his being wounded and a prisoner in Germany. In fact, he had already been killed on the Hauts-de-Meuse front. So had Charles Péguy, on September 5, near Villeroy, when the battle of the Marne was just beginning; he was one of the first infantry lieutenants cut down by a salvo, and the first French writer to die in the war.

This was a severe shock to his many friends, admirers, and readers. The news saddened Gaston and it revolted him: it confirmed his hatred of war, that unfair filler of cemeteries. To kill soldiers was understandable, it went with their trade, but to kill men like Péguy, who was only forty-one and still had so much to do, to write, to publish! And Alain-Fournier—at twenty-eight, he had barely begun his writing career! In that early winter of 1914, Gaston must have thought back with bitterness and derision on what Péguy had said to young Fournier three years earlier:

"You will go far, Fournier. And you will remember that I was the one who told you so."

1915. At Ypres, they were fighting with flamethrowers and poison gas. In Paris, Cipa Godebski was having friends in on Sunday evenings for musicales. Gallimard and Fargue, the two "literary ones," listened as Darius Milhaud, Maurice Ravel, and Erik Satie tried to outplay and outimprovise one another on the household piano.[5] How far away the war seemed.

Strangely, the ones who were enduring the war were all worried about the "slacker." Gaston could count the number of his friends by these expressions of concern, and there were many of them. In the diary he kept as a war prisoner, Jacques Rivière noted: "Right now, my friendship for Gaston is growing more youthful and deeper. I keep discovering in him treasures, resources that nothing will ever exhaust."[6]

Most of the letters Gaston received were concerned with the "morbid depression" into which he had fallen. Martin du Gard wrote Copeau: "I know that Gaston reacted with resolute energy. That is the only chance he has of coming through. His last letters terrified me: they were written by a man near death."[7]

Indeed, Gaston had really undermined his health. The fear of war made him ill. He worried that his various dodges might prove insufficient, as the conflict dragged on and grew fiercer.

His friend Fargue, a slacker like Gaston, had connections among military physicians. He found one who gave Gaston a lengthy examination and then advised a long stay in a rest home. Which, in the spring of 1915, led Gallimard to the sanatorium of Rueil. Copeau, who twice visited him there, was overwhelmed by the change in him, his physical and mental collapse.

"You're made of rubber," Gaston told him, "you always bounce back. Can't you understand that something can happen to a man and he can't recover from it?"

Then, after a moment, he got hold of himself and continued:

"You know what? I am insane. Oh, not insane all day long yet, but each day for part of the time. I think my personality is slipping away from me, and obsessions are taking over."

After spending hours talking with Gaston, Copeau was convinced that he would never get over this, and that it was all due to his horror of war, his fear of being called up in spite of his health: "That fear is his idée fixe, his madness," he wrote.[8]

At the same time, in the adversity of imprisonment and exile, Rivière "pray[s] to God to save my dear friend, my brother," after receiving a letter from his wife Isabelle, informing him that "Gaston is no better. He keeps getting thinner. It's purely nervous—something will have to be done to raise his spirits or the war will have to end."[9]

On May 23 Gallimard finally left the institution on Rue Bergère at Rueil-Malmaison, to go to Versailles and see Martin du Gard, a stopover on the way to La Ferté-sous-Jouarre. In a nearby hamlet called Le Limon, he found his friend Copeau waiting for him at his home. Gaston had come here to rest, to talk, to work, to organize, to regain a feel for life. It was either that or waste away at the sanatorium. After his long talks with Copeau he knew that with Copeau's help he would be able to readjust. "I need no other doctor but you," he wrote him.[10]

An habitué of the Brasserie Lipp would never have recognized the administrator of the *NRF* and the Vieux-Colombier. His hair was long and combed back, he had grown a slight beard, and seemed abnormally calm, his voice firm. He would often say, "We will have to be very strong," before reinventing the future with his accomplice, straightening out their plans, preparing an illustrated periodical devoted to the theater and entitled "Le Vieux-Colombier." His prewar enthusiasm was returning. Copeau felt that they were over the hump and reported these days of work together to Schlumberger, now an artillery observer, who immediately answered, "Take good care of Gaston. We would be better off each losing a hand than losing him."[11]

For he was precious. The firm had to go on, in spite of everything. From 1911 to 1914 it had published some sixty titles with a maximum printing of 1,500 copies each. The magazine itself had 3,000 readers in the summer of 1914. To keep the firm going and assure a minimum of continuity in business, Gallimard had delegated part of his powers to Berthe Lemarié, a friend of the magazine, the publishing house, and the theater. She saw to everything. Thanks to her, a semblance of activity went on. She knew everyone, the NRF founding fathers as well as the newcomers. Friendly and obliging, she invited them all in small groups to her apartment on Rue du Cardinal-Mercier, where, more than once, important decisions for the firm's future were made. Without Berthe, Gaston would not have known where to begin. Still, he was not sure what to turn to first: all the contracts that needed reviewing; the manuscripts that needed to be read; Claudel, who had to be called on at the Foreign Office on Quai d'Orsay; and all the printers who had no paper, no electricity, no personnel, but still wanted to do jobs for the NRF.

At the end of August he started going back to Bénerville for weekends, as he had done before his depression, to be with his wife, his mother, his son Claude, "a fat little chap, stark naked all day long at the beach."[12] He would have liked to use these moments of calm to write to all his friends, but was unable to overcome his revulsion at taking pen in hand. Roger was right to call him lazy and resent his brief "American-type notes." But he could not hold it against him, for he knew what he was getting over. Martin du Gard, now a sergeant in a transport outfit, wrote Gaston at length: "Your health is the main thing, one of the bases of what is important to me, our friendship as well as our common endeavor. So you have to hang on to it zealously and sacrifice all else to it."[13]

But before the year was out, Gaston was forced to go for a stay at a rest home in Switzerland, this time the Stephani Sanatorium in the high-altitude resort of Montana, to have his intestines treated.

In October Gaston arranged a meeting with Jacques Rouché, theater director, editor of *La Grande Revue*, patron of the arts, and recently appointed head of the Paris Opera, where the meeting took place. Having read Rouché's book, *L'Art théâtral moderne* (The Art of the Modern Theater), in which he introduced the revolutionary concepts of Edward Gordon Craig, the British theatrical theorist, Gaston wanted to take over from Rouché the rights he held to a Craig book, *On the Art of the Theatre*, with all commitments to the British publisher, to the author, and even to the translator, Geneviève Seligmann-Lui.[14]

Gaston was eager to have this book appear under the imprint of the *NRF*, the publishing house not only of genuine literature but also of pure theater—particularly since the beginning of the Vieux-Colombier adventure and its recent tour in England. A month later, right after Christmas, he was proud to announce another triumph to Copeau: he had persuaded Joseph Conrad's agent to give him the exclusive rights for France to all Conrad's works. Gaston did not want his house to miss out on the Polish-born English writer, whose many adventure novels and sea stories had brought the comment from Gide, "No excesses in his descriptions: they remain cruelly accurate." Gaston succeeded in getting what he wanted in every clause of the contract prepared by Conrad's agent, except for one: he had to agree to publish no less than two volumes a year. In the current state of affairs, this was manifestly impossible. After lengthy discussions they reached a compromise: the stipulation would go into effect only when the cannons had stopped, giving the *NRF* a respite, room to maneuver before starting on the publication of *Typhoon, Lord Jim, The Secret Sharer*, and so on. Such was the enthusiasm for Conrad at the *NRF* that, quite apart from professional translators like Philippe Neel and G. Jean-Aubry, who would translate most of the titles, Conrad's books were also translated by members of the *NRF* and its circle: André Gide, André Ruyters, Isabelle Rivière, and Dominique Drouin among others.

Gaston had not worked so hard since the start of the war. After

Craig and Conrad, he wanted to get Charles Péguy, the first anniversary of whose death had recently been celebrated. After publishing *Notre patrie* (Our Homeland), he asked Péguy's widow to turn the complete works over to him, so he could bring them out without any further delay.

He was staying up later and later to answer his voluminous mail, the more so since he had to keep Berthe Lemarié, his Parisian representative, informed. During the day he visited Swiss printers to see how they operated, with a view to starting his own press. He promised Copeau that from this stay abroad he would bring back "neither postcards nor photographs but catalogues of typefaces with up-to-date price lists. . . . I am well only when I am working."[15]

On the morning of January 24, 1916, just a few days after his thirty-fifth birthday, Gaston came back from Switzerland to Paris and his friend Léon-Paul Fargue. The poet was most upset by his appearance. He had never seen him with such a beard and such long hair, seemingly from the last century. Gaston's face looked troubled, his features drawn, his eyes sharply focused. The speechless Fargue listened to his friend talk on and on; discouraged by his stay in Switzerland, Gaston was convinced that the luxury hotels in Lausanne were full of German spies, lordly, good-looking personages with lavish Franz Josef sideburns who tried to outdo in elegance the equally mysterious countesses around them. He was deeply disturbed by the conversations he picked up here and there in bars and restaurants. At all events, nothing that was cause for optimism.[16]

More than ever, Gaston was determined to lose himself in his daily work. Martin du Gard understood this perfectly: "Have you found a way to escape that feeling of oppression which so disturbed you, with its excessive resonances that kept you from embarking on future projects—the only, blessed refuge, the sole source of patience and resignation?"[17]

Day by day Fargue and Gaston, working with Berthe Lemarié, made some order in the office on Rue Madame, dealing with the accumulation of books and the growing piles of manuscripts, acknowledging their receipt to authors by return mail, opening newspapers and magazines, and bringing accounts up to date. The *NRF* members who were prisoners or under arms had to know that they had not been forgotten, that their places remained unfilled, and that they were still considered "our own."

The magazine was suspended, but a few books appeared, such as Henri Ghéon's war poems, *Foi en la France* (Faith in France). Fearing that Gaston, in order to economize, might cut down on the press copies and the copies sent "in the name of the author," Ghéon urged Gide to stop by at Rue Madame and make sure that Gaston's list had not left out his friends or the Catholic papers.[18] But no, they were all there, and Martin du Gard would write of his joy at having received in the barracks a book with the *NRF* logo: "You can't imagine the pleasure I get in feeling a book from the *NRF*, in cutting its pages, turning it this way and that, like a friend."[19]

Publishing was becoming more and more difficult. There was a shortage of everything but manuscripts. Gaston was all the more frustrated, because young authors whom he had set out to launch before the war, such as Jean-Richard Bloch, were stirring with impatience. Their new books were ready and they could not understand why he, their publisher, was not. For in town, the war notwithstanding, life went on. When Bloch urged him to bring out *Et Cie* ("— & Co."), his novel describing the rise of a Jewish family in Alsace, Gaston wrote him:

> I will study your proposal. What was holding me back, of course, was the increase in the production cost of volumes at the moment, but also the question of tying up several thousand-franc bills at a time when they are scarce. No matter. Don't let my silence bother you. Your manuscript is on my desk and I am looking for a plan and a printer. But you have no idea how difficult work has become.[20]

Gaston was playing his cards close to his vest with most of his young authors, for other Parisian publishers were able to bring out books in this disturbed period, and he was determined, if the war dragged on, to stanch the exodus of writers. Gaston was to remain haunted by this period throughout his long career: suspicious that someone was trying to take away "his" authors, trying to seduce them by the most devious means. But that would never stop him— quite the contrary!—from borrowing or even appropriating his rivals' authors.

During the fall of 1916 Gaston assiduously cultivated a group of writer-diplomats through the good offices of Paul Claudel, who had just been assigned to his first ambassadorial post at Rio de Janeiro, and Alexis Saint-Léger Léger, who was leaving his position with the foreign press service to become third secretary of the French Legation in Peking. When not busying himself at the Ministry of Foreign Affairs, Gaston and his friend Fargue might invite some ladies for tea at the *NRF* office or go to movies, see plays, visit restaurants, attend picnics, explore riverside bistros, taking life easy, in spite of everything.

Gaston was in no way intimidated by the National League against Slackers. Their arguments did not impress him. He shrugged off all mention of the heroism of a namesake, Gen. Jacques Gallimard, an officer in the engineering corps who had distinguished himself at Peking in 1860 and been chief of the Ecole Polytechnique after the Franco-Prussian War of 1870. He was dominated by his own moods, nothing else mattered. But he lost some of his self-assurance and became once again frantic with worry when new regulations concerning exemptions were announced and he ran the risk of being called up again. Demoralized, Gaston turned to Fargue, who had him examined by a psychiatrist; Dr. Dupré declared that the patient was undoubtedly suffering an extreme case of "military anxiety."[21] Exempted again!

In 1917, Gaston and Berthe Lemarié were having lunch with Martin du Gard, who happened to be in Paris on furlough. They took stock of their situation and did not find it brilliant. Rivière, the managing editor of the magazine, was still a prisoner in Germany; Lanux was a war correspondent for *Le Figaro* in the Balkans; Tronche, their business manager, was in the trenches; Copeau was in New York; and most of the contributors were away from Paris. Gaston once again was depressed. Strangely, though he was the fixed center of a completely scattered *NRF*, he felt excluded; he was convinced that plans were being made behind his back. He had never been a friend of Gide's, and was therefore not surprised by the latter's occasional distance and distrust. But he was close to Copeau, and the idea that Jacques was no longer counting on him cut him to the quick.

Copeau had gone to the United States to try to set up a tour for the Vieux-Colombier, since its Parisian theater was closed for the duration. In New York he was acclaimed and immediately invited to head the local Théâtre Français. He was making plans on his own for things that Gaston would have liked both to originate and manage. In a very long letter, Copeau tried to reassure his friend while "filling him in" on what was being done without him:

> No need to tell you, dear Gaston, that I am not making any plan without including you. We will look into the matter together and then decide whether it is better for our mutual enterprise if you remain in Paris or come to New York with me. . . . I doubt that, back there on Rue Madame, you can realize what sane, reasonable activity can accomplish over here. I am not speaking only of the theater; I mean also the magazine and the publishing house. Among the young intellectual elite here, the *Nouvelle Revue Française* has a reputation without equal; you would have been moved to see young people (who themselves publish quite estimable magazines) ask me whether our circulation was over a hundred thousand. Yet we have absolutely no commercial outlet here. Not one of our books is on sale; we must without delay, not after the war but right now, lay claim to the place we are entitled to.[22]

Never had Gaston felt so isolated, so separated from everyone. He made no show of it, expressed it to no one, except perhaps Rivière, to whom he confided:

> I have reached the point where I have just about decided to leave the *NRF*, and perhaps even France. . . . A year ago that was a settled

matter, and if at the last minute I stayed on, I was kept here only by a sense of duty, an idea to which I am so unaccustomed, yet in that idea the memory of you was intimately connected.[23]

But Gaston could no longer hide his bitterness. Martin du Gard, who knew him well, quickly understood and begged him to clear up this misunderstanding, not to let the situation deteriorate, for that would hurt everyone in the group. He faulted him for the courtesy in their relationship, their fears of hurting one another, in a word, for their good manners, which were also a delicacy of the heart. Martin du Gard was convinced that things would improve between Copeau and Gaston, but also among all the NRF people, if they were less polite, and if, occasionally, without necessarily indulging in vulgar slaps on the back, they dropped the hypocrisy of society people and replaced it with the frankness of old friends. The NRF meetings might be less gracious but a lot more efficient.[24] Regarding lack of frankness and silent acquiescence, Martin du Gard considered Gaston even guiltier than Copeau, but in his Diary he noted:

> Copeau taxes Gallimard with not devoting himself body and soul to his work, with being a hypochondriac, completely stymied by the war, with not knowing English, and with not having the sacred fire. Gallimard taxes Copeau with having used and abused his time, money, and devotion, and with not making room for him in his own undertakings. He wants to be his associate, but not his subordinate. And Copeau can find room only for those under him. It is very worrisome. Both are wrong and yet at the same time both are right. But between them, there can be no open discussion of it.[25]

Gaston was disappointed, worried, yet despite it all, despite the temptation to chuck it and go away, he persevered. Contrary to what Copeau believed, he did have the sacred fire for literature and the theater, but his fire burned inwardly; very few could see it.

In March, Fargue sent him a young man whose manuscript of poems he had read by chance one evening at the home of some friends. At Rue Madame Gaston saw an awkward, long-limbed boy arrive in an infantry uniform, but so bashful that he had brought along his fiancée and two of her girl friends. His name was Pierre Drieu La Rochelle. Gaston agreed to publish his war poems at the author's expense, even though two of them, out of a total of seventeen, especially upset the censors, who told him, "See here, young man, you speak to the Germans as if they were human beings like us."[26] Despite the high quality of these poems, they were banned. Gaston nevertheless printed 150 copies instead of the originally planned 500 of *Interrogation*, and they were distributed sub rosa in September.

Since this was Drieu's first book, he was not very demanding. But Gaston had to fight with other authors, explain to them that many manuscripts were held up at the printers, and that he, as publisher, had to foot the bill for these delays, the lack of transport, and the general apathy and ill will.

Not loath to involve his authors in his problems, he often wrote them long technical letters, well aware that some of them were indeed interested in typography, the quality of paper used, and distribution. This was the case with Paul Valéry, who published the first of his books with the *NRF* in 1917. For over four years Gide, Rivière, and Gaston had urged him to collect into one volume his poems that had appeared in different magazines. Having escaped the draft, Valéry used the war years to polish and deliver to Gaston *La Jeune Parque*, which was to hold a special place in his oeuvre. The 600 copies of the first printing quickly sold out. Beyond its literary qualities, its manufacture and publishing had been carefully prepared by author and publisher working together as a team. Their exchange of letters prior to the publication of *La Jeune Parque* sounds more like a printshop conversation than one between a poet and a lover of words.

I have a new sample of Cremieu to show you in a 14-pt. Didot and also a sample of what I feel is a less attractive typeface. I am familiar with the Studium printshop; I got together with them about the publication we are planning: they have Didot only in 14 pt. . . . As you can see, we come out to 50 pages—each sheet making 16 pages, we therefore have to settle for 48 pages or else 48 + 8 = 56 pages. The latter solution would, of course, increase the production cost. But you know I have never looked upon this publication as a business matter. . . . I have somewhat arbitrarily inserted the blank spaces: some are 8 and some are 10 lines. By saving two or three lines we might end up saving a whole page. Anyway, the sinkage for each piece has been laid out on the basis of 14 or 15 lines to the page—perhaps we might equally well agree on 16 lines.[27]

The correspondence between the two was long and detailed. Valéry, not always in agreement with his publisher, came to feel that the latter tended more to "impose" than to "propose." However, Gide was able to convince Valéry and lead him toward compromise by stressing that Gaston and the *NRF* would be dishonored if his name were not in their catalogue, and would be disappointed not to feel that he was one of them.[28]

With other authors not within Gide's orbit, dynamic authors in demand, it was more difficult. Worried about the future of his new novel *"—& Co.,"* Jean-Richard Bloch warned Gaston that he had received offers from a competing firm, Berger-Levrault, and that he would not be able to hold out very long. Having no other way of retaining him, Gaston then carefully explained his own situation and asked Bloch to be more indulgent toward him than toward his competitors.

Since the beginning of the war, the whole *NRF* organization had been wiped out. The Bruges printer, who held all its stocks of paper, its lead, and its plates, was beyond reach, Belgium being under German occupation. Despite the amount of capital tied up there and the uncertainties about tomorrow, Gaston was on the lookout for other printers who, when they did accept his orders, still gave priority to their long-standing customers. It took him twice as long, to be sure, but he did succeed in reprinting some of the earlier books so as to keep them on dealers' shelves and bring in some cash flow to finance new enterprises. In this light, *"—& Co."* meant to him mainly a book of 750,000 characters, which presented a problem at a time when printers were not disposed to adding further type to their supply. For this new book of Bloch's and the reprinting of Martin du Gard's *Jean Barois*, Gaston queried 351 printers in the provinces. He got only ten satisfactory replies and, after visiting all ten shops, decided on one at Morlaix. It was a small shop, but it was growing and might well take the place of Verbeke. Its price list was reasonable, and Gallimard foresaw that he would be its main customer, having first priority by buying into the firm. He even had it buy a Monotype, the only machine then capable of quickly setting long books without too much personnel: 8,000 characters an hour! At any rate, despite the investment that this choice entailed, it was Gaston's last chance to do any normal publishing if the war dragged on: Swiss printers were now supplying paper only to their Swiss customers, and to import paper or get earlier delivery required considerable sums.[29] As for the paper suppliers to whom Gaston had traditionally turned—Navarre or Lafuma—their stocks were largely depleted.

Jean-Richard Bloch decided he would wait. His book came out in 1918.

In the fall of 1917, Gaston was getting ready to sail for the United States. It had been decided that he would join the Vieux-Colombier troupe in New York. But before that, he was absolutely determined to settle the "Proust affair."

Convinced by Gaston, Gide, and Rivière that he had to break once and for all with Grasset and become part of the *NRF* "stable," Proust consulted Emile Strauss, a legal expert on questions of literary property, and then brought in René Blum, who had introduced him to Grasset three years before.

Proust, not one for brutal breaks, wanted to slip quietly out of his deal with the publisher. But despite all the circumlocutions and tactfulness he displayed, Grasset, convalescing in Switzerland, was furious and bitter when he read Proust's letter of termination. He had published the book at the author's expense, it was true, but the very fact that the *NRF* wanted to take him away was enough for Grasset to want to hold on to Proust. Too late. The Rue Madame cabal had convinced Proust that there was no turning back. Rather than standing on his rights, Grasset questioned Proust's loyalty to his first publisher. But in either case it was a lost cause; vanity publishing is an expedient and certainly no sign of a publisher showing confidence in an author. This being the case, it could only be a matter of one-sided loyalty.

On October 15, Gaston for the first time wrote to Grasset: "Having become the publisher of M. Marcel Proust and being currently engaged in bringing out the whole series of *Remembrance of Things Past*, by agreement with him I would like to buy back from you whatever supply of copies remains of *Swann's Way*."[30]

This occasioned the first meeting between the two publishers. A business discussion: the price of the stock—some 600 copies—was high, but Gaston wanted the matter settled. So from Grasset's Rue des Saints-Pères house to Rue Madame a handcart transferred several dozen pounds of Proust. Immediately Gaston had the Grasset covers torn off, to be replaced by the *NRF*'s, hoping thereby to erase once and for all that original blunder painfully brought to mind by this edition. A few months later there would be three-way negotiations among the author and his two publishers, and after much discussion they would iron out the remaining details of the transfer: indemnities, compensations, and royalties. The only things not settled by this accounting were Grasset's bitterness and his public disavowal. Paris gossip would long refer to him as "the publisher who dumped Proust because he didn't believe in the writer's future." Throughout his life Grasset would have to deny this legend, pointing out that the vanity publication was inevitable because of the length of the book and the costs of printing it, and that, had it not been for the 1914 declaration of war, he would have brought out *Le Côté de Guermantes (The Guermantes Way)*, much of which was already in type.[31] Gaston, for his part, would never cease to remind people that he had met Proust first, on the road to Bénerville, and that the *NRF*'s rejection of his manuscript had merely been an unfortunate misunderstanding, a slip due to the inexperience of the young publishing house and its lack of organization. One way or the other, the Proust episode marked a significant date in the history of the two publishing firms, for it was then, in October 1917, that their ferocious competition got its start.

The Garrick Theatre on Thirty-fifth Street in New York was where lovers of good French theater were most likely to catch the Vieux-Colombier company: Copeau, Charles Dullin, Louis Jouvet, Valentine Tessier, Lucienne Bogaert, Romain Bouquet—and Gaston, who did not appear on stage, but was otherwise very active.

Philippe Berthelot had made it possible for them to be there. That shrewd diplomat, cabinet secretary to Minister of Foreign Affairs Aristide Briand and later permanent secretary of the Quai d'Orsay, was a true friend of the *NRF*. He was actually the boss of Paul Claudel, Alexis Saint-Léger Léger, Paul Morand, and Jean Giraudoux, and it was Berthelot who instigated this propaganda tour in support of French culture in the United States—a roundabout way of keeping the Vieux-Colombier troupe alive despite the war and the closing of its theater in Paris, and of getting actors such as Dullin and Jouvet out of uniform.

The "angel" for the New York tour was the local patron of the arts, Otto Kahn, who was active on the board of the French Theatre, as he was on that of the Metropolitan Opera. From the outbreak of the war, Kahn, one of New York's leading bankers, had been known for his pro-French sentiments. During the three-months layoff between the two Vieux-Colombier seasons in New York, he lent the company the use of his magnificent New Jersey estate.

First Berthelot, then Kahn: in adversity, the Vieux-Colombier somehow always found guardian angels along its way. From his stay in America Gaston retained happy memories. The day after his arrival, Charles Dullin called for him at the small boarding house where he was staying, to show him Fifth Avenue. Dullin was in his Sunday best, with fine high shoes and a top hat, believing that this was the proper way to dress.[32] But he seemed hardly more incongruous than the ladies in the audience who knitted woolen underwear for the boys "over there," as they watched Copeau and Dullin trade verbal barbs on the Garrick stage.

Gaston spent some unforgettable and very useful times in New York meeting writers, critics, publishers, and even investigating presses, an old habit he had got into whenever he was traveling. He made friends with some of the printers, among them a Frenchman whose company he enjoyed as a relief from the Americans who did not speak his language. With him he could talk painting and literature and take in the sights of New York, famous and not so famous, from the Ziegfeld Follies to obscure Negro jazz clubs.[33] Gaston's nighttime companion and welcome guide in the alien big city was Henri-Pierre Roché; much later, in the 1950s, he would be the author of two novels published by Gallimard that would gain greater fame when they became the movies *Jules et Jim* and *Deux Anglaises et le continent.*

Of course not everything about this American interlude was on the plus side. After a few months of living together, the players started getting on one another's nerves. Copeau got it into his head that his friends had begun plotting against him, and that Gaston was behind it, pulling strings to undermine his authority. Gallimard, on the other hand, was finding it more and more difficult to accept Copeau's view of the troupe as an extension of himself, and of the theater as his creature. It all worked itself out after some stormy scenes, but in the process a spring had been broken.

This American tour, while hardly brilliant financially, was of great moment to Gaston. In the calm of Otto Kahn's Jersey estate, he was able to give deep thought to what his life up to that point had been, and meditate on his professional start. Once back in Paris, "I understood that the firm had to be given a commercial base and an organization, if it were to be viable. Otherwise it would just be the undertaking of a group of friends whose good will was not always enough."[34]

After six months of "liberty" in the United States, Gaston was thrust into family problems as soon as he set foot in France. The return to reality was brutal. He was immediately taken to Bénerville, where his grandmother was at death's door. There, he was treated to a

"sickening" spectacle: the old woman was being pressed, even physically, to sign some papers before she died.[35] This picture he would
never forget.

His immediate reaction was to sail right back to the United States,
to prepare future projects with Copeau—in person better than by
mail—and also to get away from the domination of his father who,
since the grandmother's death, had started playing the patriarch.

Gaston got his tickets and sailed for America on July 13, just as
the military situation was on the point of turning. The Germans had
launched their offensive in Flanders and along the Aisne River, and
were about to attack in Champagne. But the balance of power would
soon shift in favor of the Allies. Foch announced to an assembly of
all the commanders-in-chief that, despite numerical inferiority, the
time had come to go from the defensive to the offensive. A series
of thrusts by General Mangin at Villers-Cotterets, the British at
Amiens, the Americans at Saint-Mihiel, and Gen. Franchet d'Esperey
in the Balkans led up to the general Allied offensive of September
26. The Bulgarians were the first to sue for an armistice. For Germany
and her allies, this was the beginning of the end.

In Paris that shift in the political and military situation upset a
great many plans. Light could now be seen at the end of the tunnel.
After his second stay in the United States, Gaston came home for
good in January 1919. He was determined to set his publishing house
on a more solid business foundation. The financial situation was
hardly brilliant, nor did Gaston attribute this only to monetary and
managerial difficulties caused by the war. It was the spirit of things
that had to be changed. Gone was the artisanlike atmosphere of the
start. The "bureau" had turned into a real business, and the group
would have to adapt to that development and assume the constraints
of it. Schlumberger would present no problem; he had confidence
in Gaston. But Gaston was much less sure of his other partner, Gide.

At the beginning of 1918, a profound disagreement had arisen
between the two men. They had, of course, never been very close.
But their disagreement went so far that it threatened to tear the *NRF*
apart. The survival of the group hinged on their reconciliation. Gide

took umbrage at the increasingly important position Gaston was assuming both on the magazine and in the publishing house. During the war Gide had already anticipated the broad lines of the *NRF*, as he wrote in his *Journal*:

> To avoid my being made responsible for attitudes and actions which friendship alone keeps me from repudiating, it would be better soon to change the name of the firm and give up a solidarity that is both compromising and dishonest. Like Copeau, I believe that it is better for Gallimard to make the decisions and to make them by himself; but then it will be necessary for him to put his name, and his name alone, on those decisions; let the *NRF* publishing house become the Gallimard publishing house.

Such a development seemed unavoidable, not for commercial reasons alone, but also because of the antagonism between Gide and Gaston, their conflict of personalities and power which was poisoning the atmosphere. Even though they were officially reconciled in 1919, this falling out was never wholly forgotten. For many years Gaston would enjoy repeating under his breath two famous comments Fargue had made about Gide's elusive character: "He's a fistful of water," and "If he jumped out the window, he wouldn't fall."[36]

As for Gide, while admitting that he could not remember a single conversation with Gaston "out of which I didn't emerge totally turned around and agreeing with him,"[37] he would complain for many years, and often bitterly, about the distance his publisher insisted on keeping between them:

> In the nearly thirty years that I have known him and we have worked together, never once has Gaston shared a meal with me. He has never invited me. Yet I did my best. How often, at lunchtime, I would walk into his office, sit down in an armchair, and wait for an invitation. Sometimes I dropped a heavy hint, often going so far as to tell him I was alone at lunch and didn't know where to eat. But despite these indiscreet and often too obvious advances, he never asked me along. No, not once in thirty years.[38]

A man who knew them both very well, Copeau, summed up the situation perfectly in the fall of 1918, from the United States, when he wrote to Rivière:

> It was never right between them. It never will be. Gaston is weak and violent. Gide is often oblique, even duplicitous. . . . Gaston wants to be at home in the publishing house, he wants it to be his. It has to be that way or he will leave. I know him well now, having seen him close up over here. . . . He says things like, "We'll never be able to do anything as long as Gide is there." And he isn't wrong. He adds, "Gide can't leave, so I might as well pull out." You have to know about this, because it has been going on for six or seven years, keeps getting in our way, and in the end will do real harm. Gaston is right, from his viewpoint. But he is wrong in his attitude, his behavior toward Gide, which is almost always pusillanimous.[39]

Their positions seemed irreconcilable. Yet by dint of compromises and negotiations, often done by letter, which did not make anything easier, their differences were smoothed out for the benefit of the group. Gide and Gaston both realized that this was the only way to avoid an explosion.

4

The Firm

1919-1936

The war was over, France was victorious, her people had been bled white: 1,310,000 dead or missing, 1,110,000 wounded. The rich pre-1914 nation was ruined. Germany will pay, it was said. In the meantime the survivors had to start rebuilding. Slackers sometimes found it hard to face those who had come back from the trenches at Verdun or elsewhere. Gaston, proud of having escaped the inferno and a death he considered all but certain, got the cold shoulder from his family and some of his friends. "Coward," many muttered. He did not care. His mind had been made up, and he was not going to accept lessons about morals, even from authentic heroes. The hecatomb of the fallen had somewhat shaken his cynicism, true, but the death of a personal friend, Pierre Margaritis, from a poorly treated case of influenza shook him far more deeply. One figure, though, did disturb his equanimity: 450. That was how many writers had been killed in the war, according to the Writer-Veterans Association.[1]

Like all sectors of the national economy, the book business found it hard to get going again. The great prewar publishing houses seemed drained of whatever dynamism they had once had. Fasquelle was losing its influence, Ollendorff was selling out to Albin Michel, Calmann-Lévy lived off its prestigious nineteenth-century authors. The other "giants" kept going, each aiming at a separate share of the market: Plon specialized in Catholic books, Fayard in history, Flammarion in popular literature, and the Mercure de France in the avantgarde. It was time for the young. Bernard Grasset was attracting attention particularly through his persistent personal involvement in the promotion of his books and authors; Albin Michel was taking off like lightning in all directions. It exploited the Ollendorff backlist (Hugo, Balzac, Maupassant, Romain Rolland, and Paul Féval); won a flock of awards for its more recently established writers (Henri Béraud, Pierre Benoit, Francis Carco, Roland Dorgelès); and broke ground with many new names (Maxence Van der Meersch, Henri Pourrat, Roger Vercel).[2]

In the face of all this, Gaston seemed unenterprising. Actually, all his energy was absorbed in reorganizing the *NRF* and setting it on a sound basis, eliminating misunderstandings or recriminations.

As mediator between Gide and Gaston in their struggle for influence, the group looked to Rivière. During the enforced leisure of a prisoner of war, Rivière had given much thought to the future of the *NRF*, and on his return made it clear that he wanted to be the editor of the magazine. But in spite of his experience, the founding fathers thought him too young—only thirty-three—and insufficiently authoritarian; also, as Schlumberger was quick to point out, Rivière contributed to the magazine "neither money nor preponderant influence."[3] There was a drift toward another solution: Gide as editor, Rivière as managing editor. But the violent opposition of Claudel crystallized the basic problems that would be created by Gide's rule, were he officially given the title:

> I am told that André Gide is officially going to take on the editorship of the *NRF*. If that should occur, you may count on my never again giving one line of writing to this periodical. The name of Gide stands

for pederasty and anti-Catholicism. That is a shingle under which I have no intention of setting myself up.[4]

Gide was much too well known for what he was, to accept any responsibility other than an informal and shadowy one on a magazine that sought to be a meeting place, an assembly around a common moral, aesthetic, and literary viewpoint. Finally, after many discussions, it was decided that Rivière would be editor of the *NRF*, that Gaston would head the publishing company, and that Gide would withdraw to the sidelines to devote himself more fully to his own writings, while maintaining a privileged connection with the firm.

The magazine started reappearing in June 1919, after an absence of almost five years. But the very first issue sowed discord in the ranks of the group. Rivière, who had put it together, assumed responsibility for a manifesto that opted for the practice and defense of "pure" literature, which would not subordinate intelligence and thought to any nationalistic or ethical values. This opening statement was, in effect, a call to political disengagement. It created all the more discord among the group for having gone straight from Rivière's desk to the printer's without being shown to anyone, though it committed the magazine and its founders to these stated principles. Once again the specter of a schism haunted the Rue Madame offices, but it was quickly dissipated by a meeting held on July 3, which resulted in nothing concrete, thanks to the kind of compromise they all liked, except for one confirmed fact: even if the façade of the *NRF* was once again maintained, the group was definitely split in two. Gide, Rivière, Copeau, and Gaston were on one side; on the other, Ghéon, Drouin, and Schlumberger, who meant the *NRF* to be above all a fighting vehicle, judging the value of a work not by its aesthetics but by its social and moral effectiveness.[5] This meeting also marked out the differences between Rivière and the others. Just before the meeting, he said to Gaston: "I will not and cannot say anything except what I see, and not what is supposed to be said, for the very reason that as a prisoner in Germany I lived among people who never said anything except what was supposed to be said."

And about Schlumberger, with whom he was once more in opposition, he added: "On meeting him again, I am struck by how Germanic his turn of mind is. He is very much like the people I encountered there."[6]

So the war was not over—in people's minds. Its aftereffects still distorted discussions and crystallized unresolved differences.

Three weeks after this clarification session, on July 26, 1919, the Librairie Gallimard, as the new publishing house was to be generically and corporatively known, was set up. It was capitalized at 1,050,000 francs, supplied by five shareholders: Emmanuel Couvreux, Gaston Gallimard, Jean Schlumberger, Raymond Gallimard, and André Gide. The group therefore included two new names, those of men brought in by Gaston: one of his brothers and one of his best friends.

Raymond Gallimard was two years younger than Gaston. There was nothing special to single him out for the book business. After secondary schooling at the Lycée Condorcet, he had gone to the Ecole Centrale des Arts et Manufactures. A graduate engineer, he had a brilliant future before him with Panhard et Levassor, the automobile company, especially since Paul Panhard, the founder's nephew, was a friend of his. Less passionately involved with literature than his older brother, Raymond had more of a bent toward figures, accounting schedules, and business strategies.

When Gaston met with his two brothers, to explain the catastrophic financial situation of the *NRF* company at the end of the war, he scared them a bit, suggested the possibility of bankruptcy, and as always when occasion demanded, showed a great flair for sentimental blackmail, shrewdly intertwining their mutual affection with the business matters for which he was responsible.

"If you don't help me," he announced, "the business will go under, our name will be discredited—and I will move to the United States!"[7]

Raymond let himself be talked into taking over the business and administrative end of the young company. Jacques, the youngest and the only one of the brothers to have been in the war, did not want to join the firm; he preferred going ahead with the little central-heating company he had started with some Army buddies. Their cousins Pierre and Frédéric Duché did invest some money in the firm, but without becoming active participants.[8]

First with the title of delegate administrator, and then as adjunct director general and executive officer of the company, Raymond Gallimard was to play a discreet but fundamental role in the history of the publishing house that bore his name as well. His arrival at the *NRF* meant a much firmer management. He set up a systematic cost accounting for production, rather than the vague "200 pages at 3 fr. 50" that was traditional in the industry. But above all, he and Gaston would form a pair who ideally complemented each other. The Gallimard brothers had a very useful ploy: when confronted with some bothersome character—whether author, supplier, printer, or the press—they would break off the discussion with, "I'll take it up with my brother. He's the one who makes the decisions," and thus send the pest back and forth from one to the other until he was worn out. In other cases Gaston would "soften up" the customer and then turn him over to Raymond, who would "do him in" quite properly.

Of the two Gallimards, Raymond was the administrator; if Gaston had done that job for a while, it was only because of the challenge of it, and he had done it with total improvisation. The 1919 situation of the *NRF* was evidence of that. His brother's arrival was to make the growth of the company possible, with Gaston devoting himself mainly to being a publisher, properly speaking: sparking and running a firm that would develop with lightning speed.

No one has given a better picture of the fraternal duo than André Beucler in his roman à clé *La Fleur qui chante* (The Singing Flower). When the book appeared, everyone in the Parisian literary and publishing worlds knew at once that the Gallimards were the models for Olivier and Maurice Brouillard, owners of an important Parisian art gallery located halfway between the Chamber of Deputies and Saint-Germain-des-Prés.

Where Olivier was agreeable and self-assured, Maurice was gauche and importunate. . . . When the gallery was founded, Olivier had gone to reclaim his brother from the nuts-and-bolts shop in which he was a head engineer, so Maurice entered the world of the arts with precise and honest ideas. . . . Olivier took care of making the pitch to customers and suppliers, preparing them, putting them in the mood before sending them along to his brother who, while meticulous and complimentary, came to the point, confronting them with the bills or contracts. One was the brains of the business, the other its stomach. . . . The two men had for each other a kind of tacit and embarrassed tenderness, which was as much complicity as affection: Maurice knew that, in his way, Olivier was the sharpest salesman in Paris, and Olivier felt that Maurice was a fine legalist who had no difficulty in playing dumb within the dull framework of honesty. . . . Olivier was the lawyer and Maurice the executioner; one acted as the hound, while the other lay in wait for the deer or hare and finished it off.[9]

Charm and integrity, talent and competence: Gaston and Raymond Gallimard to the life.

The other newcomer among the active *NRF* shareholders was one of their dearest childhood friends. Emmanuel Couvreux, "Mané" to his friends, was the son of a famous builder of public works. He was three years younger than Gaston, and had three passions in life: devotion to the Gallimards, which was unconditional; the Jacques Dalcroze method of eurhythmics, solfeggio, and body technique, which he followed assiduously; and Louis Jouvet's theater, of which he was one of the most fervent supporters. He had gone to the Lycée Condorcet with Raymond Gallimard, and the two of them would hold endless engineering talks about their favorite subject: heaters. With Gaston, Fargue, and Pierre de Lanux he talked literature, theater, and music. Phlegmatic, indifferent to what people thought of him, majestically ignoring taunts and gibes when he sped around Paris bareheaded in a roadster without a windshield, Couvreux was often described as an eccentric by his relatives and the members of the Automobile-Club de France, where he rubbed elbows with fellow member Gaston. His friends viewed him mainly as a very rich but marginal member of the upper bourgeoisie, a distinguished and not ordinary amateur who would later sometimes indulge himself in writing a piece on Isadora Duncan and Wagner for *La Revue musicale*, while putting up some of his less fortunate artistic and literary friends at his town house in fashionable Neuilly. Couvreux, who took his position on the board of the Gallimard company very seriously, had also invested a great deal of money in the firm, so that in that sense, too, he was a dear friend.

The bylaws of the new company gave Gaston 300 shares, as founder and in consideration of what he had contributed: the property and goodwill of the existing *NRF* company and the benefit of the research and groundwork undertaken in establishing the Librairie Gallimard. Shortly thereafter Gaston informed Rivière that he was making him a gift of thirty of those 300 shares.[10] But if this was his intention, it was never carried out: all that Rivière ever got was 2,000 francs per month as editor of the *Nouvelle Revue Francaise*.[11]

Throughout August 1919, Gallimard desperately hunted for larger space than they had on Rue Madame. All he could find was a ground floor and mezzanine on Rue du Faubourg Saint-Honoré, at 60,000 francs per annum—out of the question. Bankers also proved of no help; not one would open a line of credit to him without collateral, and Jean Schlumberger, who would have lost nothing by it, refused to cosign.[12]

Gaston was in a hurry, and rightly so. First of all, he had undertaken to acquire in October part ownership of The St. Catherine Press in Bruges. Since the end of the war, Verbeke had once again become his chief printer. Then, thanks to his brother Raymond, he came to understand that in the event of an unexpected best-seller the firm would be hard put to find the cash to cover a few massive printings. This was a contingency he had to be ready for. The more so because of his faith in Proust. He had been seeing a great deal of Proust since his return from the United States, mostly at night, giving no sign of his furious impatience while the author made endless corrections and changes in the manuscript of *A l'ombre des jeunes filles en fleurs (Within a Budding Grove)*. The book was as successful, both commercially and critically, as *Swann's Way*—good enough, but not overwhelming. Quite obviously, not yet what both author and publisher hoped for. Only the winning of the Goncourt Prize might allow the complete work, long and difficult, to "take off" with the general public. In early September Proust let some of his friends know that he was being considered for it. Nor was he discouraged when the man who had been one of his mentors, old Anatole France, showing his seventy-five years, gave up reading *Within a Budding Grove*, sighing, "Life is too short and Proust is too long."[13]

Convinced that in time his work would be consecrated, Proust organized a whole literary strategy at which he was a past master, giving numerous luncheons at the Pré-Catelan and dinners at the Ritz, using his best friends and closest connections as light cavalry in his battle for final victory. The influence of Robert de Flers, Reynaldo Hahn, Louis de Robert, and Robert Dreyfus was put to work to bring round the Prize judges least well disposed toward him, Léon Hennique and Lucien Descaves. He knew that the votes of Léon Daudet, J.-H. Rosny jeune, and Henri Céard would be his, but there were still five more.

On December 10, after the traditional luncheon at Chez Drouant, the Goncourt Academy did award its prize to Proust. He was only two votes ahead of his rival, Roland Dorgelès, the author of *Les Croix de bois (Wooden Crosses)*, a realistic novel about death in the trenches of 1914, light-years removed from *Within a Budding Grove*.

At 5:00 P.M. the bell rang at Proust's, on Rue Hamelin. Céleste, his housekeeper, opened the door and saw three very excited gentlemen: Gaston, flanked by Tronche and Rivière.

"I expect you know that Monsieur Proust has won the Prix Goncourt," Gaston said to her. And then, "I must see Monsieur Proust immediately!"[14]

The housekeeper informed her employer, who was having an antiasthma inhalation. He would not be able to see them, but asked that they come back about 10 P.M. Gaston, not to be gainsaid, lost his temper and protested that he would miss the train to Deauville; he absolutely had to meet his Abbeville printer so as to avoid running out of stock. He kept insisting, beside himself, exerting more and more pressure, pacing back and forth in the vestibule. The writer finally gave in and received the three of them, now joined by Léon Daudet, who had also come to bring the good news. It was a strange, very strained encounter between the *NRF* ambassadors and the reactionary, royalist pamphleteer of *L'Action française* at Proust's bedside. Fortunately it did not last long: the writer was overcome by a violent asthma attack, took leave of his guests, and ordered his servants to bar the door to the press. Which did not keep the papers from devoting lengthy articles to the bedridden author, lauding his work in terms that would have been unimaginable a few months earlier, in most cases reducing the event of the day to no more than the crowning of a personality, and completely overlooking the literary merits of *Remembrance of Things Past*. A number of papers were mainly struck by the fact that the 1919 Goncourt winner was a socialite intellectual unknown to the public and not a war veteran.

The printing of *Within a Budding Grove* was snapped up in a few days. Using every device he could, by hook or by crook Gallimard had most bookshops restocked with it within ten days of the Drouant luncheon; the copies now had a red paper band around them reading "Prix Goncourt," a first in the history of *NRF* publishing. For a time they considered suing Albin Michel, which had put a similar "Prix Goncourt" band on Dorgelès's book, with the words "4 votes out of 10" in tiny letters underneath. But they thought better of it, deciding that suing would place them on the same level as the misrepresentation.

With this consecration of Proust, the new start of Gaston's publishing concern took place under the best of auspices. The year 1920 would maintain the momentum of the commercial success of *Within a Budding Grove* with the new edition of Martin du Gard's *Jean Barois*, which had been delayed by the war. Gallimard opened a retail bookstore on Boulevard Raspail, increased his capitalization on June 11, and launched a new magazine, *La Revue musicale* (The Musical Review), which very quickly won favor with its specialized audience. This was enhanced by the fact that, like the *NRF*, of which it was a sort of cousin by marriage, under Gaston's guidance it also created a "magazine spirit," organizing chamber music concerts at the Vieux-Colombier, offering reduced prices "to try to do for music what the Vieux-Colombier troupe has done for the theater." They put on performances of little-known, rarely played works, or modernistic compositions by Bartók, Honegger, Dukas, Milhaud, and Stravinsky.

La Revue musicale could only be profitable in the medium term for the *NRF*. It was important less for financial gain than for its indirect fallout. In his few years of experience, Gallimard had seen very well to what extent a magazine like the *NRF* provided the publishing house with new talent. What had happened at *Le Mercure de France* had worked the same way: the magazine editor was the best possible recruiter for the house. Publishing articles, reviews, first drafts, or even excerpts from books in the magazine did not represent a commitment, whereas having a publisher bring out a book presupposed at least a legal commitment, the signing of a contract, often the promise of other works to come. That was just where Gallimard came in, at the vague, informal point that separated the article published in the magazine from the book brought out under his logo. Once authors were attracted to Rue Madame, it was up to him to trap them.

What he did with the *NRF* and *La Revue musicale*, Gaston felt he would be able to repeat with other magazines, even with cultural journals. But that called for a structure, personnel, and means which he did not have. Not yet, anyway.

Moving the magazine and the publishing house to Rue de Grenelle in 1921 coincided with the firm's expanding in many directions. Since Proust's Goncourt Prize, more and more manuscripts were being submitted to the *NRF*, but there was no consistent follow-up: many authors complained that their submissions were not acknowledged, and that they didn't know whom to get in touch with. Gaston himself felt the lack of organization, despite Raymond's taking charge. Gone were the days when the *NRF* founding fathers met on Thursdays at Schlumberger's on Rue d'Assas to read manuscripts aloud and engage in Byzantine quarrels about the influence of Mallarmé's verse on the younger writers. Already during the war, as he thought about the group's future, Gaston had become aware of the metamorphosis that had to take place, if they were to compete with other publishers on an equal footing. While wanting to preserve the accommodating spirit that governed relationships within the firm, he decided to jettison the negative aspects of such a close-knit association: inbreeding, artisanship, improvisation, laxness.

With the beginning of the 1920s, Gaston, by gathering around him persons of quality, each competent in his own field and efficient when united as a team, laid the most solid bases for his future success.

Still, the context did not favor larger projects. At the 1921 Booksellers' Convention, the word "crisis" was on everyone's lips. True, pessimism had always been a prevalent attitude of the profession. But this time there were serious reasons behind it. The report made to one panel was convincing: before the war an average volume, with a press run of 2,000 copies and sold at 3 francs 50, cost the publisher 73 centimes to produce. But the cost of this same "average" volume had gone up to 2 francs 96, an increase of about 300 percent. The worldwide drop in paper production following the Armistice had made prices climb dangerously high after the British and Americans had contracted for the largest allotments, while in France there was the new eight-hour day (legalized in April 1919) and its repercussions on the employment of manpower, and the disorganization of transport, making it impossible to predict exact delivery dates, and finally inflation. Such were the new phenomena that, in the eyes of the publishers, constituted the "crisis."[15]

Tuesday, 5:00 P.M.: after a few variations, this day and time were to become those of the weekly meeting of the firm's "readers," the editors to whom manuscripts submitted by mail or through contacts were given for appraisal. There was no way to learn how to be a reader; no one could give the recipe. A single prerequisite was agreed on: to know how to "read"—that is, to sniff out, detect, study, dissect, explain, and evaluate a piece of writing, to defend it or condemn it. Nothing could be more arbitrary, more subjective. The reader might vote yes or no; he would usually give his reasons, although not always. Ever since the day Gide, the first reader of Proust's manuscript, decided that *Swann's Way* smelled of society salons and the columns of *Le Figaro* and so rejected it, writers were convinced that the reader had a tremendous influence, especially since he was usually nameless, his appraisal supposed to remain as confidential as his identity.

The tradition of secrecy and mystery is easy enough to understand: it avoided pressure before the reading and grudges afterward. This last point was essential, for nowhere more than in the Paris of literature, politics, art, and the press was there such an overlapping of interests and influences among potential authors who were at the same time theater managers, editors-in-chief, reviewers, or even other publishers' readers. The line was so ill defined that it was often breached clandestinely or even publicly, without the least scruple. Readers who also functioned as book critics of some periodical would praise in print a novel which they had earlier recommended for publication.

While other well-known publishers advertised the famous writers who acted as their reader-editors, Gallimard's editorial board would always remain a thing apart. From the earliest 1920s it was surrounded by a deliberately fostered aura of mystery.

Much later, Céline wrote a sidesplitting set piece in *Nord (North)* about the editorial board, sketched from life when a vote was taken:

> Well-to-do society people, total loafers! . . . pederasts . . . alcoholics, definitely! . . . A few murderers. . . . Editorial board! All of them incompetent! These people gauge a work! know how to "judge" it—all their lives! . . . and they speak English—and Kirghiz! . . .

From an outsider's view, this weekly editorial meeting seemed more like a secret rite than a work session. It always took place in the office the two Gallimard brothers shared. Each member had his seat, almost always the same one. One at a time, they would report on what they had read. The presentation had to be brief, the words to the point, and the conclusion speedy—at least, ideally. Often an author or book would provoke a discussion, and courtesy would give way to the most vehement frankness. If the reader was particularly enthusiastic and his report met with few objections, a manuscript might be accepted on the spot. But whenever contradictory views were expressed, the work in question was circulated to two, three, four, or even five readers. Some readers were voluble, others taciturn. Some pleaded their cases, others attacked. But it was perfectly understood among all of them that not a word of any of this was to be leaked to the outside world.

Belonging to this board was a matter of pride for anyone in the world of letters. If the *Nouvelle Revue Française* magazine was the breeding ground for the publishing house, the editorial board was its court of justice: it could judge, condemn, or acquit, often with benefit of doubt, appeal a decision, carry it to a higher court. In the final analysis, it was the chief magistrate who decided: Gaston.

> Gaston Gallimard, who took little part in the general discussion, tried to get a clear picture from sometimes disparate opinions expressed by his counselors and draw from them the conclusion that no one thereafter questioned. I frequently admired the humanity with which he exercised this magistracy and delivered verdicts, how he took into account not only the value of a manuscript, to be sure, but the charater and the sensitivity of the author. This ambience of considerateness and high intellectuality prevailing at the editorial meetings did not keep them from taking place within a framework of rigor and precision.[16]

In point of fact, each reader–editor did not merely present a summary that he wrote partly on cards, one per title. His final judgment was translated into a mark, like a grade for schoolwork. The marks ran from 1 to 4. The top grade, 1, meant unqualified acceptance. Some readers occasionally added an asterisk, which in a code known only to the committee members signified that they would not be swayed from this opinion. A 2 meant that the manuscript was to be accepted, given revisions by the author. A 3 indicated serious reservations, and 4 meant the author and his work were doomed to rejection. The reader's name as well as the text on the card were considered absolutely confidential. The card itself went into a file open only to the firm's top executives. Open to them, that is, if it could be located—which was not always easy. There were good reasons for some of the cards to get "lost," especially those on which famous writers peremptorily dismissed the work of beginners whom posterity later acclaimed.

The reading committee not only rejected and accepted manuscripts, but often in the latter case determined how they would subsequently be handled by the firm, whether they would appear as part of a particular collection or imprint. One such collection, most indicative of the turn of mind of the board, was special and hidden from outsiders. Called "Une oeuvre, un portrait" (A Work, A Portrait), it was a semideluxe edition, limited on the average to a printing of 800 copies, virtually presold by subscription to a clientèle of collectors. From time to time a short work by a well-known author would appear in it—Gide, Claudel, Rivière, or Valéry—but most often it was a vehicle for beginners making their first major public appearance. Because of the specifications of the collection (size of press run, and so on), Gaston's financial risk was minimal. But this device allowed him to publish the first works of young authors at a limited cost, and at the same time get them to sign up for their works to come; if they fulfilled their promise, they would appear in the standard formats. It was in this way that Gallimard in the 1920s laid his bets without risk on Roger Vitrac, Joseph Kessel (whose first book, *Mary de Cork*, contained his portrait by Jean Cocteau), Marcel Arland, Paul Eluard, Marcel Jouhandeau, and many others that he prided himself on having first tried out in "Une oeuvre, un portrait."

It was not a conventional procedure, but there was nothing dishonest about it. And it was the more easily accepted and made use of by the editorial board since it did not essentially depart from the editorial and moral tone set by the *NRF*. But when Gallimard decided to put profits ahead of literary quality, he met with so much opposition that he was led more and more to make decisions without consulting the editorial board. Since the *NRF* publishing house had officially become the Librairie Gallimard, he felt freer, especially toward Gide, to publish popular books that would be commercially successful. Their sales made up for the relative failures of the purely literary books, which enthralled all concerned—except the business manager, the accountant, and the banker.

The question came up with savage suddenness when Rivière, the magazine editor, saw the first two volumes of a new collection he had not even known was in preparation: Les Chefs-d'oeuvre du roman d'aventures (Masterpieces of the Adventure Novel). The two works in question, by George Toudouze and Gaston Leroux (famous for his *Rouletabille* series), although not pulp, were part of a genre, an ethic, and a conception of literature diametrically opposed to the principles adopted by the founding fathers of the *NRF*. Rivière immediately confronted Gaston in his office.

"How could you do this?" he demanded. "Why publish such trash? This is not what we worked for so hard and with so many sacrifices over the past ten years!"

"Get this straight, Jacques," Gaston replied. "I am as deeply attached as you to everything that has made the reputation of our company, the quality of the books we have brought out. But it is precisely to be able to maintain that quality in the future, to go on bringing out young authors and publishing difficult works, that I have now resolved to make certain concessions. When you bring me a work of quality that will obviously be a commercial flop, you are delighted when I agree to publish it. But each time it's a loss for the firm. Do you want to keep us in publishing, to play our role? If so, we will have to compensate for the commercially disastrous titles, or those that pay off only in the very long run, by bringing out some that are profitable. I know as well as you that Gaston Leroux and Toudouze are not the peers of a Valéry, a Claudel, or yourself. Unfortunately, they sell better, at least for the time being. So please, Jacques, try to understand; don't storm against what is necessary and unavoidable. Allow me, without compromising the Collection Blanche,* or the *NRF* logo, or the magazine you edit, to pander to the public, if need be, with books that I take sole responsibility for, which will carry the name of the Librairie Gallimard, not the *NRF*. Allow me to do that for you, to compromise myself, to sacrifice myself."[17]

That was the vital issue. Since 1919, when the company was set up under the Gallimard name, it kept reappearing in most of their projects. Gaston postponed the showdown several times for fear of bruising the sensibilities of his friends and associates. When he finally felt himself ready, he decided, against the opinion of all the others, upon a course of publishing in which the support of the best of literature was tied in with the commercial imperatives of a fully developing company. From concession to compromise, he would at times go too far, as in 1933 when Raymonde Allain, the goddaughter of Valentine Tessier and a beauty-prize winner, told how she won the contest to Emmanuel Berl, who made a book out of it and got Tristan Bernard to write the preface. Manufactured with all the ingredients of a popular best-seller, *Histoire vraie d'un prix de beauté* (The True Story of a Beauty Prize) was nevertheless a dud.[18]

The Gallimard list, with this new policy, did have a few flops that were quickly written off. They were due to all sorts of nonliterary considerations—a payoff for an unspecified service, a favor done for some judge of a prestigious prize, or political opportunism. Whoever mentioned them was met with a smile and lowered eyes, and the whispered explanation: the decision had come from the mysterious realm of the editorial board.

In 1927 the board had eleven members: Robert Aron, Benjamin Crémieux, Ramon Fernandez, Jean Grenier, Bernard Groethuysen, Louis-Daniel Hirsch, Georges Lecoq, Brice Parain, Jean Paulhan, Georges Sadoul, and Gaston Gallimard. Comparing this list to the

*The "White Collection" was the main body of *NRF* literary titles.—TRANS.

earlier and later ones, one sees that from the 1920s through the Liberation some were constant members, while others came and went.

Paulhan was probably the person who most consistently symbolized the *NRF*, both the magazine and the publishing house. He joined it in 1920, at age thirty-six, and stayed on up to his death in 1968. His family came from Nîmes and the Cévennes mountain country, but he grew up in Paris, where he got his secondary education at the Lycée Louis-le-Grand, before taking a degree in literature at the Sorbonne in 1905. Two years later he was appointed to a teaching post in Madagascar, where he taught Latin and foreign languages, and later settled there as a gold prospector. Recalled to Paris, he taught Malagasy at the School for Oriental Languages and published his first book, on Malagasy poetics, *Les Hain-Tenys Merinas*.[19] Mobilized at the start of the war and almost immediately wounded, Sergeant Paulhan of the 9th Zouaves became an airplane spotter and then an interpreter with the Malagasy troops, and published his own war book, *Le Guerrier appliqué* (The Diligent Warrior),[20] in which an eighteen-year-old conscript tries to develop in himself a warlike state of mind and comes to comprehend the measure of men's strengths and weaknesses in the face of danger, their unscrupulousness and cruelty. Hired in 1920 to be an assistant editor of the magazine under Rivière, Paulhan came into his own as the author of literary articles.

Physically, Paulhan was a tall man, large and sometimes on the heavy side, in contrast with his rather high-pitched voice. Taciturn, mercurial, fastidious, naturally refined, meticulous, he was most of all a self-effacing man. He succeeded in imposing his own manner on the firm so well that for decades everyone there spoke in whispers rather than aloud and intelligibly. Since secretiveness went well with the intimate conviction that Gallimard was the only true literary publishing house, this whispering tradition would be its hallmark for a long time. Subtle, unpredictable, Paulhan sought to achieve the unexpected in his judgments, behavior, and attitudes. A relentless enemy of all clichés and facileness, he proved himself to be the true son of a philosopher by calling everything into question, writings as well as people, prejudging nothing.

All these qualities, latent in Paulhan from the early 1920s, came to fruition when he became editor of the *NRF* magazine in 1925, at the death of Rivière. From that privileged position as the lookout of French literature, he would rapidly go on to become its *éminence grise*. That expression, commonly taken to mean "the power behind the throne," was applied to Paulhan so often that some came to feel his reputation was exaggerated and his prestige usurped. At any rate, though the title was a cliché, it perfectly suited Paulhan, who was not satisfied to be an exalted intermediary. He prided himself on being a great reader, and as a reader was meticulous, making file cards and reports that commanded respect from more than one unhappy author because of their seriousness, rigor, and exacting demands.

Mostly secretive, Paulhan once revealed a great deal about himself in answering Proust's questionnaire.[21] He expressed a preference for Jules Renard, Lao-tzu, François Villon, Baudelaire, Saint-John Perse, Braque and Uccello, Lewis Carroll's Alice, Gilgamesh, Couperin and Satie because "they don't spill their guts all over the table"; for visible energy and hidden softness in man, for the great visible softness and hidden energy of woman, for loyalty, games, friendship, the color bronze, zinnias, the martin, and the names of his friends. There was nothing that he "detests above all else," but he admitted that history held no attraction for him—"how can one be interested in what might not have happened?"—while confessing to a soft spot for Christopher Columbus and even Joan of Arc ("if what they say about her is true"). To Paulhan, the depth of misery was to be on display. He extended his indulgence to all guilty parties, would have liked to live in a little-known historical château of which he might be the custodian, dreamed of "doing something that is worth more than myself," and feared "being much too unequal to what I am doing." He would have liked being endowed by nature with the gift of "being invisible at will," and would like to die fully conscious:

"I am upset enough at having missed out on my birth." His motto summed up the man as well as his work: "Take care not to add another personal opinion to all those already abroad in the world."[22] Such was Jean Paulhan.

While extolling his qualities as an incomparable associate, Gaston more than once made a point of the distances that separated him from this odd character. The one thing they had in common was literature. Without doubt, each considered the other indispensable, but Gaston could never feel the closeness of comprehension with him that he did with Rivière, Larbaud, and Fargue. The publisher with the legendary flair did not *sniff out* anything in Paulhan. He did not much care for his sense of humor, got bored with hearing him constantly exclaim, "C'est épatant!" (That's swell!), and was not always pleased by his lack of deference and his haughtiness. But what he most held against Paulhan was that the man so perfectly embodied his own favorite saying: "The simplest things are the ones to be approached obliquely." Of course Gaston, as a courteous gentleman and a sharp negotiator, knew how to be oblique; but Paulhan's sub-tleties were often beyond him and he did not like being left in the dark; it gave him the feeling of being patronized. Their mutual esteem and lack of comprehension were to go on for over forty years.

A day in the life of Paulhan followed an unvarying rhythm. Up early, he would drink a cup of coffee, the first of many. Then came the scrutiny of a list of letters to be written; that was of the first importance. In his fine and strangely mechanical penmanship, daily he wrote to writers, of course, but also to printers, newspapermen, and contacts. And he got as many letters in return. His letters were by no means quick obligatory notes, they were *writings*, crafted with the same care as if he were writing a book.

Although one or two days were set aside each week and specific times reserved for interviews, an ambitious author knew that he might walk into Paulhan's office unannounced, carrying his manu-script. He might have to wait a while in an uncomfortable springless armchair, but he would be seen. And when Paulhan saw someone, it meant he welcomed him. He enjoyed letting strangers share in his decision-making, or at least having them think they did. This stemmed from his delight in game-playing. He would often ask those who had been waiting to see him what they thought of some article, manuscript, or author. Without seeming to, that was his way of testing newcomers: he might make up the name of an imaginary author and ask them whether they had read his complete works. Once a timid young lady said to him, "Well, Monsieur Paulhan, I have my manuscript here, and I am worried. I don't know whether it is publishable." He immediately raised his eyebrows and retorted, "Why? Is the spelling so bad?"

Sarcastic at times and even eccentric, Paulhan was a cold fish whose sagaciousness made Gaston uneasy. The publisher was never quite sure whether the apparent absurdities of this serious reader were meant to be taken seriously. One day Paulhan came in with a suggestion that left him speechless: that they compile a literary directory, in one single copy, made up of all the manuscripts the *NRF* had rejected during the year.

"It would include all kinds of unique things," he argued. "A good writer will most likely show us only himself. But a mediocre writer may show us all men, their needs, by way of myths and tales. We certainly don't lack personal expressions of viewpoint. We are overrun with them, smothered by them. Besides, nothing human should be neglected, and we could call this one-copy book *The Sunday Writers*."[23]

But for Gaston, in the final analysis, Paulhan remained the model reader-editor: one who "judged" writings for what they were and not by the reputation or gossip surrounding their authors. The manuscripts that went through his hands were annotated at length, sometimes with *ts* in the margin (Malagasy for "very good"), and his suggestions to writers were always explicit.[24]

Another important member of the editorial board was Benjamin Crémieux. Less well-known than Paulhan, Crémieux held no official title either on the magazine or in the firm; his opinion nevertheless carried great weight with Gaston. His professional conscientiousness, erudition, and discernment gave him a well-deserved reputation, though it was mainly confined to professional circles of literary criticism, the press, and publishing.

Born in Narbonne in 1888, he was descended from a Jewish family established there since the fourteenth century. By nature an active and energetic person, he had a great capacity for work and was always busy. Expansive, sometimes to the point of exuberance, he still never lost his dignity. His reviews and critical articles in numerous papers and magazines earned him an appreciative following. From 1919 up to World War II, besides turning out hundreds of articles and several books and performing his regular duties as Gallimard's reader-editor, as well as being secretary of the French section of the International Pen Club, Crémieux held the position of chief of the Italian desk at the Ministry of Foreign Affairs, in charge of day-by-day analyses of public opinion in Italy as reflected in the press and diplomatic dispatches. Next to literature, his great passion was Italy, a specialty that stood him in good stead at the Gallimard house, where he was responsible for the publication of important works of Italian literature. In collaboration with his wife, Marie-Anne Comnène, Crémieux translated and adapted almost all the plays of Luigi Pirandello from 1925 on, and introduced to French audiences the works of Verga, Borgese, Moravia, and Italo Svevo, sometimes even before they became well known in Italy.[25] In a 1945 novel, *France*, published by Gallimard, Marie-Anne Comnène painted a faithful picture of her husband. Paulhan could be proud of having brought him into the firm in 1920. A choice recruit, equaled by few others.

From the 1920s until the Liberation, a similar position in the domain of foreign, especially German, literature was held on the board by Bernard Groethuysen. A confirmed Marxist, "Groeth," as his friends called him, had spent his youth in Berlin in very cosmopolitan circles, with his Dutch physician father and Russian mother. When he came to Paris, his looks and behavior were decidedly bohemian—those of a man to whom only revolution and literature mattered. In spite of his influential position at Gallimard, he never gave up his habits or attitudes of those stormy early years. He was constantly busy, no matter when or where, jotting down the ideas that popped into his head on bits of paper that were immediately mislaid—or on newspapers, or even handkerchiefs. He was unimpressive in appearance. His face was a mobile mirror of his moods, his complexion was repulsive. But the intensity of his eyes made up for the ill-kempt face. When the committee meetings dragged on, his jacket would be all covered with ashes from the cigarettes he chain-smoked. Pot-bellied, his fingers combing his long beard, his large blue eyes fixed upon the person speaking, he could suddenly spout forth about a manuscript with such vehement conviction that it immediately overcame the most deeply held prejudices. Kind and generous with all refugees from the East, and with German Jews fleeing victorious Nazism, he often got Gallimard to give them translation jobs, and since these translations most often were anything but perfect, he would himself revise and polish them, then sign them with the original translator's name so he or she might collect the full fee.[26]

It was through him that Gallimard introduced Franz Kafka to France. As early as 1928, four years after his death, the Czech writer was published in the *NRF*. After *Metamorphosis*, translated by Alexandre Vialatte, as was the rest of his work, *The Trial* appeared in 1933, with a Groethuysen preface. Thanks to him, the editorial board took an interest in such writers unknown to them as Hermann Broch, the Austrian essayist and novelist who wrote *The Sleepwalkers*, and his compatriot Robert Musil, the author of *Young Törless* and *The Man without Qualities*. A philosopher by training and himself an essayist, Bernard Groethuysen put his duties as a great reader and his revolutionary activities ahead of his own literary work. He published very few works under his signature; the first, *Origines de l'esprit bourgeois en France* (Origins of the Bourgeois Spirit in France), in 1927, was the opening volume of a new imprint, La Bibliothèque des idées (The Library of Ideas).

Another member of the editorial board, Brice Parain, also closely followed German literature. But his speciality, which in Gaston's eyes made him a complement to the Italianist Crémieux and the

Germanist Groethuysen, was Russian literature. He had taken a degree in philosophy at the prestigious Ecole Normale Supérieure, where his doctoral thesis was an "Essai sur le logos platonicien" (Essay on the Platonic Logos), and another in Russian at the Ecole Nationale des Langues Orientales, which quite naturally led this son of a suburban schoolteacher to be in charge for a time of the Center of Russian Documentation in Paris (1924–25), before being posted to the French embassy in Moscow (1925–26). As a teacher of Russian at the Lycée Voltaire in Paris, he tried to get his young pupils to delve further into the intricacies of that language; then, after a brief, fruitless fling at banking, he hired on as one of the secretaries to Gaston, introduced by his close friend Paulhan.

That was in October 1927, when Parain was thirty. He jumped at the chance, even though he was not in total agreement with everything being done at Gallimard. When first introduced to the publisher, he made no bones about his literary tastes and philosophic convictions. "I was not joining up to turn out literature, I was joining up to make a living."[27] As a reader, he was concerned with substance, had no time for the facile and superficial, was perpetually pondering the nature of language, the mendacity of words and their power to create illusions (Parain played himself, the philosopher, in Jean-Luc Godard's film *My Life to Live*). Gallimard was quick to see his value, and Parain shortly became one of the pillars of the editorial board, shepherding to publication Mikhail Sholokhov's *Virgin Soil Upturned* (1933); Vsevolod Ivanov's *Armored Train* 14–69 (1928); Nikolai Tikhonov's verse in *Tête brûlée* (1936), translated and prefaced by the French novelist Vladimir Pozner; and a great many others, including Konstantin Fedin and Boris Pilnyak, all of whom he brought out in the Jeunes Russes (Young Russians) collection, sometimes translating them himself, as he did for Ilya Ehrenburg's *Rvač* (The Self-seeker, in French *Rapace*, 1930).

Crémieux, Groethuysen, Parain, the "foreign" trio, also had the help of the firm's outside contributors, Fargue and Valery Larbaud, who enriched the catalogue through their contacts and erudition. These two intimates of Gaston's both gravitated to circles in which literature was created. Immediately after World War I, they were both habitués of Rue de l'Odéon, where two new bookshops opened: on one side, La Maison des Amis du Livre, run by Adrienne Monnier, where Fargue daily met the best French writers of the moment and those who would soon become such; and across the street Shakespeare & Co., run by Sylvia Beach, who made it the permanent meeting place for American and English writers. Having met James Joyce as early as 1919, Larbaud worked with him on the impossible task of translating his *Ulysses*, "that cathedral of prose," into French, so Gallimard could publish it in 1937. Larbaud's role was immense in discovering both Anglo-American and Spanish-language writers for Gallimard, who through his good offices became the publisher of Samuel Butler, G. K. Chesterton, Ramón Gomez de la Serna, and Ricardo Guiraldes.

It was these "foreign" reader-editors who, through their determined search and discovery, as well as their flair, made it possible for Gaston to feel, at the beginning of the 1930s, that he had won the first round of his undertaking: to become competitive with the Librairie Stock's powerful and prestigious collection, the Bibliothèque cosmopolite (Cosmopolitan Library).

Strangely, another member of the editorial board, whose background seemed to qualify for literary cosmopolitanism—Mexican father, Provençal mother, British education—shone mainly in French. After studies at the Lycée Louis-le-Grand and the Sorbonne, and having been known until the age of twenty-five mainly for "his reputation as a racing-car-mad playboy who excelled at dancing the tango,"[28] Ramon Fernandez (born 1894) made his début in the *NRF* magazine under the auspices of Rivière, with a tribute to Proust in 1923. An attractive and restless character, Fernandez published three books under the Gallimard imprint, *Le Pari* (The Bet, 1932), *Les Violents* (The Violent Ones, 1935), and *L'homme est-il humain?* (Is Man Human?, 1936). But it is probably in a debate on morals and literature with his friend Rivière, held at Geneva and Lausanne in the early 1920s, that Fernandez best revealed the complexities of his character. The

NRF editor presented the evils of moralism in literature, whereupon Fernandez rose to its defense with arguments that tell us as much about his state of mind as a member of the editorial board at Gallimard as they do about his future political commitment, his involvement with fascism and collaboration with the Germans:

> One of my main concerns is to make my position clear, to take stock of myself, always hoping and trying to make this stocktaking provisional. And I firmly believe that a man who has made no commitment is not fully loyal to his mission as a man, and consequently that literary art, especially dramatic art, which deals with what is human, is insufficient when it does not in one way or another express that commitment, be it only to repudiate it. I speak from the experience of a Latin-American who has come to ask Europe to give some meaning to his life and who has entered with a barbarian's demands into the admirable French community.* Rivière, since he was born into this community, cannot conceive the degree to which the very perfection of French culture relieves one, allows one to forgo the problems that torment the less fortunate who are reduced to living from day to day, to build themselves up as best they can.[29]

The complete opposite of Fernandez in training, tastes, and personality, yet a member of the same editorial board in 1927, was Robert Aron (born 1898), an alumnus of the Lycée Condorcet with an advanced degree in letters, and later a historian of World War II. "Very Jewish and very French for over two and a half centuries," [30] Robert Aron, the son of the general manager of a brokerage firm, had begun in 1921 to contribute to *La Revue des Deux Mondes*, the bastion of conservative Catholicism. Not sufficiently challenged by this, he got in touch with Gaston just when the publisher was looking for a young secretary. Gaston hired Aron at 750 francs per month, a modest salary that he would have raised a bit from the start, had his brother Raymond not held him back.

Aron quickly rose in Gaston's esteem, was made a member of

---

*Fernandez became a naturalized French citizen in 1927.

the editorial board and put in charge of subsidiary rights (film adaptations and the like) as well as foreign rights. His first job, in 1922, was to write a circular letter to some hundred people advising them that answers to their communications would soon be forthcoming; the office mail had piled up for months. Next, he was given a first manuscript to read—and lost it. "Tell the author just that," was Gaston's only comment. And Aron, discovering in surprise after surprise what publishing was like, was much taken aback when the author replied, "Thanks anyway, my book wasn't really in final form. It'll be better if I rewrite it."[31]

Gaston and Aron had nothing at all in common, yet they respected each other on a professional level.[32] This promising young intellectual was never to forget the two rules Gaston laid down when he took him on: "The main thing in our business is to know how to turn a manuscript down" and "If you want to be a publisher, give up the idea of writing yourself."[33]

Worth bearing in mind . . .

Under Gaston's guidance he learned the thousand and one ways of getting rid of a writer, from "My brother Raymond doesn't see it our way" to "It doesn't fit any of our imprints." When the author was a stranger to the firm, it was of course much simpler; no need to treat him with kid gloves, especially if he had not treated you that way either.

Gaston always remembered the falling-out between his fellow publisher Pierre-Victor Stock and Georges Darien, the author of the somewhat scabrously sensational *Le Voleur* (The Thief) and *Biribi*,* in August 1903. Stock had turned down Darien's latest book, *L'Epaulette* (The Epaulet), because he did not think it would sell. He received a registered letter from the author:

Monsieur Stock,
    I am in receipt of your card. Here is my answer: If you do not publish my novel next October, I will kill you. . . . You are free to

*Biribi was a French military penal colony in North Africa.—TRANS.

act as you see fit, properly or improperly. I will wait until the month of October; if by then my novel has not been published by you, I will execute you.

Four days later, the publisher sent him an equally unambiguous reply:

Monsieur Darien,
　　You are a clown, but not a nice clown, which spoils everything. Along with that, you are a person of the greatest bad faith, which complicates matters and is very troublesome. To the letter you sent, there can be but one answer: *Merde*—which is what I say to you.[34]

The book was published, but not by Stock. It flopped.

Much too shrewd and diplomatic to use such coarse language with authors, Gaston was cynical in conversation with his associates. As soon as his young secretary came on the job, he advised him: "An author, a writer is most often not a man. He is a female whom you have to pay, knowing she is equally ready to offer her wares elsewhere. A writer is a whore."[35]

The young man was completely convinced, when Gaston quoted to him "famous names that bore out his experience as both a womanizer and a publisher." With his friends, Gaston was always a poor liar, for they saw too much of him not to be able to read correctly his embarrassment or attempt to conceal something. One day in 1918, Roger Martin du Gard had asked Gaston what was happening with the publication of his manuscript *Près des mourants* (Near the Dying). An obviously embarrassed Gaston replied:

"It's very literary, feels a bit made to order. We'll have to have a talk about it."

The writer immediately understood and in his mind translated his friend's embellishing vocabulary into clear terms. That evening he wrote in his diary, "It's not worth a damn."[36]

Beyond these two categories—authors who were friends and authors who were strangers—there was a third, much less frequent and indeed exceptional: those published by Gallimard while in the employ of the company. This applied to Marcel Arland, who joined the editorial board in 1930, having been on Paulhan's staff at the magazine since 1926.

This timid and reserved young man began his career at age twenty-three in 1922. While preparing a university degree in Latin/Greek/French, he became the literary editor of a student magazine, *L'Université de Paris*, for which he succeeded in getting pieces by Proust and Giraudoux. He then launched two avant-garde little magazines, *Aventure* (Adventure) and *Dés* (Dice), in which he published poems and articles by some of his service buddies—Georges Limbour, René Crevel, Andre Dhôtel, and Jacques Baron, among others. Then he dropped everything, left Paris, and went to live a solitary existence in the village where he was born, Varennes-sur-Armance in the Haute-Marne; locked in a garret with a skylight that opened onto the woods, he wrote his first book, *Terres étrangères* (Foreign Lands). To whom should he submit it? Returning to Paris, he immediately thought of Bernard Grasset, a dynamic and open-minded publisher who would appreciate a work done in meditative isolation, away from the bustle of Paris. But Arland belonged to a generation under the sway of Gide and his awesome position in literature. He therefore sent Gide the manuscript, and so as not to face publicly the shame of a rejection, gave his address as "M.A., Student Hostel, Rue de la Bûcherie, Paris." A week later, after going to many others with the same initials, an enthusiastic letter from Gide was finally turned over to him, thanking "this anonymous author whom I shall certainly get to meet." On the recommendation of the great writer, the manuscript was read by Paulhan, who accepted it, and lauded by Valery Larbaud in the *NRF* magazine. What more could Arland want? A contract. Gaston tendered him one.

"I'm in!" the young man exulted to himself that day.[37]

He was indeed, and remained so for a long time. His book was published in 1923. A year later, at the request of Rivière, who perfectly grasped this promising young writer's gifts of analysis and criticism, Arland gave the *NRF* magazine an essay entitled "Sur un nouveau mal du siècle" (On a New "Mal du Siècle"), which created quite a stir. With the intellectual maelstrom of the moment eddying between Dadaism and Surrealism, Arland took the daring step of adopting a solid, classical style, and the position that "morality will be our first concern. I cannot conceive of a literature without ethics."

Marcel Arland developed into a great editorial reader, esteemed as much by Paulhan as by Gaston, who was perhaps more impressed by Arland's reader's reports than by his critical articles or novels. Arland won the Goncourt Prize in 1929 for *L'Ordre* (Order), a long novel running three volumes of over 500 pages each. But the next year he wrote *Antarès*, a 150-page book, the slimness and scope of which were a disappointment to the publisher, who had hoped for an equally weighty, equally long book.

"But, Marcel, this is just a pamphlet-sized poem that you've written here!" he told him, flabbergasted.

"It's what I had to write," Arland replied simply, with no additional explanation.

"Very well, of course, do as you see fit. You are a free man."

The writer responded gratefully to this reaction.[38] In his eyes, it characterized Gaston, marked him as the great publisher of his century:

> Gaston took care not to make me feel any pressure. He might have, he certainly wanted to, and commercial considerations inclined him to. But he did not do it. And he published my books without ever having them read by the editorial board. As the years went by, we became good friends, very close. That was because I told him the truth. It was a principle of mine always to be frank, and he was grateful to me for that, because like all powerful men he was continually surrounded by yes-men. He loved books, kept track of authors and never abandoned them. When I won the Goncourt in 1929, he was happy that he had bet right. Yet he could publish a book knowing that it would not sell but in the full conviction that its author would someday be recognized. That is what you call a great publisher.[39]

Arland and Paulhan, Crémieux and Groethuysen, Parain—these men were the backbone of the Gallimard editorial board from the 1920s to the 1940s, the ones who built up the catalogue that Gaston was so rightly proud of. But in this brilliant gathering there was one discreet, unnoticed person, an ex-officio member of the editorial board; though not acting as an editor, he attended all the meetings and knew all the authors, a key man in the Gallimard firm whom none of the histories of French literature have ever mentioned, although they should have. This was Louis-Daniel Hirsch, the business manager.

Hirsch never missed a board meeting, always voiced an opinion about the sales and distribution possibilities of books, the display they might get in bookstores, and even their contents, since he read a great deal for his own pleasure. But this small, slim man with a broad forehead and beaked nose preferred listening to talking. Interested in every detail, he made constant notes about everything. On weekends or on vacation, he invariably visited the local bookstores to make sure they were properly displaying the Gallimard output.

He had a flexible character and was easy to get along with, but he also had the temperament of a man of principle who could not compromise on certain values—such as loyalty. Jean Giono found this out to his chagrin, when Hirsch heard he had signed contracts with both Grasset and Gallimard for the same books.

Like Gaston, Hirsch liked to dispel antagonisms and lead both sides toward mutual understanding. Frequently urged by his friends to keep a diary and later to publish his memoirs, he always refused, saying, "That sort of thing makes people fight with one another."[40]

Hirsch was born in Paris in 1891 to a completely assimilated Alsatian Jewish family. His father, who worked in the yard-goods business, died when he was seventeen. Louis-Daniel finished his *baccalauréat* at the Lycée Charlemagne and immediately went to work, without going on to higher studies, so as to support the family, which was now his responsibility. His first job was with a grain import-export firm at the commodity exchange. When he was called up for military service, his boss promised him an important job with the company's Romanian branch as soon as he came back. But two years later, just as Hirsch was about to reenter civilian life, the war broke out. He donned his uniform again, this time for five years more. During the war he drove a bus loaded with meat to supply the men at the front, and once the Armistice was signed, he was sent to Germany to serve with the occupation forces until the spring of 1919.

When he finally returned to Paris, everything was a shambles. "His" company had disappeared! Looking for a new job, he found a place as head bookkeeper for an importer of frozen meat from Argentina. Always the meat business, it seemed, in peacetime as before in the war. So in 1925, when a friend said he knew a publisher who was looking for a young business executive, Hirsch rushed to Rue de Grenelle. After a quick interview, Gaston told him:

"I can offer you one of two jobs: either as manager of my bookstore on the Boulevard Raspail, or else business manager of my publishing house. The salaries are virtually the same. Think about it and let me know tomorrow."[41]

Hirsch was taken as much with the man as with his business. Hirsch remembered that, at Proust's death some years ago, Gallimard and the *NRF* had been mentioned in all the eulogies. Frozen meat had never really appealed to Hirsch. Books, on the other hand, were something he liked, something he had learned to treasure. He decided publishing was for him, and stayed with the company until he died, as did most of the pillars of Gallimard. As did Gaston himself.

One of the most important components of the editorial board was the only one who could not be called formally a "member": Gide, the "preeminent contemporary," whose influence, invisible but undeniable, hovered over all the editorial meetings, because of the manuscripts and authors he attracted to them for decades to come.

November 1922, Paris: Gaston at the bedside of Marcel Proust. He had sat up with him, along with Reynaldo Hahn, Paul Morand, and a few other friends. Dunoyer de Segonzac was sent for, with his paintbrushes, India ink, and sketch pad; he settled quietly in a corner and drew the portrait of the writer on his deathbed. Just a few lines, the curve of the nose, the knitted eyebrows, and the black beard and hair stark against a white, immaculate background. Looking over the painter's shoulder, what Gaston saw was not the picture of a sick man, let alone a dead one, but rather "of an Artaxerxes archer in the Louvre, this Jewish head with the handsome mask exuding an extraordinary impression of power."[42]

Family, friends, everyone was received at the foot of the writer's bed. The room where he lay was a salon, just as the ambience of his life had been. Cocteau had just come in and was talking to Gaston about his next book, *Thomas l'imposteur (Thomas the Imposter)*.

"Jean, let me have your novel," said Gaston.

"Of course, Gaston."

The deal was made at the bedside while the corpse was still warm.[43]

The funeral, the mass in the chapel of Saint-Pierre de Chaillot, were equally Parisian. Maurice Barrès, on the sidewalk outside, was heard to mutter:

"I had always thought that that boy Marcel Proust was a Jew, but what a fine funeral!"[44]

The social and literary world was fully represented. The characters of *Remembrance of Things Past* had gathered to bid adieu to their creator, who had given them permanent life in literature: dukes and countesses, bankers and aesthetes, elegant society ladies and gentlemen riders of the Jockey Club. A great many writers, Gaston lost among them, and Gide conspicuously absent. Ravel's *Pavane pour une infante défunte* was played, then the bells rang, and the hearse moved off toward the Père-Lachaise Cemetery, followed by a parade of cars.

Beyond the event itself, one must note what it expresses, the picture that these people constituting the Republic of Letters give of themselves. Whatever the place or the occasion, it is always good for a meeting, for gossip, for consultation, for trading influence. In that context, literature is simply a way of appearing and satisfying one's vanity. More than most others, Gaston was aware of this. Though no longer an elegant playboy, he could go against his grain and blend fully into such surroundings, for that, too, was what being a publisher meant, and in this frivolous and inconsequential atmosphere one might also discover writers. Gaston, like some of his peers, knew that the stereotype of Balzac's period was a thing of the past: the writer harnessed to his task in a garret lighted by a candle, dipping his pen into the blackest ink of adversity. Grasset put it well when he described Paris as the city of compliments:

> Paris is the great market for favors. Everyone knows that gathered in Paris are a thousand different stock certificates, the market for which are the salons, where one is always sure of getting the exact change for what one is seeking without recourse to money, which would be immoral and is not done. So every compliment that you pay is credited to your account with So-and-So. When the time comes, you will be able to draw on it. If Paris is the city of compliments, it is because every Parisian wants to build up a large credit balance in his account.[45]

Through his editorial committee, through Larbaud, Fargue, Gide especially, and a few others, Gaston had feelers out in all the places that counted. At the Foreign Office on the Quai d'Orsay, Philippe Berthelot was a sure, dependable friend, with almost as many writers in his employ as Gaston had, often the same ones. Politics? Gaston had no use for it; it horrified him. For him, being politically active— on whatever side—could be only a diminishment, a mutilation that closed the mind of any decent man to culture, to freedom of criticism, to the examining of one's conscience, and especially to individualism. At any rate, the deputy from Lyons, Edouard Herriot, head of the slightly left-of-center Radical Socialist Party and prime minister in 1924 and 1925, was a faithful reader of the *NRF*. Gaston knew he could count on him. Thanks to that special relationship, in 1925 Louis-Daniel Hirsch was able to organize a promotion for a new book by Alain beyond his wildest dreams. It was called *Eléments d'une doctrine radicale* (Elements of a Radical Doctrine), and the week of its publication a copy of it appeared, well displayed, at the place of each minister at the cabinet's weekly meeting—a fact immediately noted and trumpeted by the press. What did it matter if some people questioned the connection between Gallimard and the party in power! The book had been given a great send-off, that was what counted.

In 1922 Gaston was still looking for a way to increase the influence he could exert. He felt he would have to go beyond literary magazines and get involved with a newspaper. But that would mean moving too fast, and Raymond was beginning to raise objections: the financial risk was out of proportion to the goal. Fortunately, the occasion arose without Gaston's having to make the first step. The initiative came from Maurice Martin du Gard, a journalist and writer, and a cousin of Gaston's friend Roger. The young man planned to launch a cultural weekly devoted essentially to writers. It would be a vehicle for many of the *NRF* contributors, an advertising forum for the Gallimard house. Its critics would pay special attention to the Gallimard publications. In exchange, Gallimard was asked to invest in the enterprise. Young Martin du Gard, who was an operator, made no secret of the fact that the same proposal had already been made to Grasset.

Gaston accepted. He became a member of the board of the company, which was capitalized at 250,000 francs. And on October 21, 1922, along the boulevards newsboys could be heard hawking, "Get the first issue of *Les Nouvelles littéraires* [The Literary News]! The newspaper for people who think! Only twenty-five centimes!"[46]

Gaston was not sorry to have gone along. Leafing through the weekly barely off the presses, reading the first-rate articles, admiring the impressive format, he knew he had not made a mistake. His authors, his firm, and his books would all profit. Among the bylines in the first issue were several of his authors. With a few offers to publish a first novel in the "Une oeuvre, un portrait" collection, he would have garnered most of the rest of them, too. He was right. *Les Nouvelles littéraires*, an estimable weekly from every point of view, quickly became the best of publicity outlets for Gallimard publications, as its columns were filled more and more with texts by *NRF* authors. As for eventual conflicts of interest, one literary journalist was later to sum up the situation: "How could a critic on the Gallimard payroll refuse to review or discuss Gallimard books, when the firm was bringing out about one quarter of all the best French books published?"[47]

In Gallimard's literary policy, in his strategy for getting the critics on his side, *Les Nouvelles littéraires* was only one tool among many. One of his ultimate goals was to monopolize the literary prizes, the Goncourt first and foremost. From 1919 to 1935 it went to his authors eight out of seventeen times. He was first among the winning publishers, ahead of Albin Michel (with three) and Grasset (two), and would try to keep it that way all his life.

In their will the Goncourt brothers had provided 5,000 francs for the authors of the book selected by ten judges, each of whom in turn would receive an annual income of 6,000 francs, so they might be freed "from the chores of bureaucrats and the low maneuvers of journalism." Each judge was to be "a man of letters, not a nobleman or a politician." The Goncourts gave a more precise definition to their effort to encourage talent:

> Our idea is to free talent from the material difficulties of life, to make it possible for it to work efficiently, to be productive. . . . [The prize will be given] to the best novel, the best collection of short stories, the best volume of impressions, the best work of the imagination in prose— and exclusively in prose—published during the year. [Above all, let this prize be given] to youth, to originality of talent, to the newest and most daring undertakings in thought and form.[48]

Strangely, in a country where everything is labeled, the Goncourt Prize never gave rise to a style that might have enabled critics to classify such-and-such a novel as belonging to the "Goncourt school." Instead of authors and publishers trying to conform to a Goncourt formula in the hope of winning the prize, the Goncourt Academy adapted itself to the ongoing evolution of the French novel.

In the mid-1920s, being able to put a "Prix Goncourt" wrapper on a novel began to mean big money for publishers and authors. Even though, as is usually the case, the figures announced were most often magnified, the trade had become fully convinced of the commercial value of the prize. Gallimard had had his first experience of it with Proust. He believed in the prize and did his best to monopolize it. He kept up his friendships with the judges, especially the one most useful to him: Jean Ajalbert, elected to the Goncourt Academy in 1917 to succeed Octave Mirbeau. A loudmouth and frequent pain in the neck, according to Jules Renard, Ajalbert split his activities between literature and the curatorship of Malmaison. In the 1930s he authored four Gallimard books—the least Gaston could do for him. Among the young *NRF* authors, no one seemed to doubt that Ajalbert was Gaston's special representative among the Goncourt judges. Gaston treated him royally, inviting him to luncheon at the famous Larue's, so he could introduce a young candidate for the prize, André Malraux, to him. The novelist Jean Prévost, hoping for the prize in 1930 and discussing his chances for it with Georges Duhamel, assured him, "No problem about Jean Ajalbert. Gallimard will handle that; he owns him."[49]

That was the height of cynicism; moreover, Prévost never did get the award. But another Gallimard author, who did win the Goncourt, was by contrast amazingly ingenuous in telling how he got his book published. One day in 1927, Maurice Bedel, a total novice in the world of literature and publishing, happened to be in the Gallimard bookstore on Boulevard Raspail. He bought a book by Joseph Delteil, the latest Paul Morand, and as he was paying for them he diffidently asked the clerk:

"Would you happen to know of a publisher who might be interested in a fantasy?"

"A what?" asked the clerk.

"Well, I have a manuscript, and I don't know where to submit it."

"Oh, a manuscript," was the reply. "See my boss."

He was introduced to the manager who, as Bedel took a thick sheaf of papers out of his attaché case, merely said:

"Leave it with me. I'll pass it along to the firm."

A few months later, Bedel was informed by letter that his book had been accepted for publication. One surprise following the other, sometime later he was informed that he had won the Goncourt for 1927 with his *Jérôme, 60° latitude nord (Jerome, or The Latitude of Love)*.

During the two years after Proust's winning the award, Gaston kept sharpening his weapons, and in 1922 he felt ready to go on the offensive again. He was so successful that the list of nominees for the prize included three of his titles: Joseph Kessel's *La Steppe rouge* (The Red Steppe), the first volume of Roger Martin du Gard's *Les Thibault (World of the Thibaults)*, and Paul Morand's *Ouvert la nuit (Open All Night)*. The latter seemed to be the favorite, but at the last moment the votes went to Henri Béraud. Some felt that Gaston spoiled his chances by announcing that Morand's book had already sold 30,000 copies before the award.

The following year, however, he got his revenge, then fought tooth and nail to keep on winning the prize (of which he garnered seven of the next eleven). By 1931, the salvoes that Gaston unleashed to get several of his books on the preferred list each year set off an explosion. Bernard Grasset felt it was time to go public on the subject of what the Goncourt Prize meant. Furious at having missed the prize for the past six years, the publisher attacked on all fronts. What about that annual award luncheon at Drouant? he asked in an article. "Everyone knows now that the glory they bestow is only 'paper glory,' and people are more interested in what they ate than in what they said. The time is near when the most obliging of newsmen will refuse to put himself out for so little." He did not advocate abolishing the prize, but reducing its influence, which he felt had been magnified out of all proportion. As he saw it, the prizewinners no longer excited anyone: the contest had seen its day and been overblown by an age that was given to excesses.[50]

It was no accident that the Goncourt member who rose to the defense was Gaston's friend Jean Ajalbert. He was quick to point out that each year the Grasset company reserved the table at Drouant next to that of the Goncourt Academy, so as to hear the result first, and that for years Grasset had been making overtures of all sorts to the judges. He attributed Grasset's campaign to the fact that for the past few years his company had not won the prize, while pointing out the important writers Grasset had passed up: "Yes, Marcel Proust was let go by the infallible M. Bernard Grasset."[51] He then polished him off with vitriolic comments in which he made fun of him as an industrious peddler, a seller of paper who played on the snobbery of readers by publishing limited editions , and on the self-importance of authors through vanity publications, while thinking of himself as a possible future candidate for the French Academy.

Cut to the quick, Grasset decided to break off the public debate, but without giving ground:-

> The Goncourt Prize is no longer the annual miracle of literature performed by an assembly of Gods. It has resumed its proper place among other prizes awarded to deserving writers by judges of whom the least that can be said is that they are just as qualified as our December [i.e., Goncourt] regents. And if what it takes—to put an end to an unjustified supremacy and get things back to normal—is for a publisher to come forward and say, "I will no longer play a game that, like all games of chance, profit only the house"—well, that has been done.[52]

Grasset performed his mea culpa some twenty years later. In an open letter to Gaston, he would write:

> I was a poor prophet when I foresaw the growing prestige of the Goncourt Prize as the end of literature. Today we are blessed—if that is the word—with more prizes than there are days in the year. And literature has gone its merry way. Only the customs have been changed. In 1931 a new era, if not in literature, at least in publishing, was opening up. You latched on to it before I did.[53]

Between the two world wars, Grasset did indeed believe in the commercial impact of these literary prizes. His 1931 outburst above all showed his fury at Gaston's having the Goncourts under his thumb.

One need only think back on Grasset's earlier period of glory, when he won the Goncourt in both 1911 and 1912, and remember the remarkable commercial boost that this well-publicized double victory had given him. He believed in prizes so much that, in 1922, he maneuvered his way inside a new one so it could never get away from him. This was the Balzac Prize, founded by the munitions king Sir Basil Zaharoff, giving 20,000 francs to an unpublished first novel by a new author. Grasset arranged for his firm to be used as headquarters for the prize, and offered the prizewinner a contract (for publication by Grasset, of course) with an advance of 10,000 francs on royalties. The Balzac Prize struck everyone as being too completely in one publisher's pocket. Some of the Goncourt Academy members were up in arms, and Ajalbert once again made himself their spokesman with a colorful metaphor:

"Let the benefactor relieve himself, as long as he does not do it against the wall of Chez Drouant!"[54]

The trade itself opposed it: the panel of judges, presided over by Paul Bourget and including as leading members Daniel Halévy and Edmond Jaloux, was too obviously connected with Grasset for anyone but him to benefit from the enterprise. The publishers' trade association insisted that the bylaws be changed and the winner be free to select any publisher he chose. In March this was done. In October the prize was awarded to Jean Giraudoux and Emile Baumann, who were neither new nor unpublished. It so happened that their *Siegfried et le Limousin (My Friend from Limousin)* and *Job le prédestiné* (Job the Predestined) had already both been published by Grasset.[55]

In that same year, 1922, Gaston first garnered the Femina Prize for one of his books, Jacques de Lacretelle's *Silbermann*. Eight years later the same author got Gaston his first French Academy Prize for the novel *Amour nuptial* (Conjugal Love). But 1926 was the year Gaston most obviously revealed the interest he had in literary prizes and the place they held in his business strategy. For example, one of his authors was the first to win a new prize, the Renaudot Prize, which was created for purely gastronomical—not literary—merit.

Each year the reporters for Paris's major daily newspapers who covered the Goncourt award complained regularly that they did not get to eat lunch until very late, because they had to wait for the Goncourt announcement, made after the Drouant luncheon, then pick up reactions here and there and write their pieces for their papers. So in 1926 they decided to have their lunch before the Ten (who constituted the Goncourt Academy) and, while they were about it, award a literary prize of their own. This prize was named after one of the earliest (and in a sense the patron saint) of French journalists, Théophraste Renaudot, who in 1631 had started *La Gazette de France*. So the representatives of *L'Intransigeant, Le Matin, Le Journal, Paris-Midi, Candide, Le Petit Journal, Le Canard enchaîné*, and so on, lunched at the Fontaine Gaillon, close by Drouant, and between the fruit course and dessert gave their award to *Nicolo-Peccavi, ou l'Affaire Dreyfus à Carpentras* by a young unknown novelist, Armand Lunel.[56]

This move by the newsmen of the Renaudot panel was so successful that five years later, so as not to be left out, their fellow reporters covering the Femina award on Rue du Faubourg Saint-Honoré decided to do likewise and called their award the Interallié Prize, after the Cercle Interallié, in which the women judges of the Femina Prize met. And they decided that their prize should be restricted to novelists who were also newspapermen. The first would go to André Malraux.

Shortly after that, in 1933, the librarian of the École des Beaux-Arts, an habitué of the Café des Deux-Magots at Saint-Germain-des-Prés, decided he would also start a prize, named after his favorite haunt. He collected 1,300 francs from the patrons of the Deux-Magots and turned that sum over to Raymond Queneau, for his prizewinning book *Le Chiendent (The Bark Tree)*. Queneau, finding a surrealistic way to thumb his nose at the award, blew the cash on a costly "drink on the house" for all the customers of the next-door establishment, the Café de Flore. Meanwhile, since there was already dissension among the members of the jury awarding the Deux-Magots Prize, one of them crossed Boulevard Saint-Germain—on foot—to the Brasserie Lipp and there created the Cazes Prize, named after that restaurant's owner.

In November 1927 Edouard Bourdet's four-act comedy *Vient de paraître* (Just Published) opened at the Théâtre de la Michodière. The show was in the audience as much as onstage, for those present included all the familiar names of the world of art and letters. Letters particularly, since that was the main subject of the play: the story of a literary prize and the launching of a book.

The curtain goes up on a scene in the publishing house of one Julien Moscat. Stage right is his office; stage left, the waiting room for visitors and the mail room for the books. The Emile Zola Prize is about to be awarded. Another important character, never on stage, is Moscat's competitor, Chamillard. The two are constantly at swords' points. They keep stealing authors from each other; no method seems too underhanded.

"With very few exceptions," says Moscat, "an author—I mean the ones that sell—only starts being profitable with his third or fourth book. That's the problem with bringing out new young writers. But what can one do? I like to. It's fun." And a little later, he adds, "I didn't think Chamillard was that foxy. He's learning."

The audience was stirring. People craned their necks, trying to pick out Gallimard and Grasset, while on stage Moscat was saying: "I can't hold my own in this business as I do, unless I am ahead of everyone else and never let anyone get the better of me."[57]

That could have been either Grasset or Gallimard. A funny business, publishing, the uninitiated must have thought. Because all they talk about is manipulation, tactics, moves and countermoves. Was that what publishing was like? Precisely. Bourdet drew a faithful picture. It was in Grasset's waiting room, where he was supposed to meet François Mauriac, that he got the idea for his play and started his research, making notes of everything: the comings and goings, the remarks, the insults and flattery, the publisher's fiery temper with his staff, and the placidity of the writers. He had all the time he needed to observe and sketch. His play showed that Parisian publishing was a minor theater in itself.

"How stupid you were, Maréchal, my friend! You should have come and told me, 'Chamillard is offering me twenty-five thousand francs advance for my next novel.' Then I would have given you thirty and that would have clinched it. . . . Chamillard never had the slightest idea how to promote a book! He still thinks that all it takes to sell a book is for the author to have talent! So you can imagine . . . "

At times, the satire fringed on slander. Bourdet had Grasset accuse Gallimard of misrepresentation:

"We'll print twenty thousand copies for starters."

"Twenty thousand?"

"Yes, and our thousands are *real* thousands—five hundred each!"

"What do you mean?"

"When Chamillard, for instance, talks of thousands, each thousand amounts only to two hundred and fifty copies."

During the intermission, while all eyes were on Grasset, the publisher turned to a lady friend and said—loud enough for everyone to hear:

"Really funny—and so typical of Gallimard!"

When, a little later, Moscat made a particularly cutting retort, Grasset was heard to exclaim:

"Oh, no! That's not Gallimard. That's Albin Michel!"[58]

Bourdet had been smart enough to draw on more than two Parisian publishers. In spite of that, everyone seeing the play took it to be about Grasset and Gallimard and the ferocious competition between them. Which goes to show how much the antagonistic actions of the two men were at the heart of French publishing between the two world wars. "It was just an amusing satire of the world of literature," Grasset would write a decade later.[59] That may well be, but some satires are documents; *Vient de paraître* stands as an enduring picture of a mentality that would endure long after the deaths of the two publishers.

Everybody referred to Gallimard as Gaston, and his given name identified him, as if there were no other Gaston in France, whereas very few people, only his most intimate friends, ever spoke of Grasset as Bernard. Nor was this the only difference between the two men, who were opposites in everything except their chosen profession, of which they gave a similar definition: to seek out and discover a literary value, then transform it into a commercial value before offering it for sale. They both thought that publishing was essentially a personal business, a craft. But it was in their personal ways of achieving their ends that they differed most.

Pale, abrupt, nervous, short in stature, Grasset did not cut an impressive figure. His face had some disturbing similarities to Hitler's. The same mustache, the same haircut, the same way of striking a pose. With the years, this similarity became more and more noticeable.[60] But in Grasset's eyes there was a touch of mischief, a promise of daring, and a bright intelligence that had nothing in common with the expressionless features of the Nazi dictator.

Extreme and passionate, Grasset's letters had an all or nothing quality, they were never lukewarm. And they were almost always unfair, not because he lacked judgment, but out of a kind of perversity. He was given to quick judgments—usually correct—on a person at first sight, and on a manuscript after four pages. That is known as flair, and his career shows that his did not often mislead him. Grasset was very conscious of what people said about him, and especially what they wrote. Sensitive about his reputation, he once sent a correction to a newspaper that had done a profile of him; he described himself as a man who could be either selfish or helpful, enthusiastic or icy, depending not on his moods but on the people he dealt with—a man deeply devoted to those he cared for and those he considered his responsibility.[61]

He was born in the same year as Gaston at Chambéry in the French Alps. The son of a lawyer, he naturally was sent to Paris to study law and get a doctorate in it. With 3,000 francs that he inherited, he set up his publishing house in July 1907 on Rue Gay-Lussac, before moving to Rue Corneille, and then permanently to Rue des

Saints-Pères in 1910. He learned his trade with the best of masters, Charles Péguy, publisher of *Les Cahiers de la quinzaine*, and Alfred Vallette, editor of *Le Mercure de France*. He published Giraudoux, Mauriac, the parodists Paul Reboux and Charles Muller, and Alphonse de Chateaubriant, as well as a good many "vanity" books like Proust's. But it was after World War I that his company was really put on the map and he could seriously consider competing with the famous old established firms, notably thanks to Les Cahiers Verts (The Green Books), his famous imprint run by Daniel Halévy; to several sensationally successful novels such as Louis Hémon's *Maria Chapdelaine* and Raymond Radiguet's *Le Diable au corps (The Devil in the Flesh)*; and to a group of talented and promising young writers, Emmanuel Berl, André Malraux, Pierre Drieu La Rochelle, Blaise Cendrars, and Henry de Montherlant.

The way he acquired *Maria Chapdelaine* and launched *The Devil in the Flesh* was typical of his style. In 1921 Halévy brought him a text published seven years earlier as a serial in the prestigious newspaper *Le Temps* under the name of Louis Hémon, a Breton who had spent some time in Canada leading the life of a woodsman and who died in an accident in 1913. The novel was a saga of pioneer woodsmen, a love story in which men and women were shown to be in perfect symbiosis with nature. Taking to the book enthusiastically, Grasset tried to find Hémon's heir. He was informed that two years before, in 1919, Hémon's heiress had unfortunately signed a contract with the Editions Payot, which, however, had still not published the book. No matter: Grasset knew that Payot was a Protestant, so he called him and stressed the totally Catholic character of the story. Payot was reluctant, but Grasset carried the day with his quick decisions, which allowed no time for reconsideration. No sooner did Payot mention a tentative price for the rights, than Grasset had his secretary bring him 2,000 francs and a contract. That very afternoon Grasset was the new publisher of *Maria Chapdelaine*, and the next day he was in Quimper, where Mlle. Hémon contracted with him for all the rest of the author's books. Six months later *Maria Chapdelaine* had sold more than 100,000 copies. Eventually it would reach a million in its regular edition, be translated into numerous foreign languages, and be reprinted in paperback editions.[62]

That was Grasset. Quick, energetic, throwing the best of himself into every book he had faith in. He never spared his own efforts, something rare among publishers, who too often left the necessary follow-ups to their subordinates. Grasset delegated nothing and often proceeded headfirst, full speed ahead. In 1913, while the Academy was deliberating whether to give its Grand Prize for Literature to one Emile Clermont, author of *Laure*, or to the great Romain Rolland, Grasset, who had published the former, exchanged words outside the Academy with the literary critic of the weekly *Gil Blas*, who had panned his book. Although neither knew how to handle a sword, they fought a duel, and Grasset was slightly cut on the forearm, most likely by accident. But he had shed blood in defense of one of his authors.[63]

Such impulsiveness was part of Grasset's charm, as were also his lies, and sometimes his utter caddishness—with women as well as with writers. He was not above publicly humiliating a person for his own pleasure, out of cynicism or in fun. One day Armand Godoy, a rich Cuban poet who wrote in French and had had a number of volumes of verse vanity-published by Grasset, complained to the publisher that he continued to make him foot the bill for his books, which was beginning to get expensive. Grasset replied:

"Yes, but your books are a blot on my reputation. There's no putting a price on that!"[64]

For all his excesses and contradictions, his fits of temper and unfairness, Grasset had no peer when it came to "smelling out" an author or a manuscript, and he followed his instincts no matter what. A number of his authors were more loyal to him personally than to his firm, and some even stipulated in their contracts that they would deal only with him personally and not with the firm.[65] More than one publisher would have taken that as a compliment; certainly he did. In 1935 this put him in a paradoxical situation: involved in litigation with his own company, he was barred from his office on Rue des Saints-Pères and removed himself to a rest home outside

Paris, at Garches. Some of his associates tried to have him declared insane and stricken from the publishers' rolls. He finally won out and got rid of his enemies. But the fact that many authors had sided with him was proof enough that the company bearing his name had no validity without him.

Grasset mad? True, his behavior more than once raised eyebrows. The testimony of his colleagues was clinical. "Since childhood he suffered from a neurosis that made him a hypochondriac, self-destructive, bulimic, depressive, and sadistic," said one of them.[66] "He was a cyclothymic personality with a constant background of deep melancholia that led him to the depths of depression," specified another.[67]

It was difficult to work with Grasset, to put up with the four packs of cigarettes he smoked each day, with the constant nervous fingering of his cigarette holder, and with his susceptibility to toadying, his bursts of hypernationalism, and his excessive pride. Working with Grasset in the 1920s and 1930s, one had to accept the fact that his word alone counted. While Gaston had full confidence in his editorial board and essentially read only those manuscripts it recommended to him, Grasset trusted nothing but his own judgment.

"Reading editors are advocates of the mediocre," he used to say. "They don't ask themselves whether something is 'very good,' but only whether it is 'no worse than the next thing.' I have no editorial board."[68]

No editorial board, but some editors just the same. More than once he had sharp exchanges with Edmond Jaloux or Daniel Halévy, when their opinions differed from his, and he always made the final decision. His company was based solely on his will, on his moods. In a legal sense, too, it was a personal business; only in 1930 did it become a stock company, the Editions Bernard Grasset, capitalized at 9.5 million francs. In view of his contribution, he was allotted 28,200 shares estimated to be worth 7.2 million francs.[69] But he found it difficult to admit that he had a board of directors. And so did the trade in general, which saw the Editions Grasset always as only Bernard Grasset himself and, in his shadow, Louis Brun, his cat's-paw, the negative to his positive.

Plump and somewhat red-faced, Brun, a Protestant from Toulouse, actually was the man who kept the business on track. For Grasset to be able to indulge his eccentricities and his strokes of genius, M. Brun had to hold the reins at Rue des Saints-Pères. He was the one who put out the fires the boss lit, who talked compromise with authors after the publisher manhandled them. Grasset was always categorical, Brun was oblique. They complemented each other admirably.

Grasset did not like Brun, but knew his value. Brun did not like Grasset, but admired him. Once they had this out, they got along wonderfully together, which meant that each one put up with the other's shortcomings. Unlike his boss, the general manager of the Grasset firm loved money, luxury, and collecting fine books, but did very little reading. Sometimes he insisted that some useless and obviously bad book be published, for the sole reason that its author could serve his personal ends in the business. He himself admitted it:

"The Grasset company is a whore, but a high-priced whore."[70]

Grasset chose to overlook this. For if publishing needs men like Grasset, it also needs characters like Brun. By the same token, Brun knew just how far to go and never set foot in the boss's domain, if such an initiative might go against Grasset's plans or upset his person-to-person habits. He allowed Grasset to keep his schoolboy notebooks, in which he entered at the top of the page the titles published each month, and in facing columns the date on one side and the number of copies sold opposite.[71] Brun was not always candid about his own opinion on the quality of the books that Grasset's flair moved him to publish. Above all, Brun never criticized his boss's writings, for Grasset was also a writer. Too much a writer, for some people's tastes, especially those of the authors upon whom he bestowed long prefaces, unsolicited, in the form of personal letters.[72] Grasset was the author of a dozen books, of which a good part were made up of previously published articles, prefaces, or open letters. These writings were almost exclusively devoted to two subjects: the publishing trade and morality. He was generous with his advice on writing, literature, the promotion of books, book collecting, bookselling— but also on happiness, justice, action, pleasure, knowledge. One may state without fear of contradiction that Grasset's writings made more of an impression on publishers than on moralists.

Not satisfied with publishing his own books, as icing on his cake he had some of them published by, of all people, Gallimard. This was quite a feat on the part of both Grasset and Gaston, since in their environment of hooters and backbiters such lordly manners were almost unprecedented between competitors. "What's the matter? Has he lost faith in his green silks?" sarcastically asked Jean Ajalbert, alluding to the imprint edited by Daniel Halévy.[73]

Grasset and Gaston esteemed each other. The one was a lout obsessed with his work, intolerably egocentric; the other, a sly gentleman to whom the ends justified any means. They were at total war because in the final analysis they were cut from the same cloth, were of the same generation, and more especially because their two companies expanded in the same boom at the same time, in the same market. Malraux, who was published by both, said that they had once even thought of becoming partners.[74] It is hard to imagine how they could have cohabited between the two world wars, even though Grasset was to assert later on, "The brotherhood between us was never marred by our fights as publishers. One could almost say that at certain turns they reinforced it." And as the years went by, regretting that he had remained a bachelor because of his character and because he felt that that was the only way he could devote himself totally to his work, Grasset admitted, "I sometimes look enviously at the tribe running the firm across the way, under Gaston's glorious patriarchy, the omnipotence of which is limited only by Jean Paulhan's veto."[75]

He wished to be alone, and so he remained. But while Gaston had to share the prestige of his firm with his editorial board, the general editors of his imprints, and the members of the NRF, Grasset got full credit for all his successes—and full blame for his defeats. Proud of being made an officer of the Legion of Honor by the minister of industry and commerce, "for having contributed much to the expansion of French books abroad,"[76] Grasset wanted to personalize his company to the limit, and impose his own selections against all other opinions. In the early 1920s this led him to invest large sums in book advertising at a time when most of his competitors were still holding back.

After Cocteau read him a page from his friend Raymond Radiguet's novel, *The Devil in the Flesh*, in 1923 Grasset decided to bring it out to the accompaniment of a huge advertising campaign. Sure of what he was doing, he signed the young author to a contract giving him 1,500 francs per month to allow him to devote all his time to an oeuvre that both Cocteau and Max Jacob had assured Grasset was most promising. In Grasset's eyes this was the time, if ever there was a time, to prove the rightness of his faith in advertising: the author, only twenty, had had his first poems published in *Le Canard enchaîné* at fifteen; fêted and praised to the skies by Tout-Paris, he led an unbelievably bohemian existence, and his novel, said to be partially autobiographical, had overtones of scandal. The protagonist undergoes a man's experiences with the soul of a child. He takes as his mistress a married woman whose husband is away at the front, dictates tender letters for her to send him so as to keep him reassured, and pleasures her without giving her any remorse. Such cynicism revolted a large segment of the French public in the immediate aftermath of World War I—which tended to obscure the simplicity and sobriety of the first-person narrative.

Grasset created some successful slogans around his "seventeen-year-old author," for Radiguet had in fact written the book three years earlier. Grasset took space in all the literary weeklies and fortnightlies, as well as in dailies with a religious slant; copies were sent to the entire press, to actors, politicians, and other likely groups. Then he waited, but not for long. The critics lauded Radiguet's literary gifts and waxed ecstatic over his precociousness, while expressing some reservations about his hero's morals. The veterans' organizations duly took umbrage. The book was launched, its success assured, and Radiguet was the novelist of the year. A few months later, while the book was at the height of its sales, the author gave his publisher the crowning piece of the publicity campaign: he died. Of typhoid fever, alone, in a hospital which Cocteau had refused to go to, not wanting to see his friend suffer. Cut down so young! Grasset would never have dared imagine the kind of articles the newspapers now devoted to Radiguet, nor such a funeral: the church of Saint-Honoré d'Eylau was flooded with white roses, with red ones on the coffin, white horses pulled the hearse followed by the cream of Paris in full mourning attire, behind the black jazz band from the Boeuf sur le Toit cabaret.* Truly, a most Parisian funeral, orchestrated by one of the young writer's friends, Coco Chanel.

No more was needed to convince Grasset of the usefulness of advertising. He was now persuaded that an author had to be "sold" just like any other commercial product, and was determined to go much further than the timid attempt made by Albin Michel to launch Pierre Benoit's L'Atlantide (Atlantida) with daily teasers reading, "In 15 days, this writer will be famous," and the next day, "In 14 days . . . ," and so on.

His primary aim was to strike people's imagination so that the titles and names would stick in their memory. When it occurred to him that four of the leading young authors in his catalogue were André Maurois, François Mauriac, Paul Morand, and Henry de Montherlant, all with names beginning with M, he dismissed their literary objections and lumped them together as "The Four M's." André Malraux escaped this by getting away in time to Gallimard. He was right. Grasset got his Four M's together for a press luncheon, and the atmosphere was glacial. They never lunched together again, but the Four M's advertisements continued.[77] Watching the faces of the literary reporters he had invited to the luncheon, Grasset realized that it was a bad idea: the individualism of bourgeois writers could

*The Ox on the Roof, named after Cocteau's ballet for the Ballets Russes.— TRANS.

not be toyed with in that way. He was also to come a cropper with his idea of advertisement inserts in books. If newspapers did it, why not books? He did not try this in his truly literary publications, afraid of compromising their integrity, but only in the more popular books whose authors agreed to it. But he dropped the idea when he realized the revenue from the advertising barely covered the costs of paper and printing for the inserts.[78]

Grasset was flying in the face of the critics, for he made no bones about the fact that his book advertising was meant to make a breach in the literary press's exclusive and excessive power to inform the public of the existence and quality of a new work. Jean Giraudoux (still known then only as a novelist) was not the only author whom this delighted: his courageous publisher was getting through the "screen" of the critics to bring news of his book directly to the reader.[79] But within the trade the majority of publishers, reviewers, and even authors disapproved of "vulgar advertising." Georges Duhamel, for one, detected a "lowering of moral tone," an effort to replace independent criticism by "imposing on the multitudes judgments that were based on nothing more than monetary concerns." For him, book advertising was a low artifice that the literary trade should be too proud to stoop to, in keeping with its professional dignity.[80]

In a magazine survey on the subject, publisher Georges Crès denounced advertising as "the Americanization of our business," against the opinion of several writers who advocated addressing themselves to readers and not to critics. Some spoke of "arrant mercantilism" and "grocery store mentality," while others like Henri Massis, who was a writer, publisher, and critic all in one, felt advertising was unsuitable for the promotion of intellectual products: "The reputation, credibility, and receptivity that a writer gains with his audience all demand a type of preparation that no launching campaign can replace."

Many of the people questioned by the journalist Maximilien Gauthier resented the fact that advertising tended to "create" the literary event, in an unwholesome and immoral atmosphere unlikely to develop a true writing talent. Henri Béraud, on the other hand, advocated purely informative advertising, not garish, hyperbolic, or presumptuous. What bothered him most, and rightly so, was the financial aspect of the problem, since some well-to-do writers were ready to spend large amounts to satisfy their vanity. Béraud, who saw a most nefarious inequality in this kind of book promotion, was convinced that in the final analysis the best advertising was oral: word-of-mouth, from satisfied readers who recommended a book to their friends. Nevertheless, Béraud's lucidly argued judgment was outweighed by an interview with a Boulevard Saint-Germain book-store clerk, to whom book advertising, along with the title, the cover, and the promotional wrapper provided by the French publishers were the only way to keep a book from disappearing within a week from the display counters to the reserve shelves, where it would stay until inventoried and returned to the publisher.[81]

This controversy, needless to say, only encouraged Grasset in his innovating endeavors. His conception of book advertising and publicity was simple—some said simplistic—but it worked: it played up anecdotes about the book rather than the book's content.

> Take the case of a writer we'll call Table. To publicize him, don't say, "Table has talent." Say, "Table is writing his new book at Saint-Tropez." One person will reply, "Table? Never heard of him." That's a lost cause. But the next person, trying to sound in the know, will say, "Really? That's interesting!" That's a step forward. After that, you come to the fellow who winks at you and says, "I know," and you're in. Publicity must always be approached in this anecdotal form. Advertising means having the courage to claim that what you hope for has already been accomplished.[82]

Starting from this fixed principle, Grasset chose "He is seventeen years old" over "Radiguet is a genius," and shortly after that went with "Do Irene's hats come from Lewis's? Read Paul Morand's novel," even though that author's *Lewis and Irene* had nothing to do with hats and even less with the well-known milliner Lewis. All it took was daring. But it was something Gaston could not afford. He was still battling with his editorial committee to accept writers of a non-cerebral literature based on exoticism, mystery, and adventure: the books of Joseph Kessel, Pierre MacOrlan, and a few others. Gaudy advertising was utterly alien to his temperament, but he might have agreed to it for strictly commercial reasons, convinced of its impact on sales.

Eventually Gallimard and his fellow publishers had to follow Grasset along his pioneering path, even though they lagged somewhat behind; they could not allow Grasset to dominate the display advertising space in *Les Nouvelles littéraires* without at least reminding its readers of their existence. The subsequent tendency toward larger and larger ads made at least one group happy: the literary press. In the same way, the Gallimard-Grasset competition was advantageous to a number of writers who otherwise might have had to be less demanding.

Since the Proust affair, Gaston and Grasset knew that they appealed to an identical audience. Despite their mutual respect and the many nonaggression pacts they agreed to, they went on waging total war against each other. Observers kept a tally of who was ahead, while a few shrewd authors were able to cash in on the rivalry. Grasset, hard put to recover after Proust won the Goncourt Prize in 1919, received another shock the same year, when Charles Péguy's widow took back the rights to his *Œuvres choisies* (Selected Works). Having published that volume in 1911, Grasset was sure that it would serve as a precedent and that, after Péguy was killed in the war, his widow would naturally let Grasset publish the complete works. But Gaston beat him to the punch; after reading the contract for the *Œuvres choisies* and seeing that it granted the work to Grasset for only ten years, he persuaded the widow to let him include the selected texts in an edition of the complete works. Outraged by what he considered underhandedness, Grasset was forced to give the *Œuvres choisies* to Gallimard, but wrote him, "You stole them from me."[83]

A bit later, in 1922, when Jacques de Lacretelle got the Femina Prize for his novel about Jew-baiting in a French lycée, *Silbermann*, Grasset had the same angry reaction; after all, he had given the writer his first break two years before by publishing *La Vie inquiète de Jean Hermelin* (The Troubled Life of Jean Hermelin), which had not created a ripple. Other writers, including Malraux and Emmanuel Berl, followed the same path from Grasset to Gallimard. The former sowed, the latter reaped, said certain malicious gossips. Which led one critic to formulate it much less charitably:

"Gaston is the first man to discover authors for the second time."

While exaggerated, this barb hit the mark, and Gaston was to make every effort to eliminate the truth of it. He would recoup the writers his editorial board had turned its nose up at, cover the literary milieu with a well-organized network, and support a whole flock of young writers who had promise.

Had Gaston listened to his head bookkeeper, his relations with authors would have been very simple. For M. Dupont, authors came in two categories: good ones (who never asked for advances against their royalties) and bad ones (who never stopped asking for advances).[84] By this criterion, almost all authors were detestable. But the publisher's relations with them were unfortunately much more complicated. There was one perennial story in the publishing business that called up the specter of what publishers wanted to ward off, come what may: the author's representative or, more commonly, the agent.

Flaubert, whose *Madame Bovary* had been published by Michel Lévy, thought twice in 1862 before giving his *Salammbô* to the same publisher. He stipulated outrageous conditions: the publisher would have to accept the manuscript sight unseen, could not have the book illustrated, and would pay 25,000 to 30,000 francs for ten-year publication rights to Flaubert, who in addition would have final say on the format, typeface, and so forth, and who would retain all subsidiary rights. Not quite sure he could make such demands in person, Flaubert asked the brother of one of his friends, a lawyer named Ernest Duplan, to negotiate and act as his agent. While Flaubert fully intended to stay with his old publisher, he made no bones about having received other generous proposals, which was a good negotiating tactic. To bolster his demands and not leave it all in the hands of his sometime "agent," Flaubert wrote Lévy that *Salammbô* took him five years to write and cost him 4,000 francs for research *in situ*: "I am not out to earn my living from literature. But the least I can expect is that it should not bankrupt me."[85] Finally, Michel Lévy agreed to accept the work sight unseen, paid 10,000 francs, promised there would be no illustrations, and in exchange was given first refusal on Flaubert's next book, provided it had a modern setting. But to obtain those conditions, the publisher had had to engage in long, arduous negotiations with a lawyer who knew nothing about either literature or the publishing business.

To many French publishers, agents are a pain. First, because agents know more about the law than most authors and are therefore more difficult to hoodwink. Then, because nothing cuts ice with them except legal and financial arguments. Fortunately for Gaston and his peers, French writers, as opposed to those writing in English, are much too individualistic to leave their interests in the hands of an intermediary. They turn to lawyers only for specific points or under unusual circumstances, as for instance when the Gallimard firm once lost a writer's manuscript, and he sued and won 200,000 francs in damages, for he had not lost his receipt for it.[86]

For Gaston nothing could replace direct contact between author and publisher. When a sense of interaction develops, when mutual ties are formed and affinities discovered, and when a purely commercial relationship becomes a true friendship, the work of a writer can be deeply influenced. This is so true that, without Gallimard and Grasset, French literature of the first half of this century would not have become what it is. Their dispositions, their willingness to take a chance, their pugnacity, and their conceptions of literature and the writer's trade profoundly and durably transformed the writing and publishing landscape. This could not have happened with agents as intermediaries. Author-publisher relations, harmonious or acrimonious according to the individuals, periods, and events, left their mark—discreet but present—on the quality of a work. A striking example of this is Georges Simenon, in whom critics and biographers have discovered three different styles coinciding with his changes of publishers.

Gaston devoted a good part of his time to keeping up contacts with his authors. In the mornings he continued the letter-writing tradition he had made a rule since the inception of the publishing "bureau." His letters, sometimes typed by a secretary, but most often written out in his firm and regular hand, fall into four categories: technical (printing, display, rights, etc.), intended for the record; friendly, as a means of keeping in touch; imperative, serving as urgent reminders to hurry up with an overdue manuscript; and finally informative, meant simply to notify some author (probably being published by Grasset) that the *NRF* would be flattered and the Gallimard catalogue honored to include his or her name.

Gaston was in the habit of having contracts signed at the end of a lunch at a restaurant. People are always better disposed after having consumed a fine wine. And Gaston felt more at home in this kind of social environment, where appearances count for so much, than in the office, where he could never get away from the phone or his brother Raymond. The rest of the day, when not meeting with his editors, or reading some debatable manuscript, or settling some internal house dispute, he would visit writers or receive them in his office. One question was always foremost in his mind: does this author have talent? "Talent, as far as publishers are concerned, means: 'How many books does he have in him?' "[87]

But how did one judge that, how did one guess? By instinct, of course. Did Alain-Fournier have another work in him of the quality of *Le Grand Meaulnes (The Wanderer)*? He died too young, too soon for anyone to tell. What about all those writers who failed to live up to their first work, even when that first shot was a masterstroke? On looking over the lists of literary prizes at half a century's remove, it is appalling to see how many of the winners never produced anything lasting. Even Gaston could make mistakes. His legendary instinct was not infallible. People were impressed at his early recognition of Aragon, Drieu La Rochelle, and Jacques Audiberti. But who remembered how many others, in those same 1920s, he had hand-carried and forced upon literary groups, prize judges, and literary journals—authors who left absolutely nothing that held up a few decades later?

The hits tended to obscure the flops, which were entered into the invisible catalogue column headed "Profit and Loss"—barring unlikely consecration by rediscovery. But there is no reviving enthusiasm over books that lack the required qualities to age well. Here too the important thing was a sense for durability which Gaston made one of his fundamental principles.

True, when he importuned Georges Duhamel, a notable contemporary writer, to write the *Life of Tolstoy*, he was motivated by something quite unrelated to the potential work's durability,[88] namely literary politics. But Gaston was on the road to exploration when he wrote to Rivière:

> This morning I am giving Paulhan the manuscript of a story that seems to me not at all bad. It's by a man named Jouhandeau, who some months ago gave me a manuscript. I think he has a definite talent. I asked him to come in; he turned out to be an exceedingly appealing and shy young man who told me he had never had anything published before.[89]

Gaston was right: the young man in question truly had "a body of work in him," as Sartre might have said, and he was to publish almost a hundred books with Gallimard, from his first one, *La Jeunesse de Théophile* (Théophile As a Young Man), in 1921 to volume 26 of his long-running *Les Journaliers* (The Day Laborers) in 1978. Of course not all of them were hits, far from it. Every time Marcel Jouhandeau tried to "cheat on him" with Grasset, Gaston made a point of telling him how much he had cost the firm. A lot, a whole lot. And Jouhandeau was certainly not Gaston's most ruinous investment. A few hits sometimes make up for some pretty bad flops. Which couldn't be said of a good many authors, who were reluctant to admit their failures, even if faced with the irrefutable evidence of the sales figures. In such cases, Gaston would tactfully tell them the story known as the tale of Zamora.

Charles Gounod had sold his *Faust* outright to his publisher for a mere 5,000 francs, and it made him famous. As a result, much later the composer was able to get 100,000 francs for *Le Tribut de Zamora* (The Tribute of Zamora). Toward the end of his life he met his publisher on the boulevards, and noticed that the man was wearing a very fine fur coat along with an old, disreputable-looking high hat. Gounod moved close to him, with a meaningful smile on his lips, stroked the fine fur, and said, "Aha! *Faust?*"

The publisher then pointed to his old hat and replied, "*The Tribute of Zamora.*"

For every *Faust*, how many *Tributes of Zamora* there are in the catalogues and cellars of publishers!

Once, exasperated at hearing Grasset reiterate that the publisher was much more important to a book than the writer, Cocteau responded:

"You ought to do what the movie producers do, bill it in big type as 'A Book by Grasset,' and in small type underneath, 'Words by Cocteau.' "[90]

That was typical of Grasset, but never of Gaston, whose natural inclination was to disappear behind the author. Unlike his main competitor, when Gaston decided to read a manuscript, he read it and did not stop at "sniffing" it or riffling through a few pages. He felt his criticisms and rejections had to be fully explained; he owed that to his authors. When they were, moreover, friends or permanent associates in the firm, he could not fob them off with a letter from the editorial committee. And the closer the author was to him, the harsher he might be dealt with. When Martin du Gard asked his opinion of a play he had written, *Deux jours de vacances* (Two Days' Vacation), he was met with a scowl and frank words of rejection. The characters too artificial, the writing labored, the construction faulty, and then the coup de grâce: it had been written too hastily. When Martin du Gard had put in two years on it! Though crestfallen, he was convinced the censure was apposite and utterly sincere.[91]

That was the main thing. Gaston was credible to his authors. He was not merely a banker. His friend Fargue, who kept promising books and collected advances but did not produce anything, agreed during a weekend at Bénerville to let himself be locked in his room for the whole day while Gaston and the others went off on an outing. When evening came, Fargue proudly handed Gaston a sheaf of paper on which he had tirelessly written over and over again: "I am the captain of a corvette. I am the captain . . ."[92]

The foundation of the business lay in public relations. Gaston knew this better than anyone and spent a good part of his time representing his firm to the outside world. He cast his nets in all directions. A good share of his catalogue in the early 1930s was brought in by the *NRF* magazine, Gide, Rivière, Paulhan, and a few others, who were as much recruiters collaring the best available talent for the Rue de Grenelle as filters keeping out the unwanted.

It was Malraux who wooed Emmanuel Berl away from Grasset for Gallimard. In 1929 Berl had just published *Mort de la pensée bourgeoise* (The Death of Bourgeois Thought) and was beginning to make a name for himself, after his two earlier Grasset books had gone unnoticed. And now he left him just as he was to achieve real success with his next book, *Mort de la morale bourgeoise* (The Death of Bourgeois Morality). Prior to this, Berl had been both attracted to and repelled by the *NRF* publishing house: his cousin Henri Franck had been published there at the very outset, but the firm's "Left Bank" quality and its "sort of Protestant pseudohomosexuality" kept Berl from crossing the Rubicon.[93] Malraux helped him do it.

It was Jean Prévost, a contributor to the magazine as well as one of Gallimard's published authors, who introduced Antoine de Saint-Exupéry to Gaston. After reading one or two of the pilot's stories, Gaston encouraged him to try something more ambitious. He took the advice, and *Courrier sud (Southern Mail)* became a Gallimard book in 1929.[94]

A young Frenchman who was teaching Spanish in the United States and was enamored of American literature, Maurice-Edgar

Coindreau, sent Gaston the first pages of John Dos Passos's *Manhattan Transfer* in his own translation. Gaston was won over and proceeded to publish the whole long book as a two-volume work in 1928. From then on, he trusted Coindreau's judgment and accepted everything he suggested to him. After the translator wrote an article about William Faulkner in the *NRF* in 1931, Gallimard brought out *Sanctuary*, then *As I Lay Dying*, and many more, whose success with the French public helped Faulkner's career toward its well-deserved dimensions. Gaston was fortunate in having Coindreau bring to the Du monde entier (From All Over the World) imprint the works of John Steinbeck in 1939 *(Of Mice and Men)*, Erskine Caldwell in 1936 *(God's Little Acre)*, and Ernest Hemingway in 1932 *(A Farewell to Arms)*.[95]

Actor-producer Charles Dullin got his friend Gaston to read the plays of a newcomer that he was himself performing, Armand Salacrou, and Salacrou's works became Gallimard books from 1934 on. Antonin Artaud, whose *L'Ombilic des limbes* (The Umbilicus of Limbo) Gaston had just published in 1925, was asked to recruit among the Surrealists, where he met with little success, however. But there was always Gide and his fertile network . . .

The list is long. By its diversity, and the variety of recruiters and recruits, it illustrates the scope of Gaston Gallimard's reach between the two world wars: in all directions, with emphasis on quality and durability. This was one of the most profitable of policies. Out of that logic, the jewel of the crown—the collection known as La Pléiade—was brought to Gallimard. This imprint, before becoming a prestigious literary pantheon, was an amazing adventure in publishing, typical of its time.

This unusual enterprise was started by an unusual man, Jacques Schiffrin. With his tall, emaciated figure, his sunken face and expressive eyes, he was decidedly a presence. Women were quick to notice his large, bony hands with fingers that seemed endless. Schiffrin was impressive because of his distinction, his culture, and his sharp mind. He was born in 1894 at Baku in Azerbaijan to Jewish parents. His father was both a chemist and a businessman. Totally bilingual, Jacques Schiffrin had had part of his schooling in Russia, then studied law in Geneva, taking a doctorate. He moved to Paris, married a concert pianist, and took a job with the art publisher Henri Piazza. Gifted in the visual arts, but also an avid reader and book collector, toward the end of the 1920s Schiffrin decided to go into publishing on his own. First he found quarters in Montparnasse, at the corner of Boulevard Raspail and Rue Huyghens. Next he incorporated a company with a capital of 280,000 francs, financed with the help of three other Parisian Russians: his brother Simon, later to be a film producer (*Quai des brumes—Port of Shadows*—for one); his brother-in-law Joseph Pouterman (born in Kishinev in 1890), who under his own name had already published a few fine illustrated books, some by Julien Green; and Alexander Halpern (born in 1879 in Saint Petersburg), an intimate friend, a naturalized British citizen later reputed to be one of the political advisers of the sometime cabinet minister and M.P. Winston Churchill. The company was incorporated on November 16, 1929, as Les Editions de la Pléiade, taking its name from the Russian word *pleiada*, meaning a group—the group of friends in this case rather than the celestial constellation or the sixteenth-century school of poets that included Ronsard and Du Bellay.

To start with, Jacques Schiffrin published exclusively art books, fine editions, some writings for private circulation, and the great Russian classics which he himself translated with the assistance (for their final editing) of his friends André Gide and Charles Du Bos, a writer and critic who edited foreign authors' works. But very soon Schiffrin decided to expand his business with an idea that had come to him during a train ride: an omnivorous reader, he was always twisting his pockets out of shape with heavy volumes, which were not long enough to last him an entire trip. He was not thinking of pocket books, easy to handle and cheap, but rather of a deluxe set of books in pocket-size format, impeccably produced and edited (this was the bibliophile in him), to be printed on Bible paper so that many hundreds of pages could be fitted into a book that one could easily carry in one's pocket. It was not a world-shaking idea, but while many would later claim to have thought of it first (José Corti, Henri Piazza, Henri Filipacchi, Jean Prévost, etc.), Schiffrin alone carried it to fruition.[96]

He invested a large part of his wife's dowry in the venture and, with no contemporary authors of his own, concentrated on the classics which were in the public domain and required no royalty payments. After the collected *Œuvres poétiques* (Poetic Works) of Baudelaire, which inaugurated the series in November 1931, a dozen similar editions were published. Their success was so great that, as is normal in such cases, it created a financial squeeze on the small company. Schiffrin did not even try to increase his capitalization or go into debt. He was stymied by the old habits of bookstores, which were accustomed to having all their books on consignment and refused immediate cash payments for the volumes of La Pléiade. Schiffrin was willing to forgo his economic independence, but not to give up his imprint. Then Gide came into the picture. He was to be of great help to him, and not only by getting Gallimard to entrust him and his brother-in-law Pouterman with translations of Pushkin and others in his collections of Russian Classics and Young Russians. Gide, who had closely followed Schiffrin's publishing venture—in his *Diary*, he never wearied of remarking on the high quality of those books— urged him to put his imprint under the umbrella of a more solvent publisher. Larousse, Armand Colin, Hachette, and a few others turned down the idea. Nor did Gaston take to it.

"I don't know what you see about it that is so remarkable," he kept saying to Gide and Schlumberger, who for two years fought to win him over.[97]

A contract was finally signed toward the end of 1933. Les Editions de la Pléiade were absorbed by Gallimard, and Schiffrin was named head of the Bibliothèque de la Pléiade (Pleiades Library), with a heavy participation in its profits. At Gallimard the Pléiade was much improved. The volumes were of even finer quality: the Garamond typeface used was elegant yet very readable; the leather bindings were of sheepskin; and to the texts, the best of translations, was added a scholarly apparatus incorporating explanatory notes, indexes, chronology, prefaces, variants, etc., which turned them into lasting reference works. Eventually, the number of volumes would grow to well over three hundred.

But for Gide's friendship with Schiffrin—in 1934 they made their pilgrimage to the Soviet Union together, along with Eugène Dabit and Louis Guilloux—Gallimard would never have acquired La Pléiade. But there was another side to that coin: the authors and associates that Gide forced upon him for the sole reason that they were his protégés cost the firm a pretty penny. An outstanding example of this was Maurice Sachs.

When he first came to Gallimard, Sachs's past did not recommend him. Secretary and friend to Cocteau in 1924, two years later he entered the Séminaire des Carmes, on Rue d'Assas, to study for the priesthood. Jacques Maritain acted as godfather to this converted Jew, Coco Chanel designed a special cassock for him, and soon afterward, to bring an end to this very Parisian conversion, he left the orders he had only recently taken, flanked by Max Jacob and Marcel Jouhandeau. After that, he lived off small jobs that his friends found for him: Cocteau and Jacob let him copyedit their writings, Chanel commissioned him to assemble a collection of first editions for her, and so on. Sachs's largest profits derived from signed copies he managed to extract from publishers and writers he knew, which he promptly turned into objects for speculation.

In October 1933, with the support of Gide, whom he had kept after about it, he was hired by Gallimard. Paulhan had his reservations and so had Gaston; he left it to Raymond to work out the terms of employment. As secretary to the boss, he was shortly named editor of a collection of Catholic works, no less. At various times, for instance, when he had angered Cocteau and Gide because of his repeated thefts of original drawings and manuscripts, he was threatened with dismissal. He translated some of Poe's stories (*Le Sphinx*, 1934) and in July of that year wrote an article for the *NRF*, "Contre les peintres d'aujourd'hui" (Against Today's Painters), which was so outrageous that it created a scandal and made him famous. Gaston then and there decided to ask him if he had a novel for publication.

Sachs turned over *Alias*, which was duly published in 1935 and dedicated to a friend of ten years' standing, Emmanuel Boudot-Lamotte, then a member of the editorial board. But that was no reason for Sachs to settle down. He went on living in high style, speculated, extracted a two-years' advance on his salary from Hirsch, became Gide's private secretary at his home on Rue Vaneau, and continued as a member of the editorial board at Gallimard. When Gide asked him, shortly before the Popular Front victory of 1936, to write a book glorifying the French Communist leader Maurice Thorez, he complied, but then had it published by a competitor, Denoël, with whom he also signed a contract for two more books.[98]

Beside himself, Gaston used that as a pretext to remove him as head of the Catholic collection, also pressured to do so by the archbishop of Paris, who was disgusted by the homosexual habits and dissolute life of Sachs, who was now a "Communist" to boot. One more thing drove Gaston to get rid of him, despite Gide's continued support: Sachs proved even foxier than Gaston. When Gaston heard of a small scandal that was making waves in the auction houses—at the Hôtel Drouot books by Proust and Apollinaire with lengthy autographed inscriptions to Cocteau were on exhibit—he asked the latter for an explanation. Cocteau confessed that in his absence Sachs had carried off a cartload of manuscripts, papers, and rare editions which he promptly disposed of. Gaston then called in Sachs and fired him. That very day the young swindler reappeared at the office brandishing a letter from Cocteau—forged—authorizing his friend Maurice to sell the said documents. Sachs, noticing the suspicion on his publisher's face, lit his cigarette lighter and said:

"See how willing I am to excuse Jean for his fabrications. I'm burning his letter."[99]

Gaston fell for it, but not for long. When he found out that he had been taken in, he permanently removed Sachs from all his functions within the company. With his innate good nature, however, he left Sachs the royalties on the books Sachs had edited, gave him some English translations to do, and let him run the literary and musical soirées of the *NRF*. In that way, Gaston little by little got rid of a pest who bothered him all the more since he created in him a feeling of inferiority. Sachs competed with Gaston not only on the level of financial or professional success, but also in love affairs. This well-known homosexual deployed all his energy and charm in court-ing the women that Gaston had his eye on—notably, a South Amer-ican Sachs met at Gaston's at a party—with the sole intention of detaching them from Gaston and thus scoring points against him.[100]

The very thought that a book or an author of distinction might appear under another imprint depressed Gaston. He kept track of the names that came to his attention and was not satisfied until he had recaptured those he considered to have strayed (such as André Suarès). Any means would do. He was just as determined to hold on to those who were listening to the blandishments of rival pub-lishers. It was a struggle in which no quarter was given. The courtesy and fair play that usually prevailed in relations between publishers before 1914 had given way to trench warfare between Grasset and Gallimard. It used to be that publishers had the courtesy to advise their colleagues when they were about to get hold of one another's authors; now a publisher learned of his loss when he saw a new work by one of "his" authors among forthcoming titles under another imprint, in the official booksellers' journal, *La Bibliographie de la France*. To old-established figures in the book trade, Grasset and Gallimard often seemed like buccaneers.

Gaston's relations in those years with authors as different as Mal-raux, Albert Cohen, Simenon, Morand, Bloch, Paul Léautaud, or Louis Aragon were illustrative of his flexibility, his ability to adapt to their moods, their shortcomings, and especially their individual demands.

From 1928 on, Gaston "worked" Malraux in an effort to draw him into his orbit. Malraux was being published by Grasset, with whom he had signed a contract in 1924 for three books, based only on the recommendation of François Mauriac. Grasset had never read a line Malraux wrote nor even met him, but relied completely on Mauriac's judgment. He had nothing to regret: Malraux's first essay, *La Tentation de l'Occident (The Temptation of the West)*, was well received, and it was followed by two novels that continued his Oriental meditation about man's fate, *Les Conquérants (The Conquerors)* and *La Voie royale (The Royal Way)*. A contributor to the *NRF* magazine, to which—once again—Gide had introduced him, Malraux became an habitué at Rue de Grenelle, and Gaston took a liking to this ardent young fellow (he published a short fictional fantasy of his, *Royaume-Farfelu* (Cockeyed Kingdom), in 1928. In 1929 Malraux was all set to organize, with the help of his friends at the *NRF*, an expedition to snatch Leon Trotsky from his imprisonment at Alma Ata in Kazakhstan. Gaston pointed out to him, firmly, that that was not their kind of business. Understanding that Malraux was intoxicated with the view of himself as the hero of one of his own novels, Gaston made him realize that there were limits to romanticism and publicity.[101]

When the publisher thought the young man was ready—and free, after the three books contracted for—to leave Grasset, he offered him the position of art director. It was a shrewd move to put him on the payroll, with a salary over and above his advances against royalties, in this way creating a permanent bond to the company. Yet it should be pointed out that the art director, Roger Allard, was indeed leaving and had to be replaced, and that Malraux had shown an interest in publishing: earlier he had started two small publishing companies, A la sphère and Aldes, which quickly folded, a sympathetic Grasset absorbing one of them. That experience had given the young Malraux a lasting taste for printed matter, fine paper, and quality illustrations.

Gaston was to do even better for his new protégé in whom he had such faith. In addition to this most convenient job—no set hours, no specific conditions to be met—which in the final analysis meant he was in charge of one of the collections of deluxe editions, Malraux became a member of the editorial board. He brought along a school chum, Louis Chevasson, who had been with him on his adventures and witnessed all of the Malraux saga. Being too stimulated by ideas and too much of a firebrand to be satisfied with limited edition books and reading new manuscripts, Malraux got Gaston to approve a number of new projects. Some of them were ambitious, such as his *Tableau de la littérature française* (Table of French Literature), a collaborative work in several volumes (that it would take eleven years to finish), which all the best minds of the *Nouvelle Revue Française* contributed to. Other projects dreamed up by his restless mind proved less successful, so Gaston stopped financing them and asked Malraux to concentrate somewhat more on his own writing. Which led to *La Condition humaine (Man's Fate)*, the great work Gaston had been waiting for. He had hoped for a powerful book, one that would establish the writer's fame with the general public, and—why not?—perhaps even impress the Goncourt jury favorably. *Man's Fate* filled the bill perfectly. It had everything: exoticism (China), dramatic intensity (the Revolution on the march against Chiang Kai-shek), philosophical considerations (man cannot go beyond his fate or escape his condition), political commitment (Communist activism), great ideals (liberty, loyalty, and so on), rivalry in heroism, and especially the touch, the breath of Malraux, that had been suggested in *The Conquerors* and *The Royal Way* and were here displayed in their full maturity.

It did not take long for the Goncourt Academy to decide. Malraux, at twenty-seven, became the youngest writer ever to win their prize. Gaston could well be satisfied: his vision had been correct. For neither the first time nor the last.

In 1922 Gaston had read in the *NRF* a piece by an unknown named Albert Cohen, "Après minuit à Genève" (Geneva After Midnight). From Rivière he learned that the author, aged twenty-seven, was a Swiss, originally from the Greek island of Corfu, practicing law before the Geneva bar. Cohen had sent in his article "over the transom" (in the trade expression), and it had been read and published. Gaston was intrigued. Some months later he sent Rivière to Geneva on a short visit. Happily surprised that the prestigious magazine had run his piece, Cohen was even more delighted to be called on unexpectedly by its editor. After the usual introductory remarks, Rivière came right to the point:

"I have been sent here by Gaston Gallimard to offer you a contract for your next five books."

"But I don't have any next five books!" answered Cohen, amazed at the proposition. "In fact, I don't even have one next book."

"No matter. You will have," Rivière told him, sure that this young man had a career before him. "All we want is one thing: write any title you want and sign the contract."[102]

Any title you want was easy to say. Cohen thought for a moment, then wrote, "Rapides internationaux" (International Express Trains). After which he signed the paper that committed him to the publisher. He had nothing to lose; he was short of cash, and had little interest in practicing law. After one additional interview, Rivière left. He had not been there long, but he had taken it all in: the writer's money problems and his dissatisfaction with his profession. As soon as Rivière got back to Paris, he wrote Albert Thomas, director of the International Labor Organization of the League of Nations, to recommend to him most enthusiastically this unusual man being wasted in trivial Geneva lawsuits. A week later the new entry in the Gallimard stable, without knowing how or why, was offered a job in the diplomatic division of the ILO, where he was to remain for several years.

Gaston went even further in putting himself out for a writer who so far had not delivered a single book to him. He agreed to have him start a magazine, which his company would publish and handle in all noneditorial respects. Closely connected with Zionist circles, and active from his youth in various movements, Cohen knew Chaim Weizmann, the president of the World Zionist Organization and future president of the state of Israel. After several long discussions, Cohen and Weizmann agreed that, given their limited means of publicity, it might further the dissemination of their ideas in Europe if they had as a forum a magazine of high standing with articles by well-known personalities. The WZO provided a significant sum of money to start it, and Cohen signed a contract with the Librairie Gallimard.

The first issue of *La Revue juive* (The Jewish Review) appeared on January 15, 1925. The editor was Albert Cohen, the publisher Gaston Gallimard, and the general manager Louis-Daniel Hirsch. On the masthead appeared the names of editorial board members or contributors such as Albert Einstein, Sigmund Freud, Chaim Weizmann, the famous Danish essayist and philosopher Georg Brandes, Professor Charles Gide (André's uncle), Léon Zadoc Kahn, and soon thereafter, Martin Buber. No less.

Young Cohen had really done marvels of groundwork. "He has such willpower that I am no longer surprised that the Red Sea in olden times parted for the Hebrews," wrote René Crevel, who interviewed him in *Les Nouvelles littéraires*.[103] The Review, announced as appearing six times a year, sought to be the organ of Jewish rebirth, worked to advance the idea of Israel as a nation, and promoted Jewish activity on intellectual levels.

Given to lyricism and firmly convinced of the eventual triumph of Zionism in Palestine, Cohen wrote an introductory editorial giving the magazine's position: "A faith has visited us, a discovery has seared us, but we will have the strength to affirm without the weakness of excluding." He found striking formulations—"We will think our race into being," "A race is an idea made flesh"—before more concretely delineating the nature of its sympathies and informational aims and announcing "the good news: Israel is returning to Israel." In the second year of its existence, *La Revue juive* was honored with the signatures of Léon Blum, Joseph Kessel, and Henry de Jouvenel, the distinguished French diplomat who was married to Colette, but with its five thousand-odd subscribers it went from Gallimard to the Editions Rieder, "as a result of a series of intrigues," as Cohen was to put it in his 1979 interview.

While continuing with his activism—he was made the Zionist delegate to the League of Nations—Cohen was working on his novel. In 1930 at last—eight years after his contract was signed—he delivered *Solal* (rather than "International Express Trains") to Gaston. The thick manuscript was immediately greeted with enthusiasm by its first readers—and by many more later on—for its sense of humor, its tragic dimension, and marvelous storyteller's art. It was a Jewish saga comparable to no other, patiently chiseled by an authentic cosmopolitan—Greek, Jewish, and Swiss—whose only homeland, apart from a Jewish Palestine, was French language and literature.

Fêted, applauded, and acclaimed, Albert Cohen fell in love with Paris, resigned from the ILO, and decided to stay in the French capital. He wrote a one-act play *Ezéchiel* (Ezekiel), which was staged at the Comédie-Française after the young lawyer read it and pleaded its case before that prestigious theater's play committee. Gaston, very satisfied with the promising success of *Solal*, allotted him "a very respectable monthly stipend"[104]—to keep a hold on him. With Cohen, Gaston was also learning patience. The man himself had warned him: a novel has to be thought out, refined, and worked over in joy and suffering, in the image of the destiny of the Jewish people, the flesh of his work. So Gaston waited, much as he would have liked to urge a quick follow-up to satisfy the readers of *Solal*. In 1937, noting that his publisher was showing mounting signs of concern, Cohen buckled down and out of a "sense of duty" wrote a second book in nine months, the title of which was to raise more than one eyebrow at Gallimard: *Mangeclous, surnommé aussi longues dents et oeil de Satan et Lord High Life et sultan des tousseurs et crâne en selle et pieds noirs et haut de forme et bey des menteurs et parole d'honneur et presque avocat et compliqueur de procès et médecin de lavements et âme de l'intérêt et plein d'astuce et dévoreur des patrimoines et barbe en fourche et père de la crasse et capitaine des vents* (Naileater, Also Nicknamed Long Teeth and Eye of Satan and Lord High Life and Sultan of Coughers and Brave in the Saddle and Black Feet and High Hat and Bey of Liars and Word of Honor and Almost Lawyer and Complicator of Trials and Enema Doctor and Soul of Interest and Full of Tricks and Squanderer of Inheritances and Forked Beard and Father of Filth and Captain of the Winds).

Gaston was happy. He had got himself a writer, and a real one. Cohen's manuscripts were few and expensive. Two books in sixteen years—but what books!

———

Watching Gaston perform in his dealings with writers, one might have got the impression of a changeable character. That would have been grievously misreading him. He remained "Gaston" throughout, but adapted himself to people and situations. He was able to hide his strongest reservations, hide the contempt he felt for a person, and indulge in double-talk when he had decided that a given author had to be in his catalogue. More chameleonlike, more of a fox than Grasset, he often succeeded where his rival failed, for he did not lie shamelessly as Grasset did, he lied in the Machiavellian mode, with ingenuity and charm. He got a sort of sensual pleasure out of sweet-talking one group and then another into agreeing with him, where Grasset treated everyone with unconstrained rudeness.

Theoretically, all Gallimard contracts were to be for ten books, exclusive, preventing the author from spreading his wares around other companies—in order to build up a backlist from which Gaston could hope to see results at least after the appearance of the third book. But that rule was subject to as many exceptions as necessary. Raymond Guérin, an author whose books became increasingly voluminous, insisted that his contract stipulate how many lines he was committed to Gallimard for, rather than how many volumes. Paul Claudel was given a lifetime contract after he wrote Gaston, "I don't want to have to worry about it anymore." André Maurois, usually published by Grasset, signed individual contracts for the books he agreed to do for Gallimard. Gaston found that most satisfactory: the author's novelized life of Disraeli was such a hit that it led Gallimard to start a series entitled Vie des hommes illustres (Lives of Great Men) that turned out to be a most profitable venture.

He latched on to good ideas wherever he found them, even if they originated with his rivals. And when he wanted an author, he was ready to pay the price, however much his brother Raymond or certain members of the editorial board tried to hold him back. In 1933 he decided he wanted Simenon; he got him.

Simenon was then a writer with a well-established reputation, although it was nothing compared to what it was to become later. To Gaston he was above all a writer with a quick pen and a prolific journalist, a man who under various noms de plume had already authored hundreds of articles, serials, and popular novels published by Fayard. Simenon sold well. He was a dependable product, insufficiently exploited, as Gaston saw it, the more so since the author's strong personality lent itself to more ambitious undertakings. Simenon was also the one who two years earlier, in 1931, had had the most original idea to date for launching a book.

On February 20, at midnight, he had invited—or rather "summoned," by invitations made out like police tickets—Tout-Paris and especially Tout-Montparnasse to the Boule Blanche cabaret on Rue Vavin. "Evening dress *not* de rigueur," it was specified. And there he gave a great "Fingerprint Ball": at the entrance all the guests were fingerprinted; the waiters served drinks in convicts' uniforms, the whole place resembled a penitentiary. Simenon, as fast as he could, inscribed copies of his books, a new collection of detective novels, the hero of which was Inspector Maigret, a detective sans-pareil who was rarely without his trench coat, pipe, and felt hat, whether among cutthroats or decent folk. Fayard had agreed to Simenon's plan, provided he delivered a book a month to him, with a backup supply of six for a start. But in spite of its success, the publisher did not think the idea was long for this world. That was when Gaston stepped in.

Simenon had of course heard of Gallimard. And where the new publisher considered the writer a profit-making writing machine, the writer, for his part, was somewhat leery of the publisher's "lordship going to cocktail parties" side.

Gaston phoned him and a short time later they met in his office:

"Please be seated, my dear friend," Gaston said. "Let's discuss your contract. I really want you under my banner, want you to be one of our authors. Gide is one, as you know, and he has the highest regard for you; he would very much like to meet you."

"We can see about that later," Simenon cut him off.

"Are you under long-term contract to Fayard?"

"No, I have no contract. I give him what he wants, but I am

not bound by contract. I don't believe in those interminable contracts."

"Very well," Gaston said, visibly satisfied. "Could you start in as soon as you have finished your current work?"

"Yes, but it would depend on your conditions."

"Ah! very well, then. Let's talk that over next week in a good restaurant."

But Simenon was not having any of that. There would be no cozy restaurant meetings, now or later, he told Gaston, and none of this "my dear friend" business. They would meet at Gaston's convenience in his office, with a secretary present and taking notes, and they could settle the terms of their agreement in half an hour.

After that, whenever Gaston wanted to renew the contract, he would have to come to Simenon, wherever the author might be. Because publishers came to see him, he said, and not vice versa.[105]

Gaston was dumbstruck. No author had ever spoken to him like that. But he had the man he wanted and was not going to let him go for so little. The following week Simenon came back and signed "an amazing contract": six books a year, author and publisher sharing the net profits fifty-fifty. Unheard of. Simenon imposed these Draconian demands, explaining to his publisher that he had made a deep study of book production costs, estimating in detail the expenses of paper, printing, transportation, binding, and distribution. Fully aware of the publisher's share in this outlay, he felt justified in asking for half the proceeds.[106] And anyway, it was take it or leave it. Considering the rate at which he turned out books and the level of their previous sales, he did not want to be treated in the same way as any old writer of poems. The contract was for one year, renewable every twelve months. So every year Gaston had to go after Simenon in his wanderings throughout France, to get his signature to each new contract.

That was to last thirteen years: *The Lodger, The Shadow Falls, The Man Who Watched the Trains Go By, Burgomaster of Furnes, The Widow, Magnet of Doom*—in all, more than forty works published by Gallimard. "With him, as with old Fayard, I had the friendliest of relations. However, at Gallimard I did not feel at ease in the company of some of the authors he published."[107]

For all Gaston's efforts, Simenon would never become a fully integrated member of the Gallimard house. It did not suit his temperament, and there was nothing to be done about it. His output made him the very opposite of a passing author: a house author. But the house was not in his style.

During the 1920s, publishing and literary habits underwent changes. The young were most in demand. The great elders, Gide and Valéry, were unusual in that fame had come to them late in life; their debut as writers had gone unnoticed. This was in sharp contrast to a new generation of writers—Aragon, Drieu, Malraux, Morand, Montherlant among them—who were known and accepted before they were thirty, when their careers were still in infancy, as it were. Their "main claim to fame was that they were young, they were promising, and they represented a future much more than a present."[108] Suddenly they had a public literary prominence quite out of proportion with what they had so far produced.

By the end of the twenties it was not unusual for a young writer to do minor books on commission—portraits of a city, travel notes, essays, etc.—for a diversity of publishers, while reserving his novels and major works exclusively for one. The proliferation of collections, or special imprints created for the very purpose of attracting writers already under contract elsewhere, was a hallmark of the times. While making good use of this custom himself, Gaston was disgusted when "his" authors indulged in it. When Jean-Richard Bloch asked him to allow a publisher named Arcos to publish a volume of his short stories, Gaston was inflexible.

> I cannot tell you that it makes me happy for a work of yours to appear outside the *NRF*. I like Arcos, but they regularly call upon the *NRF* authors who mean the most to me. I am perfectly ready to publish them. You tell me that it will be a run of only 750 copies; but it so happens that the problem in the book trade, except for things like

Goncourt Prize winners . . . is the sale of unlimited editions. By announcing 750 copies of almost anything, one can always be sure of breaking even; these first printings always detract from the regular editions. I might add that, in view of the new arrangements I have made for the publishing of original editions, such limited ones will undermine the economics of my operation. Finally, I have sustained great costs in order to bring together in my catalogue a certain number of writers, and you will readily understand why I guard them jealously. That being said, now that you know my feelings, let me tell you that for my part I . . . am as ever ready to print anything you submit to me. For *Carnaval est mort* [Carnival Is Dead] I await your new version of the foreword: you will be given two sets of proofs.

Gaston Gallimard
Publisher, Les Editions de la *NRF*[109]

From the dryness of the greetings and conclusion, it is easy to see that Gaston was irritated. In spite of that, Bloch stuck to his guns and during the following weeks repeated his request. But Gaston did not yield, reminding him that he had already refused such favors to friends like Jules Romains, and asserted that Tronche, his commercial manager, shared his opinion that such practices should be stopped. Gaston complained of the thanklessness of his job. To convince Bloch, he offered to show him his huge correspondence with firms like Arcos which wanted to steal away his authors "just for one book."[110]

Thanklessness—the word would often come to his mouth or pen when Gaston discussed his relations with some writers. At various times in his career he was ready to give up, chuck it all, and take off. He would say he was nothing but a grocer, or that he would have been better off as a pharmacist or plumber, publishing in his spare time the authors he admired.[111] When he felt really low, he told himself that he should have devoted his life to painting a picture or writing a book, so as to leave behind something worthwhile. When this happened, his friends knew he was on the verge of depression.

Fortunately, such moments were not frequent. Gaston had a

fundamentally optimistic disposition. He adopted a simple but effective principle: "In any profession, two people can come to terms. Why not in publishing?"[112] If all authors had been like Proust, how much more pleasant Gaston's life would have been! To be sure, Proust had his own special needs. You had to go and see him at night, since he slept during the day. He kept making tiny changes and altering sentences at the last minute, so that making out his corrected galleys drove André Breton crazy (the future founder of Surrealism had accepted the job because he was short of cash at the time). But in Gaston's view the great writer had one additional virtue that set him apart from all the others:

"Not once did Marcel Proust ask me to advance any money to him. Not once. Or to do advertising."[113]

That was something any publisher could appreciate. But it was not the only reason Gaston included Proust among his favorites, among those who had made the deepest impression on him. When in 1939 the weekly *Marianne* asked three publishers to relate their impressions of one writer, Eugène Fasquelle chose Zola, Robert Denoël Céline, and Gaston Gallimard Proust. That was not fortuitous. How could one help remembering a writer who, right after getting the Goncourt, wrote you a letter such as this?

> I take no self-satisfaction in it, knowing that it is often fashionable to select the worst books. I take no self-satisfaction in it, but I had hoped it would mean a little more money for me. . . . Dear Gaston, this perpetual matter of cash keeps plaguing me like mud that I would like to wash away by a fraternal handshake with you. And I am sure that if you were to give me some good practical advice, you would do me more good than by paying me more. A person becomes wealthier as much by diminishing his expenditures as by increasing his income. It is perhaps not very businesslike to tell you that, but it is the effusion of a friend who is very truly yours.[114]

Happy period! With Morand and Aragon, Gaston was to learn what difficult authors could be like—problem people, more devious and rapacious than their writings or their personalities would ever lead one to suspect. This was a far cry from forcing Fargue to get down to work, or coping with Claudel's anger when typesetters put "mystic" in place of his "rustic," or "humility" for "humidity."[115]

Up to 1923, Paul Morand was a charming author, greatly talented, with sterling qualities, and a pleasant friend to have. It was later that things soured. He had then published three books which had made him famous: *Tendres Stocks (Fancy Goods)*, *Ouvert la nuit (Open All Night)*, and *Fermé la nuit (Closed All Night)*. In order not to compromise his freedom of choice or his future, the author had had Article XI deleted from his first contract, the clause dealing with first rejection of future books,[116] as if he knew what lay ahead. In the campaign for *Open All Night* in 1922, Gaston had invested heavily: ads appeared with regularity in *Le Figaro*, *Le Gaulois*, *L'Action française*, *L'Œuvre*, *Les Débats*, and *Le Temps*, the most prestigious dailies of the moment. It was hard to remain unaware of Morand's new book if one read the newspapers. All the more since Gaston also succeeded in having innumerable feature articles and reviews devoted to it. By all logic, this huge campaign should have won the book the Goncourt at the end of the year. But Morand was beaten out by Henri Béraud, and for once the blame was put on his publisher, Gallimard. Gallimard was accused of poor strategy, reducing Morand's chances and finally costing him the award—by making it widely known that the book had sold 30,000 copies, and that Morand was already an established writer whom the Goncourt Academy simply had to crown. The reaction was the opposite: the Ten resented all the publicity, and were not sorry they made the choice they did when somewhat later Gaston admitted that the printing had actually not gone beyond 7,000 copies.[117]

Was it really Gaston's fault? At any rate, Morand made no secret of his resentment. But his entourage wondered which upset him more, the loss of prestige or of the sales that the Goncourt guaranteed. Gaston began to understand that Morand's nonchalance, indifference, and professed high-mindedness were suddenly dropped when it became a question of money. This was confirmed to Gaston on several occasions. In some countries with very poor exchange rates such as

Romania, booksellers were willing to stock many *NRF* books in return for large discounts. Gaston agreed to sacrifice his own profit from such sales, not even trying to recoup his overhead expenses, and asked some of his authors to forgo their royalties on these sales. He explained the advantage of such an arrangement, since if they refused, not one of their books would get into those countries. Gide, Jules Romains, and Schlumberger agreed. But not Morand, who for all his success was still a newcomer and might have been expected to show a bit more humility and less greed. During the same period, Gaston offered to act as intermediary for Morand in the sale of the original manuscript of *Fancy Goods* and a draft of "La Nuit catalane" (Night in Catalonia), one of the short stories in *Open All Night*. This was customary at the time, and more than once the publisher found an "angel" as a favor to his authors. But Jacques Doucet, the couturier-collector, was not willing to pay 4,000 francs. He offered only 2,000, so nothing came of it.

Only thirty-five, Morand had a well-paying job at the Foreign Office and came from a well-to-do family. Yet he showed an almost unbelievable venality, which could not be explained entirely by the high life he was leading, the crowd he associated with, and his taste for travel and for sports cars. Grasset caught on to this more quickly than Gaston. He wanted Morand. More than any other, this "quick," spectacular writer, gifted with such a disconcerting facility of style, lent himself—by his personality, his subjects, and the lightness of his books—to just the kind of advertising sendoffs that Grasset was making his specialty. A glance at the contract Morand had on *Closed All Night* was enough to reassure Grasset: it would not be hard to raise the ante. At Gallimard, Morand got 1 franc 10 per copy sold up to 6,000, 1 franc 15 for the next 6,000, and 1 franc 20 from 12,000 to 20,000. He got a 2,000-franc advance on signing, and 3,000 francs on publication.

Grasset offered him a 50,000-franc advance against royalties plus a monthly stipend of 3,000 francs, promised him advertising campaigns worthy of him, and—to prove to him that these amounts committed to a single author were enormous—had Morand's life insured until the final delivery of his next novel, *Lewis et Irene (Lewis and Irene)*.[118] Grasset would say, "I made him an offer he couldn't refuse."

On October 8, 1923, Morand informed Gaston in a brief note that the book project so often discussed between them—*Lewis and Irene*, with its setting in Greece and Sicily—had been switched to Grasset. However, he reassured him: this was only a one-book "detour," his next book would be for the *NRF*. Despite the discourtesy of the notice given him and the harm done—Gallimard had already announced *Lewis and Irene* in his catalogue—Gaston went to see Morand at his Quai d'Orsay office and got his formal assurance of a "Rhenish novel" and a collection of short stories with the title *L'Europe galante* (Lusty Europe). Once their conversation was confirmed in letters, Gallimard announced these forthcoming publications in the *NRF* and in circulars addressed to those readers who habitually subscribed to Morand books. This time there could be no hitch. The publisher had made himself clear: "You owe me a novel or a book of short stories, to be called *L'Europe galante*, and if you fail to deliver, I will have to obtain it by enforcing my legal rights."[119] But only a few days later, Gaston again had occasion to be furious. Instead of the collection of short stories promised, the author sent him a collection of poems entitled *Glaces chaudes* (Hot Ices). Gaston immediately sent a registered letter to his home on Rue de Penthièvre, expressing his anger, reiterating the terms of their contract and oral agreement, and warning that he was ready "to make you feel the seriousness of the damage you have caused my company."[120]

What Morand had called a "detour to Grasset" was pure and simple betrayal. But Gaston held his ire in check, swallowed his pride, and agreed to publish *Glaces chaudes*, provided Morand gave him, before the end of 1924, his novel *Lewis and Irene* and his short stories in *L'Europe galante*. Gaston was determined to insist on his rights, all the more since the competitor was Grasset. This roused him more than if it had been any other publisher. Morand, on the other hand, was evasive, alleging that his many trips abroad on government business and his work at the ministry were causing the delay. Gaston was now demanding three manuscripts from him, and nothing was forthcoming.

In London, where he was staying at the Piccadilly Hotel, the writer tore up several drafts of a letter to Gaston. For financial reasons he had committed himself to Grasset, but on purely legal grounds he could not get out of his Gallimard commitment. Perhaps the ideal thing might be for him to alternate, giving one publisher his lighter books and the other the more demanding ones. That distinction would be in line with their respective public images. But it so happened that the two publishers were not at all inclined to share. So Morand tried to discourage Gallimard by making outrageous demands: each book had to be priced at an average of 7 francs 50, with 1 franc to go to the author on each copy sold, and a guaranteed advance on royalties amounting to what he would earn if 100,000 copies were sold.[121]

It took more than that to deter a man of Gaston's stripe. In his answer he in no way showed his irritation, but allowed himself a little sarcasm at the end: "At any rate, please believe me that I remain as always yours faithfully (unless that should seem too cumbersome to you)."[122]

Finally, Grasset won out. He published *Lewis and Irene* in 1924, *L'Europe galante* the following year, and some fifteen more Morand titles after that. He had got his revenge for Proust. Psychologically, he was the winner. Commercially too, of course, since some of the Morand titles were best-sellers.

Gaston refused to admit defeat. For four years he continued to correspond with Morand, assuring him of his empathy, his desire to be his publisher again, and his lack of bitterness and rancor. He was even touching:

> I do not think you would have any reason to complain about us. I have learned my lesson. I will know how to "create an event" and at the opportune moment start my campaign of "waves of gossip." If you feel this letter warrants our meeting, I am at your disposal.[123]

Not good enough. Gaston would have to wait almost ten years to get Morand back in his catalogue. And he would have to pay the price. Henceforth, the advances against royalties would be 100,000 francs. Moreover, beginning in 1933 Morand would have his own collection, La Renaissance de la nouvelle (The Rebirth of the Short Story), on which he would have a 2 percent override on each volume sold. Apart from his own books, under this imprint he would publish Drieu La Rochelle's *Journal d'un homme trompé* (Diary of a Deceived Man), Jean Cassou's *De l'Etoile au Jardin des plantes* (From the Etoile to the Botanical Garden), Eugène Dabit's *Train de vies* (Life Styles), and Simenon's *Les Sept Minutes* (Seven Minutes). His contract required him to bring out at least four titles a year for Gallimard, and for once he tried to abide by it. So there was no lawsuit, though Gallimard repeatedly threatened one in 1923 and 1924.

With Jean Giono he almost went to court. The author had signed contracts with both Gallimard and Grasset, giving each of them exclusive rights to all his works. Shrewdness? Duplicity? His friends back home in the South, at Manosque, had an excuse: that's the way he is, he can't say no. "Whatever anyone asked, he would say yes, and then wait to see what would happen."[124] Fortunately, Jean Giono produced enough books to keep both publishers happy.

As for Aragon, he came in for anger, contempt, and a lawsuit. Aragon had been with the *NRF* since the fall of 1919. A young soldier on furlough, he gave Gide the first four chapters of his *Anicet ou le panorama* (Anicet, or the Panorama). Without even waiting for the author to finish it, Gide, enthusiastic over what he read, asked Gaston to put Aragon under contract. Neither a novel nor a nonfiction narrative, *Anicet* was a *texte à clé* which in its time was considered avant-garde, although there appeared in it such characters as Nick Carter and some real-life French anarchist terrorists. Rivière was taken with the manuscript, although he did not hide his reservations, as he wrote Gaston:

I find Aragon's novel full of qualities of the highest order, at times very funny, and in the end a bit boring because of its endless dream atmosphere. And that is not psychology, either. But I am more and more confident about the future of our two Dadaists whom, I admit, you were a thousand times right in bringing into our fold. So if you think that Aragon, if he is turned down, will get away, you certainly have to accept his novel.[125]

He did not get away. After *Anicet*, Aragon wrote *Le Libertinage* (Libertinism) for Gallimard in 1924, a collection including plays as well as tales, nonfiction narratives, and prose poems. Just as baffling as in his previous book, Aragon caused some concern with his preface, which seemed unconnected to the rest of the book; it lent a Surrealist dimension to an incongruous collection which seemed to be a double paean to anarchism and love. Two years later *Le Paysan de Paris* (*Nightwalkers*) appeared and was erroneously listed in the Gallimard catalogue under "Memoirs, Recollections, and Correspondence," since every book had to carry a label; in fact, it belonged to no known literary genre and fell into an informal classification that at the time only the Surrealists could recognize. With no connection whatever to peasants of Paris, the peasant of *Nightwalkers* was first and foremost a man who saw his city in a new light and, through the city, the whole of life. In the manner of Fargue's *Le Piéton de Paris*, which came later, it dealt with a walk through the French capital, but in Aragon's case inventorying the sites and smells of Paris was merely a pretext for expressing his ideas on all things and his conception of poetry.

At Gallimard, from 1924 on Aragon was paid a monthly stipend that was to vary from one to two thousand francs. The sum, a very respectable one for the times, proved clearly that they did not want to let him get away. Aragon was aware of this, and took advantage of it to try to get them to accept certain books and writers over the opposition within the house. "It was only because of my personal relationship with Gaston Gallimard that certain writers were welcomed into the firm who had been lambasted by the *NRF* magazine, Apollinaire, for instance," he said.[126]

The relationship began to deteriorate when Aragon's friend Drieu

La Rochelle published in the *NRF* an open letter to the Surrealists, to which Aragon replied sharply a month later. Behind their literary dispute was an affair with a woman that pushed them increasingly apart. When Aragon learned that Drieu had asked Gaston to publish a pamphlet in which he would demolish Aragon publicly, the atmosphere became truly stormy. A few years later, it was to become absolutely intolerable, when the two men became increasingly committed, Drieu to fascism, Aragon to Communism.

Gaston acted the buffer as well as he could. His job was to make it possible for writers who often did not like one another, had nothing in common but their trade, and sometimes were on the verge of blows, to live together under the same banner. At that same period, Paulhan, having been insulted by André Breton (the Surrealists were quick to take and give offense), sent him his seconds (Crémieux and Arland). A duel! At last there would be some fun! But Breton declined the chance to get wounded—if not killed—and the affair ended with an open letter from Paulhan to his seconds, which of course the *NRF* magazine published: "Dear friends, thank you. I did not put you to this bother for nothing: now we know the cowardice behind this character's violence and filth."

Paulhan and Breton were eventually to make up.[127] An insult can be forgotten—but not an insulting book. That was what would cause a break between Aragon and Gallimard. In 1928 Aragon met Elsa Triolet, whose influence would be great on his behavior and attitudes. He was no longer altogether a Surrealist, and not yet wholly a Communist. But he was on his way. During this transition period he gave Gaston a text that could only shake up the firm, for in it Aragon squared accounts with all of established literature. At first, reading the manuscript of *Traité du style (Treatise on Style)*, Gaston was not especially put out. Discussing with Paul Léautaud the publication of the latter's *Journal littéraire* (Literary Diary), which was full of indiscretions and stabs in the back targeting associates of the company, Gaston reassured him:

"It doesn't matter to me. Why, I'm about to publish a volume by Aragon. The things he says in it about Gide! He calls him a 'stable boy.' Well, I couldn't care less. I don't involve myself with what one writer says about another in his book."[128]

Gallimard wanted all the less to be involved, since it was Gide who was dragged through the mud. Did he perhaps underestimate the effect Aragon's book would have? Had he, in fact, read it all the way through? At any rate, its publication date was delayed by pressures from Gide and Valéry, among others, who did not hide their wrath. The house mandarins laid permanent siege to Gaston. Was their self-assurance so shaky that they could not put up with criticisms from within their own ranks? Granted, Aragon eschewed any kind of subtlety, aiming as he was to outdo the Surrealists in their shock effects. He spared nothing and nobody. His *Treatise on Style* was so much target practice. It was a prose poem suffused with uncommon violence, in which he took aim at both persons and institutions.

Gide? "Neither a stable boy nor a clown: but a f . . . ing bore. Besides, he thinks he is Goethe. Which means he would like to be funny."

Benda? Morand? "Clowns."

The *NRF*? Arland? "The *mal du siècle*, a creaking concept not unskillfully plastered over and resuscitated under his pen, to strut around in the *Nvelle Rvue Frinçaise* [sic]. Some characters prefer the circus to a cabaret, but I prefer crappers to magazines. And to the *Nouelle Reüe françoise* [sic] in particular. There, they explicate every six months what happened everywhere. While in crappers what is expelled is rarely more than two days old."

Valéry? "It has never in any way escaped me that the abstract vocabulary of this author mostly hides a successful premeditated swindle, a swindle not without its charm."

With one stroke of his pen Aragon in similar manner executed the Church, religion, and conversion, all so dear to Claudel, interpreting their external manifestations from a sexual, sadomasochistic viewpoint. His coup de grâce he reserved for the army, which he methodically criticized, then called for revolt against its leaders and the French uniform, recommended mayhem, and ended by equating officers and noncoms with feces. "Well since looking cross-eyed at them on the street means sleeping in the clink, it is my great honor, at home, in this book, in this place, to say very consciously that I beshit the French army in its totality."

Any institution, even a young and open-minded one like the *NRF*, would have been shaken by less, although Gaston personally had reason to be delighted at seeing Gide, the army, Claudel, and the Church lampooned in such healthy fashion. Were the insults in the *Treatise on Style* the only basis for the falling-out between Aragon and the Librairie Gallimard, which ended up in court? We do not know. Their estrangement was to last ten years, to the great benefit of Robert Denoël, a beginner on the publishing scene, whose meteoric rise was breathtaking.

Denoël started his publishing house in April 1930 with a capital of 300,000 francs. To get this sum together and leave his cramped quarters on Avenue de La Bourdonnais and move to Rue Amélie, he went into partnership with the American Jew Bernard Steele, a capitalist but not necessarily good at business administration, a man much more interested in music than in literature. Despite the small part played by his "partner" in the company, the books were published by "Denoël & Steele." But Denoël was its complete embodiment. He spent all his time on the lookout: for money, manuscripts, writers. Tall, elegant, with a certain seductive charm, Denoël was a born optimist. Everyone was aware of his acute intelligence, his undeniable openness of mind, his lack of prejudices, his complete devotion to books and literature, but also of his appalling naïveté when it came to business matters. Belgian by birth and nationality, he had an inferiority complex about Paris, convinced that in the literary circles of the City of Light he was seen only as a brilliant provincial. Rather than associate with his fellow publishers (with the exception of Sven Nielsen, like himself a foreigner), he preferred the company of newspaper people, who returned the compliment: in proportion to the size of his company and its output, Denoël in the 1930s was the champion of the literary prize sweepstakes.

In 1930 a staff of less than ten ran this publishing house that no one in the business expected to survive: Denoël, who was the only reader, a secretary, a bookkeeper, a production head who after World War II would become a famous writer (René Barjavel), a designer, a packer, a production secretary, one salesman for Paris, and one for the provinces. That was all.[129] But it was enough to pick up Aragon, who had broken with Gallimard; to publish Blaise Cendrars, Eugène Dabit, Céline, and a psychoanalytical review that was considered authoritative; and to cop all the Renaudot Prizes from 1931 to 1939 (except for two "relinquished" to Gallimard in 1934 and 1935). The Interallié Prize of 1936 also went to one of Denoël's authors, and so did the Femina for 1936 and 1939.

Understandably, Gaston was not fond of Denoël. Younger, more dynamic, and especially heading a more flexible organization than his prestigious competitor, in 1932 Denoël gave Gaston another reason to hate him lastingly. One evening, coming home from the theater, he found on a table in his apartment an enormous package wrapped in newspaper. A second sheet with a publisher's label wrapped the ugly package, which contained three thick bundles of manuscript, nine hundred pages in all. The work had a title—*Voyage au bout de la nuit (Journey to the End of the Night)*—but no name or address anywhere. In spite of the late hour, he started to read the pile of papers. It was love at first sight: the publisher was "speechless before the book's freedom of tone, its lyricism, so powerful and new." At dawn he was still reading, "exhausted but wildly enthusiastic." Unable to sleep, he read on to the end and in the afternoon set out to look for the author.[130]

The same week, another copy of the manuscript was also sent to the Gallimard firm. The author, Dr. Louis-Ferdinand Destouches, calling himself Céline, was not a total stranger there. In 1927 the editorial committee had already turned down a play of his, *L'Eglise* (The Church). "Some satirical vigor, but does not follow through. Gift for depicting very different kinds of milieux," concluded the readers' file card. Two years later, the same had happened with the manuscript of his *Semmelweis*.[131] But this third time he was not to be dismissed so easily. The discussion went on for a week, Brice Parain remembered.[132] Benjamin Crémieux was the first to read it.

"It's a picaresque novel," he told the committee after reading a few extracts aloud. He did not have time to go more deeply into this difficult manuscript, since he had to leave for a convention at Ragusa, so he returned it to Gaston, who turned it over to Malraux, then to Ramon Fernandez and Emmanuel Berl. Their debate was long and heated. Meanwhile Denoël was on the move. But how could he find a writer whose name was unknown? He searched for the discarded wrapping the manuscript came with, and found it after going through several trash cans. He was disappointed but intrigued: there was a name, but a lady's, that of an author of pious novels he had previously turned down. She could not possibly have written this *Journey*. He asked her to come see him and showed her the package and the wrapper:

"Did you write this?" Denoël asked on the off-chance.

"Me? Write that ghastly stuff? No, it was written by my neighbor across the hall, Dr. Destouches."

Denoël understood: this lady and Destouches shared the same cleaning woman, who indiscriminately salvaged wrapping papers from one place or the other, using them mainly to wrap her slippers. Immediately the publisher sent an enthusiastic special-delivery *pneumatique* to Destouches, who got it just before he received a lukewarm letter from Gallimard saying he would publish the book if the author did some "lightening up" and made some "rearrangements." In other words, Destouches must cut out a certain number of pages deemed expendable in the judgment of the editorial committee, particularly Crémieux.[133]

With one publisher saying "yes" right away, and the other hedging with "yes, but," Céline's choice was simple. It was Denoël, even though the latter, shortly afterward, also suggested (in vain) "some lightening up." Later, Céline was to sum up the episode in a few words:

"Gallimard sniffed at my bear. . . . Not what he wanted . . . not at all what he wanted! Denoël, he jumped at the chance. . . ."[134]

Céline went to see Denoël without delay. The publisher was impressed by "this man as unusual as his book,"[135] who unfolded his saga to him: five years of work; 20,000 pages rewritten, revised, started over from scratch; disappointing contacts with publishers; the manuscript sent to Gallimard, despite what had happened before, and to Denoël because Eugène Dabit's *Hôtel du Nord* had done so well.

More and more enthusiastic in spite of the voluminousness of the manuscript—it would run to 625 printed pages—Denoël launched his attack. He sent proofs to three magazines, planted items with gossip columnists, read excerpts from "the book" to most of the people who came to see him, and was vocal in all the echo chambers of Paris about the unusualness, originality, and inventive powers of this new writer. By the end of October the first articles began to appear—violently for or against the book, but almost never luke-warm. The Goncourt campaign began, the advertising was placed, but it took over a month to beat down public resistance, for readers were used to a different tone, another kind of vocabulary, and a more classical narrative technique—especially at such length. Ten days before the Ten had their traditional luncheon at Drouant, the first printing of 3,000 copies had still not sold out. But word was getting about: *he* would get the Goncourt. Better still, Jean Ajalbert came to see Denoël and told him there had been unanimous agreement at an informal meeting of the judges. Among newsmen, the hardened bettors claimed Céline was in. Orders started pouring in to Rue Amélie, and a second printing of 10,000 was ordered. Alas, in spite of the official support of Ajalbert, Lucien Descaves, Léon Daudet, and J.-H. Rosny, the situation changed, there was a turnabout in the feelings and alliances within the Goncourt Academy of which it alone knew the secret, and the prize went to Guy Mazeline for *Les Loups* (The Wolves), published by Gallimard. It was scandalous, but no matter.

Céline got his revenge by winning the Renaudot Prize. In the next two months some 5,000 articles about him were published; 50,000 copies of the *Journey* were quickly snapped up; the publisher had to place orders with three printers to keep up with the demand; and fourteen countries acquired translation rights.[136]

Céline was launched, the *Journey* was the book of the year, and Denoël was a great publisher at the head of a small publishing house. Gaston never forgave him for having reacted with more acumen and greater rapidity than he. But the affair clearly illustrated the difference between the ponderous *NRF*-Gallimard setup and a publisher of lesser financial and commercial standing who could step more nimbly. Before Denoël and in his time, other publishers had started with the same aims, but almost all had failed. Were they perhaps less determined, less gifted, less talented than he? Even if he was never able to rid himself of the administrative problems that took so much of his time, to the detriment of his reading of manuscripts, Denoël always knew where to find capital to keep from going broke, and how to roll with the financial punches. That too was a publishing talent. This was precisely what was lacking at a small house that seemed to have a wonderful future, Au sans pareil, which for a while gave Gaston cause to worry.

As usual, one man was its mainspring, its inventor and moving spirit: René Hilsum, the son of a Dutch wood merchant and a Polish mother. Self-educated, but a great reader and devoted to literature, he began studying medicine along with a school chum from the Collège Chaptal, André Breton, and dropped it for the same reason as he: mobilization and war. In 1918 both were paramedics at the Val-de-Grâce military hospital in Paris, where they met another young man in the same situation, Louis Aragon. The three became friends, went to gallery openings together, to the Ballets Russes, and Adrienne Monnier's bookstore; the prevailing atmosphere in which they moved led them, inescapably, to the founding of a magazine, *Littérature*, in which Hilsum played his role without, however, writing for it. He managed to get hold of an unpublished Rimbaud manuscript, *Les Mains de Jeanne-Marie* (Jeanne-Marie's Hands), and published it as a chapbook in 500 copies. What it lacked was a publisher's imprint. Dadaism was then at its height, and the group wanted to stress the incongruous and above all make a total break with traditional publishing. Breton suggested appropriating the name of the well-known shoestore, "L'Incroyable" (The Unbelievable). Aragon proposed that they use the pretentious designation "Au sans pareil" (Without Peer) that was a favorite of provincial novelty shops. It was unanimously agreed upon.

Hilsum dubbed himself the publisher, and two young women they had met at the studio of the painter André Lhote lent them a small sum—and, equally important, an address, on Rue du Cherche-Midi. In his first year, he published books by the contributors to the magazine—Breton, Aragon, and Philippe Soupault, of course (the three founders of Surrealism), but also works by Cendrars, Morand (his very first book, a collection of poems), Jacques Vaché, and Francis Picabia. Picabia actually caused the first falling-out among the founding fathers, when Hilsum refused to publish his *Jésus-Christ rastaquouère* (Jesus Christ the Fraud), not because Grasset had turned it down, but because it lacked brilliance and inventiveness in its challenge to authority. Little by little Au sans pareil ceased to be the publishing house for Surrealists and Dadaists and was open to all comers. Hilsum at the same time started a bookstore under the Au sans pareil shingle at 37 Avenue Kléber and displayed, in this rather high-class neighborhood, works of Marx and Trotsky alongside those of Apollinaire and Paul Valéry, a neighbor and customer who eventually gave him some of his poems to publish.

Until 1923 Au sans pareil operated without any real editorial board, getting by on reports, advice, suggestions, and contacts of the *Littérature* contributors. And if authors did not spontaneously come to Hilsum, he sought them out, after reading their articles in magazines of scant circulation. In his contracts there was no clause about books to come. Authors signed up for a single title since the house, for want of advances against royalties or proper distribution outlets, had no way to keep Morand or Aragon from heading for Gallimard. Though a horn of plenty for a few authors who had become his friends—such as Blaise Cendrars—Hilsum no longer had the wherewithal to keep up the treasury. He shut the company down, temporarily, and under the label Le Génie de la France (Genius of France) started a collection of deluxe editions of French classics from François Villon to—well, any author dead for over fifty years, whose work had therefore fallen into the public domain. The commercial impact was immediate.

In record time he brought out 130 titles, whereas Au sans pareil had done 176 over a period of years. But this time he was no longer on his own: several financiers put up seed money. The money was still insufficient. When Hilsum set about increasing it, one of the shareholders, a banker, lent him 700,000 francs, but in 1936 suddenly demanded its return. In a stranglehold, Hilsum had no choice but to sell. There was a buyer, brought in by a business manager: Gaston Gallimard. The deal was made, and the collection was put to rest as soon as the stock on hand had been sold. Of course Gallimard already had La Pléiade as a collection of deluxe classics. But the deal also allowed him to eliminate a small potential competitor. What was Hilsum's opinion of Gallimard? "An enlightened millionaire, a dilettante who was a friend of literature."[137]

The fact is, the two men had absolutely nothing in common. Gaston was born rich, started in business rich, and surrounded himself with men who understood figures, in addition to those who knew how to read. Nothing like that in Hilsum's case, either in his past or his future: a Communist, he would be named by party leader Jacques Duclos to head the collective control of the party's publishing house, and after World War II for several decades would be an adviser to Les Editions Sociales.

Yet there were many bridges between the two firms: Morand, Aragon, and others less well known, who had their starts with the "little one" before being snatched up by the "big one." For example, the young lady of twenty-seven who in 1929 sent the manuscript of her first novel simultaneously to Gallimard and Hilsum—to Hilsum, because she liked what he was doing—and got no reply from the former, while the latter sent an enthusiastic note and published her brief tale, giving her an advance against royalties that was very modest indeed: 150 francs. But *Alexis ou le traité du vain combat (Alexis)* was out in the bookstalls, and that was all that mattered to Marguerite de Crayencour, who chose to be known as Marguerite Yourcenar.

A Gallimard mistake? There would be others. The editorial board was not a machine, and the firm was getting more cumbersome and more disorganized despite the efforts of Raymond Gallimard. Proust and Céline were the two best-known cases of missed opportunities. There was also Mauriac, whom Rivière did not welcome into the NRF when he wanted to be part of it, which did not keep them from later becoming very close friends. Gallimard would have to wait until 1978 to "recoup" Mauriac, when he qualified for a Pléiade edition. Jacques Copeau in 1914 absolutely vetoed the publication of poems by Jean Cocteau in the NRF. Malraux got Gallimard to turn down Boris Souvarine's *Stalin*. There would be the rejection of *Au château d'Argol (The Castle of Argol)*, the first story by Louis Poirier, who was beginning to use the name Julien Gracq, and whose manuscript was accepted by a courageous bookseller-publisher, José Corti: "Wouldn't you turn down a dish that someone else has sent back to the kitchen? . . . Yet the dish that someone has refused to touch is not necessarily bad."[138]

For some of the mistakes the whole firm took responsibility; others were attributed to specific editors, at least so rumor had it. The Céline affair would always be seen as Crémieux's fault, and the Proust rejection as Gide's. As recently as May 6, 1984, the *New York Times Book Review*, surveying "books that got away," referred to Gide's rejection of the Proust novel.

But sometimes Gaston himself had a share in the responsibility, as for instance in the case of Henry de Montherlant, who "got away" and was brought back only through a lawsuit after World War II. "I wrote to Montherland [*sic*] that I would not publish his book and asked him to let us see his next one," Gaston confessed to Rivière on August 20, 1919.[139] But it was too late, for Daniel Halévy and Grasset were quicker on the draw; in 1922 they published *Le Songe (The Dream)*—and the prolific author's entire oeuvre for some twenty years thereafter.

Money and contract matters, questionable deals and concessions, a competition of shopkeepers, self-interested ties with authors, few friends but many connections, the infiltrating of literary-prize panels—

was that the profession of Gaston Gallimard, publisher? Yes, it was that, too.

ZED. The three letters did not mean much. Even taken as an acronym, however hard one tried, whatever one imagined, they didn't register. Yet during the 1930s they appeared in tiny type at the bottom of the last page of a number of papers: ZED Publications. That was the name Gaston dreamed up for a corporation he started on December 20, 1928, capitalized at 700,000 francs. Its officially stated aim tells us little: publishing, printing, advertising. Actually, the corporation's intent was to be a springboard for newspapers and magazines without endangering the Librairie Gallimard. If the papers failed, the publishing house would be none the worse off, at least in theory.

Ever since he had been in full charge of the publishing house, that is, since right after World War I, Gaston had sought ways of increasing profits without going outside the world of print. He was not interested in branching into spaghetti or automobiles; even if such things had been offered him with the assurance of a short-term profit, he would have refused. That kind of thing was not Gaston Gallimard. But newspapers and magazines were another matter. They were paper, more power, and a way to give work to underemployed writers under contract to the firm. After all, the signatures of those associated with Gallimard were often found simultaneously in the *NRF*, *La Revue musicale*, *La Revue juive*, not to mention *Les Nouvelles littéraires*. And if, in addition, such an undertaking could earn some profits for the parent company, Gaston was ready to confront the most closed-minded purists of the *NRF* with the argument that, without the dose of oxygen and the powerful financial support such business could bring, their own little enterprise would go under, to say nothing of the costly limited printings of so many authors.

Gaston put Georges Kessel in charge of getting together a team to produce a new weekly: *Détective*. The title had a good sound, was easy to remember, and to the point. Unfortunately, someone already had preempted it. Not to be denied, Gallimard decided to wrest it from its owner. The owner was a former cop, now a private investigator, named Henri La Barthe (the French initials of which he turned into his pseudonym, Ashelbé), and *Détective* was the title of a kind of advertising sheet for private detectives and information agencies, in which he also published some cops-and-robbers stories by established newspapermen. Gallimard simply bought him out, lock, stock, and title. (Ashelbé, having had a taste of the written word, eventually provided the story for the film *Pépé-le-Moko*.)

Now the only problem was acquiring members for the team. Kessel wanted good newspaper men on his staff, but they all had the same reservation: *Détective* had no track record. In those days, joining the staff of a paper usually was understood to mean signing on for life—unless you hit the editor on the head with an inkwell. Most of the men Kessel approached were willing to be stringers or occasional contributors, but did not want to commit themselves wholeheartedly to the weekly. So the bulk of the material would have to come from people who were already part of the Gallimard complex. Joseph Kessel, Georges' older brother, of course; also Pierre MacOrlan; Georges Simenon, who would write weekly mystery puzzles that readers won prizes for solving; and Francis Carco, Paul Morand, and the like.

The first issue of *Détective* was on the newsstands October 25, 1928, its lead story headed, "Chicago, Crime Capital of the World." The 350,000 copies quickly sold out. It was an instant hit, and would maintain that same average circulation until 1936.

To the austere House of Gallimard *Détective* brought a note of lightness and humor, quite a break from the traditional image of the *NRF*. The weekly was looked on askance by many as a bastard of noble lineage, not to be disclaimed (impossible, given the ties between Gallimard and *Détective*), but not to be displayed either. The offices of the magazine were on Rue Madame, in the old warehouse that the publishing company still maintained there; then, when the *NRF* moved to Rue de Beaune, *Détective* inherited its quarters on Rue de Grenelle. But the geographical distance maintained between them did not keep the name writers of the company from contributing to *Détective* or occasionally dropping in to watch the purveyors of blood and crime at work, as if they were exotic wild beasts.

Often, on Tuesdays, when the magazine was put to bed, Gaston would take his brother and Valentine Tessier to Rue Madame, before the editorial staff of *Détective* wrapped it up and took off for dinner at a restaurant in the working-class neighborhood of La Villette.

"Let's take a look at the circus," he would say to them.[140]

To them, that was just what it was; it had nothing in common with the studious atmosphere of Paulhan's office. One such evening they truly got their money's worth. On their arrival, they heard shots and rushed into the city room. Preparing an exposé on the underworld, in the evening the editorial staff of *Détective* were training to defend themselves against possible retaliation—with revolvers not always loaded with blanks. The warehouse was their shooting gallery. Gaston and Raymond now understood why some of their fine editions and rare paper stock were turning up with bullet holes in them. But the training had to be called off when a shot barely missed the concierge, who was bringing in the day's last mail delivery. As it turned out, she was deaf. The cutthroats of the underworld never did attack the Rue Madame establishment. The worst scare was a visit from a gangster known as Jo-la-terreur, who had been mentioned in connection with the Stavisky scandal. But it was settled with drinks at a nearby bistro.

For Gallimard, this was a success beyond expectations, and he often told his colleague, Alfred Vallette, of the austere *Mercure de France*:

"What I lose on the *Nouvelle Revue Française*, I earn back with *Détective*."[141]

Much later, he would go further than that:

"The only time I was financially at ease in those days was when I published *Détective*. Its success was breathtaking. It was the best commercial venture I ever had."[142]

The venture's commercial success was all the more durable, since Gallimard decided to publish a series of books also called Détective.

Several of Joseph Kessel's works appeared with this imprint, to which were added works by the best writers from the weekly, in all 86 titles from 1934 to 1939.

Money aside, *Détective* brought some excitement into the lives of the Gallimards. Naturally the two brothers had nothing to do with its editing. They oversaw it with empathy and amusement, but never interfered. Yet Gaston still had to defend the paper publicly when it came under attack. For a long time it was the *bête noire* of the Commission for Supervision of the Press, and on several occasions that group threatened to ban *Détective* posters. It was subject to all kinds of verbal attacks because of "all the gore," even though its readership was known to be adults and even the elderly.

This first experience with newspaper publication also gave Gaston a chance to meet a different set of people, something he greatly enjoyed. Like his friend Fargue he loved the local color of Paris, the atmosphere of newspaper press rooms and police stations. But for *Détective*, he would never have hired the man who became the accountant of the Editions Gallimard. In one of the earliest issues of the weekly, Louis Roubaud had published a long series on the "good" convicts of Cayenne,* that is, those who were reclaimable as respectable citizens. One day a man presented himself at the Rue Madame offices and asked to see the managing editor. Paul Gruaut had spent fifteen years on Devil's Island for some farfetched affair involving love, espionage, and money. In fifteen years he had learned accounting by actually doing it.

"I am one of those that you spoke of in that series," he said to Georges Kessel. "If I can be salvaged, salvage me. Find me a job."

Gaston interviewed this unusual job applicant himself. The ex-con was put in charge of bookkeeping at the weekly, and stayed there until it was scuttled in 1939. Gaston was satisfied with his work, and developed such condfidence in the man that he brought him into the publishing house to handle his own personal accounts

*The penal colony in French Guiana.—TRANS.

as well as those of the authors, a position which M. Gruaut would fill with total competence until the end of his life.

Only a few weeks after launching *Détective*, Gallimard brought out *Du cinéma* (On the Cinema), another special-audience magazine. Starting in December 1928, three issues appeared under that title, and then, from October 1929 to December 1931, it was known as *La Revue du cinéma* (The Magazine of Film). It had three successive editors, Pierre Kéfer, Jacques Niel, and Robert Aron. But the guiding spirit of this richly illustrated magazine, which boasted articles by Philippe Soupault, Jean-Richard Bloch, Robert Desnos, and André Beucler, among others, was Jean-Georges Auriol, a somewhat difficult, brusque character who never got along with Gaston, but who knew all that there was to know about movies.

It was a quality magazine from all viewpoints, but still a magazine. Gaston, bitten by the bug of big circulation, dreamed of duplicating the success of *Détective*. In March 1931 he brought out *Voilà*, a weekly printed in sepia rotogravure, which had its offices at Rue de Grenelle, under the editorship of Georges Kessel. Just like *Détective*. But its subject matter was different. With the subtitle "news weekly," and using a great many photographs, it dealt with current events—not only courtroom and police news, but anything connected with Paris life, international affairs, or politics. *Voilà* caught on mainly because it published the "lives" of several femmes fatales ghosted by famous writers using transparent pseudonyms. Contributing also to its success were the newly popular pinups that, with a daring (for the day) display of legs, thighs, and cleavages, were the staple of its back page. Kessel remained as managing editor for a mere two years. After a serious automobile accident that forced him to wear a neck brace and left his brother Joseph limping, Georges felt he had to give up the job. Gaston named Florent Fels to replace him on *Voilà* and Marius Larique to do the same on *Détective*.

Fels, who had shortened his name from Felsenberg, would leave the most lasting imprint on *Voilà*. Self-educated and a bon vivant, friendly with painters and poets, always ready to share a dinner table or lend books, Florent Fels was what was called a "very Parisian" character, sensitive but temperamental, very like Gaston in some ways, for instance in his delight in pretty women and the company of Valentine Tessier in particular. Rough in manner but a loyal friend, he did not shrink from asking the then prefect of police, Jean Chiappe, to drop charges against several of *Voilà*'s contributors: an opium-smoking poet at whose place seven kilos of the drug had been found, or a writer with pockets full of heroin, or one newspaperman given to exposing himself. Sometimes, too, Chiappe lent Fels a hand in his editorial work by getting his cross-Channel opposite number—Lord Tranchard—to make arrangements for Fels to visit British penitentiaries and report on conditions there.[143]

In the pages of *Voilà* some writers used their own names, others did not, depending on whether it was the memoirs of a high-class courtesan or an expedition to the antipodes. In 1932 Simenon published in it a long account of a trip he had made the year before to Africa. The stir caused by its anticolonialist tone was so great among general readers that a short time later Simenon was refused a French visa for a return to the Dark Continent. At that time Parisian movie houses were showing a documentary about André Citroën's so-called "black cruise" under the title *L'Afrique vous parle* (Africa Speaks), and Simenon had subtitled his piece, "Africa speaks, and says *merde* to you." In fact, the last words of his series were: "Yes, Africa says *merde* to us—and we deserve it!"

Voilà, like most of the papers and magazines Gallimard published, gave him a chance to lighten the financial problems of a number of his authors. Antonin Artaud, between two opium cures, published two pieces in 1932, one on China, the other on the Galapagos. Fels, who was a friend of his (having published Artaud's writings ten years earlier in his magazine *Action*, as well as at the Stock publishing house), knew that he had never set foot in either place: Artaud's "first-hand reports" were in fact journeys around his room and through his library. So when Fels accepted a third article from Artaud, he left it in the file—but paid for it, for Gaston had to find ways, direct or indirect, to assist his authors financially. Especially since Artaud had been receiving proposals. Denoël was trying to take him over by commissioning translations, prefaces, and even publishing some of his writings: *Héliogabale, ou l'Anarchiste couronné* (Heliogabalus, or The Anarchist Crowned) in 1934; *La Race des hommes perdus* (The Race of Lost Men), under the pen name of John Forester; and *Nouvelles Révélations de l'être* (New Revelations of the Being), signed "The Revealed One."[144]

Because of their financial insecurity, writers were apt to treat their publisher as though he were their banker or errand boy. But what often required delicate handling with the two mass-circulation weeklies he was publishing was much less of a problem with Gallimard's next press innovation: *Marianne*.

This political-cultural weekly owed its existence not so much to intuitive genius as to a response to what was already there. Arthème Fayard had launched *Candide* in 1924, and *Je suis partout* (I Am Everywhere) in 1930, both politically conservative weeklies in newspaper format. The success of *Candide* inspired imitators: Horace de Carbuccia, head of Les Editions de France, brought out *Gringoire* in 1928, and Gallimard *Marianne* in 1932, while a year later the well-established house of Plon created a weekly with an annually changing title: *1933, 1934*, and so on. These book publishers going into periodical publication all had common goals: to diversify their activities, to provide their houses with a new outlet, to have less expensive vehicles for the advertising and publicizing of their books, and to attract new writers or those under contract to rivals by publishing their novels as serials.

More than *Gringoire*, which was considered somewhat vulgar, *Candide* irked Gaston. It was impeccably edited, and anchored solidly to the political Right. *Marianne*, then, had to be equally well done, but oriented toward the Left. This was less a matter of political conviction than of market. To run this new weekly, Gaston thought of Emmanuel Berl, two of whose book-length essays he had published: *Mort de la morale bourgeoise* (The Death of Bourgeois Morality) and *Le Bourgeois et l'amour* (The Bourgeois and Love). Berl was qualified to commission articles, write some himself, publish them, and try to win over the talent of the rival publishing houses and weeklies. After all, this was what Fayard-*Candide* was doing with the *NRF* people; it was in part to stanch this drain that Gaston started *Marianne*.

Berl, at forty, was a pure-bred product of the Parisian Jewish bourgeoisie. From a family of industrialists and academics with family ties to Proust's mother and to the Bergsons and the Francks, he came from an assimilated milieu with no religious ties, and politically of the free-thinking, moderate-progressive Clemenceau stripe. He was a close friend of Drieu La Rochelle and also of Malraux, who had weaned him away from Grasset and brought him over to Gallimard.

What Gaston wanted him to create was a weekly written by newspapermen, with pictures, articles, news, criticism, feature articles, and a lot of free publicity for the *NRF*. For months Berl, along with Malraux, worked to overcome the problems of offset printing, dummying, making page layouts, and getting the weekly to bed on time under often difficult conditions which Gallimard did not always take into consideration, in his hurry to get on the presses. Berl and Gaston had their differences, but the publisher recognized that Berl was an indispensable associate:

> He is difficult, demanding, often loudmouthed, he talks a blue streak, is terribly expensive, but aside from a few details we have the paper we wanted. Moreover, through him I think I have finally learned what Right and Left mean. That isn't so simple. Berl bubbles with ideas, good ideas and upsetting ones, but the firm, since he has made himself felt in it, has become noisy, alive, connected to the corridors of power and the backstage of the theater.[145]

Berl got the first issue of *Marianne* out on schedule on October 26, 1932. It was subtitled "Great Illustrated Literary Weekly," with Gallimard as publisher, Hirsch as general manager, and Lang as printer. On the cover was a Berl editorial, as might be expected. On page 2 was a piece by Saint-Exupéry, "Pilote de ligne" (Airline Pilot), and on the following pages political prophecies by Joseph Caillaux, a report on the new parliamentary season by Pierre Brossolette, on finances by Jules Moch (of the Chamber of Deputies finance commission), book reviews by Ramon Fernandez, Colette's beauty secrets by Josette Clotis, a theater review by Edouard Bourdet, a review of art shows by Pierre MacOrlan, of recordings by Jean-Richard Bloch, a short story by Marcel Aymé, a novel by Georges Duhamel, and the "Life of Voltaire" as told by André Maurois.

In a word, the whole damned family! The titles put on the various columns were winks to friends and initiates, recalling titles of Morand, Proust, Musset, or Chaplin: "Open All Night" for cabarets, "World's Champion" for sports, "Pleasures and Regrets" for art exhibits and concerts, "The Caprices of Marianne" for the theater, and "City Lights."

Apart from the contributions he obtained for this special first issue, Berl subsequently got articles from Edouard Herriot and Bernard Lecache, Colette and Tristan Bernard, Martin du Gard and Giraudoux, and even, in the second issue, a short story by the famous journalist Albert Londres. The tables of contents were prestigious, the articles often dense and brilliant. Gaston, now at the head of three weeklies, did not even have time to read them.

From the beginning, *Marianne* was politically labeled: moderately leftist, nonmilitant, antifascist, supportive of but not wild over the Popular Front. The newspaper stood for peace, for Briand as against Poincaré—an image, a tone, and a tendency that Gallimard had wanted, so that his weekly might be the *Candide* of the other side.

Of course the paper was also a Trojan horse for the publishing house. It was used to print excerpts from the latest novel by Colette, coming out at Grasset's, or the latest work of Francis Carco, who just happened to be one of the Goncourt judges. But if readers bought it mainly for such literary pages, its contributors were more often motivated by politics, as seen from their weekly editorial meetings on Fridays at 6:00 P.M. at the *NRF* publishing house, which was also the headquarters of *Marianne*.

The *NRF*, which tended to underplay its commercial links with its embarrassing cousins—*Détective* and *Voilà*—was rather proud of *Marianne*; it sometimes sent ideas or articles to it and was adept at using the services of a "very Parisian" weekly whose editor had unusually good contacts.

In 1932, when Gallimard published the French translation of D. H. Lawrence's *Lady Chatterley's Lover*, it created a scandal despite its preface by Malraux. Charges were pressed in court to have it banned. But on advice of the prosecutor, the Ministry of Justice did not follow through. The prefect of police was then summoned before the city council by an alderman bent on suppressing immorality. Prefect Chiappe, who wanted to accommodate two of Gallimard's powerful tools—Fels and Berl—found a way out by forbidding only the city-owned news kiosks to sell the book.

1936 marked the high point and the beginning of the end for Gallimard's weeklies. The Spanish Civil War and the growing threats to the peace of Europe took readers' attention away from the murders of retired little old ladies and the derring-do of the Belleville gangsters, which were featured in *Détective* and *Voilà*. *Marianne*, after a high of 120,000 copies weekly, declined. Though it remained the third best of the weeklies of its type, that was not enough to satisfy Gallimard. In 1937 he sold *Marianne* to Raymond Patenôtre, an extremely rich politician, who was minister of economics in the Léon Blum regime. But in the sales contract Gallimard got a stipulation that *NRF* texts and authors would still have a privileged place in it.[146]

Gaston Gallimard turned fifty in 1931. He abhorred being wished a happy birthday; birthdays for him were recognized and official steps on the way to old age and death, something he wished to conjure away. He did not look his age. Only the death of his friends and contemporaries made him conscious of it. Jacques Rivière's death in 1925 had upset him greatly. Their correspondence over a dozen years was copious and affectionate, and revealed deep and lasting bonds between them that were sincere despite the ambiguity of some of their relationships: to get over his violent love for Yvonne Gallimard, Gaston's wife, Rivière had written his roman à clé *Aimée*, in which he portrayed himself along with Gaston and Yvonne on their weekends at Bénerville. Things literary were of such importance in the ambience of the early *NRF* that they outweighed all other considerations; the moment events and situations became subjects of literature, they became impersonal. By transposing his "secret" passion for Yvonne to the pages of a novel, Rivière purged himself of it, the more fully since "the husband in the case" was also its publisher.

In 1929 Gaston's father had died. That marked the end of an era. But his father had long since ceased to be the famous Paul Gallimard: he had sold the Bénerville mansion, keeping only some of the acreage, and sold as well his great art collection, though he did retain some paintings. The amount realized on this sale has never been made public, but it became known that shortly after the Cognacq sale at the Charpentier Gallery in 1952, the dealer Wildenstein, lunching with Gaston, told him that if the Paul Gallimard collection had been sold then it would have brought in, at the least, a billion francs, which led the publisher to "whistle discreetly."[147]

Despite the sale, Gaston did inherit a few canvases of masters, notably Renoir's *The Source*, which he later sold so as not to have to borrow from banks in order to move his corporate headquarters from the now inadequate space on Rue de Grenelle to a building of their own on Rue Sébastien-Bottin (formerly Rue de Beaune), across from the town house of Cambacérès, who had been second consul to Napoleon and was largely responsible for drawing up the Napoleonic Code.[148]

Turning fifty, he still toyed with others and carried on as in the early days, when all had been free and easy, with no pressing deadlines and no cares. Despite the weight of his responsibilities, and the financial scope of his operation and commitments, he still found it hard to take himself seriously. When he left the office on Rue de Grenelle late at night, as Fargue napped on a couch strewn with file folders and manuscripts, he could not keep from saying:

"Léon, be a good fellow and leave the key across the street, will you? Good night."[149]

Across the street meant the café on Rue du Dragon.

Yet he looked very respectable indeed in his eternal navy blue suit—gray in summer—with his bow tie also navy blue, his salt-and-pepper hair neatly plastered down, his hat, and the austere reputation of the *NRF* which, willy-nilly, he had to bear. Behind that façade, however, the man was anything but ponderous. His blue eyes had a mischievous twinkle; he was always ready with a smile; a bit of a paunch bespeaking his habit of eating well either at the Brasserie Lorraine in Place des Ternes or at Maxim's; an invariably pink complexion betraying hints of bashfulness; a natural casualness in his bearing as in his speech—all these things combined to create in Gaston what everyone who knew him summed up in a single word: charm. Some even thought him rather feminine in his complexity, in the mystery he kept around his deepest thoughts, and in his skill in hiding his emotions.

He was a nineteenth-century character in the sense that he never identified with ideas, but rather with style. He claimed to have only aesthetic imperatives in matters of elegance, refinement, and quality, which led him to prize Larbaud above Malraux, and Fargue above Drieu and Aragon. He disliked people with made-up minds, and of Gide's work all he retained were the doubts, never the certainties. Sectarians, militants did not appeal to him, as he felt they were the prisoners of too rigid a yoke of principle. He likened men of principle to puritans. Going to the other extreme, Gaston occasionally carried his dissembling and vagueness to the point of duplicity. Never frank or transparent, he detested confidences, and not out of discretion alone. No one ever saw him give in totally to disgust or admiration. This man's climate was always temperate. An aesthete rather than an intellectual, preferring artists to people with ideas, he was often irritated by the tortuous sophistication and the paradoxes upon paradoxes of a Jean Paulhan. By nature he guessed right, rather than reasoning correctly.

Was Gaston a boss? On paper, of course, but not in everyday

life. He was flexible and tolerant regarding schedules, even though he himself was always punctual. Not especially generous in the salaries he paid his staff or in the advances against royalties he gave his authors, he was perfectly capable of giving disproportionate sums without collateral or guarantees to writers he liked, whose work he believed in, whose personality appealed to him. He also knew how to pay people for doing nothing, so that one day he might make use of them or get a favor from them; he had scouts and antennae wherever necessary. In society as in the office among his associates he hated to embarrass anyone, especially in the presence of a third party. He would often apologize when someone else had made a faux pas. If a waiter in a restaurant spilled a glass of water on the tablecloth, Gaston would claim responsibility, to spare the man any unpleasantness with his superior. If a proofreader let some typos slip through, he would say, "In his place I might have done the same."

He was indulgence incarnate in order to avoid any humiliation in his presence. Provided, of course, that he was not deliberately provoked. At Rue Sébastien-Bottin the ire of his extreme calm was awesome. He could not be pushed around with impunity. Unusually tenacious—"Better to stick with a bad idea than to be constantly changing good ones," he often said—he always wanted the last word, even when he knew he was wrong. At the end of a stormy argument with his business manager Hirsch, Gaston would belch and say oracularly:

"And I forbid you to throw my inconsistencies up to me!"

There was also Gaston the man of taste who loved cars, all motor cars—to drive, not to show off; who made fun of the social whirl while being a part of it; who liked luxury, refinement, and variety but wore his suits till they were threadbare, then replaced them with identical new ones; who refused to get rid of his favorite sweater that was out at the elbows, his old tweed jacket that was turning green, his antique leather attaché case from Hermès, his raincoat. A man whose only hobbies were books, theater, and women, who was comfortable with his habits, the Gauloise stuck to the corner of his lip, the fountain pen always filled with blue ink. Gaston was modest to a fault, shocked that Martin du Gard, in his memoirs published as part of his complete works in the Pléiade edition, should have discussed the illnesses of his parents.[150] Modest and discreet.

When gossip columnists trapped him in the restaurants that he habitually went to, he would tell them:

"I like the environs of Paris, *Carmen*, *Boris Godunov*, and *Louise*, *The Idiot*, *Lost Illusions*, and *Great Expectations*, Impressionism, cold veal with mayonnaise and fried potatoes, the Maupassant life style. I never escape from reality through a wardrobe mirror the way Cocteau does, and I feel no need to degallimard myself the way Claudel does."[151]

André Beucler, the writer, journalist, and screenwriter who saw a great deal of him at the end of the 1920s, had ample opportunity to question Gaston about his likes and dislikes:

"It would be quicker if you asked me what I don't like. I would start with Henry Bernstein's plays, lavallière neckties, formal ceremonies, authors who try to teach me my business in my own office, faced with the rows of books I've published! But there would be no end to the list. Actually it's after long habit that I realize what gives me pleasure."

"How about the house writers?"

"I adore Roger Martin du Gard. I like Valéry very much (when he talks about heating, sausages, and umbrellas). I am a bit leery of Gide, who is too intelligent, constantly, without ever taking a breath. I like Lacretelle, Aragon, Kessel, Berl, Etiemble. I don't mention Fargue, who is part of our family and our home. As for the rest, there are some who amuse me but whose books I don't publish, because I think they're no good, and the ones I don't socialize with, who bore me stiff with their pretensions, but whose books I publish because they're good."

"How about enemies?"

"I have a whole collection of them, even among people who have nothing to do with the literature that we like, with printing or distribution, but I will name only the ringleaders among them, whom everyone knows about anyway: Henri Béraud, Galtier-Boissière, Lucien Dubech, Henri Massis."[152]

"What do you read for your own pleasure?"

"Right now I am rereading La Bruyère, in small doses, at night, before going to sleep."[153]

All the facets of Gaston are there, between the lines, except one: the dimension of secrecy. He was a secret man, who enjoyed secrets and who therefore might be trusted to keep them. In brief, the ideal publisher. But what did his authors think of him?

Valery Larbaud: "If Gaston Gallimard were not one of my oldest friends, I wouldn't care about the sale of my books. Proper cultivation of my property at Valbois would bring me much more income."[154]

André Beucler: "A great leader, who was more like a big brother to everyone. A familiar, understanding, patient boss, who dominated in a gentle way because of his obvious intellectual superiority or, better put, because of an elegant facility to express with talent and humor simple ideas which would have been commonplace in the mouth of one who lacked his seductiveness and shadings."[155]

Max Jacob: "He is judicious, harmonious, delicious, melodious, yes, of course, we all know that, but he's also something of a Lucifer, isn't he?"[156]

Benjamin Crémieux: "Gaston Gallimard is something like this. If you ask him for a raise, he moans that he can't afford it, that business is too bad. On the other hand, if you tell him you dropped 10,000 francs at the gaming table, he'll give you that amount right away."[157]

Roger Nimier: "The tyrant under whom Jean Paulhan lived did not know how to wield the iron scepter, much less control atoms. He created a kind of authority which has no connection with American matriarchy, Portuguese paternalism, or French infantilism. The pleasures of this tyrant are books. Gaston, first of the Gastonides and founder of the Gastonate."[158]

Jean Dutourd: "Gaston the First, king of publishing, general of literature, prince of the novel, protector of poets, lord of all printed lands. Generations of writers have had no other dream than to wear his coat of arms, which as everyone knows is argent with lines of gules and sable, and in fess-point the monogram *NRF*—in other words, to be published inside his famous white cover with its thin red and black lines. At twenty, I would have sold my soul for that."[159]

Céline: "Monsieur Gallimard is very rich . . . In six months he can make you the greatest writer of the century!"[160] "The bastard won't let go of me. I've bawled the hell out of him, called him all kinds of names . . . dirty pimp."[161] "I dedicated *Normance* to Gaston Gallimard and Pliny the Elder, and neither one of them thanked me."[162]

François Mauriac: "A dogfish shark."[163]

Some of these writers knew Gaston when he was fifty, others earlier, others later. But when they passed judgment on the man— and not on particular situations—their opinions were never anachronistic, for in the 1930s the qualities, characteristics, and shortcomings of the publisher were already clearly established, and they were never to vary. Whatever aspect of him one might describe between the start of the 1920s and the end of the 1930s, Gaston remained faithful to his image. Named in 1924 to the administrative council of the Cercle de la Librairie,* he promptly delegated his brother Raymond to hold that position for him, since he hated the professional aspect of his trade and would always feel that way. He did not relish his profession in the company of fellow publishers, however brilliant, but in hunting, tracking down, and bringing forward new talents. He did not pride himself on a fine annual financial statement, but on having been the first in 1919 to read some magazine pieces by Joseph Kessel, an unknown twenty-one-year-old, to have asked him to collect them into book form, to have published *Mary de Cork* and *La Steppe rouge*, Kessel's first two books, and to have gone on to publish on the average one a year up to 1939. He prided himself on having published, at the same period, Samuel Butler, translated and prefaced by Valery Larbaud, the works of G. K. Chesterton and of Henri Michaux. Always with this principle in mind:

*The French publishers' trade association.—TRANS.

to make the best-selling writers pay for those who brought in no profit.

"A play is put on for what happens during the intermissions," Gaston once told his friend Louis Guilloux.[164] That was typical of him. He liked show business for what it was, what it had to offer, what it *presented*—but on both sides of the footlights, in the audience as well as on the stage. For a long time the theater was the focus of his passions. Copeau's theater, of course, but also the lighter Boulevard plays, which often, in his eyes, had the merit of being constructed according to the rules of the craft. He attended every opening, sat in the orchestra along with those in the Parisian swim, and often went backstage, since he enjoyed the company of actresses. But the experiment of being a theater administrator cooled his ardor. In 1924 he and his partners dissolved the Vieux-Colombier Company. Henceforth Gaston was to be more cautious in such ventures. He would not again be caught investing large sums of money in a theater.

When not attending Giraudoux's latest play put on by Louis Jouvet at the Athénée, he went to the movies, had dinner at Maxim's or the bistro where the *Détective* staff went—it did not matter which— and finished the evening at a night club or cabaret. La Boeuf sur le Toit was probably the one he liked best. The spirit of the place and the people who went there appealed to him. Gaston had followed the Boeuf from its birth through all its peregrinations, but mainly when it was on Rue Duphot and then Rue Boissy-d'Anglas. This club had caught on quickly, with its Dadaistic décor, when it was bruited about that Tout-Paris went there evenings for fun, elegance, relaxation, and especially music. Darius Milhaud and the other five of the group of composers known as "Les Six," seeing that writers and artists had their own cafés but musicians did not, had suggested to Louis Moysès that he open the club. A man of impressive build, always cordial and ready with a hearty handshake for his many friends, Moysès was the animating spirit of the Boeuf. Familiar with his customers but not overly so, knowing just where to draw the line, he needed no explanations and knew his customers in all their diversity: those who wanted a quiet table on the side, or those who wanted to see and be seen. Ministers and whores, artists and athletes, the snobs of the Jockey Club and the staff of *Les Nouvelles littéraires*, all rubbed elbows there, provided they had a name and stayed in character.

Cocteau was of course the godfather of the Boeuf. When the tourists disappeared around midnight, leaving the place to the regulars, however many real crowned heads may have been in the room, Cocteau was the only recognized king, and Radiguet his prince, despite the heterosexual lapses of the youthful author of *The Devil in the Flesh*. When the latter died suddenly, Tout-Paris, never at a loss for a pun in bad taste, dubbed Cocteau *le veuf sur le toit* (the widower on the roof). At Cocteau's reserved table, where the wit flowed as freely as the champagne, one would regularly find Gaston Gallimard with Valentine Tessier, Joseph Kessel, Dunoyer de Segonzac, and Darius Milhaud.[165]

Gaston a fifty-year-old young man? He was willing to act it, and those around him found him quite chipper. But to a very few he confided his bitterness toward an often thankless profession and admitted that his health was no longer what it once had been. In 1928 he went to Vichy to "take the cure" for his liver for the first time in his life: "I feel I am on the threshold of another age," he wrote Jean-Richard Bloch. Two years later, when he broke his heel in an accident, it depressed him greatly: he could not stand being bedridden. In 1928 he had bought a place at Pressagny-l'Orgueilleux, a small village on the Seine west of Paris, eight kilometers downstream from Vernon. It was a fine bourgeois home with spacious grounds surrounded by quickset hedges. He had a tennis court built, and later enlarged the holding by the acquisition of two adjoining estates. It was there at Pressagny, by the river, that he found rest, when he was not at Le Tertre, the château that Martin du Gard had bought from his father-in-law, at the edge of the Bellême forest, in the Perche plain, also just outside Paris. The writer kept on renovating its interior over five years, altering and rearranging the building under Gaston's interested and amused eye.

Half a century for Gaston also coincided with his divorce from Yvonne Redelsperger, which gave official recognition to a separation that had taken place long before, and his second marriage, on July 23, 1930, at the city hall of the Fourteenth Arrondissement, with Jeanne-Léonie Dumont. But this marital reorganization brought about no change in his habits. He remained a "man covered with women" (to use the title of one of Drieu's novels) and a raconteur whose reputation was not exclusively intellectual or ethical. The women who knew him—and they were legion—still speak of him with dreamy eyes and smiles, inevitably recalling his charm and availability, whether they knew him at forty or at seventy.

To his friends and associates he was certainly a man who loved women. His extramarital relationships were never a secret; more than once close collaborators related how they carried on their work sessions with Gaston around Valentine Tessier's dinner table. During the entire period between the two wars, Valentine played a dominant role in his life. She had already made his tour in the United States with the Vieux-Colombier during World War I unforgettable. In 1931, when Gaston reached fifty, she was thirty-nine. "She is a fine fruit at its peak," Gide said of her. A critic recalled: "For all those who at that time loved the theater, Valentine Tessier symbolized gracefulness, charm, and in a word, Womanhood."[166] After the dissolution of the Vieux-Colombier in 1924 and Copeau's retirement to Burgundy, she joined Louis Jouvet's Comédie des Champs-Elysées, where she became the center of the plays of Jean Giraudoux, the arcane novelist turned playwright.

In 1933 she made her movie début with Gaston. That is, she starred, and he put up the money. But while his father, in the late nineteen hundreds, could easily afford to put on plays for his protégée in his own theater, Gaston came very close to having to mortgage the precarious financial future of the publishing house.

In an earlier film-related experiment, in 1925, he had made Albert Pigasse editor of a series called Cinario (contracting *cinema* and *scenario*), to give what was then called "the seventh art" its own literary voice and engage the more visually minded and spectacular of the house authors, the Kessels and MacOrlans, to write directly for the screen. Shortly afterward he started another series, Cinéma Romanesque (Cinema Novels), publishing novels adapted from movie hits. As for the *Revue du cinéma* (the forerunner of the much-later *Cahiers du cinéma*), Gaston first cut down the number of its pages and the production costs before dropping it altogether in December 1931: it had been a costly failure, never living up to the hope that it might become for the film what the *NRF* was for the written word.

In 1933 the man in charge of movie-related matters at Gallimard was Robert Aron. Gaston asked him to set up a small production company, the NSF, or Nouvelle Société de Films (New Film Company). Discovering that it was possible to finance part of a film by discounting distribution commitments and putting up only a small amount of cash, young Aron—with Gaston's but not Raymond's support—set about producing half-hour shorts, to be shown before the main features, as was then the custom.[167] Gaston was completely indifferent to the hypothetical profits; all he wanted was to give Valentine Tessier a worthy showcase for her talent. Once again, Raymond tried to put a brake on Gaston's enthusiasm, but his brother would not listen. And when an agent of Flaubert's publisher Fasquelle offered the screen rights to *Madame Bovary*, Gaston agreed to the purchase. Valentine would play, of course, Emma Bovary.

For director they engaged Jacques Feyder, and the treatment and screenplay were naturally entrusted to Gaston's friend Roger Martin du Gard. A luncheon date was made at Larue's, but the first meeting turned sour. Feyder, a top director at the time, could not envisage Valentine in the part. They broke off before even getting started. Martin du Gard, disappointed by the turn of events, now also bowed out. Gaston was not so easily discouraged; with Aron's help, he got together almost as impressive a crew. The director, Jean Renoir (not yet quite of the stature of Feyder), son of the painter and old family friend, brought along his customary associates, several of whom were members of his family: his brother Pierre to play Charles Bovary, his nephew Claude as assistant cameraman, and Marguerite in charge of editing. Of the three artists who designed the sets, Georges Wakhévitch was the most famous. Darius Milhaud did the musical score. Acting alongside Valentine and Pierre Renoir, Max Dearly played the pharmacist M. Homais, Pierre Larquey was Hippolyte the clubfoot, and Le Vigan was Lheureux the draper.

Euphoria! Nothing could be better. They were ready to shoot.

To Aron it seemed too good to be true: "I signed an agreement with a new distribution company, CID, which, delighted to have such a superproduction in its program, issued a flood of commitments which Gaston Gallimard, always the grand seigneur and imprudently trusting my financial competence, one evening as he was leaving the office countersigned for me on the verso, without even looking at the other side to see what he was letting himself in for."[168] All the while, Raymond Gallimard warned of the impending storm; but no one would listen.

The shooting started at Billancourt in the fall of 1933, the exteriors having been shot on location in Normandy shortly before. The company was made up of friends. Renoir called it "the ecstasy of intimacy." Every evening the entire company, actors, crew, and staff, gathered around Gaston and Valentine for laughter and chatter. In this relaxed atmosphere on location, in August in a Normandy village, Gaston forgot all about Rue Sébastien-Bottin, his authors, his contracts, and even Grasset; his movie was all he could think of.

The editing took an inordinately long time—and so did the film: it ran over three hours. No theater would want to show that long a film. So, despite the opposition of the director and the producer, the distributors made their own cuts. The film was brought down to two hours for theatrical release. Renoir was outraged, feeling betrayed, amputated: Would anyone have dared cut a couple of chapters from a novel just to make it shorter? Gaston agreed: it was a massacre. Especially since they had run it full-length five or six times for audiences at the studio, and they had liked it.[169]

The gala première took place in Paris at the Ciné-Opéra on January 4, 1934. Gallimard and Renoir, together as their fathers had been forty years earlier, although not in the same context, were worried. The audience was polite, but what would the critics say? Georges Champeaux in *Gringoire* did not hide his high regard for Renoir—or his disappointment in the film. "He has made neither a successful psychological film nor one of atmosphere. He has depicted neither Mme. Bovary's ardor nor the boredom of the provinces. He has told us, without conviction, the story of a woman who commits suicide because she is short 8,000 francs." In other words, it was Flaubert who was being murdered, and that was a very serious thing to Gallimard, not the producer but the publisher. Fortunately, the critic spared Valentine: "The only praise one can give M. Jean Renoir concerns his choice of a star. Mme. Valentine Tessier was truly the right woman for the part and one can only regret that more was not made of her gifts."[170]

Madame Bovary proved a total flop. It was quickly withdrawn from release. Everyone had an explanation for the catastrophe: the cuts that mutilated it, its theatricality, the unenthusiastic reviews. But there was no need to look for excuses: in the early weeks of 1934, Parisians had something more important on their minds than a drama of small-town adultery in nineteenth-century Normandy at the Ciné-Opéra. The scandal-tinged swindler Alexandre Stavisky had just died, the Chautemps cabinet had had to resign, and day after day the streets were the scene of violent demonstrations, forerunners of the bloody February 6 to come.

The company distributing *Madame Bovary* went into bankruptcy. For Gaston, who had countersigned all their drafts, this was catastrophic. The whole financial structure of the operation was in collapse, unraveling when the first link broke. The creditors, from studio owners to film suppliers, and even the renter of the sound truck, all came to dun Gaston, who turned a deaf ear on them. They threatened that his signature would be discredited, his assets seized, that they would go public with the scandal—but to no avail. He would not be budged. The creditors wanted Aron's neck and demanded that he be fired. Gaston refused. He barred his door to them. Finally, he won out by dint of patience and determination. They accepted his lordly conditions: all debts would be paid off proportionately, *pari passu*, out of the receipts.[171]

Raymond proved to be right. Gaston did not care, he had had his fun. As for the failure of the film, he applied to it, as he did to his books, the long view, and convinced himself that, a few decades hence, informed audiences would find *Madame Bovary* to be Jean Renoir's masterpiece. But he did promise not to dabble in the movies soon again.

Still, when Berl approached him, in 1936, with an idea conceived by Denise Tual, Gaston agreed to organize a company called Synops; the *NRF* was its major shareholder, along with Tual, Myron Selznick (the famous producer's brother), and Constance Collier. It seemed a good idea: to mine the enormous reservoir of stories in the Gallimard list, adapting appropriate ones and submitting them to producers and directors.

In 1932 celebrations were in order at Rue Sébastien-Bottin—champagne on every floor. An alliance with Hachette, France's mightiest distributor of printed matter, had been concluded. For months that possibility had been the main subject of conversation in the house. Now it was a fact: the contract was signed March 29, 1932. Thanks to this very technical document Gallimard was going to become in actual fact what the satirical magazine *Le Crapouillot* had nicknamed him: "Gaston I, King of Publishing."

Since the late 1920s René Schoeller, head of the Messageries Hachette, had pursued single-heartedly the aim of expanding to books what he had already achieved for newspapers and magazines, a virtual monopoly on their wholesale distribution. It was the best way to diversify and extend the power of his company, while at the same time imposing bonds of dependency on the publishing houses. Schoeller's strategy started in July 1927 when the Librairie des Champs-Elysées had been signed up. But Schoeller needed a truly prestigious publishing house, whose agreement would be the most promising precedent for Hachette to sign up other publishers.

That house could only be the *NRF*. It had the proper profile.

Moreover, Schoeller was on friendly terms with Gaston, dating to the time when he distributed *Détective* for the firm. They had done each other favors. Hachette offered Gallimard what he had already offered several other publishers: he would sell his entire output to bookstores at the same discount the publisher himself had been giving them. The margin allowed the wholesaler varied from company to company, depending on the numbers of copies purchased outright. For several months Gaston had been playing a very tight game with regard to this variable discount schedule, deploying his considerable negotiating skills. He was arguing from strength, since the offer had not come from him. He used this advantage to impose his own conditions: he published about 250 books per year, with an average printing of 3,000 to 5,000 copies, according to category (novels, essays, and so on), and he wanted Hachette to guarantee him 75 percent of their sales outright. Everything depended on that guarantee. No other publisher had got or ever would get such terms. Gallimard insisted, and he got them.[172] In his hand he held an unrivaled card: the *NRF* magazine, the prestigious back list, the established name.

To outsiders, the deal and its ramifications appeared enigmatic. Some speculated that Hachette was investing in Gallimard's company. The trade, according to Paul Léautaud's *Diary*, took the deal as indicative of serious financial problems, heavy losses by the *NRF*, overstock of unsold books, and chronic disorder in the Gallimard operation.

By getting what he wanted, Gaston with one stroke eliminated three of the stumbling blocks that had undone a number of aspiring publishers: the risk of publishing unknowns, the threat of returns, and financial dependency. Whatever he did henceforth, he was sure that a good part of his annual production would regularly be bought and paid for. No one could ask for more. To top it off, beginning in 1935, the man handling relations with Gallimard would be Hachette's new vice president in charge of book distribution, Henri Filipacchi. Gaston had met Filipacchi through his friend Schiffrin when he bought out La Pléiade, and it was Gaston who barely a year earlier introduced Filipacchi to Schoeller; the latter had taken him on as a trainee. Although delighted by this, Gaston never dreamt that young Filipacchi would move up so rapidly at Hachette and become his personal contact with Schoeller.

For Gallimard, it was a wonderful deal. For Hachette as well. By October 1935, Fasquelle also signed an exclusive distribution contract with Hachette. Others would follow.

5

Taking Sides

1936-1939

June 5. Popular Front. Start of the Blum experiment. Gaston really liked Léon Blum. Léon Blum was one of the trio of politicos—with Edouard Herriot (who had written a *Life of Beethoven* for him in 1929) and Philippe Berthelot—he always mentioned to prove that he did not hate the whole profession.

Blum was the author of *Souvenirs sur l'affaire* (Memories of the Dreyfus Affair), which Gallimard had published in 1935, as well as *Nouvelles Conversations de Goethe avec Eckermann* (Further Conversations of Goethe with Eckermann) and *L'Exercice du pouvoir* (Exercising Power), published in 1937.

Now, as head of the Socialist government, Blum was a friend, a connection in power. Gaston certainly had nothing against that. But by mid-June he was beginning to be a little less happy with him, when the new laws on collective bargaining, paid vacations, and the forty-hour-week were enacted. Until now, Gaston had done his best to keep his company under control through the best kind of paternalism. Adequate wages, not too much strictness about working hours, a temporary loan here and there just before the end of the monthly pay period, if necessary. Gaston had always applied his own social laws, case by case and instance by instance. So he did not care for social legislation applied from above. He grumbled but had to conform, especially since Louis-Daniel Hirsch, his firm's general manager, saw to it that the new rules were scrupulously applied and respected. It was not worth fighting over. The Socialists would surely give them other grounds, at higher stakes.

On August 13, two days after the new law nationalizing war industries, Jean Zay, the minister of national education, introduced a bill to reform publishing contracts and authors' rights, no less. And it was not an improvisation: its fifty-six headings were proof of that. Publishing houses were first alarmed, then furious. Didn't the government have anything better to do—what with the sitdown strikes in the factories and the so-called nonintervention in Spain—than to monkey around with publishing contracts? The bill drafted by the legal services of the ministry was long, dense, and well argued. How could it be combatted? What should be advocated instead? The trade did not have any prepared position, but a man true to his character— Bernard Grasset—decided that the bill called for an all-out attack on the government, and swore not to give up until he had won. Those who knew him well were reassured, for he was the ideal point man for this kind of fight. Feistier than ever, he urged his fellow publishers to join the fray, asking each to bring his own pressure to bear against the bill. As for Gaston, he soon found out that one of his own authors was a member of Jean Zay's ministry: a former editor at *Le Mercure de France* and onetime coworker of Jean Paulhan's in the ministry of information, Jean Cassou had six titles in the *NRF* catalogue.

Anxious to stir up public opinion and have it on his side, Grasset concentrated his fire on that part of Zay's bill which tampered with the duration of exclusive rights in a given work or the body of works of a given writer.

For Grasset and Gallimard such a clause would mean the death of their business, at least as they understood it. They were shrewd enough not to condemn the entire bill, and to admit the need for it: for there was no encompassing law regulating authors' rights and publishing contracts, only piecemeal precedents, and it was a good thing to update those old rulings to apply to radio broadcasting and phonograph recording, among other things.

So far, so good. But this Article 21, which they considered especially deadly, questioned the very principle of publishing. Wrote Grasset: "The job of a publisher in fact consists essentially in building up a backlist, that is, in acquiring for himself and his successors the largest possible number of lasting values."[1] He pointed out that in this trade the emphasis was not on quick returns; a publisher had to acquire more and more titles so as to build up profits *in the future*; any publisher satisfied with immediate turnover would be a suicide in no time. If deprived of the income from a work over its lifetime, a publisher could not decently be of service to literature. The message was as clear as the bill: to this they were diametrically opposed.

The Zay Bill questioned an author's authority to cede his work to a publisher for an indefinite period; it replaced it with a cession the duration of which, in terms of posthumous rights, might be summed up as follows. For the first ten years the royalties would continue as before to go to the author's estate; for the next forty years, the heirs would be empowered to sell the rights to the highest bidder; and a half century after the author's death the work in question would fall into the public domain and be free of royalties.

The fury of a number of publishers was understandable. Yet curiously it was not shared by all: a broad survey of opinions about the bill in the evening paper *L'Intransigeant* in September 1936 revealed that not all—Flammarion, for one—were as vehement as Grasset. There were even some, like Robert Denoël, who heartily endorsed Jean Zay's bill because it would encourage free competition.

Not letting the matter rest there, Grasset fired up his public opinion campaign by publishing at the beginning of 1937 *La Doctrine française du droit d'auteur* (The French Doctrine of Authors' Rights), a book written to order for him by three eminent jurists, Jean Escarra, Jean Rault, and François Hepp, law professors and recognized legal experts. They said the same things as the feisty publisher, but in more moderate terms, with supporting arguments, quotations, propositions, and a competency lending great weight to their critique of the Socialist bill.

Grasset's campaign bore fruit. In June 1938 the discussion the government hoped to hold was postponed because of some sixty amendments. A year later it was postponed again because the commission rapporteur Albert Le Bail, was overwhelmed by the piles of letters that came in daily from writers', artists', and publishers' associations, exerting sustained pressure. On June 1, 1939, the long-awaited debate finally began in the Chamber of Deputies. Zay, the minister, as well as his cabinet secretary Pierre Abraham and Julien Cain, the administrator of the Bibliothèque Nationale,* were present. Everyone, supporters and opponents alike, were in agreement that new legislation was needed, but their opinions differed concerning it. No formula had been found guaranteeing the interests of both authors and publishers, interests sometimes in conflict. Le Bail set the tone at the start:

> The main purpose of this bill is to do away with the notion of literary property which has been the source of so many abuses. We do not want the publisher to continue to be a regular business manager. We want the author to be allowed to turn over to him only one right, the one that corresponds to the publisher's occupation. That is the most natural way: each publisher will stick to the role for which he was made. If he is a book publisher, he is not a filmmaker.[2]

As Le Bail saw it, there were two kinds of publishers: "good ones," some of whom were pure philanthropists, and "bad ones," some of whom were pure scoundrels. Between the two, there was an "intermediate category of quite respectable people who are businessmen-publishers, who try to the best of their merchandising ability to get the maximum profit from the works entrusted to them."

*The national library, corresponding to the Library of Congress.—TRANS.

He met with loud applause. The bill had been reworked and honed for three years. Sales of rights for a lump sum, for instance, something that had not at first been covered, were now forbidden. But what still bothered some of the deputies was a new clause mentioned by Le Bail: the creation of arbitration courts to settle conflicts between authors and publishers. "Various objections on the left and the right," the official minutes recorded. But Le Bail went on: without such a court, the bill is meaningless.

In the original draft, he explained, there had been a provision for unilateral contract cancellation by the author, which of course made publishers howl. That meant the end of backlists. What was now intended was merely a "review" of contracts, which this special court would undertake.

"All that the publishers are asking is to be allowed to continue diffusing French thought throughout the world," one deputy protested at the end of a long, impassioned speech against the Zay Bill.

The next day, the session went on. François Martin, consulting rapporteur for the Commission on Commerce and Industry, referred again to the matter of short-term contracts. The bill, as a careful study of it revealed, allowed a writer to take back his rights at the end of ten years. On behalf of the publishers, he quoted Gide in strong opposition:

"What publisher would be crazy enough, generously crazy enough, madly enough in love with belles lettres, and wealthy enough to undertake the publication of works he knows he will be stripped of before the public has time to recognize their true value?"[3]

Three hundred and fifteen deputies had wanted and demanded this debate, but only a handful bothered to attend. It was Friday, just before the weekend, and in 1939 there were other concerns more pressing than literary property rights. Grasset was to relate later how Zay called him in to inform him personally that he was withdrawing his bill:

"I have understood that the risks you take and the patience you show must have compensation, and that that compensation can be found only in the monopoly rights of use that the present laws assure to you."[4]

Publishers' pressures, amendments, World War II, and the assassination of Jean Zay by the fascist militia in 1944 would spell the total end of the bill.

The three years between the Popular Front experiment and the start of the "phony war" were as intense for the country as they were for the publishing trade. The latter had seemed stagnant; now it was in turmoil. The specter of the Zay Bill was partly responsible, of course, but in publishing houses too circumstances and personalities were changing.

The death of Alfred Vallette, the head of the Mercure de France, was followed, in November 1936, by that of Arthème Fayard, of the house bearing his name. Grasset, meanwhile, sorely regretted having lost sole control of his company and felt that his board of directors was impeding him. At the end of 1938 he was obliged to reduce the capitalization of his company to 3.8 million francs: as a result of a new evaluation of what he had contributed to the firm, the face value of shares was marked down from 250 to 100 francs.[5] What a glorious time it was for him, when he was not accountable to anyone but himself! Or at most to Louis Brun. But that could no longer be: during the summer of 1939, his number 2 man had been murdered by his wife with two pistol shots. Acquitted of the crime, during the Occupation she would sell at a profit the thousands of rare and inscribed books that her husband had carefully accumulated over the years.

At the beginning of 1936 in Paris, Jean Bardet and Paul Flamand, two young Catholics active in Christian leftist movements, such as the magazine *Esprit* and the Personalists, joined forces with a publicist who had ventured into publishing, Henri Sjöberg, to lift his nascent Editions du Seuil above the artisan level. At the same time, in London, the British publisher Allen Lane was bringing out André Maurois's *Ariel, or The Life of Shelley* in a sixpence paperback to be sold through the Woolworth stores. The book trade looked askance at this, but not book buyers, who enthusiastically welcomed this first Penguin Book, the forerunner of all pocket books. It took four years for the idea to cross the Atlantic and inspire similar editions by American publishers, and an equal number of years to cross the Channel and be picked up by Robert Meunier du Houssoy, the president of Hachette, in a series of inexpensive pocket books called the Collection Pourpre (Purple Books).

Let us not jump to the conclusion that, once again, all good ideas had to be imported from abroad, for it was a thirty-five-year-old Frenchman who for some ten years headed Les Editions Sequana, the very first book club in the world. Each month René Julliard, with the help of a committee that included André Maurois, Paul Valéry, and Marshal Lyautey, among others, would select a title from forthcoming lists. Julliard then brought it out in a special edition for his many subscribers, all French at first, but soon from overseas as well. The idea was revolutionary, and profitable for all concerned; it would have many imitators.

At Gallimard also, things were on the march. Since its founding the Librairie Gallimard, originally known as Les Editions de la *NRF*, had four times increased its capital. The development of the company, the increase in personnel and overhead, the successive moves to ever larger quarters, the outside investments in news publications and printing plants, not to mention movies and advertising, the growth of its annual business turnover, the greater and greater number of books published every month, the new imprints added, the advances given to authors against royalties—all made the Gallimard house a substantial company.

Gaston brought his only son Claude into the firm. At twenty-three, Claude had graduated from the Ecole Libre des Sciences Politiques and gone on to a doctorate in law. Unlike his father, he tended toward a legalistic and commercial turn of mind, and was oriented accordingly upon his arrival at Rue Sébastien-Bottin, while participating in the editorial board meetings on the same basis as Gaston and Raymond Gallimard. Claude wrote a book, which was published a year later—by Gallimard naturally—in a series that already included volumes by names such as Keynes, Jouvenel, and Hoover. The book was called *Le Change, évolution et technique* (Foreign Exchange: Its Development and Technique) and was based on his doctoral thesis, *Des opérations de change international sur devises* (On International Currency Trading). Claude married the daughter of André Cornu, a future senator of the Radical Party,* and state secretary for fine arts, who had been the editor-in-chief of *Marianne* since Gaston sold it to Patenôtre. At twenty-five, Claude had little in common with his father, either in tastes or in personality: they were both members of the Automobile-Club de France, but that was about all they shared.

September 1938. France's prime minister Daladier came back from Munich, where he had signed an agreement that was hailed as assuring peace for our time. The phony peace. There was much talk of a cowardly feeling of relief, and of a Pax Germanica. A new insult entered the vocabulary: Munichist! It was hard to tell the doves from the hawks.

Munich was the center of discussion: should France have gone there or not? Should Daladier have signed or not? The debate filled the papers. The *NRF* as well—the magazine, that is; the publishing house did not have to follow so closely the somersaults of political life. Still, a few of the outstanding titles on its 1938 list are symptomatic of the concerns of the moment: *Le Réveil de l'Europe* (Europe Wakes) by Bertrand de Jouvenel; *La Nausée (Nausea)* by Sartre; *The Metamorphosis* and *The Trial* by Kafka; *Introduction à la philosophie de l'histoire (Introduction to the Philosophy of History)* by Raymond Aron; *La Fin de l'après-guerre* (The End of the Postwar Period) by his brother Robert Aron; *Bahía of All Saints* by Jorge Amado; *Au pays du grand mensonge* (In the Country of the Great Lie) by Anton Ciliga; and *Nietzsche, sa vie et sa pensée* (Nietzsche, His Life and Thought), in six volumes, by Charles Andler.

*Only mildly progressive, despite its name.—TRANS.

Starting with the November issue, the *NRF* magazine reacted to the Munich debate. In an article entitled "Discours pour les copains après la mobilisation de septembre 1938" (Speech to My Pals after the Mobilization of September 1938), Armand Petitjean put the readers on guard against those who claimed to represent France—politicians, journalists, bankers—and suggested that these latter be sent on a tour of the Maginot Line, to get a breath of air "a few kilometers from Death." Julien Benda explored the attitude of the democracies toward Germany and predicted that, if France were subjugated by Germany, "a larval fascism" was likely. Jean Schlumberger expressed his wish for a peace that was not a humiliation. Marcel Arland, back from a short trip around France, was struck by the fatalism, the fear, the resignation that he found in conversations everywhere. As if France were preparing to die.

Henry de Montherlant, for his part, sent the *NRF* the parts of his *Diary* that the rightist *Candide* had censored. He did not spare the pacifists and all those who reacted to the Munich agreement with a sense of relief: "Like it or not, cowardly fools, a day will come when the stench of your feces will be smothered by that of your blood. Unless you forever avoid bloodshed through your shame." And while Denis de Rougemont tried humor in writing the chapter on "Leçons sur la crise des minorités en 1938" (Lessons on the Crisis of Minorities in 1938) for some future history textbook, Jacques Audiberti related an ordinary evening of anti-Semitic hatred on the Champs-Elysées. The Collège de Sociologie (Roger Callois, Georges Bataille, Michel Leiris), although refraining from opinions outside its domain of expertise, called for awareness "of the absolute mendacity of current political forms, and the necessity of reconstituting through one's principles a way of collective existence that will go beyond all geographical or social limitations and allow people to behave with some dignity when death threatens."

Was the *NRF* a nest of rebels? A den of warmongers? At any rate, it too had joined the battle, a battle that this time had nothing to do with literature. The magazine was attacked by a man who a year before had been on the Gallimard payroll: Emmanuel Berl. The onetime editor of *Marianne* was now publishing the paper of his dreams, *Pavés de Paris* (Paris Bricks), entirely on his own. The bold headline across the front page spoke for itself: "La *NRF* contre la paix" (The *NRF* against Peace). But while he specifically attacked Benda and Schlumberger, his main target was Gaston Gallimard. It was a violent attack and had all the more impact for having a basis in truth:

> Of course the *NRF* is no longer what it used to be. It has lost most of its importance. In the depths of Jacques Rivière there was a preacher. Now there is Jean Paulhan, a prankster. . . . So warlike a policy is, more than anywhere else, unacceptable in an organ founded and run by M. Gaston Gallimard. I have been M. Gaston Gallimard's friend. I no longer am. I have worked with M. Gaston Gallimard. I no longer do. It is not pleasing to me to have to take a stand against him. I should no doubt not have done it on any other subject. I have seen a very changeable, very vacillating M. Gaston Gallimard in just about every area. On only one point have I seen him firm and constant: that point is his horror of war. He did not fight in the 1914 war. He succeeded in avoiding the draft in spite of his age, in spite of his excellent health. He defended himself even when he was not attacked, by insisting on his inability to support any war, whatever its origin, whatever its circumstances. . . . [Yet] he remains passive in the face of the offensive against peace carried on by the *NRF*. That is perhaps the one thing that he has no right to do, not only in relation to others but in relation to himself. For twenty years he was a conscientious objector, a man to whom war was synonymous with evil. . . . His anarchist philosophy made it all too easy for him. But to let the *NRF* play the warmongering game . . . he could permit it only by departing from that minimum of honor a man must maintain, at least toward himself. And here, precisely, he does not have the right to say, as he is wont to do: "I am a publisher. I publish everything: Léon Blum as well as Léon Daudet, Léon Daudet as well as Léon Blum." Because, after all, when he sees a threat to his publishing contracts, he knows very well how to say, "I am not merely a businessman. I have a duty to the mind." And for him the mind implies first and foremost taking sides for peace against war.[6]

A flag-waver, Gallimard? A saboteur of Franco-German reconciliation? Orchestra leader for a warmongering *NRF*? Berl made very
precise accusations. But they had less to do with the attitude of
pacifists toward Munich than with the ambiguities of an individual
named Gaston Gallimard, heretofore the responsible head of a magazine and publishing house with prestige and influence. It was his
conception of his profession that was being challenged. Publish
everything? Communists and fascists? Aragon and Drieu? The position seemed likely to become more and more untenable. The rising
tide of dangers made such ecumenicism very difficult.

Until the early 1930s Gaston had adopted it as a principle, a way
of life. As early as the fall of 1919, the question had been unequiv-
ocally posed. The *NRF* was preparing the publication of an article
by Jean Schlumberger entitled "France d'abord" (France First), some
antireligious phrases of which—beginning, notably, with "if I were
a Catholic"—made Gaston as well as Rivière jump. "Clarté," a group
created by several writers, had just published a manifesto based on
ideas of motherland and religion. Although Gaston claimed to belong
to neither side, he felt obliged to respond to Schlumberger's piece:
"I believe this to be necessary for some of my authors, for some of
my friends, for our firm, and perhaps for myself. . . . I have too
much interest in our undertaking to allow misunderstandings about
our respective tendencies."[7] If he had to take sides, Gaston would
choose "Clarté," despite the low opinion he had of some of its
promoters, because "this party expresses feelings rather than ideas,
while the other does not even have ideas, it has nothing but politics."[8]

Feelings rather than ideas: the whole economy of Gaston's
character could be summed up in that phrase. He would never
deviate from it. He was delighted with the eclecticism and the open-
mindedness of the *NRF*, with its contempt for all extraneous considerations. In December 1932 it published a list of grievances signed
by eleven young writers of every stripe, from Paul Nizan on the Left
to Thierry Maulnier on the Right, eager to show the public the
tenuous link binding together all the rebellious young intellectuals.

The riots of February 6, 1934, a watershed date, a break that would remain as a point of reference.* It was the year that Gallimard published, for example, Blandine Ollivier's *Jeunesse fasciste* (Fascist Youth), which was not to everyone's liking. And a year later it was *Six ans chez les Croix-de-feu* (Six Years among the "Fiery Crosses") by Paul Chopine, a blistering attack on the right-wing action group of that name led by Colonel de La Rocque (who, incidentally, was having his *Service public* [Public Service] published by Grasset).

One Wednesday evening early in 1936, the concierge of the *NRF*, while in the cellar, heard two blasts. He ran upstairs and found his wife bloodied, her clothes burnt away. She was screaming, "Fire! Fire! Call the firemen!"

Taken immediately into the offices of *Marianne*, she died eight hours later. Gaston, who had run to the scene, explained to the reporters:

"The concierge was doing some hot-wax polishing over a can of gasoline, and the vapor from it caught fire."

But he was immediately contradicted by Gabrielle Gras, who was in charge of production:

"The Fiery Crosses had threatened that if we published Chopine's book they would 'blow us to smithereens.' One of them, seeing the lobby dark and the last visitors and employees gone, must have thrown in some explosives."

The police and fire experts inclined to the political attack theory. Word went out to play the matter down in the press. The stairwell was blackened by smoke; walls were cracked, the electrical wiring exposed. A passerby commented:

"So they finally struck the *NRF!*"[9]

It would take more than that to intimidate or discourage Gallimard. Since the times were political, book publishing was political, too. In

---

*On that date both Left and Right took to the streets to protest the corruption of the Stavisky and related affairs, which continued to fester until the electoral victory of the Popular Front in 1936.—TRANS.

1937, after Gide's famous *Retour de l'URSS (Return from the U.S.S.R.)*, Gallimard published the French translation of *Down the Years* by Sir Austen Chamberlain, the onetime British Conservative leader, as well as Blum's *L'Exercice du pouvoir* (Exercise of Power), the *Discours* (Speeches) of the onetime premier of France Pierre-Etienne Flandin, and *La CGT, ce qu'elle est, ce qu'elle veut* (The General Confederation of Labor: What It Is, What It Wants) by Léon Jouhaux, secretary general of the Communist-aligned labor organization of that name.

As for literature, it was still being honored, and so was the *NRF*. In 1937 it was given a double consecration. Gaston traveled to Stockholm to be present at the award of the Nobel Prize for Literature to his old friend Roger Martin du Gard, and in Paris he attended a historical, precedent-setting event: the creation at the prestigious superuniversity, the Collège de France, of a chair of poetry to be filled by Paul Valéry. There could be no better publicity for the firm on Rue Sébastien-Bottin. Especially as it was amplified by a new and unexpected resource: Radio-37, the newest of the private radio broadcasting stations in Paris. Started a short time before by the industrialists Jean Prouvost and Henri Béghin with the help of Marcel Bleustein, it included on its board a friend of the House of Gallimard, the dramatist Armand Salacrou, while one of its staff writers was the *NRF* novelist Marc Bernard. Beginning in 1938, Radio-37 would have a regular Tuesday night program at 9:45 P.M., called "Le Quart d'heure de la *NRF*" (The *NRF* Quarter Hour), on which such figures as Claudel, Gide, Henri Calet, André Suarès, Jules Supervielle, and Julien Benda would appear. It was a valuable echo chamber and a new dimension for the *NRF*, which would later continue the program on the government radio with Bernard and Paulhan.[10]

In 1938 and 1939 Gaston evidently decided to straighten out some ticklish situations with certain authors. He asked Emmanuel Boudot-Lamotte, a member of the editorial board, to maintain contact with Paul Morand and inform him that the company was delighted soon to be publishing his next book, *L'Homme pressé* (Man in a Hurry), and that, with this in view, "Gaston is working on new sets of figures in order to give you the most honorable terms possible."[11]

Denise Tual was entrusted with convincing Georges Bernanos to forsake Plon permanently for the *NRF*. In 1938 the famous Catholic writer was thinking of leaving France for South America. Denise Tual found him in the port of Toulon, about to sail, and quickly grasped that Gaston had chosen the perfect time to wean away the author of *Le Journal d'un curé de campagne (The Diary of a Country Priest)*: he was deeper than ever in debt. The advances he had received from Maurice Bourdel, the strongman at Plon, had long since proved inadequate to his needs. In fact, Bernanos was desperate. It was the right moment to pluck the great writer, whom Gaston could not bear to see published by anyone but him. Yet, what about Bernanos's exclusive contract with Plon?

"Authors are always ready to go back on their contracts; no one is more dishonest than authors—except publishers," Gaston assured Denise Tual before she left on her errand.[12]

Gaston sent along a 25,000-franc check for Bernanos, on account, to get him to make up his mind. It did the trick; Bernanos accepted. But he did not wish to enter Gallimard's list with just any old manuscript. In his drawer he had something called *Un mauvais rêve* (A Bad Dream), written at Majorca, but that was not good enough. *La Vie de Jeanne d'Arc* (The Life of Joan of Arc)? That he had already promised to Fayard, from whom he had also received an advance against royalties.

He left for Paraguay, but then settled in Brazil, where he wrote not one but three books for Gallimard, which he sent along to his friend, Father Bruckberger. The Dominican was both his intermediary and his editor for these three books, which appeared in 1939: a brief biography, *Saint Dominique*, that came out in the Collection catholique, and two pamphlets, *Scandale de la vérité* (The Scandal of Truth) and *Nous autres Français* (We French). Bruckberger, who typed the manuscripts and corrected the proofs, decided—on his own authority, considering the geographical distance between author and publisher—to angle them on the criticism of the reactionary Charles Maurras and conservative Catholic circles, while eliminating their other polemical dimension: the apologia for Edouard Drumont,

Bernanos's master, whose selected and quoted pieces, while not expressing the anti-Semitic venom that had made the success of Drumont's *La France juive* (Jewish France) forty years earlier, ran the risk of discrediting Bernanos at this troubled time.[13]

With the mounting fanaticism on both sides, the least misstep was pounced upon and immediately exploited. In the corridors of Rue Sébastien-Bottin, relations among authors got testier. Some avoided each other, others traded insults, with Gaston acting as buffer. He was more and more uncomfortable, terrified by the violent hatred that surfaced in people's conversations and relationships. In spite of himself, the publisher of "Léon Blum and Léon Daudet" had to make choices. Some reproached him for his laxity, his readiness to oblige even Communist authors. So he acted. He asked Jean-Richard Bloch to settle his account: Bloch no longer had time for novels, yet he had been drawing a monthly stipend since 1926 as a writer. The accountant, M. Dupont, had the figures: Bloch owed the company 78,000 francs. Since 1931 he had promised several works, but it was now 1937 and he had still not published a thing. Certainly his job with the new Communist evening paper *Ce soir* was not going to leave him time to fulfill his commitments.[14]

On the Right also, Gaston cleaned house. Drieu La Rochelle, who had acquired stock in the firm, wanted to leave. He had felt mistreated since 1936, persuaded that his fascist opinions were being held against him, that he was being discriminated against because he was not on the Left, like all the others, that Gallimard showed little enthusiasm in promoting his books. When the time came to sign the contract for his big novel *Gilles*, he balked. He would go elsewhere, probably to Grasset, but he could not leave without paying his overdraft of 45,000 francs. Gaston tried reasoning with him: he appealed to his sentiments, pointed out that leaving would amount to blaming the entire firm, which would cause it harm and be all the more unjust in that Gaston had always believed fully in the future of his literary oeuvre. Alternately diplomatic and hard, Gaston explained that one simply did not do such a thing just when the tree was about to bear its ripest fruit. It would be an insult to his profession

Gaston Gallimard at the turn of the century.
(D.R.)

Gaston at the beginning of the 1930s.
(Roger-Viollet)

André Gide seated and, from left to right, Jean Schlumberger, Jacques Rivière, and Roger Martin du Gard at the "Entretiens de Pontigny" (Pontigny Conversations) in 1922.
(*Archives de Pontigny-Cerisy*)

The Gallimard brothers in their office: Raymond, left, and Gaston.
(Roger-Viollet)

Robert Denoël.
(D.R.)

Bernard Grasset.
(D.R.)

Jean Paulhan, editor.
(Roger-Viollet)

Gaston and his nephew Michel Gallimard,
with friends at Cannes, 1942.
(D.R.)

Bernard Grasset between his lawyers during his trial.
(Agence France-Presse)

Gaston in the late 1950s.
(René Saint-Paul)

Louis-Daniel Hirsch, right, general manager of the Editions
Gallimard, with Bernard Pivot of *Le Figaro littéraire*.
(D.R.)

A Gallimard cocktail party at Rue Sébastien-Bottin. In the
foreground, Marcel Arland, left, and Jean Paulhan, back to camera.
(René Saint-Paul)

Gaston with Albert Camus shortly before the latter's death.
(René Saint-Paul)

Gaston with Paul Léautaud, left.
(René Saint-Paul)

Gaston with Marcel Jouhandeau.
(René Saint-Paul)

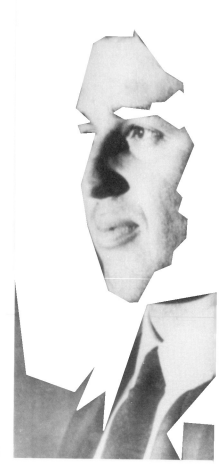

The Gallimard dynasty: right to left, Gaston,
Claude, and Christian.
(Lelièvre)

Gaston in his later years.
(René Saint-Paul)

as a publisher. And he pointed out, not unreasonably, with his particular gift for the telling phrase:

"When advances of 80,000 francs are made to a writer with your kind of sales, they are not advances, but loans."[15]

It would not be enough to reimburse the advance. An author could not be quits with his publisher by just closing out his debit account. The debt could not be expressed in figures. Drieu threw in the towel. He stayed on and signed the contract. Gaston had won again.

With Marcel Jouhandeau the falling-out took on another dimension. It was not a matter of money: Gaston wanted him to tone down his political extremism. There were, after all, limits to what a person could decently publish—limits that the editorial board did not have to spell out, since they were obvious. Robert Denoël might very well publish *L'École des cadavres* (The School for Corpses), feeling that Céline was in line with the French pamphleteering tradition and that if he turned him down, rival publishers would rush to take over the star author.[16] (However, it should be pointed out that in September 1941, in an article in *Le Cahier jaune*, Denoël would state that Céline's three anti-Semitic pamphlets contained "the essential teaching" and that "if we want to bring France back to its feet, this is where we will find wise advice, useful reflections, and the proper method. It's all there. You have only to help yourself.")

The *NRF* finally printed what ought to be said of such a work:

"This garbage is sometimes magnificent and most often ignoble, but it is beyond the scope of criticism."[17]

So Gallimard was happy to publish Jouhandeau's *Chroniques maritales* (Marital Chronicles) and *Le Jardin de Cordoue* (The Cordova Garden), but when it came to *Le Péril juif* (The Jewish Peril), the author would have to go elsewhere—to Sorlot, for instance. Jouhandeau did not hide his disappointment:

> The profession of anti-Semitic faith I made in October 1936 meant the voluntary abandonment of all my friendships and the acquiring of an incalculable number of enemies, and I received nothing whatsoever in

return. Against Jews, I remain and wish to remain alone. . . . From my friends of the *NRF*, for which I had been writing for seventeen years, I might have expected a little consideration, a little respect: that, in honor of what I believed to be true, right, and equitable, I turned away from those who, having become our masters, might have advanced my interests. . . . Moreover, by declaring war on the Jews, I gave up literature itself: I withdrew from the presses of Gaston Gallimard—who can attest to it—two books that were ready for publication, to mention only those, as I did not wish to weaken my manifesto by publishing a single line that was alien to it.[18]

In moments like those Gaston, the uncompromising enemy of political passion, took refuge more than ever in literature, genuine literature, the kind that kills no one and gets no one killed. He found his consolation, in the year of the Munich pact, in publishing Jacques Audiberti's *Abraxas* and especially the books of Marcel Aymé: *Gustalin, Derrière chez Martin* (Behind Martin's), *Les Contes du Chat perché* (*The Wonderful Farm*). Aymé was the kind of writer he liked: ever since his second novel in 1927, *Aller retour* (Round Trip), Aymé had published on the average a book a year with Gallimard. His work, full of fantasy, satirical spirit, and a rural and provincial atmosphere, infinitely diverting (in the nonpejorative sense of that term), met with great public approval, as evidenced by the best-selling *La Jument verte* (*The Green Mare*) in 1933. Gaston put more and more stock in the short-term success of such books as the future looked darker and darker. There was nothing scientific in this; nor did it mean that he favored only noncerebral literature.

Among his new writers there was the thirty-two-year-old Jean-Paul Sartre, whose manuscript he accepted only because his hand had been forced. For two years the young philosopher had been trying to breach the doors of the *NRF*. Through his friend and fellow alumnus of the Ecole Normale Supérieure, Paul Nizan, who already had a novel published by Gallimard, *Le Cheval de Troie (The Trojan Horse)*, Sartre got the manuscript of *La Légende de la vérité* (The Legend of Truth) submitted to Paulhan. It was rejected. He submitted another, *Melancholia*—rejected again. But he was not to be discouraged. This time he called upon his most highly placed contacts: Charles Dullin, the actor, Gaston's old friend from the Vieux-Colombier days, and Pierre Bost, novelist, contributor to the magazine and one of Gallimard's most respected reading editors. That did the trick. Sartre was summoned to Rue Sébastien-Bottin, where it was explained to him that there had been a misunderstanding—they had thought he was submitting his material to the magazine, not the publishing house—and he was assured that Gaston himself had read *Melancholia*, a first novel of undeniable quality of style and a very original plot. This time the editors who read the manuscript were, it seemed, impressed by its literary metaphysics, the attitudes and doubts of the hero, Antoine Roquentin, and especially by the new description of that intangible feeling, nausea, that gripped him and made his consciousness aware of his body. It was published, but Gaston didn't like its awful, sales-defeating title; without even asking, he rechristened it *La Nausée (Nausea)*, so much more obvious, easy to retain and to ask for in a bookstore. The reception of the book was promising, to the point that it was considered for the Renaudot. Gaston felt that it was now or never if he was to break Denoël's exclusive grip on that award. Everything encouraged his optimism. At the final preaward meeting of the judges, a clear majority seemed to favor young Sartre. To be ready for the event, one of the judges, the journalist Georges Charensol, took Sartre over to the studios of Radio Luxembourg a few days before the announcement was to be made, to record a brief message of gratitude for broadcast right after the event: "I am very happy to have been awarded the Renaudot Prize."[19]

Unfortunately, the voting did not go as planned. Several of the judges, leery of seeing the award go unanimously to Sartre, switched their votes without consulting one another. When they were all tallied, Sartre had been beaten out by Pierre-Jean Launay's *Léonie-la-bienheureuse* (Blessed Léonie)—published by Denoël, of course.

Deep disappointment, but no matter: Sartre was on his way. He was now part of the house. The reviews were encouraging, and

Gallimard was prepared to publish a second book, *Le Mur (The Wall)*, a collection of five stories in a neutral, spare, but effective style. So Sartre was established. He could now bring in other people's manuscripts, in the very first instance those of his companion Simone de Beauvoir. But the editorial board turned down *La Primauté du spirituel* (Primacy of the Spiritual), which it felt was poorly constructed. Sartre was more persistent than de Beauvoir and submitted it for her to Henry Muller at Grasset—with the same result. He would have to wait a while longer before his word was enough to force the acceptance of manuscripts.

Aymé and Audiberti, Sartre and Albert Cohen, all of them were fine, full of promise for the future, but even when reinforced by the battalions of heavy sellers, the Kessels and the Simenons, they were not enough to keep a firm afloat. Something more was needed. But where to find it?

Among the manuscripts under consideration, there was one that the editorial board did not think much of. They turned thumbs down on it. Yet Gaston liked it: the drama of the American South, during and after the Civil War, seen through the tumultuous and passionate relations of its two protagonists, Scarlett O'Hara, beautiful, selfish, and impetuous, and Rhett Butler, a totally charming rake. It was a rich story; the descriptions of the Georgia landscapes were unforgettable; and love, hate, and war were ever-present without being overbearing, thanks to the skill of the narrative. A novel of the kind they didn't dare write anymore.

However, there were problems about bringing the book out in French: it was very long and therefore expensive to translate, and the sales price would have to reflect that. Moreover the author, Margaret Mitchell, was thirty-eight years old, unknown in France, and this was her first book. Gaston did not want either to reject or to accept the manuscript. For months he thought about it, had it read and reread by those around him. He knew that his rival Stock—which as the leading publisher of translations had had first look—had rejected it. And Stock was not apt to make mistakes; they published the big hits from abroad. Remarque's *All Quiet on the Western*

Front and Louis Bromfield's *The Rains Came* were theirs. This expert firm was not taking *Gone with the Wind,* leaving it to others. Not a good sign. Yet the book was good. Perhaps Stock's reaction was just another of those things to be written off under "mysteries of publishing."

Jacques Chardonne, a writer who was also one of the main editors at Stock, insisted that critics and booksellers had nothing to do with the success of a book. Stock published forty foreign novels a year, of which two or three reached printings of 200,000 to 300,000 copies. The firm lived on those, they paid the freight; all the others fell flat. There were virtually no reviews, since critics did not discuss foreign books, and few review copies were sent out. So why did two or three books catch on and not the others? No one knew.[20]

The people at Stock could make mistakes despite—or because of—their great familiarity with English-language books. Weariness. The effect of repetition. Had it not been because of the number of manuscripts submitted by retired officers that the two main editors at Grasset, Henry Muller and André Fraigneau, groaned when they received *Au fil de l'épée (The Edge of the Sword)*—just another soldier voicing his opinion about the next war—and barely glanced through it before returning it to the sender, a certain Colonel de Gaulle?[21]

So what should be done about *Gone with the Wind*? Gaston wanted another opinon, so he gave it to Hirsch, his business manager, telling him that he was not crazy about its literary quality but thought it might sell. Hirsch read it, liked it, and gave it to his wife to read:

"It'll sell like Delly*," she predicted.

Hirsch, not wanting to offend his boss, rephrased this:

"It should sell more than a hundred thousand copies."

"Care to bet? A good meal, and not just any old place, eh?" Gaston replied.[22]

But that still was not enough to make him decide. The publishing department of Hachette finally acquired the rights to the book on the advice of a news syndicate man who knew American novels,

---

*A writer of cheap popular romances. —TRANS.

Paul Winkler. That settled it. Gaston still was not sure how he felt about the book. But when he heard that Margaret Mitchell had won the Pulitzer Prize, that the sales of her novel in the United States were exceeding all expectations, that it would set a new record for the number of sales of foreign translation rights (including editions in Braille), and especially that a major Hollywood film studio was preparing a superproduction, which would star Vivien Leigh and Clark Gable, he had only one idea in his head: to get hold of the rights to the book and bring it out as soon as possible. Now he was sure: it would be a smash. But he had to find his opening. It came at a trade association meeting at the Cercle de la Librairie. Hearing Robert Meunier du Houssoy, the president of Hachette, bemoan the high cost of translating the book and its inordinate size, Raymond Gallimard offered to take the property off his hands. A deal was quickly struck, at a very reasonable price, and *Gone with the Wind* was published by Gallimard in 1939. It went on to sell over 16 million copies worldwide, including 800,000 in the French edition.[23]

For once, the enthusiasm of French readers and reviewers coincided—an unhoped-for result. At Gallimard its like had not been seen in a long time. A glance at one of the then most influential political and literary periodicals, the right-wing *Je suis partout*, is illustrative. On March 10 Robert Brasillach* let his readers know:

> We will have more to say about this masterpiece, one of the most admirable novels, if not *the* most admirable novel, ever to appear in America. But for now we wish to alert you to this tender, romantic, and profound story of the Civil War . . .[24]

Louis-Daniel Hirsch and his boss had a fine luncheon together at a restaurant, and it was Gaston who picked up the tab.

---

*The well-known film historian shot after World War II as a prime Nazi collaborator.—TRANS.

6

Collaborate or Resist?

1939~1944

June of 1939 was drawing to an end. That Friday there was much excitement at Rue Sébastien-Bottin. And many people, for the editorial board had never had more members: Marcel Arland, Robert Aron, Rainer Biemel, Benjamin Crémieux, Bernard Groethuysen, Louis-Daniel Hirsch, Malraux with two of his friends, Emmanuel Boudot-Lamotte and Louis Chevasson, Albert Ollivier, Brice Parain, Jean Paulhan, Raymond Queneau (already the author of six novels), Maurice Sachs, and Pierre Seligman (who had once been one of Gaston's secretaries). Fifteen in all, not counting the three Gallimards: Gaston, his son, and his brother.

Naturally, all of them had friends and contacts. On cocktail party days such as this, there was not room enough to accommodate them all. Listening to these people talk, who could dream that catastrophe was on the horizon? And yet there were indications: Jean Giraudoux had just been named commissioner general for information by Premier Daladier. And soon there would be others.

In these hectic times the best source of information was the *Journal officiel*,* which offered no commentary, just the bare facts, the important, decisive ones. On August 26 it carried the news that President Albert Lebrun had signed a decree authorizing the seizure and suspension of publications detrimental to national defense. Not a good omen. The Communist dailies *Ce soir* and *L'Humanité* had been seized the day before, shortly after the signing of the German-Soviet pact in Moscow. On August 28 came another presidential decree concerning the control of the press and publications: from that day forward, all printed matter, as well as scripts of movies and radio broadcasts, had to be submitted for advance approval to the General Information Service, which was empowered to suppress them.

This was censorship, just as in wartime.

And September 1 brought general mobilization.

Generally speaking, the jurisdictional limits of the censorship coincided with the territorial limits of each of the country's military regions, except for Parisian publishers, whose books were printed in the neighboring departments of Seine-et-Oise and Seine-et-Marne: their censor had his offices on Rue Rouget-de-Lisle.[1]

At any rate, dealing with censors was now in the hands of some underling of the firm: Gaston and his entourage had left. Just before the declaration of war, he had received a phone call from his friend Giraudoux:

"It would be prudent for you to leave Paris."

Giraudoux was, after all, commissioner general for information: he had to know what he was talking about. Gaston had the more confidence in Giraudoux (who had always been a Grasset writer), in that he had just published for the first time one of his books, *Pleins Pouvoirs* (Unlimited Authority), a political essay much in the spirit of the times, about the danger threatening France: "vassaldom."

So as August passed into September, Gaston retreated to the properties he owned near Avranches, with a certain number of his

*The official daily record of all government actions.—TRANS.

associates: Jean Paulhan and his wife, Emmanuel Boudot-Lamotte and his sister Madeleine, who was Gaston's new secretary, Pierre Seligman, and Raymond Gallimard. One Friday at 1:00 P.M. a caravan of five cars, their trunks filled with hastily assembled files, manuscripts, and the *NRF* treasury, departed the Seventh Arrondissement for the department of La Manche, leaving only enough employees in the offices to take care of mail and phone calls. The Germans were still far away, but Gaston, even without the warning from Giraudoux, had decided to leave as early as possible, convinced that air raids on Paris and its environs were imminent.

So the center of gravity of the *NRF* moved from Saint-Germain-des-Prés to the region of Granville. The general staff of the *NRF*, or what was left of it, set up either at Mirande (near Sartilly) on the estate of Gaston's mother, or else close by at Bacilly, in a property under construction which he had recently acquired. Jacques Schiffrin, the head of the Pléiade, who had a home in the area, came by as a neighbor.

Mirande was a fine Norman villa surrounded by meadows where cows grazed and from which one could clearly see Mont-Saint-Michel, but Gaston found it boring. He was more restricted there than he had anticipated: by decision of the military authorities, the coastal departments—hence those on the Channel—had no telephone connections with the outside world. Gaston wrote many letters to Paris, trying to have his contacts—particularly one of his most highly placed friends, César Campinchi, the famous lawyer and deputy from Corsica who since April 1938 had been minister of the navy—arrange exceptions and privileges for him, so he could move about more easily. It was impossible to do anything worthwhile, anything interesting, so far from Paris. In the Norman woods Gaston felt useless. The magazine was coming out, sometimes late and with its contents a jumble, but out nevertheless. As for the publishing house, obviously it could not be run from a secondary residence.

February 27, 1940: at 6:00 P.M., Gaston was temporarily in Paris to preside over a special meeting of holders of charter shares in his

company. Its capital of 3,450,000 francs had just been raised by
150,000 francs. That money had been reinvested from the previous
year's surplus. In half an hour the meeting was over.

June 1940: the Germans in Paris, the armistice having been signed
at Rethondes. At Gallimard, as at the Foreign Office on Quai d'Orsay, papers were being burned: correspondence, documents that might
be embarrassing to certain authors—the plan for Malraux's expedition to free Trotsky, for example. As an unintentional final touch,
during the exodus to the South one of the trucks loaded with company files—the contract files, specifically—burned on a road in Tou-
raine.

As Gaston and the NRF withdrew from the Channel coast toward
the South, in Paris Brice Parain, vice president of the Librairie Gallimard corporation, took over the day-to-day management of the
publishing house: payroll disbursements, finishing production of books
already well along, and so on. Gaston left Mirande by car with his
wife Jeanne and drove across the France of the rout, that familiar
scene of overloaded baby carriages and fugitives on foot. He met up
with the Paulhans at Villalier (Aude) near Carcassonne in the south-
west, at the home of Joë Bousquet, the poet "whose life was paralyzed
by a bullet"—a bullet lodged in his spine since 1918, that had kept
him in bed in a room with closed shutters, where he devoted himself
exclusively to his work and correspondence.

There were twelve NRF "survivors," "Gallimard castaways,"[2]
who assembled at Bousquet's bedside: Gaston and Jeanne, Paulhan,
Germaine and her mother, Dupont the accountant, his wife and
daughter, two drivers, one woman employee, and Kyriak Stameroff,
manager of the warehouse. Gide was not far away, at Carcassonne.
Benda, Aragon, and others often dropped in on this improvised
branch office of the company. Young Pierre Seghers, the founder of
the magazine PC 39 (PC standing for "poètes casqués" [poets in
helmets]), met Gaston there for the first time. "They all looked like
lost souls," Seghers would remember,[3] especially Gaston, who had
no news of his son Claude, presumed to be a prisoner of war. Or

at least so Gaston hoped, as he refused to think of the worst; he suddenly seemed to have aged from the worry and the waiting.

What were they waiting for? How long? And which France was one to live in now: the free zone or the occupied? Gaston no longer knew. He met a great many authors; some, like Saint-Exupéry, turned manuscripts over to him, others discussed their works in progress, and most urged him to return to Paris and put the magazine and the publishing house back into full operation. Apart from any moral, ethical, or political considerations, proper functioning of the House of Gallimard meant, for them, the normal payment of salaries and royalties.

Gaston was undecided. He did not want to pursue his trade under the direct control of the Germans, as the local newspapers and the rumors coming down from Paris led him to believe he would have to.

"That's silly, but rather endearing," Paulhan commented.

"Endearing, mostly," added Paul Léautaud.[4]

Gaston hoped that the fall of 1940 would clarify the situation in Paris. Like many other Frenchmen he still felt himself on summer vacation, as if nothing had happened, which was understandable, at least in the free zone. He traveled about a great deal on the Mediterranean coast. At Cannes, where the company actually did have a branch, and Gaston had his own rooms at the Hôtel Cavendish, he took long boat trips with his nephew Michel on the eight-meter sailboat Michel's father had bought him. At Hyères Gaston became better acquainted with Father Bruckberger, whom he had been paying for some time to "edit" Bernanos for the NRF. In the long talks they had, the Dominican became convinced that Gaston had changed, that he had developed, and that his contacts with Saint-Exupéry had made him aware of the virtues of heroism. Another sign of the times: Gaston, the slacker of 1914–18, the "priest eater," made a strange request of Bruckberger:

"I wish you would write for me, just for me alone, a few pages explaining what priesthood means and purity. . . ."[5]

Still without news of his son, depressed by worry and doubt, Gaston felt less sure of himself than ever. He seemed thrown from the saddle. However he twisted and turned the dilemma, it came down to this: to let the Germans requisition his company and run it themselves, or to give them, as so many would soon urge him to do, an assurance of cooperation—in the form of himself running the publishing company while leaving the magazine to Drieu La Rochelle, a writer whose political views harmonized with those of the occupiers. As he told Bruckberger:

> The first solution would suit me better. I have enough money to retire to America and wait for the end of the war there; my paper supply is such that I would make more selling it by weight than turning it into books. But have I the right to abandon what I am still allowed to defend? Not to mention the fact that I have to go on giving my writers the chance to be published. And I know only too well what could be done by publishing only carefully selected passages from Péguy and Proust, for example, to mention only dead writers—the twisting of great works to achieve anti-French ends. With me there, that could not happen. The magazine, true, would be in the hands of Drieu La Rochelle, but then Drieu alone, not I, would be responsible for it. And they could find someone who was worse than he.[6]

To whom should he listen? The few who advised him to remain aloof, appealing to his conscience as a publisher, a man who had made a pact with the mind, as he had often said, and who on that score had a moral, political, and intellectual responsibility that put him on a different plane from just another business executive? Or the many who wanted everything to go back to the way it used to be, especially the money machine? And how could one turn a deaf ear to Schlumberger's argument: that those who remained in Alsace after 1870 had been more effective in preserving the French ways in that German-annexed province than those who had emigrated elsewhere in France?

As Gaston vacillated, one thing continued to influence him, out of professional habit: the attitude of his competitors.

Robert Denoël was resuming his activities. Mustered out of the Belgian army, he had returned to Paris with only one idea in mind:

to reopen his firm. It did not take him long to get the Germans to remove the padlock they had clamped on his place on Rue Amélie, where he hâd published so many anti-Nazi books before the war. He was trying in every way to find additional capital. For the past three years he had been without his partner Bernard Steele, who had refused to countenance publishing Céline's anti-Semitic pamphlets; Denoël had bought Steele out and then appealed in vain to various people to buy in—but not to other publishers, and especially not to Gallimard, as had been suggested to him. Denoël could see no way whatever to work for Gallimard.[7]

Evidently no problem of conscience kept Denoël or those in charge at Stock, or almost all the other Parisian publishers from reopening their doors, no matter under what conditions. There was only one exception: Emile-Paul frères. As early as August 1940 the brothers had made their Rue de l'Abbaye office into a "letter drop" from which Jean Cassou, Marcel Abraham, and Claude Aveline incautiously put out leaflets signed "The Free French of France" and later "Friends of Alain-Fournier," in memory of the author of *The Wanderer*, the book that had long been the firm's proudest publication. Almost immediately this improvised group merged with another at the Musée de l'Homme, which used the publishing house as depository for their bulletin, an arrangement that functioned over four years.[8]

From the beginning of August on, French publishers knew approximately where they stood. On August 3 Otto Abetz, the German ambassador to France, settled the matter of cultural policy for France with Hitler at his headquarters in the Berghof near Berchtesgaden in Bavaria. The diplomat was disturbed by the efforts of some of the German services to deal with the Parisian intelligentsia with a rigid, heavy hand, a method he considered counterproductive. The Führer drew the line:

Germans have a pedantic way of wanting to mix into everything. The censorship services of the army high command must restrict themselves to making sure that nothing in the press, on the radio, or in books, films, or theater politically energizes the French public or imperils the security of the army of occupation.[9]

But the vagueness of the statement encouraged a clash between different groups of the occupation. Nevertheless, on August 5 a note was sent by the Propaganda Command to the trade association of publishers, booksellers, and distributors forbidding the sale of works by German émigrés (Thomas Mann and the like) or books dealing with the Führer, the Duce, or their régimes. Bookstores were ordered to return to the publishers their stocks of such materials, or to junk them themselves. Three weeks later, with lists in hand, various German police detachments raided bookstores to seize copies of the proscribed works.[10] That was a foretaste.

Willy-nilly the publishers accepted, when indeed they did not welcome, such "purging." What about Grasset? Grasset was the one Gaston worried about most when he thought of his competitors' attitudes. The publisher on Rue des Saints-Pères had been extremely active since the armistice. This was no bolt from the blue to him, nor was he discouraged or conscience-stricken. On July 13 Grasset sent a memorandum to Minister François Pietri, pointing out that he had been the "leader of the movement against the Zay Bill." He asked for an appointment by Vichy as its negotiator and delegate for all matters concerning publishing. His stated goal: "To unify the regulation of all writings in France by dispensing with the fiction of the existence of two different zones."

From Nontron, a subprefecture in Dordogne where during the débâcle he had taken refuge with a few associates, most of his financial records, and some valuable manuscripts, Grasset offered his services and carried on a voluminous correspondence. Too impatient to wait for Vichy to come to him, he went directly to the spa where Marshal Pétain's government had been set up. Like so many others coming from who knows where, he patrolled the corridors of the main hotels, the restaurants, and the cafés, trying to find some of the highly placed personalities he had known before the war, who might be in a position to hasten his appointment. From his room at the Hôtel National, Grasset wrote to his friend Friedrich Sieburg, asking the famous German journalist, whose sensational *Dieu est-il français?* (Is God French?) he had published a decade earlier, for a helping hand. Perhaps Sieburg, taking advantage of the stay in Paris of Pierre Laval, now vice premier of the new French government, could bring pressure on the latter and get other important Germans to do the same. The program offered by Grasset as potential commissar for publishing was simple, at least as expressed in his letter to Sieburg: French publishers must consent to the censorship of the occupiers voluntarily, without orders or regulations. That would provide the basis for a future "statute of French publishing acceptable at the very least to all true Frenchmen."[11]

Grasset's strategy worked. On August 4 he was able to write Hamonic, his Paris representative, that Laval had granted him an audience the previous evening and officially put him in charge of representing publishers in their negotiations with the Germans. All that remained was the approval by the occupying authority. But there Grasset felt a bit less sure of himself. Not that his political ideas were "out of line"; but he feared that his having published Otto Strasser's polemical *Hitler et moi (Hitler and I)* in 1940 might be held against him. To have this "error" overlooked, he suggested that his Paris man point to the other aspects of his output: the four Sieburg books, of course, but also *France-Allemagne* (France-Germany) in 1934 and *La Gerbe des forces* (The Sheaf of Powers) in 1937, whose respective authors, Fernand de Brinon and Alphonse de Chateaubriant, were fervent collaborationists, as well as Hitler's own *Principes d'action* (Principles of Action) in 1936.[12]

But it was especially in a book of his own, written in September 1941 and published in December, that Grasset revealed the substance of his thought. The departure of the occupiers was not a primary concern. If that were to happen, "the worst could then be anticipated in France. In the first instance, Pétain would be exiled. I wonder whether there is a single Frenchman who wishes that," he wrote in *A la recherche de la France* (In Search of France), which was subtitled *Notes à leur date* (Notes at Their Dates). It was a clear, categorical appeal that Grasset addressed to his fellow publishers: to leave the free zone and come back to work in Paris. "For my part, I am determined to assume as large a place in all things French as I am permitted to. I mean that I will submit to the occupying authorities texts that are the most French in inspiration and manner. Whether by me or by others. I shall recognize no limits other than those imposed upon me." In the mind of Bernard Grasset a French publisher could exist nowhere but in Paris; one would have to be not "a true Frenchman," or to dread one's former compromising links with the old regime, to remain outside the occupied zone. He took umbrage at the fact that Montherlant planned to spend the winter in Nice, "when it is only here that he can play his part, and that part can be great."

True to himself, Grasset at least had the virtue of being unambiguous. His apologia for collaboration did not beat around the bush, and he took total responsibility for his propaganda on behalf of the new order: "Once and for all the French remaining in the free zone must understand that the occupier respects everything that is respectable. In Paris it is possible to be entirely French and to carry on one's trade with honor."

Honor?

One might wonder at what level to look for that honor when, as early as September, publishers were bending to the demands of the Germans if not indeed anticipating them. The occupiers were shrewd: rather than censor the books, they got the publishers themselves to censor them—according to the principles and laws of the new National Socialist Europe. This was the system used in prisons supervised by select prisoners, in the concentration camps run by Kapos. A publisher who was undecided could still have manuscripts read by the censor, who would tell the publisher what he was to think of them. The complement of this self-censorship was the allotment of paper supplies. Publishers were under the jackboot.

Reading the censorship agreement, one is confounded at the alacrity with which French publishers, almost to a man, decided to collaborate, even before the Montoire interview had taken place and before the Hitler-Pétain handshake had graced the front pages of all the papers.

Warning

The association of French publishers has just signed an agreement with the occupation authorities. The text appears below. The publisher hereby knows the limits within which he can exercise his activity, free of any administrative hindrance. By signing this agreement, the German authorities have expressed their confidence in Publishing. The publishers, for their part, have the aim of allowing French thought to pursue its mission, while respecting the rights of the victor. They hope they have succeeded therein.

In the application of this censorship agreement, the German authorities are publishing a first list, known as the "Otto List," of works withdrawn from sale either by their decision or on the publishers' own initiative. Other lists may follow, inspired by the spirit of this agreement. An impartial examination of the Otto List shows a large number of foreign authors who have found asylum on our French territory, whose works have begun to overcrowd our domain. French thought has reached so high a point in the history of the world that we need have no fear. Thus purged, it will express itself in its fullness and carry on its expansion.

Agreement on the Censorship of Books (New and Reprints)

In order to organize a coexistence without difficulties between the German army of occupation and the French population and, beyond that, to establish normal relations between the German and French peoples, French publishers assume the responsibility for organizing production in conformity with these intentions. With that aim in mind, between the head of the German military administration in France and the president of the publishers' trade association it has been agreed as follows:

I Each French publisher is fully responsible for his own output. Therefore the publisher must make sure that the works published by him:

a) Can neither openly nor surreptitiously in any way whatsoever damage German prestige or interests.

b) Are not the work of any author whose works are banned in Germany.

II When the publisher cannot on his own initiative make a decision according to clause a) of paragraph I above, the publishers' trade association will take charge of prior censorship. The decision of the publishers' trade association may take one of the following forms:

a) The trade association sees nothing objectionable. It takes the responsibility of authorizing the publication.

b) The trade association has objections. The work is therefore to be submitted, with the critical passages marked, to the Propaganda Staffel* at 52 Champs-Elysées.

c) The publishers' trade association does not feel competent to make a decision or authorize publication. The work in question will be sent for examination to the Propaganda Staffel, Publications Section (Gruppe Schrifttum), at 52 Champs-Elysées.

III The works coming under clauses b) and c) of paragraph II as well as those examined on its own initiative by the Propaganda Staffel are censored in the name of the German military administration in France by the Propaganda Staffel.

IV By reason of the primal importance of intellectual production to the establishment of relations between the German and French peoples, any violation of the above regulations will be subject to appropriate sanctions against whoever (publisher or trade association) assumed responsibility for the publication.

V It is expressly stated that the responsibility lies with the publisher and not with the printer of the book.

In application of the directives enumerated above, an action has been undertaken to eliminate undesirable works. French publishers commit themselves to reexamining with all possible care their catalogues and stocks, including such stocks as may be held by printers or binders. Works to be suppressed as a result of such reexamination are to be delivered, along with a list of them, to the Propaganda Staffel.

*Detachment in charge of propagating the Nazi ideology.

French publishers are obligated to transmit to the Propaganda Staffel (Publications Section, Gruppe Schrifttum) two copies as file copies of all their reprints and new publications.[13]

It is all there, in overwhelming condemnation; no need to read between the lines. Three months after the armistice and three weeks after the official recognition of political collaboration at Montoire, the president of the French publishers' trade association, in their name, cosigned this document on September 28. At the same time the first Otto List—probably so named for the German ambassador, Otto Abetz—was circulated, and few publishers escaped it. As the preamble states, the main aim was to withdraw from bookstores and sale any books "which by their lying and tendentious spirit have systematically poisoned French public opinion—in particular, the publications of political refugees or Jewish writers who, betraying the hospitality France has accorded them, unscrupulously push for a war by which they hope to further their selfish ends."[14]

It was a long list. In the *NRF*-Gallimard column there were about a hundred names with an average of two works per author. Among the foreigners were Chesterton, Ciliga, Churchill, Alfred Döblin, Freud, Magnus Hirschfeld, Irmgard Keun, Emil Ludwig, Thomas and Heinrich Mann, Walther Rathenau. Among the French were Malraux, Denis de Rougemont, Daniel Guérin, Paul Nizan, Jacques Rivière, Claudel, as well as a number of Jewish writers: Benda, Fleg, Georges Friedmann, Robert Aron, André Maurois.

In the absence of Gaston, Brice Parain was in charge of everyday business and thus of relations with the Germans, "which consisted exclusively in carrying out the orders resulting from the drafting of the Otto List, with natural concern for minimizing their effects."[15]

On October 22 Gaston came back to Paris for good. That was where he belonged, not on the Riviera. All the publishers were working, preparing their lists for the beginning of 1941. It was time for Gallimard to get back into the swing. Censorship agreement? Otto List? Statute on Jews? Well, this was war. All the companies had resumed operation, teachers were teaching, civil servants were serving civilly, doctors were practicing. People had to live, they all said. But what about that memorable "pact with the mind" that Gaston claimed separated him from other businessmen—him, the "publisher of Léon Blum and Léon Daudet"? In such troubled times the publisher's responsibility could be measured by the yardstick of the paper allotment: to get paper, one had to go by way of the Germans, their demands and desiderata. So be it: collaboration it had to be.

From the minute he got back to Paris, Gaston understood that it would not be an easy game, that he would have to be more of a negotiator than ever and have recourse, even more than in the old days, to the double-talk people so often accused him of. Shortly before he got there (October 10, 1940), one of the most hateful of the collaborationist papers, *Au pilori* (To the Pillory), published an article by one Paul Riche[16] which certainly did not augur well:

> . . . a gang of malefactors has operated in French literature from 1909 to 1939 under the orders of a gang leader: Gallimard. Thirty years of underhanded propaganda in favor of anarchy, of revolutionaries of every stripe, of "antis": antifascists, antinationalists, anti-anything. Thirty years of literary, mental, and human nihilism! Gallimard and his gang created a distinguished hoodlumocracy.
>
> Corydon-Gide, Breton the seller of ectoplasms, Aragon the archbishop of *Ce soir*, Naville the anarchist banker, Eluard the rotten fruit, Péret the insulter, and all the other monomaniacs, narcotomaniacs, and hospital fodder, that was the Gallimard team of twenty years ago. It made progress. The Surrealists, pacifists, Trotskyites, and their friends carried the firebrand of revolution everywhere. Cassou-Gallimard helped Jean Zay in 1936 in his job as national educator, Malraux-Gallimard helped the Spanish Reds string their necklaces of severed ears, Jules Romains-Gallimard distilled humanitarian poison in the deep river of his propaganda novels. . . .
>
> Now Gallimard wants back! Already, the Gallimard Negroes,* Negroids, and Negrophiles are at the Deux-Magots waiting for their next thirty pieces of silver. . . . Gallimard, murderer of the mind! Gal-

---

*The standard French term for hack writers or ghost writers.—TRANS.

limard, bringer of rot! Gallimard, chief malefactor! French youth vomits you up!

The tone was set. But the vehemence and source of this article do not clear Gaston Gallimard of responsibility for his present or future activities. It must be understood that on many occasions *Au pilori* took a position far to the right of the occupiers and looked upon the Vichy régime as too soft, too liberal, too ready to hold a hand out to the enemy. A hostile article in such a publication would never constitute proof of one's belonging to the Resistance.

Ambassador Abetz allegedly made a statement that became as famous as it was impossible to verify:

"There are three powers in France: Communism, the big banks, and the *NRF*."

With time, the quote would change in its components, but the *NRF* remained in every version. In the eyes of those in charge at the Propaganda Division (Propaganda Abteilung, part of the Wehrmacht), the German Institute (run by the embassy), and Berlin's "observers" of French intellectual life (such as Friedrich Sieburg), the House of Gallimard was anti-German and Judeo-Bolshevistic by definition.[17] That being the case, it would seem a matter of course that on the morning of November 9 the doors at 5 Rue Sébastien-Bottin were officially sealed shut. But it did not last. That action had been undertaken by the military authorities, and it reflected the rivalry among the various German services administering literature and publishing. During the month of November Gaston went repeatedly to the Propaganda Staffel to try to regain possession of his premises. Regularly, Sonderführer Kaiser threw his "anti-Nazi attitude and Judaization" up to him, quoting specially selected parts of his catalogue and running through the list of his associates and the members of his editorial board. Gaston had only one thing in mind: to get his company back as quickly as possible, for at the time he was one of the Parisian publishers who held a large supply of paper. On the other hand, he could not quite see what the Germans were after. On November 23 it all became clear. The Sonderführer suggested that Gaston take on a German bookseller-publisher as the commissar in his firm and turn over 51 percent of the shares of Librairie Gallimard to the Germans. Gaston said no—out of the question. He balked. He wouldn't put up even with a Frenchman, and a German in such a role would be altogether out of the question. Impasse. Gaston squirmed out of it by negotiating with Counsellor Rahn about the magazine. Finally Gallimard and Rahn agreed that the *NRF* magazine would be edited for five years by Drieu La Rochelle, who would moreover have "extensive powers over the whole intellectual and political production" of the firm. This arrangement was acceptable to the Germans, who agreed to tie the fate of the publishing house to that of the magazine, the presence of Drieu at the helm representing for them a guarantee that "your publishing in its overall aspects will refrain from anything hostile to Germany, but will on the contrary make a precious contribution to the new idea of the political coordination of Europe, the construction of France, and the collaboration between Germany and France."[18] For the German propaganda services this was a happy conclusion; they were not trying to take over the Gallimard company, only making sure that it would supply "a product corresponding to the spirit of our times and the task of the future."

The matter was closed: Gaston could get his premises back. Shortly afterward, a gray frontwheel-drive car drove up in front of 5 Rue Sébastien-Bottin. Two German officers got out. One was a captain of the Feldpolizei (military police) who in civilian life was a French teacher, the other—Gerhard Heller, a lieutenant of the Propaganda Staffel in charge of book censorship. As one removed the seals from the locks, the other unlocked the doors of the silent, empty building. When they reached the second floor, Heller sat down at Jean Paulhan's desk and phoned:

"Monsieur Drieu La Rochelle? I am at Rue Sébastien-Bottin. The building is open, everything is in order. Please be good enough to advise M. Gallimard; he will receive the official notice in writing tomorrow or the next day."[19]

The building was open, the business could go on as before, and the magazine reappear after a five-month interruption—thanks to Drieu. He was the pledge and the alibi, the ideal fascist, the indispensable collaborator. With Drieu editor-manager of the NRF, publishing went back to normal. Rarely had the operation of magazine and books been so closely intertwined. In December 1940 this was a patent truth; in September 1944 every effort would be made to disguise it.

"He did it for the sake of Gaston and the whole company," Brice Parain was later to say.[20]

The table of contents of the first issue of Drieu's NRF, dated December 1, 1940, was well stocked as usual: Drieu of course, Jouhandeau, Péguy, Audiberti, Aymé, Giono, Fabre-Luce, Morand, Fernandez, Alain. With a copy in his pocket, Gaston set about trying to convince the dispersed writers to contribute their pieces to this new NRF from which Paulhan was officially absent. He lobbied, he double-talked. To Léautaud, he alleged that Drieu and the Germans had made the arrangement behind his back; that he was forced to put up with a situation beyond his control. He did not come right out and say so but suggested, in his own way, that they had done it without consulting him.[21] To Gide, whom he went to see on the Riviera, he explained that the reappearance of the NRF had to be understood as an act of resistance and not a promise of collaboration. When he left, his last words remained etched in the writer's memory, for they clearly reflected Gaston's determination and state of mind in that December of 1940:

"Paris is the only place to be."[22]

It was in Paris and not in the free zone that the short-term future was being worked out. Everything was decided there. Action was swift in all sectors. At the publishers' trade association, the greatest fear was what was considered unfair competition: namely, from the free-zone publishers. As early as the end of October, René Philippon, comanager of Les Editions Armand Colin and president of the trade association, went with Grasset, who headed the association's general literature section, to the office of Dr. Kaiser to discuss the opening of the free zone to Parisian publishers. Grasset found it unacceptable that their competitors in the other zone should enjoy advantages that they themselves lacked: lower production costs, absence of censorship, and the ability to circulate their books through all of France despite the regulations.

For once the association was right and farsighted: one of the main features of literary life and therefore of publishing under the Occupation, apart from the amazing zeal of writers to produce, was to be the decentralization of magazine and book publication. The center of gravity shifted from Paris to Algiers (Editions Charlot, Max-Pol Fouchet's magazine *Fontaine, L'Arche, La Nef*), Lyons (René Tavernier's *Confluences*), Villeneuve-lès-Avignon (Pierre Seghers's *Poésie 40*), London *(La France libre)*, New York (Editions de la Maison Française and the books published by Jacques Schiffrin), Switzerland (*Les Cahiers du Rhône* with Albert Béguin, and Les Editions de la Baconnière), and Argentina (Roger Caillois's *Les Lettres françaises*).

For the association, this was unfair competition. Nor did it take the Germans long to convey to French publishers their idea of collaboration. Several times a week the heads of the association were summoned to the Propaganda Staffel, most often to be reprimanded on matters that seem slight when compared to the Otto List and the censorship agreement. One day the Germans complained of having found in the boxes of the second-hand dealers along the Seine quays books signed by Jews or Communist sympathizers, or of having discovered, during a routine inspection, that the bookshops around the Hôtel Majestic (where the Germans had their offices) were putting translations from the English into their windows as if in defiance of the occupiers. Another day some German officers severely chastised the representatives of the association and the booksellers because of illustrated books which ridiculed the German Army of 1870 or 1914:

"For instance," one of them said, "the cathedral of Rheims may be shown in flames, provided the picture is not accompanied by a caption indicating that this situation resulted from German bombardments."[23]

Obviously there were no such problems in the free zone. However, it would be wrong to conclude that Parisian publishers submitted passively to the occupier's yoke. They rushed to meet it halfway. As early as the end of November, Grasset, in a circular, called on booksellers to help give the best possible display to the new collection he was launching, starting with a book he himself had written, which also lent its name to the collection, A la recherche de la France (In Search of France). Announcing the names of the authors who agreed to appear in it—Jacques Chardonne, Bernard Faÿ, Alphonse de Chateaubriant, Drieu La Rochelle, Paul Morand, Abel Bonnard—he specified the sole object of the collection: "French order independent of any question of external politics."[24] That was vague enough, yet sufficiently precise to indicate the path it had chosen: the one that Vichy and the Propaganda Abteilung had laid out.

A sign of the times: much turnover in the personnel of publishing houses. In the corridors people's paths crossed, some leaving as others moved in. At Gallimard the Jewish Statute expelled some of the key elements from the firm: Robert Aron, but especially Hirsch and Crémieux. Having taken refuge with his wife at a farm near Saint-Flour in Auvergne since June, the business manager of Les Editions Gallimard was raising sheep. Crémieux, for his part, was in Provence after being mustered out of the armed forces. With nothing to do, he still tried to work on preparing a *Dante*, which he hoped to deliver to Gallimard, "if he can publish it," as he wrote to his friend Pierre Brisson, concluding, "I might emigrate to the United States or to Argentina, but the soil of France sticks to my feet."[25] He was to die at Buchenwald in 1944.

February 21, 1941. Paris, 3:00 P.M., in the meeting rooms of the Cercle de la Librairie building, on Boulevard Saint-Germain. After lauding Pétain, "who gave a rebirth to hope and proved that the honor of France remained intact and erect," and the heads of the Propaganda Division "who have shown toward us a breadth of view affording us significant facilities," President Philippon reminded his listeners:

"Last September the twenty-eighth a censorship agreement was signed, representing the keystone of the edifice of collaboration we are building, thus marking our will to proceed on the path the Chief of State traced for us a short time later, after the Montoire meeting."[26]

Nothing could be clearer. The trade was collaborating fully. The bookseller-publishers who resigned from the association, and those who went underground (such as Les Editions de Minuit) or stayed where they were while ignoring the Otto List and the censors and therefore publishing less for want of paper (as in the case of the brothers Emile-Paul), were the few exceptions who confirmed the rule.

At the start of the year the occupiers began preparing a catalogue to alert French readers to the works—of propaganda, of course—they were to read. "For the first time we were able to convince the largest French publishers that public advertising in favor of collaboration must be attached to the names of their firms," revealed a report of the Propaganda Staffel. *Miroir des livres* (Mirror of Books) was the title of this catalogue, the fruit of the unnatural marriage between the Third Reich propaganda machine and the seven largest French publishers—Gallimard, Grasset, Plon, Flammarion, Stock, Denoël, Payot—as well as seven smaller ones: Baudinière, Boivin, Corrêa, CEP, Editions de France, Le Livre moderne, and Renard.[27]

Only a catalogue, one might say, but full of promise. One must look elsewhere for the roots of this collaboration. An article in the magazine of the German Institute summarized the main reproaches, directives, orders, and advice of the occupiers to French publishers. Entitled "Echanges intellectuels et collaboration dans l'édition" (Intellectual Exchanges and Collaboration in Publishing), it came out in reaction to another article in the same publication in December 1940 signed by Grasset. Written by Karl Rauch, a Düsseldorf publisher and the head of Rauch Verlag, it pointed out that the Reich's propagandists did not mean to impose upon the French intelligentsia—and therefore in the first instance on publishers, who were the vehicles of French thought—a foreign culture or imported traditions. The failure of French nationalism between the wars, Rauch said, could be attributed to "the international spirit such as not long ago presided over literary exchanges—in large part of Jewish origin, as Bernard Grasset has also pointed out—which twisted the appearances of publishing, erased its characteristics, compromised the possibility of literary collaboration, and did the utmost harm to the peoples." For Rauch, French publishing between 1930 and 1940 committed a deadly error, the consequences of which were still being felt: it had welcomed and circulated "émigré literature," that is, the works of Thomas Mann and Stefan Zweig, Alfred Döblin and Erich Maria Remarque. He even tried to apportion the share of blame of the French publishers and these anti-Nazi writers for the defeat of June 1940.

Asserting that French publishers had not finished paying for the consequences of this gross error of judgment whereby they honored the "bad" Germans at the expense of the "good," Rauch felt that, while their fellows on the other side of the Rhine might also have made mistakes, they had at least always disseminated the best of French literature, that part of it containing "the wholesome and positive strengths issuing from the French soil": Raymonde Vincent, Jean de La Varende, Saint-Exupéry, Marcel Arland, and Robert Brasillach. For the numerous German translations of these authors, how many French translations were there of Hans Grimm or Ernst Jünger? That was the basis of the problem, the first step in the process which, according to the cultural policy of the Third Reich, would allow French publishing to add its voice to the great concert of National Socialist Europe. "France will have to make up the several years it has fallen behind," he insisted, hoping that the paucity of exchanges in the area of translations during the period between the wars would become only a bad memory.[28]

The message was quickly and clearly received by those addressed. Various circulars were distributed to French publishers, requiring them to publish German classics, and sometimes books much less than classical. Advised by Bernard Groethuysen, who knew the field thoroughly, during the war Gallimard published a certain number of translations from the German, in full accord with the wishes of the occupiers, beginning with Goethe, the classic par excellence, less read and less well known in France than Thomas Mann, to the dissatisfaction of Berlin. Given the strategy of the occupiers, it was much more important to distribute the works of Goethe than those of any National Socialist ideologue. As Abel Hermant of the French Academy would write: "Goethe on the German side is the one in whom the spirit of collaboration has been truly embodied." From one century to the next, the author of *Faust* was brought back for the cause of Greater Germany, the cause of the purest German spirit.

From 1941 to 1943 Gallimard published Goethe's *Gespräche mit Eckermann (Conversations with Eckermann)*, his correspondence with Bettina von Arnim, *Iphigenie auf Tauris (Iphigenia in Tauris)*, *Maximem und Reflexionen (Maxims and Reflections)*, and especially his complete dramas in the Pléiade edition, with a preface by André Gide. At the same time Groethuysen, Parain, and Gaston located half a dozen extremely varied titles which, after a volume of Meister Eckhart's treatises and sermons, would all appear during 1943: Theodor Fontane's *Frau Jenny Treibel*, Richard Wagner's *Correspondence* with Minna Wagner and Franz Liszt, Karl Hampe's *Das Hochmittelalter* (The High Middle Ages), Walter Elze's *Friedrich der Grosse* (Frederick the Great), Carl Rothe's *Die Zinnsoldaten* (The Toy Soldiers), and E. T. A. Hoffmann's *Kater Murr*. A few of these titles corresponded exactly to the wishes of the Propaganda Staffel; others were considered a lesser evil, less dishonorable than some published by Grasset or Sorlot. Gallimard also published a few works, the scientific character of which probably escaped more than one reader in those dark years, as for example, Herman Lommel's *Die alten Arier* (The Ancient Aryans), whose introduction leaves little doubt about the author's intentions:

> We are becoming deeply conscious of the origin and character of our people and of its rank within humanity. But we must also, especially if we wish to take for ourselves the name of Aryans, become conscious of what connects us to these ancient Aryans and understand their spiritual character. And that consciousness of our being (as it was formed by historical evolution and biological heredity), that feeling which is racial consciousness, coincides with the renewal of the moral sciences.

Lommel goes on to interpret the Vedas and Upanishads, Schopenhauer and the Sacred Cow, to explain and justify the future of the said Aryan race.

On the initiative of Karl Epting, the Francophile director of the German Institute, and in concert with the French publishers, a "Matthew List" was established: it included some one thousand titles of German works to be translated and published in French, to make up for the "errors" of the 1930s and render the Germans (if not the Nazis) acceptable and attractive to the French public.[29] The results of this aspect of Franco-German collaboration were not slow in being felt, for in 1943 the journalist Georges Blond wrote glowingly of it, saying that 250 German books had been translated since the armistice. He pointed with praise to the works of Goethe in the Pléiade edition and of Friedrich Sieburg at Grasset.[30]

In response to a German circular asking for clarification of his translation plans, Gaston made it clear that he differentiated between the contracts signed for books that he was translating to meet his obligations—Richard Benz, Georg Britting, Ludwig Klages—and those he was publishing because they appealed to his own taste. He said he was negotiating with the publisher of the philosopher Martin Heidegger for the latter's *Kant and the Problem of Metaphysics*, with that of Karl Jaspers for his *Nietzsche*, and with Braun Verlag of Karlsruhe, which owned the right to Wagner's correspondence with Ludwig II of Bavaria.[31]

But of all the German authors published by Gallimard during the Occupation, one had a special place: Ernst Jünger. As early as August 6, 1941, Gallimard bought the rights to four of his books from his Hamburg publisher. A hero of World War I, a nationalist but "in opposition" to the Nazis, officer Jünger had fought in the French campaign. Except for a period on the Eastern Front from October 1942 to February 1943, he spent the Occupation in Paris. His regiment was on guard duty in the French capital. The author of *In Stahlgewittern* (*Storm of Steel*) ("the finest war book I ever read," according to Gide), which in Germany had made him a famous, prizewinning author, who was still popular despite his being in "internal exile" since Hitler's coming to power, Jünger, with his company, relieved the guard at the Hôtel Continental and led the parade formation before the Tomb of the Unknown Soldier. He also censored the mail sent out by the military personnel of the general staff of the Greater Paris command. But it was more often in fashionable salons that Gaston met him, became familiar with him, and learned to appreciate him—at the Morands', on Avenue Charles-Floquet, where they also met Jean Cocteau. Often Jünger did not leave his French hosts, whoever they might be—but in those circles, they were interchangeable—without being given as a token of friendship some rare edition, beautifully bound, or an autographed letter from some prestigious writer of the nineteenth century. Gaston himself presented him with a full set of the Pléiade editions.

More than once he met Jünger in the best restaurants of the city, which they both frequented assiduously: Maxim's, La Tour d'argent, Fouquet's, Drouant, or La Pérouse—but of course not in the underground black-market bistros such as Chantaco or Le Périgord, which the Germans officially came to only on police raids.

Gallimard published three of Jünger's books during the war: *Auf den Marmorklippen (On the Marble Cliffs)*, *Das abenteuerliche Herz (The Adventurous Heart)*, and *Afrikanische Spiele (African Diversions)*. The writer Julien Gracq, who has since become one of his most fervent admirers, at first responded in a way indicative of the times and the prevailing atmosphere:

> I came across the work of Jünger during one of the darkest periods of the last war. Although his *Storm of Steel* had already been translated into French, his name at the time was totally unknown to me. And, in those years when publishing in France had become a Propaganda Department, an understandable defensive reflex—when a French reader met the name of a German author in a bookstore display—led him to pass it by.[32]

While Jünger seems to have been the most widely read German author in France at the time, it is hard to say what the reaction of the French public was to German translations. But there is no doubt that, for French publishers, that concession to the occupiers was one way of getting paper stock. Even more than the cinema, or the theater with its limited audience, during the Occupation the book was king. Even more than radio, which was not entertaining enough and too politicized, whether on Radio-Paris or the BBC. If there had been no restrictions on paper supply, French publishers would have done even better business, for books were at a premium, in Paris and in the provinces, as a remedy against boredom, deprivations, and gloom.

"At that time, all books sold. If we had printed the phone directory, I have a feeling it would have sold just as well," says Sven Nielsen, the son of a Danish bookseller who after the armistice converted his book-exporting business by buying out Les Editions Albert-Premier, to publish deluxe and semi-deluxe editions of Stendhal, Voltaire, Flaubert, and others.[33]

A Catholic journalist, Hubert Forestier, had the good idea in those days of making a survey of the principal Paris publishers. At Plon, on Rue Garancière, the literary director M. Belperron responded:

> The two books with the best sales are unquestionably René Benjamin's novel, *Printemps tragique* [Tragic Springtime], of which we distributed 30,000 copies, and *Après la defaite* [After the Defeat] by Bertrand de Jouvenel, of which we sold 20,000. Those two books just sold themselves. But apart from this double success, we note a real revival of the sale of Alexis Carrel's *l'Homme cet inconnu* [*Man, the Unknown*], which has run to some 250,000 copies and is still selling at the rate of 5,000 a month. We have a definite impression that the public is looking mainly for serious books and that, while not giving up novels entirely, they choose titles corresponding to their current concerns, history and political, economic, or moral questions. The Carrel is symptomatic. It has always had steady sales, but never so high as now. Moreover, wars have the advantage of making people read a lot. During the Great War we saw the same thing: people read enormously. After the armistice books took second place to dancing. But I almost forgot Georges

Suarez's book, *Le Maréchal Pétain* [Marshal Pétain], the sale of which has already reached the huge figure of 96,000.

At Flammarion on Rue Racine, the literary director, M. d'Uckermann, had this to say:

The return to the soil, the restoration of peasant dignity are in the foreground of the national policy of renovation. So Henri Pourrat's *L'Homme à la bêche* [The Man with the Spade], an admirable canvas of peasant life down the centuries and in different countries, is having a considerable success. . . . Likewise, people are much concerned with dietary matters, so they read such books as: *Nourris ton corps* [Feed Your Body] by Charles Geffroy, *L'Elevage du lapin* [Raising Rabbits] by Dr. Lissot, *L'Apiculture familiale* [Family Beekeeping] by Corn, and *La Pomme de terre* [The Potato] by André Gault. These substantial and useful books are unquestionably among the ones most read at this time.

At Gallimard Forestier could quote only "a spokesman":

Today's big success is Herman Melville's famous novel *Moby Dick*, translated by Jean Giono. This success indicates the public's interest in big novels. Published on June 1, *Moby Dick* has already been reprinted three times. . . . The works of Péguy are undergoing a very considerable revival. Their sales have doubled, compared to the figures before the war. Among the new works very well received by the public and the press one can cite the novel by Sigrid Undset, *The Faithful Wife*, translated from the Norwegian; and in our historical collections *L'Eminence grise* [The Gray Eminence] by Monseigneur Grente and *La Vie de Mallarmé* [Life of Mallarmé] by Prof. Henri Mondor. Marcel Aymé and Robert Francis continue to enjoy public favor. . . . We are going to publish the *Oeuvres poétiques* [Complete Poetic Works] of Charles Péguy in the Pléiade. . . . Immediately after the exodus, reading resumed with the classics. Since then, there has also been a run on documentary and historical works.

At Denoël the interviewer was received by Robert Denoël himself:

The book most read in my firm is Céline's *Les Beaux Draps* [A Fine Kettle of Fish], which came out at the beginning of March and in three months has reached a sale of 28,000. I can guarantee you that that is no inflated publicity figure. The entire oeuvre of Céline has had the advantage of an extraordinary new vogue, to the point that in the last few months we have sold about 30,000 of his various books, not counting the latest one. . . . By agreement with the German Institute, Parisian publishers are going to bring out a number of works meant to familiarize us with the German effort in the artistic, literary, and social areas in the last few years. But German publishers have also bought a large number of French works that they will translate into German. . . . I'm optimistic! Because in the new France the book is beginning to win back its place as number one.

At Calmann-Lévy, one of the oldest publishing companies in France, the interviewer found himself facing a new general manager, who had come by his position through doubtful means, to say the least:

Since March 11, I have signed fifty-four contracts, including one with Colette, who is going to let me publish *Mes cahiers* [My Notebooks]. In this firm there are five authors who sell big: Pierre Loti, Anatole France, René Bazin, Alexandre Dumas père, and Guy Chantepleure. . . . Given the present circumstances, I will be publishing many books of history and memoirs. I expect to have a dozen or so out within the next two months.

At Stock there was no surprise: they were selling mainly foreign translations, and Louis Bromfield's *The Rains Came* in particular:

The public, it is obvious, likes a pièce de résistance, a long book. But what is important to the success of the large volume is that it be full of life, adventures, emotion, and humanity. Of course the success of *The Rains Came* was already apparent before the war, but it has grown since; we have sold 200,000, and it's going at the rate of five to six thousand copies a month. . . . The terrible condition of France after the defeat inspired the Librairie Stock to create a small collection of books devoted to research on the characteristics of our country, its history, geography, mores: a sort of moral and political inventory that would allow us to move toward a truly French future in a new world. . . . That is our contribution to national reconstruction.

Forestier interviewed many more publishers during his lengthy survey, which lasted from July through September 1941. Everywhere he heard the same thing: everything was for the best, publishing was booming. A similar unanimity was to be found in a complaint—an odd lamentation, considering the urgent problems of the day—voiced by every one of the publishers: we do not have enough paper and are short of raw materials (paste, thread, leather); supplies are being exhausted without our being able to replenish them; supply can no longer keep up with demand. At the end of this X ray of the profession taken in its daily activities after a year of German occupation, the journalist concluded: "It appears that French publishing, through the voice of its directors, has taken as its own the motto of the Chief of State, 'Work, Family, Motherland,' and has placed itself at his disposal to make that slogan penetrate our national life through the powerful medium of the book."[34]

One could hardly put it better. That was probably what Gracq had in mind when he reminded us that French publishing at that time had become "a propaganda department."

So much for the publishers. What of the writers?

It would be unworthy to dismiss the question, as some try to do, by considering them as a category of workers with duties similar to those of other categories: civil servants, schoolteachers, and so on. That would be denying the very essence of their craft: their responsibility as intellectuals. That special responsibility, which *ought* to have applied to the publishers also (if they did not see themselves purely as businessmen), presented a problem to those men of letters during the war who were also men of conscience.

To publish under the jackboot or not? That was the dilemma. Being a French writer in Paris in 1941 and submitting a manuscript to be read at Gallimard, meant being willing to have it judged by a committee that included, besides Marcel Arland, Brice Parain, and a few other old-timers, the likes of Ramon Fernandez, the devoted lecturer of the Cercles Populaires Français (French People's Circles), contributor to the newspaper *Le Cri du peuple*, and a member of the politburo of Jacques Doriot's PPF (Parti Populaire Français)—all of which were committed to total collaboration with the occupiers. Despite his undeniable moral and intellectual qualities, and a certain independence of mind (he dared to publish moving tributes to two proscribed Jews—Bergson and Proust—in mid-Occupation), Fernandez was still the counterpart of Drieu La Rochelle, and not at the *NRF* magazine, which was alleged to be separate from the rest of the firm, but in the very bosom of the *NRF* publishing house, the sanctum sanctorum, the editorial board purged of its Jewish members. No more Robert Aron or Benjamin Crémieux; instead, Ramon Fernandez.

Authors were not supposed to know the composition of the editorial board, but from newspapers, radio, rumors, and everything that made up the temper of the day they knew that nothing was published in France without being submitted to two censorships. First, that of the publisher, who since September 1940 had agreed not to publish Jewish or Gaullist authors (the Communists would be proscribed somewhat later, when the Nazi-Soviet pact was nothing more than a bad memory), or books criticizing the policy or principles of Franco-German collaboration, German National Socialism, or Italian Fascism. And second, that of the occupying authorities, which came into play not only when the publisher's self-censorship proved deficient, but in a much more regular fashion. To publish a book in Paris in 1941 also meant carrying on as if nothing had happened: sending press copies to the Parisian journalists, submitting it to their reviews in the hope of rating an article in a daily or weekly of the City of Light—a legal and authorized article, to be sure, one that had also been censored by the identical Propaganda Staffel services, and therefore collaborationist.

Nothing was published without the approval of the occupier. To get that, one had to go through a series of acts of allegiance, whether direct or implicit. This was not, properly speaking, Collaboration. But it certainly was not Resistance, as so many were later to claim. It was an infinitely complex attitude, quite in harmony with the character of a Gaston Gallimard or a Jean Paulhan.

In actual fact, submitting to the law of the occupier—a law that one had drawn up jointly with him—meant agreeing to republish *La France* by Charles Péguy (an author who had to be republished as soon as possible, because he sold well) with the elimination of the following passage. It was removed in the fall of 1941 from the text published in 1939 in Gallimard's Catholic collection.

> The Germans, who went for centuries without founding their empire and then founded it only on our ruins . . . are, and always have been, empire men. The Holy Germanic Empire. And that again is why no true philosophy of freedom has ever been able to emerge in Germany. What they call freedom is what we would call good servitude. What they call socialist is what we would call a pale center-left. And what they call revolutionary is what we on our side would call good conservatism.[35]

That sort of thing did not sit well with the Propaganda Staffel, whose wishes were commands. Even though the family of the writer probably gave its agreement for publication under such conditions, one is moved to meditate on the unjust posterity of Péguy, killed in battle by the Germans in 1914, and then mutilated by them twenty-seven years later—with the help of the French.

Faced with German censorship, Gaston, unlike Grasset, played a very careful hand. His only short-term aim was to amass the greatest supply of paper he could. He made sure not to offend anyone, and was more tactful than ever before. Gaston and Grasset adopted exactly opposite attitudes in their dealings with the occupier. It is interesting to compare their reactions in similar matters occurring at the same time: June 1941.

Grasset sent a letter of complaint to the German censors, to Lieutenant Heller; he was dissatisfied and like a good Frenchman made himself heard, loudly criticizing the malfunctioning of the censorship service! As if he were in a restaurant! The reason for Grasset's wrath was the upcoming publication of François Mauriac's *La Pharisienne (Woman of the Pharisees)*. To forestall problems, he had taken all necessary precautions, advising the author to go to the German Institute and ask its director, Karl Epting, to be good enough to authorize his book's publication "and to inform him of his desire to resume his literary activity." The authorization was given without reservations. The book could be launched on the market. With this favorite author Grasset generally started with a press run of 20,000. But because of the paper restrictions, he was holding it down to 8,800, which was quite a handicap. Then he learned that the Germans had authorized only 5,000 copies—a catastrophe. The point was that Mauriac was being paid 9,000 francs per month as an advance on royalties, plus an additional monthly sum of 11,000 francs as an advance against the royalties of his *Mémoires* to come. If *Woman of the Pharisees* came out in only 5,000 copies, Grasset could not break even on it—to say nothing of covering at least part of that 20,000-franc monthly advance. Outraged, he did what Gaston would never have done: he wrote directly to the Propaganda Division to complain of the damage caused him by their decision. As a final act of desperation he made use of an argument that he hoped might get through to the Germans: if you go on this way, limiting the press runs of the Parisian publishers, who are all loyal to you, you will encourage our authors to go and get published in the free zone.[36] Was he courageous, or simply obtuse?

Gaston, for his part, was neither. In June 1941 M. Schultz, from the Hôtel Majestic, wrote him to express indignation over the publication of a novel by Violet Trefusis entitled *Les Causes perdues* (Lost Causes). Arguing that the book was published under a contract that predated the war, Gaston answered him with a real effort toward appeasement:

. . . we were, of course, not unaware that the author was English, but we never thought that she was Jewish. . . . We can therefore assure the Arbeitsführer that any idea of provocation was far from our thoughts when we published this work, and that we would not have included it in our catalogue had we known that such publication might be disagreeable to you.[37]

The officer at the Hôtel Majestic did not really think that Violet Trefusis's novels were so dangerous either. He had been alerted by a denunciation, a "friendly bit of advice" from one of those extremist collaborators who often kept a sharper eye on what the publishers brought out than did the German censors, and with greater competence, since they were dealing with French authors. The denunciation in this case was a typed text of five pages sent anonymously to the Propaganda Division, which took it into consideration. It was entitled, "Violet Trefusis, M. Gaston Gallimard and the Intelligence Service." After enumerating former Jewish employees of Gallimard (Hirsch, Schiffrin, Fels), the writer accused Trefusis of being a British spy, of having seduced various influential Parisian newspaper editors and book publishers to get them to publish British propaganda in the guise of novels, and maintained that Gaston Gallimard knew all about it: "He is not a fool: he is a sly one who has always played the Jewish card in France and who continues to play it. And just as he published Léon Blum, now he publishes Violet Trefusis."[38]

The informer did not sign his name. Doubtless some embittered person, possibly one of the many writers whose manuscripts had been rejected by the Gallimard editorial board. But there are clues as to who might have instigated the denunciation: the informer suggested that Gaston Gallimard be removed from his publishing company through a forced purchase of it by the Société Le Pont, run by Gerhard Hibbelen, who in Paris directed a veritable press empire for the German embassy, and that Violet Trefusis's two estates in France be ceded to the Bernheim interests administered by Louis Thomas, who was to turn up again in the matter of the Calmann-Lévy company.[39]

Gaston's attitude toward the censors should not surprise us. Don't stir up trouble, don't make waves—that was his makeup. Never mind the means, the end alone mattered. But the writers? Were they automatically accomplices of a publisher who cooperated with the occupiers, merely by having him publish one of their books?

This is a complex matter, if one is not satisfied with a Manichaean good-versus-evil historiography and studies the behavior and individual paths of certain Gallimard authors without regard to the reputations they concocted for themselves in September 1944 and thereafter.

During the preceding years French writers had had plenty of leisure to think about their position during the Occupation. Mussolini's seizure of power, then Hitler's, and Franco's—to mention only the West—drew into France a part of the intelligentsia of those countries: men and women who chose exile rather than work in a totalitarian country, and who had been confronted with the same problem—censorship, self-censorship, silent approval, the acceptance of a hated régime. The Germans who had been welcomed in France between 1933 and 1940 were familiar with this dilemma, this struggle of conscience.

It was all plain to see in the Germany of 1935: to remain in that country under the jackboot, to publish books and articles there in official publishing houses and publications, meant resigning oneself to the auto-da-fés, the repression—in a word, collaboration. During that period French intellectuals had followed closely developments across the Rhine. From the action of Goebbels's satraps in the Ministry of Propaganda and Alfred Rosenberg's in the "Literary Office," they had a foretaste of what lay ahead if, by chance, the Germans invaded France. Hitler himself had given a clear warning, in the famous interview he gave Bertrand de Jouvenel in February 1936 for *Paris-Soir*:

> If I succeed in bringing about a Franco-German rapprochement such as I wish, that will be a rectification worthy of me! I will write my

rectification into the great book of History! . . . Once the rapprochement is accomplished, there will be no dearth of French writings that will also have to be rectified, eh? Because they do not always treat us tenderly![40]

Four years in advance, he was announcing the Otto List.

A violent debate among the "internal émigrés" and the "external émigrés" was tearing apart the German intelligentsia, with the former throwing up to the latter that they were fighting without running any physical danger, that they were not confronting the enemy where he held sway, and above all were deserting the Fatherland. All shades of people and opinions were to be found in these cleavages: Jews, who were the most numerous in the battalions of the refugees, Communists, Germans of no special label who had sworn never again to speak their native tongue as long as the swastika flew over Berlin, socialists, pacifists. Also involved were writers of the Right like Ernst Jünger and Oswald Spengler (whose *Decline of the West* Gallimard was to publish), who kept apart from those named above, but steered equally clear of the regime in power.

In a fit of "rehabilitation" the Third Reich had dubbed Goethe and Schiller "the first National Socialists"—its forerunners, as it were. It also tried to make use of the living: those intellectuals who had not "deserted." In 1933 the Nazis were proud that Gerhart Hauptmann, Nobel Prize winner for literature in 1912, one of Germany's greatest playwrights, was still having his plays performed as before. Gottfried Benn, one of the most important poets and essayists of his time, rallied to the new masters. In the spring of 1933 he read over the Berlin radio his essay *Der Neue Staat und die Intellektuellen* (The New State and the Intellectuals) and published, a year later, *Kunst und Macht* (Art and Power), both attuned to the spirit of the times. Considering his prestige and the respect in which he was held by German intellectuals, this conversion dismayed many of his compatriots in exile—and drove many within the country from doubt to despair. In such instances one could see the full measure of the intellectual's responsibility. From Le Lavandou in southern France, Klaus Mann, Thomas Mann's son, wrote him:

> What could have brought you to put a name which to us symbolizes the highest intellectual order and an uncompromising purity at the disposal of individuals whose insignificance is unprecedented in European history and whose moral ignominy provokes the disgust of the entire world? How many friends you will lose if you thus make common cause with people worthy only of contempt! And what friends can you make, in the end, on that wrong side of the barrier?

Benn answered Klaus Mann in this way:

> I declare myself in favor of the new State because it is my own people carving out their own path in their own way. Who am I to isolate myself? Do I know more than the people? No. I may try, within the measure of my abilities, to direct them where I would like to see them go, but if I do not succeed, they are still my people. A nation is no small thing! My spiritual and material existence, my language, my life, my human relationships, the sum total of my brain—all this I owe to the people.[41]

It was around the person of Thomas Mann, Klaus's father, that most of these debates crystallized. That was due to the influence exerted over a whole generation by this writer, who was sixty-eight when Hitler came to power and had behind him the great novels *Buddenbrooks* and *The Magic Mountain*. It was due also to Mann's total, categorical, and uncompromising position from the very outset against the National Socialist regime. On February 11, 1933, he left his country for a lecture tour, with little luggage. The tour lasted many years, Mann refusing to return to a Germany governed by persons against whom he had never ceased to warn his people. He settled in turn in various foreign countries, complaining of having lost his home, his friends, and especially his roots, the vital base of a writer from which rose the sap of his work. But, unlike those who swore never to write in the language of Goethe as long as it was also the language of Goebbels, he remained faithful to German, "that authentic and inalienable Fatherland which I carried with me into exile and from which no potentate could drive me."[42] He considered it absurd to write in English, as had been suggested to him. His novels appeared more or less normally in Germany until 1936, the date of his national excommunication. He summed up his position in two sentences: "It was impossible to practice culture in Germany while the abominations we know of existed. That would be equivalent to embellishing corruption, to adorning crime."[43]

The German experience was there as a precedent; the French intelligentsia could not plead surprise, at the end of 1940, on being confronted with the dilemma: to leave or to stay? Should one resign oneself to the exigencies of collaboration or turn one's typewriter into an instrument of war? Should one submit or act? Put down one's pen for the duration of the Occupation, or continue writing as before?

As June 1940 ended and July began, confusion still reigned. Emmanuel Berl—a Jew!—was writing Marshal Pétain's speeches and slogans: "The soil never lies."[44] He was to come to his senses shortly thereafter and, like many of his coreligionists, take to the countryside, first on the Riviera, then in the Corrèze. Louis-Daniel Hirsch, Gallimard's business manager, dismissed because of the statute on Jews, received a letter from Gaston informing him of this and assuring him that his salary would continue. After living in Auvergne, the Hirsches, harassed, from the fall of 1941 to the end of the war found refuge in the Lot on a farm where they could raise cows. The salary sent from Paris diminished gradually in value as the war progressed, so when they were ready to buy the house they lived in, they turned to Jean Schlumberger, who immediately lent them the necessary money.

By the end of 1940, after Pétain's meeting with Hitler at Montoire and the daily pressures on publishers by the occupying authorities to accelerate and amplify their collaboration, any doubt about who was in charge evaporated.

Who went into exile?

Raymond Aron went to England, André Breton and Saint-John Perse to the United States. Georges Bernanos remained in Brazil, and Robert Caillois in Argentina. Jules Romains and André Maurois were in the United States. A handful. A sign of the times: by the summer of 1940 Albert Cohen, who had tried in vain to recruit a Jewish military force to fight alongside the Allies, fled to London—at the very moment when Paul Morand, head of the French Economic Mission to the British government since 1939, was precipitously leaving London for Vichy, to offer his services to Pétain. Yet some years before—centuries, it would seem—Cohen had got Morand to contribute to his *Revue juive*.

In July 1941, in Buenos Aires, Caillois launched a new magazine, *Lettres françaises* (French Literature), intended to uphold the prestige of French language and letters in the Americas. In its second issue he defined the duties of exiled writers as follows: "to make themselves the attentive interpreters of their comrades who are reduced to expressing themselves in whispers." As he saw it, one should not keep silent because one was far from the field of battle, but on the contrary commit oneself—yet refrain from misusing one's liberty of expression and dispensing too much good advice. The émigré writer had to speak for the writer who stayed behind; the two were bound by an invisible chain. Caillois reproduced in *Lettres françaises* some pieces by Emmanuel Mounier which had already appeared in France, pointing out: "These labors, these concerns, these voices had to be relayed. Unpublished material could wait."[45]

Seen from South America, the situation in occupied France appeared simple, Manichaean. In Caillois's mind the choice for the writer back home was clear: either join the maquis* or write articles for the abhorred *Je suis partout*. But the majority of intellectuals in

---

*Underground resistance: the maquis is wild scrub land, the kind of countryside where Resistance fighters found cover.

France had in fact chosen a third path, as had most Frenchmen: *l'attentisme* (wait-and-see-ism).

Jean Guéhenno chose to write but not publish anything as long as the Germans were there, so as not to dishonor himself by submitting his manuscripts to them. René Char became Captain Alexandre, a leader in the Maquis, and meanwhile wrote his *Feuillets d'Hypnos (Leaves of Hypnos)*, which he was to publish only after the Liberation. Their attitude, characteristic of those intellectuals who refuse to compromise, was clear-cut, just as unambiguous as that of Drieu La Rochelle, Ramon Fernandez, Marcel Jouhandeau, and other writers who had aligned themselves with the National Revolution. But the position taken by the majority was ambiguous.

Aragon and his wife Elsa Triolet decided to make use of the contradictions of Occupied France. On the one hand they published their books under totally official imprints—Aragon's poems *Le Crève-coeur* (The Heartbreaker) and his novel *Les Voyageurs de l'impériale (The Century Was Young)* at Gallimard, and Triolet's *Mille regrets* (A Thousand Regrets) and *Le Cheval blanc (The White Charger)* at Denoël—while on the other hand they published some of their writings underground or in the free zone. A cynic might say that they were having it both ways. Aragon and Triolet called it their "smuggled prose." Their gamble was that "such reading, without arousing the censors, would smuggle in a certain hope, a desire to change things in the hearts of patriotic readers."[46] A questionable gamble, to contribute to the underground magazine *Les Lettres françaises* (not the one published in Argentina), which kept repeating that the publishers who had signed the censorship agreement were "traitors" and "collabos."

Paulhan, in October 1940, did not want to return to his job at an *NRF* magazine purged of its Jews and anti-Nazis. He found the idea repellent. For a time he thought of applying for a job as a writer in the Ministry of National Education. But at Gaston's request he stayed with the firm. Officially he was in charge of the Pléiade editions, but discreetly—in an office close to Drieu's—he helped draw up the magazine's table of contents. Too many authors had ties to him, and he remained their friend despite their political commitments, for the sake of literature. As before, he read manuscripts, looked for authors, tried to publish what appealed to him. In August 1941, Jouhandeau and Arland arranged for him to meet with Gerhard Heller in an upstairs restaurant on Rue de Ponthieu. Though a Francophile and a liberal, Heller was still a German, an occupier, a lieutenant, and a censor at the Propaganda Staffel. As a token of friendship Paulhan gave Heller a fine old edition of Voltaire. The two men were to meet often again, in more discreet places, such as the mosque in the Fifth Arrondissement.[47] Which did not keep Paulhan from joining with Jacques Decour in launching the underground magazine *Les Lettres françaises*.

Brice Parain, as a member of the editorial board, was directing a new collection aimed at academics, La Montagne Sainte-Geneviève, in which he had full freedom to publish scholarly works. Apart from his own thinking about linguistics, he published Georges Dumézil's *Jupiter, Mars, Quirinus*, an essay on the Indo-European concept of society and the origins of Rome. "Some people were in the Resistance, I was in science," Dumézil said later. And added, "Let history be the judge," recalling the famous example of Bopp.

A well-known German linguist, Franz Bopp had labored for several years at the Bibliothèque Nationale in Paris on Sanskrit conjugation. That was in 1813, when Prussia was at war with France. Possibly he was criticized for that in his day. But history has judged, and posterity has named him the father of modern linguistics. Men do not remember his presence in Paris while his nation was fighting the French, but no one has forgotten his monumental work, *Vergleichende Grammatik (Comparative Grammar)*. Bopp was the model scientist to Georges Dumézil and a few others who felt that their work was more important than messages or politics. That scholarly research was an absolute, concerned only with its results, and with the long term, independent of fleeting circumstance. In 1938 Dumézil had come to the conclusion that Roman tradition was much more important than Greek tradition; having established this, he decided to devote his life to that line of study, oblivious of contemporary developments.

In the spring of 1941 Jean-Paul Sartre, only recently freed from a prisoner-of-war camp at Trier, together with Maurice Merleau-Ponty created the intellectual Resistance group known as Socialisme et Liberté (Socialism and Liberty), and tried unsuccessfully to make contact with the Communists. During the summer he bicycled across the free zone to organize a resistance movement. But when schools reopened in September, he began teaching preparatory courses for the prestigious Ecole Normale Supérieure at the Lycée Condorcet, and so dissolved Socialisme et Liberté and devoted himself to writing articles, novels, essays, and a play, *Les Mouches (The Flies)*, which represented "the only form of resistance open to him."[48] In 1974 Sartre was to explain that that was his way of resisting: writing *L'Etre ou le néant (Being or Nothingness)* at the Café de Flore (where Simone de Beauvoir was delighted never to see a German, quite incapable of imagining that the officers of the Propaganda Staffel might be there in civilian clothes); submitting it to the censorship of the occupiers and having it published by Gallimard; writing plays under the same conditions; and publishing articles in underground magazines like *Les Lettres françaises*.[49] He preferred the intellectual's pen to the machine gun of the Maquis, although the latter had the advantage of being unambiguous. Sartre also suggested that, unlike René Char, he had neither the physical makeup nor the temperament to take part in the actual fighting. Jean Prévost, who was the same age as Sartre, died fighting in the Maquis very near the end of the war. Benjamin Crémieux and the historian Marc Bloch, both over fifty, paid with their lives for their Resistance activities: the former in a Nazi concentration camp, the latter before a firing squad. No one ever died of philosophizing at the Café de Flore. Nevertheless, at the Liberation Sartre would be considered in "the upper echelon" of Resistance writers.

In October 1941 the Propaganda Staffel organized a first trip to Weimar for French authors to take part in the Congress of European

Writers. Those invited included Drieu, Fernandez, André Fraigneau, Brasillach, Chardonne, Arland, and Morand. Of the seven, four were *NRF*-Gallimard people, including two members of the editorial board and the editor of the magazine. Finally Arland and Morand did not make the trip, but were replaced by Jouhandeau and Abel Bonnard.[50]

To appear or not to appear? That was the real problem, not: to publish or not to publish. Jean Guéhenno, noting that the table of contents of Drieu La Rochelle's *NRF* was not confined to names of collaborators or glorifiers of the New Europe, suggested an explanation:

> The man of letters is not one of the noblest of human species. Incapable of living very long in obscurity, he will sell his soul to see his name *appear*. A few months of silence, of disappearance, drive him to his wits' end. He can take it no longer. His only concern now is the size, the typeface in which his name will be printed, the position he will be given in the table of contents. It goes without saying that he is full of good reasons: "French literature," he says, "must go on." He thinks he is French literature, French thought, and that it would die without him. . . . This is the time for writing for nothing, for the pure pleasure of it.[51]

Those who did not wish to publish under the jackboot in 1941 could publish in the free zone, in Algeria, or abroad. But what point was there in *appearing* anywhere but in Paris, the intellectual and artistic capital of France—Lyons and Algiers notwithstanding? As for the underground, that was by definition anonymity.

In 1941 Jean Bruller and Pierre de Lescure created Les Editions de Minuit, an illegal publishing house that did not submit its manuscripts to German censorship, did not depend on the goodwill of the occupying authorities for its paper supply, and did not distribute its books through Hachette and other wholesale services under German control. Bruller decided to use the pseudonym of Vercors, and would be known by that name for the rest of his life. A thirty-nine-year-old illustrator, he had published several books of prints before the war. Though not a writer, he worked in publishing.

Unwilling to take part in the collaboration set up in September by the Cercle de la Librairie, he changed trades, set his pens and pencils aside, and became a carpenter on the outskirts of Paris.[52]

De Lescure and Vercors refused to accept prevailing conditions, to compromise with the occupiers, to recant. They sought an alternative. After mentioning one of his friends, a brilliant literary critic who had now begun to contribute regularly to a collaborationist publication, de Lescure heard another colleague answer:

"I wonder whether he isn't right. After all, his business is book reviewing. He has to stick to that. You don't criticize a waiter in a café because he serves a beer to a German. It doesn't keep him from thinking his own thoughts."

As for Vercors, while doing some carpentry work for Henri Membre, secretary of the International Pen Club House, he heard him say:

What's so bad about that? I understand them. The Occupation is going to go on and on. A Duhamel, a Mauriac, a Malraux can wait. It doesn't hurt them to remain silent: their reputation is established, it's solid, and they'll find it waiting for them intact. But take me, for example, with *Non-lieu* [Nol Pros; Gallimard, 1929], my only novel that got good reviews, and two others that were scarcely noticed; if I don't publish anything for five or ten years, I'll be forgotten and have to start over from scratch.[53]

Forty years later the historian Henri Michel commented that the *NRF* authors had been free to write—provided that they censored themselves. "Their signatures, appearing alongside attacks on Jews, on democracy, on England, helped to justify those attacks and make them acceptable."[54] Goebbels at the Propaganda Ministry and Ribbentrop at Foreign Affairs were waging internecine warfare over the cultural policy to be followed in occupied territories. The Führer sided more often with Ribbentrop, who in a directive dated November 30, 1940, said that his "cultural" goal was above all "to assure that German foreign policy had the best possible conditions for achieving its ends."[55] Despite the real or supposed Francophile leanings of an officer posted to Paris, the occupying authorities supported cultural enterprises with the sole aim of better subjugating France. Sometimes Frenchmen forgot this. However great his admiration for French literature, Karl Epting, the director of the German Institute, nevertheless wore a swastika on his lapel.

"How much more dignified it would have been," Henri Michel was to write, "if a few of the great voices had remained silent from the moment the armistice was signed."[56] It is true that Malraux refrained from "appearing" under the Gallimard logo during the Occupation; that he published *Les Noyers de l'Altenburg (The Walnut Trees of Altenburg)* in a free country, Switzerland; and that even though he did not enter the active Resistance until 1943, he was one of the rare writers whom no one, at the Liberation, could reproach with having made any compromise with the Germans. The extraordinary thing is that this should impress us. After all, Victor Hugo spent eighteen years in exile on Jersey and Guernsey for a cause less momentous.

In the early months of 1941 there was still doubt and debate among some who wondered even while their work was appearing, whether it should appear. Yet after six months of Occupation, the direction of the Vichy régime and the German embassy hardly left room for doubt. One Resistance group, that of the Musée de l'Homme, had already come to life and died out. Paul Valéry, Paul Eluard, André Gide, and Eugène Guillevic had articles printed in Drieu's *NRF* alongside notorious collaborators. They were still looking for their own answers—but finally found them. Gide, as we have seen, in reaction to Jacques Chardonne's articles, wired Drieu no longer to count on him, not for a single line, and announced his decision in *Le Figaro* at the beginning of April, an action that Gaston considered a stab in the back—yet another!—since Gide's withdrawal undermined his patient work of recruiting for the "normalized" *NRF*. As for Eluard, he was to say that his poems had been lying in Paulhan's desk drawer and Drieu took them without asking his permission. Guillevic, for his part, would explain: "At the time I thought that poetry was above all such considerations, or—even better—that its revolutionary force acted on its own, regardless of where the poems appeared."[57]

Sartre, among others, would justify his plays *The Flies* and *No Exit* by the Resistance message they were supposed to have carried—provided one knew how to read between the lines.

A man who used such stratagems was Ernst Jünger. When his book *On the Marble Cliffs* was published in Germany in 1939–40, he was harassed a bit, suspected, but was immediatly vouched for by Hitler himself, because of his glorious military past: "Nothing will be done to Jünger," Jünger reported the Führer saying.[58]

Fourteen thousand copies were sold in a week, his publisher told the author in uniform.

On the Marble Cliffs was without any doubt a coded book, a symbolic book. The "great forester," the enigmatic dictator, could represent nobody but Hitler; his packs of wild dogs were the SS divisions. After the war Jünger's admirers were to anthologize this book as anti-Nazi literature. Later George Steiner, in a preface to the English edition, was to opine that it was the only major act of resistance, of internal sabotage, that was displayed in German literature under the Hitler régime[59]—a somewhat unfeeling remark, considering those intellectuals who paid with torture, deportation, or death for a book, a few pages, an article, or a leaflet in which it was not necessary to read between the lines in order to discern a call to resist Nazism.

Sartre and Jünger are ambiguous figures. Their intentions were at the very least equivocal, and remain so despite the efforts of those who since the Liberation have been determined to rebuild their heroes as they would like them to have been: pure and beyond reproach, even in times of great doubt.

Jünger revealed that in his own mind the great forester represented a "type of dictator much more powerful, more diabolical," even, than Hitler. "To me, *On the Marble Cliffs* takes place within a dimension greater than that of the political life of this period," Jünger would explain. His dictator had no fatherland, but might appear any place in the world where he could express his hatred of culture and his thirst for violence.[60]

Gaston just wanted to carry on as before. But, to eliminate the obstacles created by the Occupation, he had to resort to double-talk, and to move in circles where collaborators and their masters were to be met—for it was there that power (censorship, paper supply, and safe-conducts) was to be found. Yet at the same time he allowed some of his offices to be used as informal meeting places for the people from the underground magazine *Les Lettres françaises*. Drieu on one hand, Paulhan on the other, the magazine, the books— connected by the visible and invisible strings that Gaston the illusionist pulled from inside his office, so that this whole antagonistic crowd might live together in the name of literature alone.

His contradictions, his ambivalence, his varied attitudes were revealed not in a book or a catalogue but in *Comoedia*, a newspaper that might have been conceived exactly in the image of Gallimard in those dark years. It was not by chance that he besieged and infiltrated its pages, as in earlier times he had *Les Nouvelles littéraires*.

Comoedia, an old show-business weekly that also covered books and the arts, founded in 1906, reappeared June 21, 1941, four months after the resurrection of *Je suis partout*. It was a quality publication with an intellectual tone that set it strangely apart from its competitors: it had a pleasing layout, fascinating articles, and prestigious bylines. Like any other paper published in Paris, it was subject to censorship, hence the officers of the Propaganda Staffel had to approve its contents. But the tone of *Comoedia* set it radically apart from the other weeklies of the period, for it was never polemical or insulting, it did not denounce others, and it attempted to review new books on strictly literary criteria. That was what made it dangerous— by simply being inoffensive, harmless, uncommitted. It would be truly naïve to imagine that the Germans allowed the appearance of a newspaper which in no way served their purposes. *Comoedia* helped to improve the image of Occupied France that they were spreading abroad: a country whose brilliant culture had not been snuffed out by the Occupation, quite the contrary. *Comoedia* had another advantage in the eyes of the Propaganda Staffel: the Germans could get their ideas and messages published on a page entitled "European Page"—a sugarcoated euphemism for a column devoted to furthering National Socialism. All books translated from the German were praised to the skies in it. It carried sympathetic reports of the huge cultural congress of the Hitler Youth at Weimar, the Mozart weeks in Paris and Salzburg, the glories of the Bayreuth Festival, and so on. This was subtler than the forthright propaganda of the newspapers most subservient to the New Order. One might indeed wonder whether the rest of the weekly was not merely a pretext for this "European Page," so as to insinuate into the minds of wait-and-see or lukewarm Pétainist intellectuals the ruling ideas of National Socialism. The historian Pascal Ory comments that

> *Comoedia* did not play a secondary role in the erection of a collaborationist culture: French to the point of Parisianism, European to the point of Pan-Germanism, the weekly of show business, arts, and literature assured all who would listen of the profound continuity that connected the Comédie-Française with the Schiller Theater, and Hauptmann with Claudel. These were rapprochements which did not have to await the signing of a nonbelligerence pact.[61]

René Delange, the editor of *Comoedia*, a highly respected journalist in prewar Parisian press circles, was one of the honored members of the French delegation invited to Vienna in November 1941 for the celebration of the one hundred and fiftieth anniversary of the death of Mozart, "a pilgrimage more Nazi than Mozartian."[62] This same Delange appears as a friend of the Sartre-de Beauvoir couple in the latter's *Memoirs*. Of course the powerful editor of *Comoedia* was one who liked to do favors. He made it possible for Sartre and de Beauvoir to "live penuriously," as they put it, by getting her some work in 1943: he recommended her to his friend who ran Radio-Vichy, for whom she wrote a few radio skits.

Delange particularly favored Gallimard authors. In column after column of his paper, Gallimard critics plugged books by Gallimard writers. Gaston was delighted. One could not find a shrewder type of promotion in that troubled time. Marcel Arland, Valéry, Fargue, Cocteau, Montherlant, Giraudoux, Jean-Louis Barrault, Jacques Audiberti, Arthur Honegger, Charles Dullin, and Jacques Copeau wrote regularly for the paper, alongside the most official of collaborationists. Those reluctant to cross the Rubicon and do articles for Delange were encouraged by the presence of the others, which reassured them. Henry de Montherlant, who certainly did not need such encouragement, would later justify himself by saying that, at the inaugural luncheon of *Comoedia*, he had rubbed elbows with writers who would later be known as Communists and active members of the Resistance. So why should he not have felt a "clear conscience,"[63] working cheek by jowl with them on this weekly?

In the first issue of *Comoedia* Sartre published a dithyrambic article hailing the appearance of *Moby Dick*—published, naturally, by Gallimard. But shortly thereafter he ceased contributing to it, realizing what the paper stood for, as de Beauvoir later explained. *Comoedia*'s editor, however, "defended works that opposed Fascist values and Vichy-type morality."[64] The intellectuals who, twenty years after the fact, were busy justifying their accommodations were obviously not bothered by one more contradiction. In de Beauvoir, again, we find:

> While I condemned *all* collaborators, I felt a sharply defined and quite excruciating personal loathing for those of my own kind who joined their ranks—intellectuals, journalists, writers. When artists or men of letters went to Germany to assure the conquerors of our spiritual loyalty, I felt I had been personally betrayed.[65]

Such a feeling commands respect. But what publication opened its columns to those people if not the organ of Delange—Delange the friend and benefactor of Sartre and de Beauvoir? A figurehead of the intelligentsia under the jackboot, he was also one of those who participated in the trip to Germany. The facts are stubborn. It was in *Comoedia* that the writings of Sartre and de Beauvoir received the warmest welcome and the promptest promotion: Marcel Arland did a laudatory review of her *L'Invitée (She Came to Stay)* in August 1943, and on October 30 Jean Grenier wrote in it of his high regard for Sartre's *Being and Nothingness.*

Paulhan, inconsistent to begin with, became more so. In *Les Lettres françaises* he upbraided those intellectuals who gave tokens of esteem to the occupiers. But not with his own signature, as this was an underground publication. However, in 1942 and 1943 he himself regularly contributed articles to *Comoedia* under his byline. He refused to have his name appear alongside contributors to Drieu's *NRF*, but in one issue of Delange's weekly it appeared next to that of the notorious collaborationist Jacques Chardonne.[66] In a letter to Louis Guilloux, in June 1941, Paulhan clarified his position, if that is the proper verb:

I believe a writer is responsible (and *terribly* responsible) for what he writes. I believe in dangerous ideas (and what could be dangerous, if not ideas?). I believe in heresies (and the necessity of repressing them). But that a writer may be held responsible for other writers who appear alongside him, this is something that escapes me.

People say: "By contributing (say, to *Comoedia*), you are playing the game of the protecting authorities, who allow the publication only of what serves them. So keep silent!" But:

1) If the protecting authorities have the power (and the intelligence) which you attribute to them, how can I know that it is not my silence they want? That my silence does not serve their purpose? After all, I am silent at the moment; they encourage my silence, etc. Who can judge? For:

2) Why do you take as a fact that the protecting authorities are more intelligent than I (who even so know myself better than they do)? And what if I feel that my contributing does them a disservice?

3) Carry your logic to its conclusion. What you mean to say, in your policy of total negativism, is: "The protecting authorities find it in their interest that journals of good quality appear in the occupied zone. By contributing to them, you enhance that good quality." That

may be, but then the proper conclusion would be: "Contribute, but *bad stuff* (so as the better to emphasize the noxious influence of the protecting authorities). Write *especially* inept essays and stupid novels. Etc." (like H. de M.).* But I don't favor such a policy of total negativism.[67]

Anyone who cannot understand these contradictions in Paulhan and in the character of *Comoedia* cannot grasp the opaque and multifaceted character of Gaston Gallimard and his business, or realize the full significance of the request sent at the beginning of 1941 by Drieu La Rochelle to Lieutenant Heller:

"Please make sure that nothing happens to Malraux, Paulhan, Gaston Gallimard, and Aragon, whatever allegations may be made against them."[68]

This is no longer the realm of politics. It goes beyond the circumstances of the Occupation. It belongs to an area that has no name, in which friendship, loyalty, and literature all come together.

1941 brought upheavals in the habits and daily life of Gaston Gallimard. The restrictions on heating, the charcoal shortage forced him to move back into his old family building on Rue Saint-Lazare. He had moved away in 1930, when he remarried, so as to live far from all the other Gallimards, establishing himself on Rue Méchain close by Les Editions Fernand Nathan and the Santé prison, in an apartment with white walls and Art Déco furniture.

Henceforth, under the law of November 16, 1940, reforming the structure of corporations, he became president and chief executive officer of his company—to the great distress of his friend Mané Couvreux, who had taken very seriously his own position on the board of directors. As for ZED Publications, Gaston had his accountant Charles Dupont named head of it.

But the future did not look too bleak. The editorial board had plenty of work. Some of the manuscripts were promising. One of

*Probably Henry de Montherlant.

them met with a rare unanimity of approval: a few early readers, then Paulhan, Malraux, Gaston himself, and finally even Lieutenant Heller, the censor who was now a silent partner on the editorial board, were all enthusiastic over *L'Etranger (The Stranger)* by Albert Camus, which had been brought in by his friend Pascal Pia.

Business was good. Returns of books by bookstores to the distributor Hachette were nothing compared to what they had been before the war. Everything sold. On the black market, copies of *Gone with the Wind* were fetching high prices. *L'Homme pressé* (Man in a Hurry), Paul Morand's new novel, sold 22,600 copies as soon as it appeared in the summer of 1941, and Gaston immediately sent the author a check for 20,336 francs in addition to the 50,000 francs he had advanced three years earlier, when the contract for it had been signed.[69]

When the new season began in September, the Propaganda Division circulated two reports for internal consumption, one dealing with French publishing, the other with Parisian bookstores. The first, painting a picture of the profession before the war, drew this conclusion: the trade had been corrupted by the influence of "Judeo-Masonizing capitalism" in the publishing houses, on the panels of judges of the literary prizes, in radio, and in the press. According to the report, for French publishing to be saved: publishers had to be freed from the domination of money; readers had to be reeducated out of the habit of buying books at discount prices ("the Frenchman is interested only in cheap editions at 3 to 5 francs, whereas he will pay 40 to 50 francs to see a stupid show"); impartial literary critics had to be trained; relations between authors and publishers, and between publishers and booksellers, had to be changed; and the French Academy had to be reformed, deserving individuals assured free access to it, and young authors supported.

The second report was more significant. It was based on a survey of bookstores in the twenty arrondissements of Paris initiated by the Propaganda Division; each agent had been equipped with a standard one-sheet questionnaire listing the date, name, and address of the bookseller, the number of employees, size of the store, its specialty, the type of catalogue, whether the bookseller also acted as a publisher, type of books and titles most often requested by customers, whether the bookseller was a subscriber to the *Bibliographie de la France*, whether he displayed a small poster that had been distributed by Hachette, and the bookseller's views on Franco-German collaboration, with additional remarks (e.g., was the owner Jewish?).

The author of the report pointed out at the very start that the data gatherers had run into a major problem: the refusal of the bookseller to engage in conversation. By insisting, the agents could elicit views on some technical questions—but not on collaboration.

> We overcame this difficulty as follows: our agents identified themselves as coming from the Cercle de la Librairie, to make an unofficial survey of booksellers and record their grievances. We were given the warmest welcome. Our agents skillfully led the conversation around to Franco-German relations. . . . Generally speaking, they noted the small number of true booksellers: out of the 1,498 bookshops indicated on official lists only 269 are worthy of the name, the rest being general stores and drygoods shops that sell books on the side. . . . And out of those 269 bookshops only 167 subscribe to the *Bibliographie de la France*. This clearly shows that the French bookseller is not even aware of his need to stay informed. . . . As for the small posters, they are not to be found in any shop. Finally, neither the new pamphlets issued by the Institute on Jewish Questions nor the pamphlets on current events are put on display. In this, the French bookseller reflects the state of mind that exists among his customers: a wait-and-see attitude and an increasingly open hostility toward anything German or imagined to be of German inspiration. . . . This survey has allowed us to come to two important conclusions:
>
> Booksellers complain of poor supply services and hold the Hachette company responsible. On this point there is complete unanimity.
>
> The bookselling business is currently very active. People travel less, stay home more—some, we were assured, even read at the table, to forget their appetites.
>
> Foreign translations sell well, while French books sell poorly. English translations seem more than ever in favor with the public, as a way to demonstrate its Anglophile sympathies. As for the working-

class quarters or suburbs, a painful conclusion must be drawn: the French worker does not read. The booksellers themselves of the Thirteenth, Fourteenth, Fifteenth, Eighteenth, and Twentienth Arrondissements do not read. This reveals the state of total degradation of the working-class world. From degradation to servility there is but one step.[70]

The reporter, a Frenchman working for the Reich, did not realize the full truth of his words. In the weeks that followed, Parisians flocked to the exposition "The Jew and France," a hundred or so hostages were shot, and Pétain met with Goering at Saint-Florentin. The Occupation in all its aspects.

At the end of 1942—at 11:30 A.M. on December 29, to be exact—Gaston Gallimard presided over a special general meeting of the Librairie Gallimard, flanked by his brother Raymond and Emmanuel Couvreux, who were the largest stockholders. On the agenda: to increase the firm's capital by plowing all or part of the profits back into it.

"Fiscal 1941–42, ending last June 30, showed a profit," Gaston announced.

The new capital of the company was henceforth 12 million francs, divided into 24,000 shares at a par value of 500 francs each. Thinking back to the board meetings of 1937–38, they could decidedly feel that the Occupation was not so bad for publishing. For Gaston and most of his fellow publishers Maurras's "divine surprise" had concretely translated itself into figures in the profits column.

In February 1942 Les Editions de Minuit published *Le Silence de la mer (The Silence of the Sea)*, the tale of a strange cohabitation: a German officer in the home of an old Frenchman and his niece, who meet the officer's enforced monologue, his craving for a dialogue, with silence and dignity rather than hostility. The impact of this book published under the counter was not only literary but also political and moral.

The Silence of the Sea and, a few months later, the first mimeo-
graphed issue of the weekly *Les Lettres françaises* were a breath of
hope, even if their initial distribution was limited. It was proof that
typewriters could be turned into tools of war, that one could publish
without "appearing" and assume one's function as an intellectual
without toadying to the occupier. Other publications outside official
control and therefore by nature subversive also helped to free the
atmosphere.

Gaston had never been more visibly active. His attitudes were
as opaque as the times. The little facts of daily life give a truer picture
of the contradictions in the literary world of the period than do
partisan views and positions.

February 1: Rue de Verneuil, in the salon of Mme. Boudot-
Lamotte, the mother of Gaston's charming secretary. Cocteau gave
a reading of his new play, *Renaud et Armide*, before a select audience:
Lieutenant Heller, Captain Jünger, Horst Wiemer, the German commissar at Hachette's, Gaston Gallimard, the actor Jean Marais, and
others.[71]

February 21: Place Saint-Michel, at the Rôtisserie Périgourdine.
The Parisian publishers gave a farewell luncheon for Bremer, the
assistant director of the German Institute, "who didn't give them
too much trouble while he was here."[72] He was leaving for the
Eastern front, where he was to die.

March 5: funeral mass for Gaston Gallimard's mother. On arriving at the church of La Trinité, Marcel Jouhandeau was not sure
whether to seat himself between Paulhan and Groethuysen or next
to Drieu La Rochelle. He solved the dilemma by sitting through the
ceremony with the first two, and then leaving with Drieu. Literary
diplomacy.[73]

March 11: on Rue Sébastien-Bottin Gaston met with Jünger to
mark the forthcoming publication in French of Jünger's book *On the
Marble Cliffs*, attended by his secretary Madeleine Boudot-Lamotte
and his new business manager, Stameroff. Upon leaving, Jünger
noted: "Gallimard gives an impression of enlightened energy, as
intelligent as it is practical—the very thing that should characterize

a good publisher. There must also be a bit of a gardener in him."[74]

June 2: Tout-Paris of the world of publishing and literature crowded into the Hôtel Drouot auction rooms for the sale of the library of Louis Brun, Grasset's associate, who had been murdered by his wife. Crazy prices—a typewritten copy of Charles Maurras's *La Musique intérieure* (Interior Music) with a few corrections in his handwriting fetched 20,000 francs. And 185,000 francs for one of the five copies on Japan paper of *Du côté de chez Swann (Swann's Way)*, together with some handwritten letters signed by Proust.[75]

July 10: Afternoon reception, with champagne and tartlets. In the crowd Gaston conversed with Maurice Toesca, whose novel *Clément* he was publishing. This Frenchman—formerly a teacher of German—was in charge of relations with the occupying authorities in the office of the prefect of police, Amédée Bussières.[76]

Gaston was exercising more caution than usual. "Events," as they were called, required a great deal of circumspection. Convinced that all of this would soon be over, he did not want to incriminate himself in such a shifting world. So he kept Drieu on one side and Paulhan on the other. Agreeing to publish some German classics, using Goethe as a "flag of convenience,"[77] he avoided having to publish truly Nazi writers as if they were the flower of German literature.

In 1942 Gaston did not write many letters. Rather than put everything in writing, as is a publisher's normal tendency, he went whenever necessary to the German embassy, the German Institute, or the Propaganda Staffel to express orally his reactions to the decisions of the occupiers. That was the safer way, even though he was sure—as indeed was the case—that the German services kept written records of everything. In this, he adopted an attitude far removed from that of his competitors Grasset and Denoël.

Gaston's position was all the more delicate, since he had to keep both sides happy. When Lucien Rebatet in June submitted his manuscript of *Les Décombres* (Rubbish) to Stameroff, who was both a contributor to the collaborationist paper *Je suis partout* and, in his capacity of business manager, a member of the Gallimard editorial board, Gaston was most embarrassed. He could not publish a propaganda piece of such violence, a book so overtly labeled, with the *NRF* imprint. But he could not reject it on the basis of its content without the risk of antagonizing a good part of the collaborationist press. So after two weeks' deliberation he instructed Stameroff to accept it on condition that the author cut the huge manuscript (664 book pages) by almost half and agree to a limited printing of 5,000 copies. As expected, Rebatet refused; he took it to André Fraigneau and Henry Muller, at Grasset, who reacted with enthusiasm. But Grasset himself objected—too many of his friends ("that venomous hyena of a Mauriac," as Rebatet would say) were pricked if not insulted in *Les Décombres*, the "chronicle of the long decline, the successive crumblings that produced an enormous pile of rubbish"— the rubbish of France in ruins, of its beliefs and institutions, as the author explained in his foreword. Rebatet then took his manuscript to Denoël, despite the latter's perpetual financial problems, for Denoël at least represented "an acceptable label," given the presence in his catalogue of Céline, Brasillach, and Maurice Bardèche. Fortyeight hours later Rebatet signed a contract and received a 25,000franc advance on royalties of a first printing of 20,000 copies. Denoël asked for and was allowed just one cut, a small one, forestalling the German censor: a few lines condemning the German annexation of Alsace.[78]

The success of *Les Décombres* was overwhelming. It was the literary (and political) event of 1942—and of the two following years. At Denoël's they had not seen such a public craze, such sales figures, so many autograph sessions since *Journey to the End of the Night*. A new printing was immediately needed and then another, to keep up with demand. Denoël was finally seeing light at the end of the tunnel; he even expected to show an annual report in the black, now that he had acquired a partner (since October 1941), the Berlin publisher Wilhelm Andermann, who for 180,000 francs acquired 725 shares in the company. It was understood that although Denoël remained the sole manager and editor of the firm, he accepted, by Article VIII of their contract, that Andermann had a right to review the management.[79] This unhoped-for supply of new capital allowed Denoël to meet the commercial demands growing out of the wild success of *Les Décombres* and a few other books of that fertile 1942 season, notably *Mille regrets* (A Thousand Regrets), a collection of Elsa Triolet's stories that was lauded to the skies in the Parisian press, particularly by Pierre MacOrlan. These developments rescued Denoël from being financially strangled by his wholesaler-distributor, Hachette, which held two liens on the assets of his company. By the end of 1942 he would at last be able to cancel his exclusive distribution contract with Hachette and announce that, as of January 1, 1943, his firm would sell directly to the trade.[80]

Gaston was certainly sorry to see such sales get away from him, especially when he saw customers fighting to get copies of *Les Décombres* in Rive Gauche, the large pro-German bookstore on Boulevard Saint-Michel—but not sorry that he had passed on the book. It was too dangerous, too clearly committed. To be sure, so was the *NRF*. Its tables of contents, even if at times Paulhan's hand could be felt in them, were so many pledges of loyalty given to the occupiers. Drieu, its editor, was indisputably a fascist, and without any doubt whatever he had superimposed his own image on the magazine. When he went to Germany to visit the studio of the sculptor Arno Brecker, Goebbels's propaganda services distributed the picture of their meeting with a caption that read, in part: "this writer belongs to the *Novelle Revue Française*, a periodical interested in National Socialist and fascist problems."[81] On his propaganda trip beyond the Rhine, Drieu, along with a few companions, represented French literature. By 1942 he had had enough. Enough of the trip—and of the magazine. He no longer wanted to be the "house collaborator." He was willing to continue running the *NRF* only if he could have the help of a committe of "wise men" and a managing editor. He would then remain the editor in name only, the one responsible before the law. For the committee of wise men, names were suggested: Claudel, Gide, Montherlant, Mauriac, Giono, Jouhandeau, Valéry, Fargue. But however they were combined, there was no way of getting them to agree; above and beyond the Paulhan-Drieu division there were too many mutual hatreds, jealousies, and fallings-out among these "great writers" who talked primarily the language of competition. Drieu, firmly decided to resign, had his letter ready, but once again Gaston found persuasive words:

"The magazine on the whole is good and everyone respects its editor. . . . If you did not intimidate me so, you would get a better feeling of how much affection I have for you."[82]

Drieu agreed to stay; the magazine went on.

On the editorial board of the publishing house there was a new-comer: the twenty-six-year-old Dionys Mascolo, a friend of Michel Gallimard, Gaston's nephew and Raymond's son; they had been classmates at the Ecole Alsacienne. Self-educated and avidly inter-ested in literature, Mascolo at the beginning of the war had been an errand boy and then an administrative secretary at the Nonferrous Metals Trade Association. Then he renewed his close friendship with Michel Gallimard, who regularly gave him the best of the company's output to read, and occasionally asked him to comment on difficult manuscripts such as Maurice Blanchot's *Thomas l'obscur (Thomas the Obscure)*. One evening, after a concert, Michel introduced him to Gaston, who took them out to dinner and during the evening's conversation tested the young man. Shortly afterward he offered him a spot in his secretariat and on the editorial board, at 3,000 francs per month—500 less than he had been making at the Nonferrous Metals. Mascolo accepted, despite the problem for his family, whom he had to support. As soon as he got to Rue Sébastien-Bottin, he set to work reading all the latest books and some of the manuscripts, meeting authors, arguing for or against submitted material before the editorial board.[83]

There was no dearth of work. The Occupation had not stemmed the creative inspiration of writers—quite the contrary—and war was far from being their central theme. Two authors at Gallimard were representative of the spirit of the times in 1942: Camus and Saint-Exupéry. After the appearance of *The Stranger* in June, Gaston started its author on a monthly salary, over and above advances against royalties. Officially, Camus was carried on the books as a reader-editor, a common custom for assisting financially strapped authors.[84] Gaston had great faith in him, convinced that he was a really important writer. The enthusiasm that greeted *The Stranger* and its lasting reputation bore this out. But it was only when pressured by his editorial board that in October of the same year Gaston published *Le Mythe de Sisyphe (The Myth of Sisyphus)*, the philosophical counterpart of the novel which analyzed the absurd and suicide. The chapter devoted to Kafka was suppressed by order of the German censors, as the Czech writer appeared on the Otto List because of his Jewish origin. Gaston had so little faith in the book that he ordered only a small printing: half that of *The Stranger*.[85]

Shortly afterward, Gaston sent to Lieutenant Heller the manuscript of Saint-Exupéry's *Pilote de guerre (Flight to Arras)*, which was given his approval if not his enthusiasm. This meant permission to print and publish plus a paper quota. However, two conditions were set: the printing was to be limited to 2,100 copies, and one phrase had to be cut: the six words, "Hitler, who started this crazy war." Well, if that was all . . . It was cut. The book was published, and then the scandal broke. The collaborationist press went wild. Some were offended because one of the heroes of the story was named Israel and was described as "one of the most courageous and modest" of the pilots in the group. "He had heard so much talk of Jewish craftiness that he probably mistook his courage for a form of craftiness. To gain a victory is to act craftily."[86] Such a statement was considered inadmissible and offensive to those then in power. The author, it was said, "glorifies Jews and warmongers."[87] *Flight to Arras* was a veritable "weapon of war fired by an antifascist publisher," a book "which justifies the loss of the empire and the wiping out of France."[88] Vichy did not wait for the press campaign to develop: at the first "denunciations" by anonymous Frenchmen protesting the antinational character of the work, Gallimard was asked to recall all the copies that had been distributed. Lieutenant Heller was reprimanded by his superiors for having passed such a manuscript. As for the underground publishers and printers, they latched on to it with delight, so as not to leave to the Americans alone the distinction of having published the original edition of the book on February 20, 1942: in Lyons, a group of typographers set and printed a thousand handsewn copies of *Pilote de guerre* in December 1943, and the same was done shortly afterward in Lille by Resistance printers.[89]

Gaston was distressed. This affair cost him money and, for a time, put the spotlight on his firm, something he thoroughly disliked. The next time he would be more careful. To help him in this, the Propaganda Staffel reinforced its system of prevention and suppression. Once again, lists and bans.

"French publishing, so cruelly tried by events, has refused to abandon its mission," wrote one literary commentator. "And there is nothing more moving, more praiseworthy than the efforts it is making to be worthy not only of its past, but also of the New Order."[90] A few weeks later, René Philippon, president of the publishers' trade association, sent a circular to all his members asking them for greater docility, servility, submissiveness. He was merely echoing the lecturing he had had to undergo for hours in the offices at the Hôtel Majestic. The Germans were surprised that despite paper restrictions Parisian publishers were publishing so many titles, chosen with so little discrimination, obviously unwilling to take seriously the "advice" of the occupiers. They warned the trade association that if it did not police itself, they would step in and do it. The heads of the trade association, to exhibit good faith and a spirit of discipline, offered to form a commission to supervise the quality of books to be published, a somewhat vague project, but a first concession, meant to show a willingness to cooperate. In his circular, Philippon was firm: no more random publishing of books based on the premise that anything sells; rather, careful selection of works of commanding stature or that respond to popular demand. Otherwise: "Publishers called to our attention by the Propaganda Division as not having conformed to this discipline will be stricken from the roll of those receiving paper distributions."[91] That was the ultimate sanction, the one most feared.

The situation was clear: it was time for severity and obedience. A new era, compared to which self-censorship was liberalism.

Henceforth three institutions would regulate Parisian publishing, with the trade association acting as messenger:

(1) the *Comité d'Organisation du Livre* (Committee for the Organization of Book Production), created by decree on May 3, 1941, as part of industrial production, its responsibility limited to economic and technical problems;

(2) the *Conseil du Livre* (Book Council), created by decree on June 9, 1941, as part of national education, concerned only with the intellectual orientation of books published. Among its first members were Drieu La Rochelle (then editor of the *NRF*), André Bellessort, Paul Morand, André Siegfried, Dunoyer de Segonzac, and the publishers Gillon, Bourdel, Arthaud, and Grasset;

(3) the *Commission de Contrôle du Papier* (Paper Control Commission), created by decree on April 1, 1942. This most recent and least known of the institutions set up by the government to regulate publishing held its first meeting on May 23 at the Bibliothèque Nationale on Rue de Richelieu. It quickly became apparent that its members were not there only to discuss wholesale paper problems.

"Perhaps we should go a step further," said M. Haurigot, who was representing the state secretary for information, "and ask ourselves whether the role of our commission should be not only to determine what should not be printed, but also what should be printed. The commission will make its selections on the basis of love of country and love of French literature."

Twice a month regularly, if we can trust the minutes that were kept,[92] this commission's members met at either the Bibliothèque Nationale or the Cercle de la Librairie. At their June 8 meeting Haurigot asserted that publishing houses must no longer be considered free commercial enterprises on a par with other industrial companies. Given the paper shortage, "any work published will henceforth have to be a contribution to the rebuilding of France or to its intellectual influence—either by literary value or pertinence." Haurigot also made a plea for "a censorship of quality and usefulness," concluding:

"I am happy to say, after meeting with some of the best-qualified publishers or their representatives, such as Gaston Gallimard, Bernard Grasset, Albin Michel, Robert Denoël, René Julliard, Baudinière, that they are in agreement with me."

This set the tone. The commission immediately went to work. Haurigot, who had been delegated full power, displayed a written order from Paul Marion, the state secretary for information.

"He expects Denoël's reissues of the works of M. Louis-Ferdinand Céline to be given every priority, in consideration of their value and interest."

At the meeting of June 24, a list of political works was submitted to this high tribunal of "paper allotters," who in the final analysis held sway over the life or death of most new works. They had immense power, combining as they did the function of censors with those of paper suppliers. That day, several titles were considered: *Les Intellectuels français devant le désastre de 1870* (French Intellectuals and the Disaster of 1870) by Michel Mohrt, *De Jaurès à Blum* (From Jean Jaurès to Léon Blum) by L. O. Frossard, *L'Amérique juive* (Jewish America) by Pierre-Antoine Cousteau, *Mémoires* (Memoirs) by Joseph Caillaux, and *Les Décombres* by Rebatet.

In this thicket of services, censorships, lists, and authorizations, publishers were losing their way. The president of their trade association complained of the slowness with which the control commission issued authorization numbers. The final lists had not even been drawn up yet.

Those who did the reading for the censorship services were hard pressed. Their speed was the determining factor in what the publishers could bring out. They were paid on the average 150 francs for a novel of approximately 300 pages. But the Germans did not accept all of their decisions. At the July 15 meeting of readers, some took umbrage at the fact that authorizations had been refused not only to the *Larousse élémentaire,* a standard dictionary, but even to *Scènes de la vie future (America the Menace; Scenes from the Life of the Future)* by Georges Duhamel of the French Academy.

"We cannot accept these rejections without explanations," Philippon averred. "The commission must consult with Schultz of the Propaganda Division."

It did so in short order, and was successful.

In principle and from experience they all knew that no list was ever final. The bans could always be modified, deferred, or dropped. All that was needed was a little tact, and connections. But one should never take a stand for a book that was not worth it.

On July 28 the commission drew up a first balance sheet. As of that date, 2,230 books had been submitted, of which 1,170 had been approved, although the Germans eliminated twenty-two of these. The criteria were less and less precise. Referring only to Gallimard books, it may be noted that on the same day that the commission reinstated Léon-Paul Fargue's *Déjeuners de soleil* (Sun Food) and Paul Valéry's *Mauvaises Pensées* (Evil Thoughts), both of which had been rejected in the first instance, it approved Camus's *Myth of Sisyphus* and rejected Robert Desnos's *Le Vin est tiré* (The Wine Is Drawn), which would also eventually be reinstated. It resembled a school exam, but with this difference: behind these graders with their strange tastes stood the officers of an army of occupation.

Realizing the extensive powers of the members of this commission with an innocuous name—"Paper Control"!—the publishers started lobbying. "Special representations," as they were called, were made to obtain quick imprimaturs for Jouhandeau's *Triptyque* (Triptych), Claudel's *Seigneur, apprenez-nous à prier* (Lord, Teach Us to Pray), and even Jünger's *The Adventurous Heart*. More than once, decisions were reversed even though they had at first been unanimously made. With the influx of manuscripts, the readers were overwhelmed, and some of them proved incompetent. They needed reinforcements. Marcel Arland was invited to join at the October 21 meeting; Ramon Fernandez let it be known that he was willing: he was selected along with Brice Parain. All three were members of Gallimard's editorial board: the best reader-editors were to be found at Rue Sébastien-Bottin. A sign of the times.

In July 1942 a new Otto List was circulated, replacing the earlier one, now two years old. In his foreword the president of the trade association pointed out the newcomers in this enumeration of undesirables: translations from English (except for classics) and from Polish; books by Jewish writers (with exceptions for scientific works), and biographies of Jews, even when written by "Aryans." Thus the lives of Offenbach, Milhaud, and Meyerbeer had to be withdrawn from bookstores. Once again, some hundred Gallimard titles were blacklisted—virtually the same ones as in September 1940. But five new ones were now added: Eve Curie's *Madame Curie*; Gide's *Retour de l'URSS (Return from the U.S.S.R.)* and *Retouches à mon retour de l'URSS (Afterthoughts on My Return)*; and finally *Il court il court . . .* (He Runs, He Runs . . .) and *Les Causes perdues* (Lost Causes) by the well-known Foreign Service spy Violet Trefusis.

Fortunately some warehouses still had supplies of these banned books, alongside piles of the illegal works of Les Editions de Minuit.

Booksellers were important both to the Propaganda Staffel and to the Resistance. Without their cooperation a book might remain unknown to customers, or on the contrary . . . The underground publishers were quick to understand this, sending out a bulletin virtually indistinguishable from the *Bibliographie de la France*. The bulletin denounced at length publishers and booksellers who were collaborating with the Germans. In the second issue of this counterfeit publication they ran "Six Commandments for Resistance Booksellers":

1. When thou receivest books, thou shalt sort them carefully.
2. Books by traitors thou shalt keep out of sight.
3. Likewise those from the German propaganda mills.
4. And in thy shop display nothing that smacketh of Pétain.
5. And as long as thou resistest, Honor shalt thou have.
6. Thou shalt honor the French spirit and it alone shalt thou serve.[93]

It was a breath of fresh air between the two Otto Lists.

Meanwhile in the United States *Life* magazine in its August 24

issue published a blacklist of some forty names of French collaborators. A forerunner, as it were, of the postwar purges, it brought
together, in an indiscriminate jumble, the music hall star Mistinguett,
the collaborating writer Jacques Chardonne, the actor and playwright
Sacha Guitry, Pétain, and Darlan, among others.

In Paris efforts were made to list and catalogue all banned books;
paper was apportioned sparingly to nonconforming publishers but
generously to the docile ones. The Propaganda Division had now
gone the Otto List one better: what might be called the Otto An-
tilist—that is, the titles that the Germans wished to promote in Occupied France. Banning was not enough; now certain books were
pushed, imposed on publishers.[94] This list was broken down not by
author or publisher, but by theme: Against Liberalism and Democracy; Against England; Against Gaullism. A substantial number, including five published by Gallimard: *Notes pour comprendre le siècle*
(Notes for Understanding Our Age) by Drieu La Rochelle; *La Grâce*
(State of Grace), a novel by Marcel Arland; and three biographies—
Luther, Liszt, and Gluck. These were the books which those in charge
of cultural propaganda in Occupied France considered conducive to
a closer relationship between the two countries and the perpetuation
of the Thousand-Year Reich.

These lists shed light on the thinking behind the cultural policy
of the occupiers. But in the columns of names, titles, and publishers
some of the recommendations are surprising, some omissions inex-
plicable.

For this, Bernhard Payr serves as an invaluable guide. From the
start of the Nazi regime he held a privileged observation post in
Berlin. Alongside Alfred Rosenberg, the theoretician responsible for
political and intellectual training in the NSDAP (National Socialist
German Workers' Party), Payr was in charge of the so-called literature office.[95] He scrutinized German and foreign literature, examining books either to suppress them through the censors or endorse
them. Payr, a specialist in French literature, was a man of undisputed
power and influence. In mid-Occupation (1943) he published in Germany *Phönix oder Asche?* (Phoenix or Ashes?),[96] an overview of French

collaborationist literature. Applying the National Socialist view-point, he discussed the works of Rebatet, Georges Blond, Brasillach, Alfred Fabre-Luce, Chardonne, and Jouhandeau. Outspokenly op-posed to the royalist *Action française* (too narrowly nationalistic for his taste), he praised only those writers who went beyond Franco-German collaboration to a European commitment. But most inter-esting is his criticism of Céline. Though acknowledging that Céline's enemies (Jews, Communists, Freemasons) were also Germany's, he taxed him with "savage, filthy slang" and "brutal obscenities." Of the pamphlet *Les Beaux Draps* he said that it was "made up of ex-clamatory prose and snippets of sentences adding up to hysterical outcries that cancel out the author's good intentions." Though he considered Céline untranslatable into German, Payr nevertheless rec-ognized that "he always starts from correct racial notions."[97]

The temper of the times had curious repercussions. Gaston, for instance, who regarded collaborators with derision and avoided meeting with the Germans as much as possible, at least according to those who were close to him, nevertheless proclaimed himself an Aryan. Not publicly, of course, but with discretion. Admittedly, there was a personal reason.

The moment that Vichy's anti-Semitic legislation went into ef-fect, Jewish heads of companies were expropriated without "due process." In publishing the main targets were three: Ferenczi, Na-than, and Calmann-Lévy. Their companies had to be "Aryanized," to use the prevailing expression—purged of all Jewish presence both with regard to personnel and to investors. In the case of the textbook publisher Fernand Nathan, professional solidarity provided a happy ending. Some ten publishers joined in buying the firm, thus rescuing it from a buyout by the occupier and subsequent management by one of his agents. On the one hand, the Aryanization rules were complied with, and on the other, Nathan was assured that this move was made so as to keep his publishing house intact—it would be returned to him when the Germans left France. An interim admin-istrator was appointed. On the day Paris was liberated, Nathan went to the office of the group's delegate and was handed the keys with the words: "You are back home!" All that remained was the formality of buying back the company at a price indexed to the market value of the inventory. Honor and dignity had prevailed, everything returned to normal.

At Calmann-Lévy's it was a different story. This traditional and prestigious house was the object of much desire. Michel Lévy had been the publisher of the great nineteenth-century writers and his backlist and catalogue were coveted. Aryanized, the firm seemed about to be sold. In the meantime, a manager pro tem, by the name of Capy, had been appointed. The owner of a hotel near the Madeleine, Capy appeared to be the straw man of a decidedly shady character who from the very start of the Occupation had taken every opportunity to profit from the collaborationist enterprises in journalism and publishing: Louis Thomas. Thomas, undoubtedly an agent of the Propaganda Division, carried on a subtle war against the guiding spirits of the German Institute, who were also coveting the Calmann-Lévy company. The "intellectuals" of that institute finally won out and had Jean Flory named as provisional administrator, but that was only the first step. The second was more difficult: to buy out the company, which was held jointly by Georges and Gaston Calmann-Lévy, Michel Calmann, and Georges Propper, a family that occupied a unique place in the French publishing landscape.

As with Nathan, there had initially been the idea of a publishers' consortium taking over the business to protect it from German capital. One person was the pivot of this initiative: Renée Drouelle, an employee since 1911, who had been secretary, then executive secretary, and finally one of the chief executive officers of Calmann-Lévy.[98] The family trusted her implicitly, and she was able to hold on to her job, the only one of the original staff, until July 1941, when Louis Thomas had her dismissed as well. She carried on discreet and delicate negotiations—on the one hand with the publisher Durand-Auzias, who was willing to approach and organize a group of fellow publishers, and on the other hand with the heirs of the main backlist authors (France, Loti, Bazin, Renan), so that when the day of sale came, the capital might remain French and the management honorable.

Pending that date, which had not as yet been set, the provisional administrator Jean Flory received several offers of purchase, among others from Albin Michel[99] and also from Gaston. On January 20, 1942, he sent Flory a registered letter, with a copy to M. Regelsperger, of the Central Commissariat for Jewish Affairs:

> We herewith confirm our offer to buy the publishing and bookselling firm known under the name of Calmann-Lévy. . . .
>
> This offer is based on a price of two million five hundred thousand francs payable in cash. It is understood that the Librairie Gallimard (Editions de la Nouvelle Revue Française) will not absorb the Calmann-Lévy company, which will remain autonomous and have its own editorial board, of which Messrs. Drieu La Rochelle and Paul Morand will no doubt agree to be members. We wish to inform you at this time that the Librairie Gallimard (Editions de la Nouvelle Revue Française) is an Aryan firm backed by Aryan capital. . . .[100]

The offer was specific. It enumerated everything that was likely to be part of the transaction: goodwill, commercial name, profits, overhead, authors' contracts, stock, machines, office furnishings, receivables, third-party notes, income from rights sold, payment of taxes and fees, lease for the premises. This was the offer of a businessman ready to deal.[101]

Was Gaston acting in his own name? Was his offer a matter of personal initiative, or only a trial balloon on behalf of the publishers' consortium? The question remains unanswered. But the letter cannot be denied.

The sale was finally made to four men—Louis Thomas, René Lelief, Albert Lejeune, and Henry Jamet—acting on behalf of Gerhard Hibbelen of the German Institute. The business was Aryanized. Calmann-Lévy as a company no longer existed: it was now Les Editions Balzac.

In January 1943 Gaston Gallimard turned sixty-two.

Hitler had decreed "total war." In France it had been two months since the difference between the free and occupied zones disappeared; the Wehrmacht now occupied the entire country. Pierre Laval, as head of the Vichy government, was more powerful than ever: he alone was empowered to sign laws and decrees. Parisians flocked to see Marcel Carné's film *Les Visiteurs du soir (The Devil's Envoys)*, while on stage Montherlant's *La Reine morte* (The Dead Queen) was all the rage. In the South, the first Maquis were beginning to organize. It was almost three years since France had become German.

Publishing was in mourning. Albin Michel died, then Pierre-Victor Stock. Called Albin, as Gallimard was called Gaston, Michel had been an odd figure in the book trade. A hearty, high-living man who set up shop within a stone's throw of a cemetery, he had been immediately successful. His experience, daring, and strokes of genius won the respect even of scoffers. In an interview he gave a simple— if not simplistic—definition of his profession:

> In my selection of authors I am not guided by any concern for literary schools or circles. I look for well-written books that are solidly con-structed and of interest to the general public. That, to my mind, is the principal aim of publishing: to reach the masses. . . . The backbone of a firm like mine, and very few people are aware of it, is books like *The Key to Dreams*, *The Handbook of the Perfect Gardener*, or pulp editions sold at 25 centimes. The sales of such properties are assured and con-stant. Literature is a kind of luxury.[102]

A kind of luxury . . .

For Pierre-Victor Stock it had been more a game. He had the good sense to acquire the backlist of the bookseller-publisher Albert Savine; to develop his department of foreign translations to the point of making them the hallmark of his firm; and to maintain a balance between the traditional and the innovative. After a serious crisis and some injudicious deals, Stock was forced to sell his firm to his young secretary Jacques Boutelleau (later known as the author Jacques Char-donne) and the latter's brother-in-law, Delamain. Gradually Stock faded from the picture. At the Cercle de la Librairie people said, "He was a great publisher." At the Cercle de la Presse they said, "He was a great poker player." Ten years before his death he worked in the casino where he had lost his fortune. A sad ending for a man of taste and culture. Stock decidedly belonged to the nineteenth century. The big thing in his life had been the Dreyfus Affair, into which he threw himself body and soul—on the right side.

The Propaganda Division's next move was a circular announcing that all translations from English, with the exception of textbooks and classical authors, were to be recalled immediately. Possible exceptions: Bernard Shaw, because he was Irish, and Rabindranath Tagore, because he was Indian. Kafka, banned in German as well as French because he was Jewish, was being read under cover in English: *The Castle, The Trial.* Mazo de la Roche's *Jalna* series was among the best-sellers. Saint-Exupéry had published *Le Petit Prince (The Little Prince)* in New York. Sartre was keeping a cool head: he refused to publish a collection of his articles as Gaston and Raymond Queneau had proposed, alleging that it would be premature.

Despite his outspoken sympathy for the cause of collaboration, despite his connections and the variety of his literary output, Grasset was not doing well. The comparative figures of his annual business over a five-year period told the story. From a figure of 7,153,450 francs in 1938 he had jumped to 18,922,634 francs by 1941, then declined to 10,005,665 francs in 1942, and to a bare 8,289,589 francs in 1943.[103]

At Gallimard as well, 1941 seems to have been the best of those years. What could the falling off in the later war years be attributed to? The eternal paper problem. There never was enough; the measly allotments of paper to even the most compliant of publishers did not provide for big enough printings, and as the war went on, paper got even scarcer. In July 1942 Gallimard had been allowed, by decision of the paper committee, an allotment of 3.2 tons, which dwindled to 1.3 tons by the third quarter of 1943, then stabilized at 2.0 tons the following quarter—less than Hachette, Larousse, or Les Presses Universitaires de France.

Grasset was all the more exasperated, because demand was

unprecedented. How could he explain it to the stockholders? True, he still held the largest block of shares, 25,390 out of 38,000. But there was that multitude of small holders of registered stock, and the owners of bearer shares who wielded great influence: Giraudoux (10 shares), Mauriac (8), Morand (8), Henry Muller (10). His three largest stockholders (with 200 shares each) were in no position to cause him problems, for the actress Mme. Simone (née Benda), André Maurois (né Herzog), and the industrialist Paul-Louis Weiller, being Jewish, were all in exile![104]

At the Lapérouse restaurant on the quays, Paulhan, Heller, Gallimard, and Valéry had lunch with Drieu. They were trying to put together a new editorial board for the magazine, since Drieu was now definitely leaving. The NRF would be publishing its last issue before suspension on June 1. Drieu had lost his enthusiasm for it: he knew, especially since Rommel's defeat at El Alamein in November 1942, that Germany would lose the war.

Gerhard Heller did not hide his admiration for Gaston, "the model of the perfect publisher." The firm had always been, thanks to Heller, surrounded by "a sort of protective barrier."[105] To such an extent that on the door of Heller's office Céline once scribbled "NRF" in chalk, shouting, "Come on, everybody knows you're a Gallimard agent!"[106] His support enabled Gaston to ward off attacks, wherever they might come from—and the blows came from the French more often than from the Germans. The collaborationist press had not forgotten his rejection of Rebatet's Les Décombres: "Not enough paper, he said. But for Aragon's enormous volume Gallimard solved the paper problem without any trouble. There's a political coloring there that you can't miss."[107] Gaston had learned his lesson from the scandal that followed his publication of Flight to Arras. For Aragon's The Century Was Young no review copies would go out to reviewers. Thanks to that little stratagem booksellers could display it in their windows, have piles of it in their shops, and above all put in a supply in case it might later be banned and have to be sold on the black market. When the reporters caught on, they were furious, but it was too late. The "ultra" newsmen accused Gaston of having two standards, one for Saint-Exupéry and Aragon, the other for Rebatet: "It would seem that M. Gallimard shows a lack of discernment in the choice of the horses he backs. Unless he truly prefers renegades and runaways, Jews and traitors."[108]

Fortunately not all authors posed similar problems for him. Most of his 1943 books were innocuous. *Either/Or* by Kierkegaard, James Joyce's *Portrait of the Artist As a Young Man*, *Montherlant, homme libre* (Montherlant, a Free Man) by Michel Mohrt, *Lecture de Phèdre* (On Reading *Phèdre*) by Thierry Maulnier, *Faux-pas* by Maurice Blanchot, *Le Passe-muraille (The Walker-through-walls)* and *La Vouivre (The Fable and the Flesh)* by Marcel Aymé, *Der Hochwald (The Great Woods)* by the Austrian writer Adalbert Stifter, and novels translated from Norwegian and Danish. He also published a collection of stories, *L'Eau vive* (Fresh Water) and the *Théâtre* (Theater) of Jean Giono, who was more and more pressed for money. Before asking Michel Gallimard to find a buyer for two of his original manuscripts, the poet laureate of Manosque wrote Gaston: "I have a wife to support, and a few pigs to feed before they in turn feed me. Perhaps if you could go as high as 15 or 20,000 francs . . ." Shortly afterward he came back again: "Isn't there a small credit on my account? You can't imagine how painful it is always to have to ask—one really must be desperate to do it."[109]

Gallimard had dozens of Gionos. Writers chronically in debt were even more so during the war. That was only one more worry, one more demand in this troubled, intense period when the slightest event could take on a dimension out of all proportions. Sometimes a little nothing could bring panic to Rue Sébastien-Bottin. One morning an unknown German, a Sergeant Walter Heist, had someone call to ask for information about an author whose novel he had seen in a shop window. Heist wanted to know more about him. Panicky, Gaston called Maurice Toesca, the author in question, who immediately reassured him: the man making the inquiry was the former editor-in-chief of the *Volkszeitung* of Mainz, a childhood friend he had long carried on a correspondence with, who was now trying to locate him again through Gallimard.[110]

Sometimes it was Gaston himself who caused the upsets at the company headquarters. Twice, his frequent patronizing of black-market restaurants and his attachment to a few lofty principles nearly got him into real trouble. The first time, he created a scene by demanding to be served the same runny omelet as the one that had just been served to a German officer at a nearby table:

"Why him? Why not me?" he demanded loudly.

Another time, when there was a police raid and the restaurant owner was hurrying all his guests out through the kitchen, Gaston energetically refused to hide—"I have nothing to be ashamed of!"— was arrested, and spent the night in jail, not without alarming the whole House of Gallimard at a time when the German police were selecting hostages at random from local police stations.

For all his contacts, his way with people, and his power, he knew he had to be cautious. Times had changed: many devoted supporters of Vichy, riding high only a short time back, had been locked up or deported. No one was immune to a "misunderstanding" or an "interservice rivalry" within the occupying forces.

In May 1943, in an apartment near Saint-Germain-des-Prés, at 48 Rue du Four, the first meeting of the National Resistance Council was held. Sixteen men, all of them representing parties, resistance movements, or trade unions, gathered there, despite their differences joined by one common goal: to liberate France. Jean Moulin, General de Gaulle's delegate, had called the meeting.

Resistance? Gaston had other things to worry about, personal problems requiring short-term answers. That evening, along with his nephew Michel, he was pacing the sidewalk on Avenue Niel, outside the home of Maurice Toesca. He was waiting to see him, not to talk about his next novel, but again to ask him to intercede in his capacity as cabinet secretary to the prefect of police. The two men waited there for two hours, finally sitting on a public bench, until Toesca finally came home after dining out with friends, and immediately invited them up to his apartment. Gaston was extremely worried: that afternoon he and his nephew had received summonses to appear at the Service du Travail Obligatoire (Labor Service), the feared and hated STO. They were convinced that someone had denounced them, which seemed inevitable after all those articles in the pro-German papers.

"You have to do something for us," Gaston pleaded.

"Don't worry, at your age you're too old to be sent to Germany," Toesca reassured him. "It must be a mistake."

"It's probably me they're after," Michel Gallimard suggested.[111]

The very next day Toesca—the "screen," the "representative of poetry at the prefecture," as Jean Genet was to say a few months later in a thank-you letter—checked the lists of the labor department at the prefecture of the Seine, and to set Gaston's mind completely at ease arranged a meeting for him with the chief administrator of that service, who assured him he would be able to cancel any such decision by the Germans. Leaving the prefecture, Gaston fell all over himself with apologies and thanks, making a thousand promises to this author to whom he was indebted. He invited him to lunch on several occasions, and out for the weekend at his country estate or that of André Cornu, his daughter-in-law's father. But Toesca was not the only person to whom the Gallimards were indebted; on the German side, too, they were protected from the STO. Captain Ernst Jünger, whose novel *The Adventurous Heart* Gaston had published and whom he often met in Parisian salons, had been able to knock at the right door: that of General von Stülpnagel, the military commander for France. "I've mentioned it to Stülpnagel. It's all taken care of," he would say.[112]

Gaston now learned where the "blow" came from. A political article in *Je suis partout*, devoted to something entirely different, concluded, ". . . or else they better send M. Gallimard to Germany"![113] In his eyes, the article was as good as signed—by the clan bent on making him pay for rejecting *Les Décombres*. In this France at civil war, "bad" Frenchmen were more of a threat than "good" Germans.

On June 25, after the police came to Rue Sébastien-Bottin to pick "relief" people (for work in Germany) from among the staff, and Gaston made many phone calls to high places to ward off the measure, Michel and his friend Dionys Mascolo seriously considered leaving France for England.[114] They remained in France, but Mascolo went into the Resistance, joining the movement headed by François Mitterrand (the MNPDG) and Camus's newspaper *Combat*. In his desk drawer at the Gallimard offices he now kept a revolver handy among the papers and pencils. Gaston knew it but said nothing, just as he did not try to make Paulhan stop steering authors toward *Les Lettres françaises* and the underground Editions de Minuit. That was one of the facets of the strange game he was playing.

In 1943 Gaston began organizing concerts. After publishing, the theater, newspapers, movies—it was now music. But it was not just a music lover's fancy: it was his way to get all his authors together regularly, the stay-at-homes as well as the nomads, Parisians as well as provincials, in a pleasant and nonpolitical setting. And—who knows?—in these times of deprivation when Tout-Paris crowded to any entertainment at all, it might even not lose money. Denise Tual, with whom he had launched the Synops Agency before the war, took charge of the organization. Gaston provided the title, "Les Concerts de la Pléiade"—a subtle cachet on the performances which linked them to his prestigious collection. The gala première took place on March 22 at the Charpentier Gallery. After the initial weeks the programs began to strike audiences as "charming ear-teasers," to quote Arthur Honegger.[115] No longer satisfied with such familiar fare as Rameau's *Indes galantes* or Fauré's *Pleurs d'or*, the organizers tried an innovation. Before a handpicked audience politely seated between paintings by Renoir and Toulouse-Lautrec a new work for two pianos was presented, *Les Visions de l'Amen*, by an unknown composer, Olivier Messiaen. The first performance, timed to the minute so as not to violate the curfew, took place on May 10 with Gaston in attendance, of course, since he never missed any of "his" concerts, but also with an informal gathering of *NRF* people on hand: Valéry, Paulhan, Cocteau, Mauriac, Dullin, and young Pierre Boulez.[116]

The Pléiade Concerts became successful, offering well-balanced programs to an audience of habitués who came as much to hear the music as to mingle with their own crowd. The drama critic Tony Aubin saw this clearly:

> Is this a retrospective of the elegant painting of the last century? Is it a social rendezvous, where Art and Letters meet High Fashion and Cinema, showing one another that they are still alive? Or is it a musical gathering for the purpose of hearing works that are seldom performed, not widely known, but worthy of respectful attention? A little of all these things. A group of artists under the name of Pléiade invites us into the incomparable setting of the Galerie Charpentier for concerts of French music. There, politely seated on folding chairs, are all those in Paris who are happy to be alive. [117]

Happy to be alive . . .

And the war? The front was far away, but the attacks on the occupiers, the taking of hostages, and the torture were right there in the city. That did not keep people from a frenzy of entertainment, as if tomorrow were Judgment Day: movies, stage plays, concerts, cabarets, restaurants all were crowded. "La vie parisienne" in all its splendor rubbed elbows with war in all its horror. As the playwright and actor Sacha Guitry was to say, "I resisted in my own way by diverting Frenchmen during those tragic hours."

In the wake of his successful concerts Gaston dared to do what Grasset had done twenty years earlier: he created a new literary prize: the Pléiade Prize, as of course it had to be called, since that name was now a registered trademark. The books of the collection that Jacques Schiffrin edited until 1940 were so widely esteemed and sought after in Europe and the United States, that in Rome the rarest of them, out of print, were fetching 2,000 francs a copy, and in New York some went for as high as 5,000 francs. [118] In Paris the propaganda bookstore Rive Gauche, the board of which included four Germans among its ten members (one of whom was Brasillach), included a large proportion of Pléiade books among the French works regularly sold and shipped to German universities. [119]

To earn the salary Gallimard paid him, Camus not only read

manuscripts, but was also in charge of selecting those books that would be entered as candidates for literary prizes, the Goncourt and others.[120] For the Pléiade Prize, a house prize if ever there was one, selection was particularly tricky, considering that editorial board members were also on the prize panel: Marcel Arland, Maurice Blanchot, Joë Bousquet, Albert Camus, Paul Eluard, Jean Grenier, André Malraux, Jean Paulhan, Raymond Queneau, Jean-Paul Sartre, and Roland Tual.

The creation of the prize was announced in August, and its terms specified. Carrying an award of 100,000 francs, it was meant to uncover a truly young writer. All genres were eligible, provided the work in question was unpublished, original, and written in French. The winner would be free to have his book published by any publisher he chose—a recollection, it would seem, of the lesson of Grasset's overly house-oriented Balzac Prize. Submissions were to be made at Rue Sébastien-Bottin before November 1, addressed to the Prize secretary, Jean Lemarchand. Date of the award: the first fortnight in February.[121]

Reactions were not long in coming. Apart from the snide, who feigned surprise that a publisher should act as both judge and party in the case, or who congratulated Gaston Gallimard on at last making public the collusion that existed between publishers and prize panels, the ultracollaborationist press mainly attacked the composition of the panel of judges: "On what grounds does Gaston Gallimard find André Malraux to be worthy to select the typical writer of the present generation, which of necessity must be revolutionarily European?" asked some,[122] while others wondered at the inclusion of Jean Paulhan,[123] or whether the 100,000 francs might not go to "Ilya Ehrenburg, the Party comrade and house author, who has written such charming things about the need to wipe out Paris."[124]

Among the judges for the Pléiade Prize, one was particularly active wherever the Parisian intelligentsia met, and yet he did not draw much criticism from the collaborationists: Sartre published his books and articles without encountering the censorship problems or public scandals that plagued Aragon or Saint-Exupéry. He was on his way up; the four years of the Occupation were an unexpected springboard for his popularity. In April he brought out *The Flies*, his first play, a three-act drama set in the mythical past of the city of Argos, whose master married Agamemnon's wife after murdering him, then punished and terrorized his city to make it expiate his own crime. But at Gallimard it was not Sartre's book that raised great hopes, but rather his companion Simone de Beauvoir's first novel, *L'Invitée (She Came to Stay)*. "If I had been awarded the Prix Goncourt that year, I should have accepted it with wholehearted jubilation," she was to write in her memoir, *La Force de l'âge (The Prime of Life)*.[125] Indeed, she was considered for it. At Gallimard she was told she had a good chance. At the National Writers' Committee (the organization of Resistance writers), "they"—who "they" were is not clear—told her she could accept it, provided she did not permit any press interviews.[126] The day of the award, de Beauvoir sat in great excitement at the Café de Flore waiting for a phone call. Alas, it never came.

Against all expectations, Sartre was the one who finally was glorified. Not for the play in book form but for the play when it was staged. Rehearsals, the dress rehearsal, and the premiere were announced and commented upon several times in *Comoedia* before it published a major interview with the author of *Nausea* and *The Wall* (his book of philosophy *Being and Nothingness*, published a few weeks after *The Flies*, went entirely unnoticed). "The subject of my play," he said, "might be summed up in this way: how a man acts in the face of an action he has committed, for which he does not shirk the responsibility or consequences, even though this action may at the same time horrify him."[127]

On June 2 *The Flies* opened, directed by Charles Dullin at the Théâtre de la Cité, previously known as the Théâtre Sarah-Bernhardt but now rebaptized, because a French theater could not be named for a Jewish actress, however great. There was a full house: the public, friends, contacts, and the leading personalities of Parisian intellectual collaborationism. The editors of all the Parisian newspapers had their own reserved seats in the national theaters and the best seats in private theaters; they always attended dress rehearsals.[128] Also present were many Germans in uniform, and some in mufti. Twenty orchestra seats were reserved for the Propaganda Staffel. This was normal: after all, they were the first to read the scripts of the plays proposed for production. Since German officers were generally not stupid, or masochists, or Gaullists, one can assume that they would not approve works that glorified the Resistance. Yet after the premiere a well-known German was reported to have said, "*The Flies* are us." Much later, after the war, justification for publishing and producing this play in 1943 (twenty-five performances in June and a revival in the fall) was sought by revealing its subversive message: it repudiated one of Marshal Pétain's favorite themes, the call for expiation. Some even went so far as to see in it "a revolt against the regime of moral and social order then in power."[129] But Sartre was not the only one whose virtues were discovered after the fact.

Paul Claudel's successive elegies to Pétain and later to De Gaulle, only four years apart, are enough to allow us to judge the man if not the poet. On November 27 at the Comédie-Française, for the premiere of his *Soulier de satin (The Satin Slipper)*, the author was sitting, alone, in a box just before the curtain rose. Lucien Combelle, a journalist seated in the adjacent box, observed him. Suddenly there was a small commotion in the audience: Ambassador Otto Abetz and the military governor of Greater Paris were making an entrance in dress uniform, escorted by members of their staffs. Before taking their seats, they stopped in front of the author's box. Claudel stood and deferentially bowed, and the two representatives of the Third Reich clicked their heels and gave him a military salute.[130]

After that, the show could begin. The original nine-hour play had been cut to "only" five hours. It was full-bodied, rich, and original, and the feelings of Don Rodrigo for Dona Prouhèze carried the theatergoer far beyond Renaissance Spain into such Claudelian themes as the fate of man and the mystique of Christianity. Jean-Louis Vaudoyer, then administrator general of the Comédie-Française, could consider it a success: not only was the play acclaimed, but also his whole company, the director Jean-Louis Barrault, the composer Arthur Honegger, and the cast of Pierre Dux, Madeleine Renaud, Marie Bell, Mary Marquet, and others. But there were some who did not hide the fact that they had been bored by the five-hour marathon. Sacha Guitry, as he reread the *Satin Slipper* poster afterward, said, "Thank God there were not a pair of them!" No one dreamed of suggesting, however, that hidden within the text was "a call to resistance"; after all, it had been written between 1919 and 1924. Still, the production constituted "without question the theatrical event of the whole Occupation."[131]

In February 1944 Gaston attended the church of Saint-Pierre-du-Gros-Caillou, not to pray, but to remember. It was the funeral of Jean Giraudoux. Everybody who was anybody attended, the élite of literature and diplomacy—all except those in exile. Academicians and ambassadors, former ministers and high-ranking civil servants, Jouhandeau and Heller, Georges Suarez and Edouard Bourdet, Jean Paulhan and Jean Fayard, Madeleine Renaud and Arletty, André Thérive and Pierre Renoir. Always the same people. It was a church, but it might as well have been a salon or a concert auditorium. Except for the tribute to the deceased, the conversations were just the same.

In this early February, at the *NRF*, much conjecture was devoted to the upcoming award of the first Pléiade Prize, set for February 23. Camus and Lemarchand had eliminated all but about thirty manuscripts. A penniless young bohemian with the funny name of Marcel Mouloudji seemed likely to win it. Arland and Paulhan felt his writing was a bit hurried, frothy, and decadent in the negative sense of the term. His story of a perverse and troubled childhood did not make too much sense to them. But the author was strongly backed by Camus and especially Sartre, who did battle to get him the prize. They won out, and Mouloudji received his 100,000 francs.

Sartre was everywhere. He took part in the public tribute to Giraudoux; infiltrated the Pléiade Prize; wrote a play for which he had already selected his friend Camus as director and leading player;

gave courses at Dullin's on Greek drama while still teaching philosophy at the Lycée Condorcet; participated in all kinds of celebrations; appeared in Picasso's play *Le Désir attrapé par la queue (Desire Caught by the Tail)*, privately staged at Michel Leiris's home; and yet found time for daily visits to the Café de Flore, where he met and befriended a young man named Jean Genet, just released from jail where he had spent eight months for robbing a bookstore. Genet was a habitual criminal. Jean Cocteau had testified at his trial with grandiloquence: "You see before you the greatest poet of the century." Genet's friends, many of whom were in the Gallimard-*NRF* orbit, arranged through Maurice Toesca to have him supplied with paper and pencil in his cell.

It was a strange period. At the Paper Control Commission it was announced that the Propaganda Staffel had postponed four publication permits requested by Gallimard: two for Dostoyevski *(The Idiot* and *The Possessed)* and two for Saint-Exupéry *(Night Flight* and *Southern Mail)*. Grasset, meantime, was fuming because he had to postpone *Our Contract Bridge System*. He pleaded the case, stressing that the authors were international champions and former prisoners of war and that their book would certainly appeal to other prisoners. The permit was granted. At the General Commissariat for Jewish Questions an inquiry was started—in March 1944—into the racial ancestry of Elsa Triolet. After a month it reported: "Elsa Triolet is the literary pseudonym of Elsa Kagan, a Russian Jewess who some ten years ago was the mistress of the Soviet poet Maikovicz [Mayakovski]. She is presently living in Avignon with one Aragon, a French politician known before the war for his close connections to the Popular Front. It is said that Aragon is half-Jewish, in that his natural father, unknown or said to be so, was a Jew. But this is questionable." Then, a month later, the report continued: "We now are almost certain that the subject [Triolet] is Jewish. But we will take no action until we have firmer grounds."[132]

In the spring of 1944 France found itself embroiled in a real war—no longer a war of words on the radio but one fought with weapons. The Dordogne region was being put to fire and sword. Wehrmacht commando units cheek by jowl with the French Milice* were trying to take the Plateau des Cilières, which the Maquisards were holding. Pétain denounced terrorism. Twenty-five large French cities and towns were subjected to heavy Allied air raids. The maquis reached a new peak of activity.

Meanwhile in Paris the theater went on. Gaston had not lost his taste for it. He regularly attended premieres, more than in the past, since there were so many new plays. Certainly he was not about to run a theater again, but when he could pull strings in favor of a play he was interested in, he did not hesitate to use his influence. For one of the members of his stable, Sartre, he even turned producer. After *The Flies*, Sartre wrote a one-act drama, *Les Autres* (Others), which he would shortly retitle *Huis clos (No Exit)*. The play was ready—but where should it be put on? The problem was not the censor, who had approved it without any problem, but the theater itself. Restrictions and curfew regulations made performances difficult. In March a new decree ordered that theaters be closed four days a week; by June all that was left was two days a week, and electricity for an hour and a half. It was risky for both players and audience, who had to worry about air-raid alarms and spending time in cellar shelters.[133]

Gaston thought of a solution. With the script of *No Exit* in his pocket, he went to Rue Eugène-Flachat, to the town house of his friend Anet Badel. They had not known each other long, but sufficiently to do each other favors. Badel, a former lawyer, had gone into the fuel business and been alert enough to switch from oil to charcoal, of which he sold a great deal to everyone, French and Germans alike. Devoted to the theater, Badel had recently bought the Vieux-Colombier auditorium, which was the occasion for his meeting Gaston, who had been a founding father of the prestigious avant-garde theater. That spring the Vieux-Colombier was one of the few theaters, if not the only theater, to be running normally. Not only did Badel have the necessary permits, but the building also

---

*Milice: A militia (homeguard) instituted by the Vichy government. Worked closely with the German occupation forces, often outdoing them in zeal.

had a retractable roof that facilitated performances in natural light late in the day, plus its own generator.

On May 27 *No Exit* opened at the Théâtre du Vieux-Colombier to a full house. Sartre was once again good for a huge turnout. He had personally invited all the important personalities, including those newspaper people whose ideas were at the opposite pole from *Les Lettres françaises*: Lucien Rebatet, Alain Laubreaux, André Castelot, and even Jean Galtier-Boissière, who complained of not having "a very good seat: the choice ones were reserved for the gentlemen in Feldgrau uniforms."[134] On stage were three characters who had died and were meeting in hell, shut in a room with walled-up windows and faced with a sentence they had never expected: each was to be the executioner of the other two. No couple could emerge from this infernal triangle; they were victims and hangmen both, bound together, inseparable, and unable to go out the door when at last it opened.

Some of those present would remark that hell was not "others" but the theater itself, which was infernally hot. Others would allege that the "others" were the Germans, and the bareness of the décor that of a prison cell for Resistance fighters. Those who listened to the radio could think that hell was the French cities bombed by the British, or the untenable positions of the Maquisards in Auvergne on the Plateau de la Margeride. On the whole, the Occupation press praised the rigorous construction of the play, the guilt feelings of the characters, the sobriety of the direction. It was as kind to *No Exit* as it had been a few months before to Jean Anouilh's *Antigone*. It was only after the war that drama criticism would attribute political intentions to Sartre or Anouilh.

Gaston could feel satisfied. He had been right in believing in Sartre, at thirty-nine, against the opinion of some of his editorial board, who thought Sartre would last five or six years, no more, just the time of a literary fad. But Gaston was embarrassed a month later, on June 24, at the Théâtre des Mathurins, when he attended the dress rehearsal of Camus's *Le Malentendu (Cross Purpose)*. It was a flop. He sat placidly in his seat and dutifully applauded, persisting even amid boos and hisses.[135]

The play was the closing one of the Parisian theatrical season, just as the Allied landing in Normandy had started to toll the death knell of the German Occupation. An era was ending.

It was August 1. In the last few days the fall-back position of the Maquis on the Plateau du Vercors was overrun, Soviet forces reached the Vistula, and at Avranches, in Normandy, General George Patton's tanks broke through the German front, opening the way to the offensive that would liberate Paris. In that city, at Passy, Paul Valéry was giving a reading of his three-act *Faust*. A few people were invited to enjoy this privilege: Georges Duhamel, Edouard Bourdet, Louis de Broglie, Henri Mondor, Gaston Gallimard, Armand Salacrou, Maurice Toesca, and some literary ladies. It was warm, and the text somewhat long and monotonous. Gaston was bored. He was saying to Toesca:

"Valéry is a failure, and he knows it. Everything he comes up with these days is just dug out of his pile of notebooks. The great work he had in view will never be done now. But what is appealing in Valéry is that he is a gambler, and a good loser: nothing can upset him."[136]

Outside, life went on. There was fighting a few hundred kilometers from Paris. Rennes, then Le Mans, Alençon, and Chartres were liberated. During the night of August 13, before leaving France, Lieutenant Heller dug a six-inch-deep hole on the Esplanade des Invalides, in which he buried an oblong tin box wrapped in rubber to keep out air and moisture. In it he had hastily put some precious papers: his Occupation diary, a few letters from writers, and some fifteen pages of *Der Friede* (Peace) written by his friend Jünger.[137] The Germans were folding their tents; likewise, in their wake, the ultra-collaborationists of the Parisian press. People were no longer asking for *Je suis partout* [I Am Everywhere] but for *Je suis parti* [I Am Gone].

In the maelstrom of this débâcle some were still striking good deals. For a long time Gaston had had his eye on the town house at 17 Rue de l'Université, which had a prestigious history. It had the additional attraction of abutting, in the rear, 5 Rue Sébastien-Bottin, the *NRF* building. A few days before Liberation, Gaston was able to pick it up "for a song."

Paris was martyrized, Paris was in revolt, Paris was liberated. Through it all Gaston walked, whistling softly, his hands in his pockets, with his nephews and a few friends, along the streets of the Saint-Germain quarter, while over at the Hôtel de Ville a few diehards were firing on the wildly rejoicing crowds. The Occupation was over, the war would soon wind down, and everything would be just as before. He was serene, happy, light-hearted. He was smiling. He had nothing on his conscience; that, he was sure of.

Not everyone agreed.

7

Settling Accounts

1944-1945

September 1944: time for the settling of accounts. Should one or should one not have published, edited, written, collaborated, become resigned, become reconciled, compromised, done nothing, resisted? In literature and publishing, this debate took a curious turn.

Some said: people had to live. Writers had only their pens to earn a living with, and no one thought of blaming government employees who stayed on the job when Vichy took over. Or: writers had to publish their works, because literature provided moral support for oppressed Frenchmen. Or: we should distinguish between those who merely wrote in defense of ideas (albeit fascist) and those who wrote to denounce by name their political enemies, thus personally lending a hand to the policeman and the executioner. Or: if the Occupation had lasted two or three times as long as it did, the writers' silence would have irreversibly damaged culture, the French intellectual heritage—it would have been a crime against the mind.

Others replied: it would have been better, more honorable, if for the four years writers and publishers had decided not to compromise themselves. One cannot call it an act of resistance to submit novels or essays or plays to the enemy for his approval, his deletions. Many writers could have found teaching jobs, subsisted on their salaries, and managed without royalties in wartime. The 140 publishers who signed the Otto List and the censorship agreement might at least have waited until political collaboration between Vichy and Berlin had been made official, before beginning to obey the occupying authorities. Their unanimity and their alacrity, the profits and advantages they reaped make them participants in the German cultural strategy for occupied France.

Alone among the occupied countries, France was continuing to produce works of high art, in the opinion of the British weekly *The Observer* on July 11, 1943.[1] This praise was ammunition to both sides—which shows how ambiguous the debate was. Two men summed up well the opposing positions.

Jean Galtier-Boissière, magazine publisher, bookseller, editor, and writer, who was asked by Jean-Louis Vaudoyer, the wartime administrator of the Comédie-Française, to help him draw up a file in the latter's defense, sent him a note that ended as follows:

> I know that the ultrapure of the Resistance, especially those just back from Honolulu, maintain that during the Occupation painters should have smashed their brushes, writers thrown away their pens, and actors gone fishing. I am not of that opinion and feel, on the contrary, that it was meritorious to persevere in one's work, even under the Nazi jackboot.
>
> The people in directorial positions in the arts, letters, or the theater were absolutely obliged to have contacts with the occupying authorities. I believe that we, who out of principle had nothing to do with the authorities, should be grateful to those who in spite of their disgust courageously undertook—certainly not without risks—to plead with our enemies the causes of artists and writers, and to maintain through dark times the continuity of French thought.[2]

At the opposite pole from Galtier-Boissière was another memorialist, Jean Guéhenno, a brilliant academic and writer who during the Occupation opted to write but not to publish anything, except a few fragments of his diary for Les Editions de Minuit under the pseudonym of Cévennes. Guéhenno judged it intolerable that his fellow writers "should think only of making a career out of the disaster, maintaining their reputations, and becoming thereby the entertainers of servitude." Commenting upon what he called "the honor of the prisoner," he said:

> . . . at a time when you had to stifle the only thing you wanted to shout out, if you were not absolutely forced to "appear" because of the need to earn a living, the least you could have done was to be silent as well about everything else, for everything else was no longer that important. . . . We should never have agreed to play the jailer's game, we should never have done what the jailer hoped we would do—that is, to "appear," to look as if we were still living and having fun as before, when we were free. . . . The whole world should have been made to feel that, where in normal times so many lights shone, there was nothing now but a great black emptiness, from which no longer came any word, any thought, and that this emptiness brought shame upon the world.[3]

Gaston watched these polemics with an interested professional eye, but not for an instant did he feel guilty. He had carried on with his job, that was all; he had not played the Germans' game, but kept his firm from being invaded by financial investment from across the Rhine (as had happened to Denoël, Sorlot, and Cluny).[4] Unlike Grasset, Gaston had not published "propaganda" books. As he saw it, the question should not even be asked, and he was outraged at the idea that he might be subjected to "purging," the more so since in the camp of the "purgers" were many whose fortunes he had made—Aragon, to begin with. He read and reread his catalogues for 1940–44 and found nothing to make him blush. Céline would later say:

"He had a catalogue that warranted his being shot every day. He could be locked up forever!"[5]

Beyond the German classics and modern German authors, as well as the French literature already discussed, most of the Gallimard production during the black years falls into a number of categories. There were major biographies, novels translated from English (but only until 1941), works of entertainment and travel, some North American history, and scientific and historical books.

Nothing dishonorable, especially in comparison with the catalogues of some of his fellow publishers. It was true that a few Gallimard titles were truly the occupier's meat: *Notes pour comprendre le siècle* (Notes for Understanding This Age) and *Chronique politique* (Political Chronicle) by Drieu La Rochelle—not to mention the magazine. But if Drieu made the *NRF* into an instrument of collaboration, "it was not out of the Germanophilia of a dreamer who had stumbled into politics, but quite rationally: for international fascist solidarity against so-called decadence, parliamentary democracy, racial corruption, and Communism."[6]

Parisians were still not over the days of madness and joy that had followed the liberation of their city. The war went on, but farther off, elsewhere, leaving only a few reminders in the French capital: food rationing, military censorship. In the first aboveground issue of *Les Lettres françaises*, Gallimard's advertising was not without guile: Aragon's *Aurélien*, "written while in the underground," and his *Les voyageurs de l'impériale (The Century Was Young)*, "published in 1943 and banned by the Germans"; Malraux's *Le Temps du mépris (Days of Wrath)*, "banned by the Germans"; and Saint-Exupéry's *Flight to Arras*, "published in 1942 and confiscated by the Germans." In the columns alongside these ads, traitors were held up to public obloquy, and there were denunciations of the objective complicity of "those writers whose attitudes or writings during the Occupation brought aid and comfort to the oppressor."[7]

The atmosphere of those September days in publishing comes across quite clearly in the newspapers that had sprung out of the

Resistance. "The publishers' trade association served the enemy," wrote the daily *France libre*, listing the officers and principal board members. That newspaper did not feel it was enough to punish writers who had collaborated; "those who supplied the material means for the distribution of works tending toward the enslavement of French thought" should also be held responsible, particularly the publishers' trade association. From the very first days of the Occupation, the association "put itself at the disposal of the German propaganda services" and signed the censorship agreement, "which constituted outright treason," as well as the Otto List. *France libre* further noted that since the president, secretary, and treasurer of the association held those positions during the Occupation, it was scandalous that they should have retained them after the Liberation, and pointed out that these three officers, themselves publishers, were not initially affected by the Otto List, since they published mainly scientific or law books.[8]

By the end of September *Les Lettres françaises* refused to accept any further advertisements from publishers in a questionable position, unless and until they had been cleared by the justice of the purge.

The justice of the purge in this case meant the Publishers' Purging Committee. It was made up of Messrs. Repessé (representing the government), Meunier du Houssoy (of Hachette), Durand-Auzias, Fayard (former officers of the trade association), Gay, Vercors (of Les Editions de Minuit), and Seghers and Sartre, both representing the National Writers' Committee.[9] They solemnly met at the trade association headquarters on Boulevard Saint-Germain, around the oval table in the main conference hall. Examining cases one by one immediately gave Seghers the uncomfortable feeling that "it will be the small companies that will be hit."[10] As for Sartre, he seemed to be representing Gallimard as much as—if not more than—the National Writers' Committee.

The National Writers' Committee insisted that the behavior of the publishers during the Occupation be judged by a mixed commission of jurists and writers. It easily won its point, even though the Purging Committee's composition left something to be desired. The Writers' Committee suggested as "punishment" that those found guilty should be deprived of the means of influencing public opinion and be required "to indemnify out of the profits they reaped during the Occupation those authors whose rights they had sacrificed—and this, above and beyond any sentences for criminal conduct imposed by courts of law."[11]

Vercors quickly found out that the Purging Committee was powerless. With a few others, he fought to have it made official, recognized by the government, and given muscle: "In vain. We remained unofficial. The pressure of the large publishers was too strong for our little group."[12] The large publishers had their people within the committee and in key positions. Sartre, seconded by Paulhan, continually pleaded the cause of Gaston Gallimard, while Mauriac was for purging everyone except Bernard Grasset. Vercors was one of the few among the would-be purgers who owed nothing to the publishers, the trade association, or the Germans.

In agreeing to serve on the committee, he hoped to effect sanctions against the responsible heads of the firms that had signed the Otto List, junked banned books, and received paper from the Germans. One measure was seriously considered: forcing these guilty publishers to retire early, if need be, and having them replaced by competent employees of their firms who had held a sufficiently important position and had not been compromised with the enemy. For the *NRF*, two names were brought forward: Jean Paulhan and Louis-Daniel Hirsch.[13] To sit in Gaston's seat.

Vercors did not hide the fact that he was aiming mainly at two companies, Gallimard and Grasset, the most significant in the prewar era if not during the war. But while the Purging Committee generally followed him along these lines, it refused to place the two firms on an equal footing. Gaston, who had merely acted as a smart businessman, deserved retirement, and the *NRF* magazine would go out of existence. But Grasset had collaborated shamelessly. Even though he had not specifically denounced anyone to the authorities (the worst of crimes on the purge's scale of values), he had offered to become the *Gauleiter*, the Nazi commander, of publishing, and had published works and signed articles that were clearly pro-German. Hence he had to be made an example of.

More than once, committee members met outside the official meetings—in particular Vercors and Sartre, who held long discussions in the latter's hotel room on Rue de Seine. Vercors argued unremittingly for sanctions against Gaston, while Sartre pleaded for indulgence.[14]

The purging of the publishing industry seems to have been a special case. It was as if those in high places had decided that nothing was to be done. This formed a startling contrast with the purge in journalism—another terrain of print and thought—a purge that did not wait for official approval before going into action. In the immediate aftermath of the Liberation, the editors and staffs of the newspapers, bulletins, and broadsides published underground during the war took over the quarters of the dailies and weeklies that had kept on publishing under the jackboot—presenting the authorities with a fait accompli. In publishing, such a takeover was inconceivable, for there would not have been enough people to fill the void: 140 publishers had accepted the Otto List—virtually all of them.

While the Resistance newsmen were taking over the desks of their collaborationist colleagues, the only immediate change in book publishing was the return of Nathan, Calmann-Lévy, and Ferenczi to the companies from which they had been expelled. No change beyond this was contemplated—at least by those in power. Vercors learned this for certain in September. After he had given hearings to Mauriac, Aragon, and Eluard, General de Gaulle invited Vercors to break bread with him at the Ministry of War on Rue Saint-Dominique, where he was living. The author of *Silence de la mer* (*The Silence of the Sea*) hoped, thanks to this unexpected and privileged contact, to be able to advance the work of the Publishers' Purging Committee and receive official support. But publishing did not come up once in the course of the dinner. De Gaulle discussed current events, and Vercors found it impossible to bring the conversation around to his own subject. The general nevertheless showed what he was thinking when he said that it would be bad for the image, the prestige of France abroad, if *L'Illustration* and the *Nouvelle Revue Française* were not allowed to resume publication. Vercors was among those who wanted to punish these magazines precisely because of their prestige—to show the world that the guilty were paying for their crimes. But there was no dialogue. Vercors left, convinced that the general, in whose eyes Gallimard and Grasset represented French literature, would rather condemn writers than condemn publishers. Vercors would have liked to discuss this at length, but he was so impressed by De Gaulle that he dared not raise the subject or ask for a second meeting.[15] The subject would never be raised.

At the end of November, after working for three months, the committee drew up a kind of balance sheet. Files had been completed and were ready. For several weeks the National Writers' Committee had been circulating a list of banned writers: Henri Béraud, Céline, Drieu La Rochelle, Maurras, Montherlant, André Thérive, Pierre Benoit. The National Writers' Committee was already getting some results, but what about the Purging Committee? Despite repeated urgent requests, it had not been given a legal statute empowering it to mete out punishments to the trade. Some of its members threatened to resign, and in the meantime suspended work.

Seghers was the first to walk out. What made him leave in disgust was an advertisement from the publisher Sorlot announcing forthcoming books. As if nothing had happened. Vercors, too, was deeply upset: "The firms [the committee] has wanted to condemn calmly announce their new products, which is the same as thumbing their noses at it. They thumb their noses at a corpse: the Purging Committee no longer exists." He wrote this in an article entitled "Gangrene," which appeared boldly on the front page of *Les Lettres françaises* of January 20, 1945. He went on to denounce the immorality of the situation in which the newspapers that reported the executions of collaborationist writers were also running advertisements—on the very same pages—for the publishers of those writers during the Occupation.

The publishers had succeeded in stymieing the Purging Committee. This was no small victory. Clearly, they would slip through the mesh of the net, as had so many corporation heads and industrialists. Despite their so-called "pact with the mind," the publishers' business activity came under the heading of "economic collaboration." The only sanction against the contractors of public works who actually built the Atlantic Wall for the Germans turned out to be fines,[16] while many minor black-market dealers were given prison sentences. In the same way, the publishers of Robert Brasillach and Paul Chack would not be in any real trouble, though "their" authors went before firing squads. This imbalance in the scales of justice was particularly galling in that many writers had "appeared" only to satisfy their vanity, whereas the publishers were in it only for their profits.

"People have criticized the weeding out of collaborationists because it dealt more severely with those who talked approvingly of the Atlantic Wall than with those who built it. To me it seems utterly unjust that economic collaboration should have been passed over while Hitler's propagandists were punished." So Simone de Beauvoir would write later on, although she did make a distinction among the propagandists, contrasting those who were guilty merely of aberrant opinions with others like Brasillach, who through "his denunciations, his advocacy of murder and genocide constituted a direct collaboration with the Gestapo."[17]

In 1945 publishing was still living under censorship rules. This time the rules were French and military, much lighter than the preceding ones. A first list of books to be withdrawn from sale, put out by the War Ministry, affected mainly Grasset, Denoël, Sorlot, and Baudinière—but not Gallimard. A little later the Military News Control clarified the matter: "These lists were established to withdraw from circulation not only books of a collaborationist turn of mind, but also books inspired by the principles of the National Revolution or the Pétainist ideology." It also underlined that these proscriptions affected only the specific works and not their authors in general.[18]

Prior approval of books—a mellow euphemism for censorship used by the provisional government—would cease at the end of hostilities.

The execution of Brasillach (on February 6, a symbolic date to Frenchmen); Drieu La Rochelle's suicide and his interment at the old cemetery in Neuilly, attended notably by Gaston, his son, and Brice Parain; the first trial in the high court of justice and the sentencing to life imprisonment of Admiral Esteva; the Yalta agreements and the bombing of Dresden—these events set the tone for the first months of 1945.

"The only time in my life I met M. Gallimard . . . was at the German Institute," Brasillach had stated at his trial in January 1945.[19] This was the kind of snidely murderous phrase that Gaston was most afraid of. Gaston had used double-talk so skillfully that no one knew exactly what kind of man he was, and writers returning from exile with no idea of what life in Paris had been like during those four years were often quite receptive to a Resistance version of the story of the NRF during the Occupation.

Even though Gaston, along with a few friends, affected to be above the battle and to disdain the attacks from the Resistance ultras, and even though he tried to play a cynical hand, he was deeply troubled by this new climate of suspicion, this settling of accounts and naming of names. Those close to him reported that he was deeply hurt when sometimes he saw his own name or that of his company included with those of traitors and inveterate Nazis. He had been preparing for this postwar period at least since 1943, sparing certain authors, trying not to give offense to the future. In the transitional days immediately following Liberation he contacted without delay one of those rare men who had remained a writer and publisher all that time without compromising himself: Pierre Seghers. Gaston had Paulhan set up a dinner including the poet André Frénaud, at a Rue Chabanais restaurant. He did not wait till dessert to formulate his proposal to Seghers, a founder-member of the National Writers' Committee who was also to be one of the pillars of the ephemeral Publishers' Purging Committee.

"I would like to launch *Marianne* again," he told him, "making it a great cultural and political weekly as it was before the war, when Berl was there. I would like you to edit it for me, and also have your 'Poets of Today' imprint be under the Gallimard banner, with you as its general editor, in offices on Rue de Grenelle."[20]

Taken aback, Seghers asked for twenty-four hours to think it over. He could not treat this offer lightly, if only out of loyalty to a man to whom he already owed much. Gaston had acted as Seghers' sponsor when Seghers applied for admission to the publishers' trade association. And during the summer of 1944 Gaston had recommended him to one of his printers (Dupont, at Levallois-Perret) and to his paper supplier, enabling Seghers to publish his magazine in Paris. And when Seghers was preparing to launch his famous collection Poètes d'aujourd'hui (Poets of Today), Gaston had granted him permission to reprint poems by Michaux, Eluard, Max Jacob, Apollinaire, Claudel, Supervielle, and Robert Desnos to which the *NRF* held the rights—a good share of the first twenty volumes of the imprint. This had been deeply appreciated.

All of which gave Seghers cause for thought. Twenty-four hours later he came back to see Gaston.

"I've thought it over and the answer is no. I'm afraid of newspaper work, I have no experience in it. And as for the collection, I want to be the captain of my ship. I want to publish it, but on my own."[21]

Gaston lectured this fellow publisher, twenty-five years his junior, who had turned down such an offer, but he did not hold it against him. He understood him.

In 1945 Gaston was ready to defend himself by any means. He counted his friends and tried to win over the others. It was then that he learned who were the most sincere among his authors, and who the most self-interested; who would not stick out their necks for him, and who would risk their reputations to support him. Sartre and Malraux pulled all kinds of strings. Aragon, who had a key role in purging writers, defended him. But Emmanuel Mounier, the

Catholic writer who just before the war had had two books published in the Esprit collection, now wanted to switch from Gallimard to Le Seuil; despite his friendship with Brice Parain, he considered his contract invalidated by the events under the Occupation and wanted to cancel it.[22] On the other hand, Paul Léautaud assured Gaston of his total support from the very beginning of the crisis:

> I have been told so many things concerning you: ostracism, expulsion. Such behavior! What a period of proscriptions we are going through! And among Frenchmen! Your letter leads me to think that nothing has or will come of these measures. Two lines assuring me of this would make me very happy.[23]

In 1945 many of the books published by Gallimard had a political, not purely literary, importance: Raymond Aron's *De l'armistice à l'insurrection nationale* (From the Armistice to the National Uprising); Camus's *Lettres à un ami allemand* (Letters to a German Friend); André Chamson's *Ecrit en 40* (Written in 1940) and *Le Puits des miracles* (The Well of Miracles); René Char's *Seuls demeurent* (Alone Remain); Jacques Debû-Bridel's *Déroute* (Rout); the two novels in Sartre's *Les Chemins de la liberté (Paths of Freedom)* series; Saint-Exupéry's *Lettre à un otage (Letter to a Hostage)*; Picasso's *Le désir attrapé par la queue (Desire Caught by the Tail)*; Léon Blum's *A l'échelle humaine* (On a Human Scale); Julien Benda's *La France byzantine* (Byzantine France); and de Beauvoir's *Le Sang des autres (The Blood of Others)* and *Les Bouches inutiles (Who Shall Die?)*. It might have seemed that all the members of the National Writers' Committee were meeting by prearrangement in this catalogue, which must have caused some wry smiles inside the prisons of the purgation.

Writers die, but publishers remain.

Some of the titles were unvarnished political propaganda, three in particular that appeared in a collection entitled Problèmes et Documents (Problems and Documents). *Le Maréchal Défaite* (Marshal Defeat) by Charlereine (a pen name for General Odic) put on trial "the crimes of Pétain and his clique," called Pétain "the Macbeth of dung," and accused him of having entered a *ménage à trois* with Hitler and defeat. *La France trahie et livrée* (France Betrayed and Handed Over) by Charles Dumas, a member of the executive committee of the underground Socialist Party, was primarily a study of the role of the capitalist bourgeoisie in the war and the defeat, which concluded: "What was corrupt must be eliminated." The call for a purge, not only in certain privileged sectors such as literature but in all public areas, and the need for a collective, total reform in the recruiting of personnel for the large government services were even more clearly expressed in *La République à refaire* (The Republic to be Remade) by the Socialist André Ferrat, who at the time was on the executive committee of the National Liberation Movement.

These publications were Gaston's concessions to the spirit of the times. He urgently needed them, because a file was being prepared against him. In his defense he requested some thirty men of importance to write affidavits attesting to his good conduct during the war, the concealed favors he did the Resistance, his courage as a publisher under the jackboot. They argued that it was the *NRF* magazine edited by Drieu La Rochelle that was guilty of the crimes and misdemeanors—to clear the publishing house. In other words, during the war Les Editions Gallimard was a haven for the Resistance—especially Paulhan's office—as opposed to the magazine, which was in the hands of a notorious fascist installed by the occupier and imposed on the other members of the organization. The magazine and the publishing house had absolutely nothing to do with each other. The defenders seemed to forget that the bookkeeping, the address, and the name of the owner had been the same in both cases.

Each of the exculpatory witnesses for Gaston brought in such facts and emotions as were dictated by his own experience.

André Chamson: "The total break with the *NRF* magazine by those writers who remained in contact with the Gallimard firm seems to me to indicate the way the problem was faced by the most scrupulous of consciences."

Armand Salacrou stressed that he had never allowed a play of his to be produced on a Parisian stage during the Occupation, then said: "Nevertheless, I had no scruple about Gallimard publishing them, since he was also publishing Triolet, Aragon, Eluard, Saint-Exupéry." Acknowledging that he had been a frequent visitor to Rue Sébatien-Bottin between 1942 and 1944, the playwright judged that "it was obvious that, with the full knowledge of M. Gaston Gallimard, the house was a Resistance center."

Dionys Mascolo, a reader-editor at Gallimard as of January 1, 1942, recalled that the firm ran a great risk by "lending" its offices to men who were leading double lives: it served as a letter drop and meeting place, with the help of Gaston and those around him. A member of several Resistance groups (MNPGD, Combat, FFI), Mascolo asserted: "Perhaps nowhere in Paris, at that time, could one have found a spirit of resistance to the Germans and Vichy so resolutely affirmed and unanimous. I do not hesitate to say on my own account that my contact with him played a large part in my decision to join the Resistance."

Professor Henri Mondor recalled, as an author, that his conversations with the Gallimard brothers during the war were anti-German and pro-British, Gaston having fought to keep his firm out of German hands: "The Gallimards used their skill to save not only their publishing house but the spirit of resistance that animated most of their authors."

Raymond Queneau, whom Gaston had made general secretary of the publishing firm at the beginning of 1941, even though fully aware of Queneau's political opinions, attested: "During the three and a half years of Occupation, I always saw [him] turn away collaborationist authors, torpedo all projects of German origin, and on the other hand courageously publish works of authors who were not in good standing with the occupiers and were notorious anti-Nazis."

Bernard Groethuysen, indebted to Gaston for his "warm support" when he translated German literary classics contrary to the direction desired by the Propaganda Division, remembered: "Our editorial board meetings were always between people of like opinions. This let us maintain in the publishing house viewpoints consistent with loyalism and the spirit of resistance."

Father Bruckberger, who was in prison when Gallimard published his *Ligne de faîte* (Watershed) in 1942, stated: "For my part, I should not have been willing to have contact with his publishing house, let alone be published there, had I not been aware of the immense services it rendered to the cause of France."

Jean Paulhan: "I can certify that not one of us—I speak for Groethuysen and Queneau as much as for myself—would have gone on working for Les Editions de la *NRF* between 1940 and 1944, if its separation from the magazine, which the German authorities took over in 1940, had not been complete and the break absolute. I also wish to say that, being present daily in the Rue Sébastien-Bottin offices, I never observed the least deviation from this rule. Not once did I bump into either the editor or any of the regular contributors to the magazine."

Joë Bousquet, who had put up Gaston's family and staff between June and October of 1940, declared that he had always known him to have "deeply French convictions." More than once, despite the risk of censorship, Gaston had written him that he wished "for the victory of our arms." If he returned to Paris, it was at the urgent request of his authors, to watch over their material interests "and struggle with all his strength against all forms of German propaganda." In summation: "I am absolutely convinced that Gaston Gallimard performed a task worthy of the Resistance by accepting a thankless post that we begged him to hold to the bitter end."

André Malraux, minister of information for the De Gaulle government, made no bones about his position in the fall of 1940: "I felt that since the publishing house had been closed and put under seals by the Germans, and the magazine was slated to reappear anyway, it was necessary to safeguard the backlist of the publishing house by not opposing its reopening under whatever management. The more so since, as the management was to be literary, Gide, Valéry, and Eluard agreed to work with it."

Paul Eluard recalled that it was in Paulhan's office in 1941 that he first met Jacques Decour*: "Despite the risk from the imposed presence in your building of the wretched editor of the magazine, I never felt the slightest concern in coming there. I felt protected—by you and by those around you."[24]

Roger Martin du Gard, recalling Gaston's problem of conscience in September 1940, concluded: "The break between the publishing house and Drieu's magazine was complete. I am surprised to have to give testimony to a thing so little open to debate—and upon which there can be no doubt in the minds of men of good faith."

Pierre Brisson, the editor of *Le Figaro*, recalled that, from October 1940 until it suspended publication in 1942, its literary supplement in Lyons, *Le Figaro littéraire*, never ceased opposing Drieu La Rochelle's *NRF*, the positions it took, and the writers who contributed to it. "This state of war in no way interfered with my allowing Gaston Gallimard at the same time to publish my *Molière*. And in the beginning of 1944 I also gave him my second book, *Les Deux Visages de Racine* (The Two Faces of Racine). His devotion to the best writers of the underground Resistance, the support he gave them; the remarkable anti-German activity of his immediate associates, such as Paulhan, Queneau, Groethuysen; the sometimes very daring publication of writers like Aragon, Saint-Exupéry, Eluard, Sartre, and others—all these things gave one the best possible guarantees about the spirit of the publishing house."

Georges Brissac, a member of the Liberté group and later of Combat, and from 1941 on a national delegate in the liberated territories for the intelligence service of the National Liberation Movement, testified that during the Occupation he saw a great deal of the Gallimards; that the distinction between magazine and publishing house was very clear; that the publication of anti-Hitler books by Gallimard was for the comrades "a deeply comforting sign of the

---

*Jacques Decour, the pseudonym of a professor of German named Decourdemance, was, with Paulhan and Pierre de Lescure, the originator of the National Writers' Committee and one of the founders of *Les Lettres françaises*. He died before a German firing squad.—TRANS.

maintenance of a free French literature"; and that Claude Gallimard had often put him up in his home while being fully aware of his underground activities.

W. E. Moulder testified to Gaston's courage in keeping her as a secretary from 1940 to 1944, although she was British by nationality. Rue Sébastien-Bottin was a nest of resistance, according to her.

Albert Cornu, the father of Gaston's daughter-in-law, recalled meetings attended by notorious collaborationists at which he often had to remind Gaston to be cautious: "Always, despite the real danger of such behavior, he took the floor to denounce the Vichy government, the occupiers, and to call for and predict the victory of the Allies."

The last two affidavits, from Sartre and Camus, must be set apart because of the writers' prestige, their links with Gallimard, and the substance of their letters. Sartre wrote:

> . . . As a private person, I wish to say that I have great esteem for Gaston Gallimard, whom I consider a friend. I had books published by him *(Being and Nothingness, The Flies)* during the Occupation and would never have done so had I had the slightest doubt concerning his attitude toward the Germans or Vichy. I feel, therefore, that any blame put on the house of Gallimard touches Aragon, Paulhan, Camus, Valéry, and myself—that is, all the writers who were part of the intellectual Resistance and published by him. On the contrary, Gaston Gallimard constantly showed us, by deeds, what his real feelings were. He had full knowledge that his publishing house was being used as a meeting place for members of underground organizations, yet he never stopped helping resisting writers. If under German pressure he was forced to turn the *NRF* magazine over to Drieu, it was done only after consultations with Malraux, Gide, and Martin du Gard, all of whom advised him to comply.

As for Camus, he recalled that the distinction between the magazine and the house was "public knowledge," and that the publication of Aragon and Saint-Exupéry had convinced the writers in the Resistance of Gallimard's allegiance.

I consider it my duty to bear witness that the house of Gallimard helped me during several difficult periods. In 1943 and 1944 my office at the publishing company always served as the meeting place for the militant members of the Combat Group who happened to be in contact with me. Although not aware in detail of this activity, Gaston Gallimard knew the nature of it and always provided cover for me in this regard. The fact that—at a critical moment in May 1944, when the Paris Combat Group was being actively hunted down—the Gallimard family took me in and protected me constantly obligates me to declare here the loyalty and esteem I feel for them. But what seems the most important to me is this: many writers in the Resistance continued to have their books published by the Gallimard firm during the Occupation, and they made use of it to maintain what they thought they had to maintain. These writers, of whom I am one, cannot today withdraw their support from the house that printed their works. Any judgment against this firm is a judgment against them. Personally, I would consider myself, as would other, more famous colleagues . . . to be condemned by such a judgment.

How, after such a statement, could one consider purging this publishing house?

The above letters,[25] exculpatory affidavits, come from men who for the most part were under obligation to Gaston. Practically all the letters were written in November 1945, with copies sent to the Consulting Commission for the Purging of Publishing, with a covering abstract:

All these writers, who refused to contribute to the magazine, agreed to sign or renew contracts with the Librairie Gallimard and to be published by it, thus establishing solidarity with the house. The fact that they agreed to be part of the Librairie Gallimard is a warrant of the latter's attitude during the Occupation and of the distinction they made between the house and the magazine. . . . Since its resumption of activities at the end of 1940, the Librairie Gallimard followed a policy which seemed, to it, best to conform to French interests, and in all circumstances it made every effort to adhere to that policy. It retained on its editorial board Arland, Groethuysen, Malraux, Parain, Paulhan,

Queneau . . . and added to them anti-Nazis such as Blanzat, Camus, Mascolo. . . . It published backlist authors who were anti-German (Saint-Exupéry, Aragon), and it was for this that Gallimard was summoned to the Propaganda Staffel and threatened with having members of his staff drafted for labor service. . . . It brought out, of the Germans, only classics, historians, or scientists, selected by Groethuysen or Parain. . . . It did not use the translators suggested by the Germans, but others, even Jews. . . . It founded the Pléiade Prize with a panel made up mostly of Resistance writers: Arland, Blanchot, Bousquet, Camus, Eluard, Grenier, Malraux, Paulhan, Queneau, Sartre, Tual, and the Gestapo became alarmed at this and demanded the addresses of all the members of the panel. . . . It never let itself be deflected from this policy by the attacks of the collaborationist press.

Gaston would long keep the originals of these affidavits in his desk drawer. Just in case. When he sent their copies to the Consulting Commission for the Purging of Publishing, he attached—in addition to the covering abstract—a compendium of press clippings from the Occupation period, articles that had dragged him through the mud.

The file of incriminating evidence was slight indeed: one letter, sent by a Sonderführer of the Propaganda Division on November 28, 1940, to Gaston Gallimard concerning the reopening of his company and confirming recent conversations the publisher had had with German officers, during which he turned down an offer of foreign capital to be invested in the firm and named Drieu to edit the magazine for five years.

With such a file, there could be no doubt about the outcome. But in May 1946 an investigator for the National Interprofessional Purging Committee decided to reopen the matter, to the great distress of President Durand-Auzias: What good did it do to have a consulting commission, if the Book Industry Trade Association did not accept its decisions? But it so happened that the association was not willing to forgo sanctions against Gallimard and simply file and forget the whole affair. It wished to go deeper in its investigation, to judge what had already been judged. But two years later, at the end of a report covering the same materials as in the file, it concluded:

In light of these facts, it is impossible to place Gallimard among the persons covered by the ordinance of October 16, 1944 (modified and completed by the ordinance of March 25, 1945), for having "encouraged the enemy in any way."[26]

In the end, the only sanction asked for and obtained was the banning of the *NRF* magazine and the publication of that decision in the press. As early as the fall of 1944 Gaston agreed to sacrifice the magazine—by accusing it of all the sins under the Occupation. And Paulhan had designated himself, with the approval of Gaston, the National Writers' Committee, and the Purging Committee, to be the one to liquidate the magazine with which he had been identified for twenty years. The magazine was dead; long live the publishing house!

In June 1948 the Gallimard Affair was closed.

For the publisher of the "Four M's," the purging was more difficult. Grasset, first of all, did not have the nervous makeup to face such an ordeal. And he was alone, abandoned. True to his temperament and political ideas, he had made a personal commitment during the war—to the wrong side.

He was arrested as early as September 5, 1944, two days before Pétain and Laval left France for the castle of Sigmaringen. At first interned at Drancy, he was shortly released to house arrest in a rest home outside Paris, in view of his nervous condition. On two occasions Grasset had been under treatment at the psychiatric clinic of Dr. Bonhomme at Sceaux, before his arrest from March to August 1944, and now again from November 1944 to August 1945. He suffered from a serious depressive melancholia, from which he could be roused only by electroshock treatment. When he was finally released from the clinic, those close to him still found him in a state of physical and nervous weakness that, to say the least, was worrisome.

Under attack from all sides, he would need at least six or seven weeks to prepare his defense, and merely concentrating on a subject that caused him such concern was likely to aggravate his illness. Dr. Laufer, head of the medical services for the prefecture of the Seine, made no secret of the fact that only a shortage of beds kept him from returning Grasset to a psychiatric clinic. Meanwhile, Grasset was writing and phoning everywhere. He ran through his address book, reread his authors' contracts, and racked his memory for those who might hold out a helping hand. But all the writers seemed suddenly to suffer amnesia; they forgot the publisher he had been to them before the war and even under the Occupation. The man was suddenly a social leper. It was not good to be seen with him. François Mauriac appears to have been one of the few to be willing to let bygones be bygones and take Grasset's side in spite of what he had done. And Grasset had done a lot. . . . The purgers' file on him, after a careful search through the archives, was thick and overwhelming. To cite just one example, this letter from Grasset to one of the highest of the Nazi leaders, Josef Goebbels, dated October 21, 1941:

Your Excellency,

The state of my health does not allow me to come to Weimar for the meeting over which you are to preside. But one of my closest associates, André Fraigneau, will tell you first of all what happiness it is for me to be your publisher, and all the hope we base upon an ever closer Franco-German intellectual collaboration. . . . I would be very happy if André Fraigneau could speak to you of all the problems we have in our trade and especially about the matter of paper, which is a serious worry to us. People more or less everywhere tend to forget that a book has an influence and a longevity not equaled by newspapers, and for that reason it warrants a certain privilege. Please believe, Your Excellency, that I am most respectfully yours, . . .

P.S. It is a joy for me to send you as a tribute a copy of my first book, *Remarques sur l'action* [Remarks About Action], which I hope will interest you. If you should like to receive my other works, I will send them to you with heartfelt good wishes.[27]

Goebbels's book, *Vom Kaiserhof zur Reichskanzlei (My Part in Germany's Fight)*, had indeed been bought, translated, and printed by Grasset's house, but it never appeared. The wind was beginning to turn. This did not change the fact that the French publisher had really "wanted" the book, as evidenced by another letter, equally fervent and enthusiastic, which he sent a few months earlier, on April 25, to Eher Verlag, Goebbels's Munich publisher.[28]

It is easy to understand the attitude of the investigators on May 28, 1946, when the National Interprofessional Purging Committee met to examine the Grasset Case. He was accused of having assisted the enemy by putting his publishing house at the disposal of German propaganda and the de facto government. It was held against him that between 1940 and 1944 he had published works "of collaborationist tendencies," notably that of one Drieu La Rochelle, *Ne plus attendre* (To Wait No Longer), and between July 1940 and November 1942 had sent letters to the Propaganda Division in which he expressed racist and collaborationist sentiments.

On the defense side, Grasset brought out the fact that his firm had been closed by the Germans, and that he had reopened it only to prevent them from bringing out a large number of collaborationist works under its label. He also pointed out that, of the some 200 books he had published on Rue des Saints-Pères from 1940 to 1944, only about fifteen could be held against him, that is, a matter of 2 million francs maximum as against his overall business turnover of between 40 and 44 million francs. Moreover, allowance should be made for his "peculiar psychological state," in other words, his health problems: despite the admitted principle of his guilt, this consideration should mitigate the sanction.[29]

Bernard Grasset was condemned to three months' suspension of activity. But the Consulting Commission for the Purging of Publishing was only an advisory body. Grasset's troubles were not over. The commission suggested its sanction to the national commission. Meanwhile both the criminal and civil courts took charge of the Grasset Case—or, rather, of the two Grasset Cases: one dealing with the publishing house, the other with the individual.

In 1948 the house was ordered dissolved. Grasset, himself convicted, asked for clemency. At sixty-seven, his complexion pasty, his eyelids drooping, his face wracked by tics, he played nervously with his cigarette holder as he rose to defend his firm—his child—before the criminal court.

"I started out without a sou. I have never had any wealth of my own outside of my publishing house, which was an extension of myself. Today I am back where I started. This house is my life's work. I entreat you to return it to me intact."

His lawyer, a leading member of the bar, Maître Charpentier, added: "If the dissolution of the house is ordered, there are those who would buy it at a bargain price. Today's prosecution serves only the pecuniary interests of those who have attempted to ruin the house's name."[30]

Since Grasset had unfortunately been named to defend and represent the firm, the association made between the individual and the company was immediate and permanent. Thus the company was held responsible for personal letters written by Grasset (who was never interrogated about these documents during the investigation leading up to his own trial). The prosecutor made his case against the man and not the company, proceeding from the assumption that the publisher was everything and the author nothing. The defense lawyers asked him why, then, Brasillach and Rebatet had been condemned although their publishers were not bothered. Pressed to explain why he charged Grasset for having published *Le Solstice de juin* (The June Solstice) but did not charge Montherlant for having written it, the prosecutor stated that the publisher of a work was "a thousand times more culpable than its author," since a text could not be considered harmful until it was printed and distributed.[31]

Despite the arguments presented by Maîtres Charpentier and Géranton, the Grasset company was condemned to dissolution with 99 percent of its assets confiscated. Out of consideration for the authors, this sentence was later reduced to a 10-million-franc fine.[32] Early in 1949, after a meeting of the Superior Council of the Magistracy, President Vincent Auriol granted clemency to the Grasset company, treating it as if it were a physical person, in view of the services it had rendered to contemporary French literature. Apart from the first publication of Proust, the four "M's," and Giraudoux, the President of the Republic was especially motivated by the fact that Grasset had discovered, launched, and sold hundreds of thousands of copies of Louis Hémon's *Maria Chapdelaine!*[33]

Finally Grasset, after repeated stays in psychiatric clinics and rest homes, returned in person—under amnesty—to run his company. A second career began for him, less brilliant and briefer than the first. His five years of purgatory at least allowed him to learn who his friends were—few among authors, many among publishers. When Grasset, desperate, once asked his faithful associate Henri Muller to call his fellow publishers to his assistance, not one refused. "But by far the most generous was Gaston Gallimard. Old rivalries were forgotten in the face of misfortune."[34]

The Goncourt Prize for 1944, because of "events," was awarded with a year's delay; it went to Elsa Triolet for *Le premier accroc coûte deux cents francs (A Fine of 200 Francs)*. Said Paul Léautaud tartly:

"The Goncourts killed three birds with one stone: the Triolet lady is Russian, Jewish, and a Communist. The red stitching shows."[35]

Triolet's publisher was in hot water with the purgers: Denoël had also published Lucien Rebatet and Céline. Being optimistic and rather naive, however, he was only moderately worried during the joyful days that followed the Liberation: the hunting down of the Milice, women with shaven heads, arbitrary imprisonments—these things had nothing to do with a publisher. He refused to panic, as was testified by two people who had seen him daily for months if not years: René Barjavel, his production chief, and Jeanne Loviton, better known under the pen name of Jeanne Voilier, his companion, who was also a good friend of Paul Valéry.

At the beginning of September 1944, Denoël told her several times:

"I am confident. I am counting on the Aragons. They are not ingrates, they will remember all I did for them."[36]

But he was growing impatient, for that couple was slow to act. Finally he received a luncheon invitation. He went there in high spirits, convinced that he had nothing to fear from the purges, given the influence of Aragon and Triolet in the literary and political circles of the Resistance. When he came home after this long-expected re-union, he looked haggard. His assurance was gone, and he had to search for words when Voilier questioned him:

"I asked them to help me. They answered: that is impossible. We put up with you during the war, but you cannot imagine what an ordeal it was for us to be published alongside Céline and Rebatet, under the same imprint."[37]

After this sledgehammer blow, Denoël lost faith in everything. Discouraged, he even hesitated to respond to his detractors, who started their attacks in the press and at mass meetings. Without telling him, Voilier went to the Quai des Orfèvres, the Criminal Investigation Department of the police, asking to speak with the inspector in charge of publishing affairs.

"Since you are the one who has the file on him," she said, "you should at least know that Robert Denoël helped the Jews on this list I have here to pass over into the free zone; that at Aragon's request he kept his valuables for him; that on several occasions he lent him sums of money, of which I have an exact account here; and that he allowed Elsa Triolet to be published in the free zone by sending her money. Don't you think, inspector, that they ought to be questioned?"

"Absolutely. Thank you for this information. I will have them come in for questioning."

"They may not come, and may later testify against Denoël. It would be better if you could send them a specific list of questions requiring yes-or-no answers, based on the information I have given you. That would be more effective."

The suggestion was followed and an inspector called at the home of Aragon and Triolet to ask for yes-or-no answers to purely factual questions.[38]

Voilier, who was attending the meetings of the publishers' trade association as owner of the Domat-Montchrestien company, which she had inherited from her father, was convinced that the trade had formed a plot to clear itself of its own activities during the Occupation—by making three publishers the scapegoats: Grasset, Denoël, and Sorlot. She assisted Denoël in the preparation of his defense by spending months, day and night, going through piles of books published between 1940 and 1944 by the publishing community, and making notes on those that were apologias for collaboration. The thick file that Denoël compiled also contained the advertisements that all Paris publishers had placed in the *Bibliographie de la France* during the Occupation. This was a convincing way of showing that other publishers had published as many "pro-German" books as he had, if not more. He was determined to set the record straight—not to run down the publishing profession but to save his own company at a time when his competitors were again publishing without any problems. He showed the file to his associate Barjavel, saying:

"If I am going to take it in the neck, at least I won't be the only one!"[39]

His trial was set for December 8, 1945. The week before, on December 2, Denoël went with Voilier to a theater in Montparnasse. On the way, near the Invalides, a front tire of his Peugeot 202 went flat. Voilier went to the nearest police station to try to find a taxi, while Denoël set about taking off the wheel. When she got there, she heard that a man had just been attacked near the Invalides. Returning immediately with the emergency police squad, she found Denoël unconscious, a large-caliber bullet in his back. He died shortly thereafter.

Was it merely a mugging? Or a political assassination? Or the result of a plot? All these possibilities were aired in the press, which abounded in speculation and conjecture, but the police finally dismissed the case for lack of evidence. Any of the hypotheses might have held water, especially six days before the trial of the Denoël company, which the publisher promised would be open and forthright, with documents to prove his points. Not to incriminate others, but purely in self-defense.

Who was it that was killed that night on Boulevard des Invalides? The publisher of Céline and Rebatet? A business partner? A man on the defensive ready to denounce his colleagues? Or just an unsuspecting passerby?

In 1945 street attacks were not rare in Paris, especially at that spot, because of the slopes that made it easy for attackers to get away. On that night there were three other felonies in the same area. Parisians were not even surprised: such crimes were often the work of American army deserters who took advantage of the blackout to carry out a reign of terror. Every night shots were heard, and they were always from the weapons of professionals, according to the police. Those who resisted noisily were killed but not robbed, for want of time and fear of attracting a crowd. In Denoël's pockets 12,000 francs were found.

Robert Denoël was dead. Three years later, the criminal court delivered a verdict of acquittal against his publishing house.

The publishers finally survived the purging without too much harm. The sanctions imposed by the National Interprofessional Purging Committee were benign enough, considering the vigor with which the criminal courts took over and handled the same files: three months of suspension for Grasset, an unpublicized finding of guilty for Sorlot, Baudinière barred from holding a managerial position within the industry.[40] And even that was not much, considering the death sentences of writers whose pro-German works had been published by these houses. Had Drieu La Rochelle failed in his last suicide attempt, his trial would have been fascinating, rich in revelations and lessons, and very hard to take for Gaston and a number of Gaston's associates. Much harder than the ten-year quietus imposed on the *Nouvelle Revue Française*.

The publishers had benefited from the enormous backlog of investigative files on the desks of the overworked judges; their cases, when tried in 1948 or 1949, no longer mattered to anyone. They also benefited from being treated like the heads of any other company, like businessmen whose "pact with the mind," differentiating them from an automobile manufacturer or a yard-goods maker, was opportunely shoved out of sight. Officially, in high places, it was considered time to put a brake on the natural and spontaneous movement that had led to firing squads and rather indiscriminate bannings from professions. The France of reconstruction needed its bureaucrats and heads of companies to restore the country and be able to face the Allies.

The publishers, meanwhile, did not wait for the purgers to finish their job before resuming the old competition. In the fall of 1944, when the first punitive commissions were assembling their files, most of the publishers were already busy discovering, publishing, and promoting the writers of the postwar period.

8

New Blood

1946-1952

In the world of literature at the Liberation, the National Writers' Committee was in the saddle. It was a small group of authentic Resistance writers, including some characters who wanted to be considered such.[1] But as early as 1945, it began to lose a bit of its standing as some of its best people fell away, scared off by the growing importance of the commissars of culture in the service of the Communist Party. Two years after the end of the war, Paulhan, Schlumberger, and Duhamel no longer belonged to the committee, nor did Mauriac, referred to as Saint Francis of the Assizes, who could not decently attend meetings alongside Aragon while at the same time preaching pardon for the purged before the bar of justice.

This was a key period, a period of a new literary generation. Demographic factors began overtaking the consequences of the great purge.

In the wake of World War I, fifty-year-olds (Gide, Valéry, etc.) had dominated literary life, their juniors having too often not returned from the murderous whirlwind of war. After the Liberation, it was the other way around: the older ones were dead (Jean Giraudoux, Romain Rolland) or discredited (Céline, Béraud, Montherlant), leaving the field free to those known as the Resistance writers (Sartre, Camus, Malraux, Vercors), who remained together despite their differences of opinion because they all identified with that label.[2]

It was this group that seemed to embody the future. Gaston had no need to go after them; they were already his. To give continuity to this spirit, this tendency, which could not be called a "school," Gaston was ready to launch a new magazine, "born of the Resistance" like the great daily papers that now dominated the field. He needed it all the more as there was no longer an *NRF*. Such a magazine was indispensable to the good operation of his publishing house, not only because the firm could find new authors there, but because it would always be, in Fargue's famous words, the laboratory and testing ground for the literature of tomorrow. When the company moved into an old bourgeois apartment on Rue de Grenelle in 1921, it was not entirely by chance that the offices of the magazine had been set up in the kitchen.

Prodded by Denise Tual, Gaston revived *La Revue du cinéma* in the fall of 1946, but he declined to do the same for *Détective*, as had been suggested in 1945 by two former staff members of that magazine, Marcel Montarron and Marius Larique.

"My good friends," he told them in his office, "I had enough trouble in the Occupation with another magazine, the *NRF*. And they're not over yet. I am not looking for more with *Détective*. I trust the two of you. I'll gladly sell it to any buyer you select."

The deal was worked out, and the magazine was sold for 5 million francs.[3] For Gaston the important thing was to face the new situation: *La Table ronde*, *La Nef*, *L'Arche* were new magazines just itching to take the place of the late *NRF*. Sartre was to furnish him with the means to hold that ground.

With Simone de Beauvoir, Raymond Aron, Michel Leiris, Maurice Merleau-Ponty, Albert Ollivier, and Jean Paulhan, Sartre set up, soon after the Liberation, a committee to launch a new publication. Camus, too busy with his daily newspaper *Combat*, begged off. Malraux likewise, but for personal reasons. The team found a title, *Les Temps modernes* (Modern Times, with a wink at Charlie Chaplin), and had a dummy layout done by Picasso that was finally jettisoned in favor of a purely Gallimard format. At the beginning of 1945 the future magazine applied for and was granted printing stock without any problem—although getting paper was not so easy as it might have seemed—thanks to the minister of information, Jacques Soustelle, who nevertheless expressed reservations about the presence on the brilliant board of one anti-Gaullist, Aron.[4] Gaston lent them his offices and administrative services. Everything was ready.

The first issue appeared October 1, 1945. At the end of its presentation Sartre wrote: "In 'committed literature,' the commitment must in no case make one forget the literature . . . our goal must be to serve literature by infusing it with new blood, no less than to serve the community by giving it the literature it needs." The whole spirit of the new magazine was encapsulated in those few lines. In the postwar intellectual landscape the magazine's importance was immense—because of the quality of its articles and its contributors; because of the impact of its ideas, presented at a time when existentialism was triumphant; and because of the influence of its chief mover, Sartre, on certain circles and a whole generation.

By offering it asylum on his turf, Gaston was giving a pledge to the Left, to the Resistance, and to the purgers. With Aragon now head of *Les Lettres françaises*, which had come under the control of the Communists, Malraux, de Gaulle's minister of information, and Sartre running *Les Temps modernes*, Gaston could relax. His crossing of the desert was proving much less painful than anticipated. Yet very quickly it turned stormy. In June 1946 Aron and Ollivier left *Les Temps modernes*. But it was Malraux who, a little later, created the scandal—in response, it is true, to attacks in the magazine. First, early in 1946, Maurice Merleau-Ponty, who was also the production supervisor of *Les Temps modernes*, had loosed a few barbs at him.[5]

Two and a half years later, an article appeared in the *New York*

Times of February 14, 1948, in which Cyrus Sulzberger wrote, among other things, that Malraux still said that if Leon Trotsky had won his political struggle against Stalin, Malraux today would be a Trotskyite Communist. Shortly after that, the *New York Times* published a short answer by Natalia Sedova Trotsky in which she violently attacked the author of *Man's Fate*, portraying him as a notorious Stalinist, an enemy of Trotskyism, and Jesuitical in the positions he had taken as a minister in de Gaulle's cabinet (which included Communists). "Malraux gives the appearance of having broken with Stalinism," she wrote, "but he is still serving his old masters by trying to establish a link between Trotskyism and the reactionaries."[6]

Malraux would not have cared so much, had the polemic remained in the pages of American publications. But *Les Temps modernes*, it seemed, took malicious delight in giving it wide publicity, translating and reproducing these articles and following them up with a long commentary by Merleau-Ponty:

> Giving in to intoxication with self, Malraux ceases to be a cause in politics, and allows himself to be taken over by the wave that Sulzberger is talking about. . . . If we hold something against Malraux, Koestler, Thierry Maulnier, and Burnham, against the "league of lost hopes," the "intellectuals in retreat," it is precisely this: that, having either lived or at least understood Marxism, . . . they have fallen short of it, they have not tried in spite of everything to blaze a path for the humanism of all men, but each in his own way has agreed to chaos and gone into retreat. Each has shirked the task of laying out the minimum program Trotsky had in mind.[7]

When the storm broke, Malraux was one of the closest companions of de Gaulle, who had named him his chief of propaganda of the RPF (Rassemblement du Peuple Français),* an important person, a notable, who reacted in terms of this exalted position to what

---

*The Rally of the French People—the name de Gaulle gave to his movement.— TRANS.

Merleau-Ponty had written in Sartre's magazine. Beside himself, Malraux remarked to Aron:

"He dares call me a coward, when he never fought anywhere but in his office!"[8]

He especially let loose his wrath in Gaston's office and demanded that the publisher choose: them or me! Malraux threatened to leave the firm, taking his copyrights with him as well as his books to come, if *Les Temps modernes* remained under Gallimard sponsorship. If his demand was not met, he warned, he was in a position to reopen some of the still-smoldering files of the Occupation period, the file of the Calmann-Lévy company, for example. Gaston believed him. Malraux was one of the few *NRF* authors who could permit himself this kind of dramatic display without a blush, having never in any way been compromised with the occupiers. Gaston took his dilemma straight to Sartre, who fortunately accepted the matter with good grace. There would be no scandal; Malraux would get his way. Was the firm so small that rising glories could not coexist within it without excluding one another?

Sartre took his magazine across the street to 30 Rue de l'Université, to the firm of René Julliard, one of Gallimard's competitors. The magazine got a new production manager, but Sartre stayed on as before.

"Now *he* is a real democrat," said a relieved Gaston.[9]

Gaston avoided another scandal involving another magazine. This was *Le Cheval de Troie* (The Trojan Horse), a magazine of religious doctrine and culture with the declared aim of bringing faith into confrontation with the modern world. Its first issue came out in June 1947. The originator and driving force of the venture was Father Bruckberger, the most Parisian of churchmen, who had no trouble in rounding up brilliant contributions from Bernanos, Malraux, Aymé, Sartre, Jouhandeau, Camus, Parain, Jules Roy, Jacques Maritain, and Blaise Cendrars.

Heartsick about the Jesuitical contamination which, on a moral plane, was threatening his own Dominican order, and about the

Saint-Sulpice style of preaching, he had decided to react in his own way by launching a magazine. The publisher immediately agreed, taken not so much by the ideas (Gaston tended to be an atheist and freethinker) as by the enthusiasm, fire, and output of Bruckberger, of whom Bernanos used to say, "This is a young monk you can go tiger-hunting with." It was not the least of Gaston's paradoxes for him to support this undertaking, this war against "the godless" in general and against those "who dream of the extermination and elimination of Catholicism" in particular.[10]

The magazine indeed acted as a Trojan horse within the House of Gallimard. The writing personnel of both were often the same. They were not stingy with their help to the young Dominican, nor were those few society women who made and unmade literary reputations, whom the witty Raymond Queneau lost no time in dubbing "bruckbergères et bruckbrebis."[11]*

The Dominican was in charge of the editorial end, with the publisher supplying office space, administration, and distribution. So far, so good. But at the end of eight issues there was a problem. The rigidness of the magazine's positions was an embarrassment to the French Church's drift toward modernism.[12] The Dominicans of Paris rejected the magazine's viewpoint, and the Provincial of Toulouse came to Gaston to ask him to stop this maverick periodical. With tears in his eyes Gaston reported the meeting—and his decision—to Father Bruckberger, while holding out the hope that the magazine might one day appear again. Beaten, Bruckberger gave up, not understanding the machinations behind this dark affair. But he was still full of admiration and gratitude toward Gaston, of whom he said, "He was the greatest publisher of this century, along with Robert Denoël. Their places have not been filled."[13]

To forget this misadventure, Bruckberger left for the Sahara desert in Algeria and joined the community of the Little Brothers of Jesus.

---

*The last half of Father Bruckberger's name means "shepherd" in French; the ladies thus became "Bruckshepherdesses and Bruckewes."—TRANS.

Not all the postwar magazines brought out by Gallimard caused controversy. Gaston did dream of reviving the *Nouvelle Revue Française*, but he did not want to rush things. Time had to do its work. Some years more would be required, before people stopped associating the *NRF* with Drieu La Rochelle. Jean Amrouche, who had been editing *L'Arche* along the same lines as the old *NRF* and was most anxious to see the two magazines merged, kept pressing Paulhan to revive it. He even arranged a meeting during which the silences of Paulhan, Gide, Camus, and Schlumberger were broken by the choppy voice of Malraux:

"You will never bring out a worthwhile magazine unless you pay high prices to competent people to read books they are not supposed to talk about."[14]

But if they couldn't have the *NRF*, there could be a substitute, to see them through until times and tempers improved. Gaston agreed with that proposition, and from April 1946 until the spring of 1952 he published *Les Cahiers de la Pléiade*—still keeping that trademark alive!—a kind of deluxe *NRF* in an oversize format and on special paper, meticulously designed and printed, and appearing at irregular intervals. The articles were ably done and of first-rate quality. Again, the catalyst was Paulhan. In this undertaking Paulhan was assisted by a thirty-nine-year-old former journalist, Dominique Aury. Fluent in English, retiring by temperament, she eventually would join the Gallimard editorial board and become managing editor of the future *NRF*.

Her arrival at Rue Sébastien-Bottin coincided with a period of renewal, purging, and maintaining the status quo. The firm was winning almost no prizes; Julliard was grabbing nearly all of them. But certain traditions of literary politics were still maintained—such as the cocktail parties whose fame had spread well beyond Saint-Germain-des-Prés. For a long time they had been held in the gardens of the two adjoining town houses, every Thursday from April to June. There was even a time when, between the buffets at which more drinking than eating was done, Gaston had had the idea of setting up a ping-pong table. Around that table some of the greatest French writers—a few Nobel Prize winners, and several Goncourt laureates—exchanged something other than ideas. The Gallimard cocktail party was not only an institution, it was a ceremony that one simply had to attend. One had to be seen there, and not damage the lawn. Claude Gallimard, the heir apparent, often drew up the list of invited guests.

The parties were so much a Parisian event that when Henri Calef and, a little later, Marcel Pagliero each did a documentary film of Paris and Saint-Germain-des-Prés, they included several sequences shot among the assembled guests of the *NRF*. It finally became apparent that more people were coming for the refreshments than for the literary atmosphere, so formal invitations were printed and required to be shown at the gate.

When Gaston asked some of his associates to identify a small group of people who were laughing very loudly, and it turned out that no one knew who they were, it was decided to space out these costly affairs, the returns from which were doubtful. The weekly parties became monthly and then annual affairs before disappearing completely—to the great regret of the "Duhamel gang," that happy ray of black light which had been so successfully cast across the immaculate cream-colored covers that were the trademark of the *NRF* and Gallimard.

This particular phase began with the Liberation. Its hero was named Marcel Duhamel. At forty-four he had tried his hand at everything: an advertising head of prewar illustrated magazines, he had also had a fling at the stage, the movies, film dubbing, and innkeeping. Something of a curmudgeon, as impassive as an English lord, but coming to life when pranks were in order, he was the self-educated fellow traveler of the Surrealists, a friend of Jacques Prévert and Henri Filipacchi. Duhamel admitted to one passion: English and American books. One day in August 1944 he left Marcel Achard's home with his pockets full, not of leaflets but three English novels, two by Peter Cheyney and one by James Hadley Chase. He translated them. But where could he get them published? During the Occupation he had met Michel Gallimard under rather special circumstances: a friend had told him that publishers were having trouble finding kraft paper for packaging their shipments, so through a contact Duhamel got his hands on large quantities of it and thus became a supplier to several companies. It was only natural, therefore, that he should bring his three translations to Rue Sébastien-Bottin, where his manuscripts seemed to meet with approval.

A distinctive cover and a title were needed for the collection, since if these three caught on, others would be published on a regular schedule—"small," "light" books, which by definition would be "popular." The firm's art director, Roger Allard, suggested a sketch to Gaston: green flowerlets against a white background.

"A bit bucolic for a series that will furnish gore by the bucketful," said Duhamel,[15] who then asked his wife Germaine, a professional designer, to draw a cover, and his friend Jacques Prévert to come up with a title.

"Why not just call it the Série noire [Black Series]?" said Prévert casually, while Germaine was drawing a cover of that color with a thin yellow line around it. Duhamel was happy with that, but the Gallimards were not. He needed a great deal of tenacity to overcome their resistance to what they considered a funereal note.[16] The Série noire was born. Duhamel went off to a winter sports resort, and immediately got a wire from Gaston asking for his return: there was work to do. To have translated the first group of their English novels was not enough; the rights to them had to be acquired. Paris and London were no longer cut off by the war, so Duhamel was rushed to England in search of books of a similar type. Gaston also urged him to look beyond the confines of his Série noire and find other kinds of books suitable for translation into French. The first time he had walked into the Gallimard offices, Duhamel made the mistake of saying, in a somewhat sarcastic tone, that he was probably the only one there fluent in English. Now they were making him pay for it.

Duhamel flew off to London with two documents in his pocket:

one from the minister of information, Jacques Soustelle, authorizing his trip, and another signed by Gaston saying that Duhamel was empowered to speak for the firm in England. Upon his arrival, he was greeted by the buzz bombs that were still falling at regular intervals. But no one except him seemed to pay attention to them. Chase, in his squadron chief's uniform, signed a contract with him. Cheyney did likewise, after a number of toasts with good Scotch. Then Duhamel contacted the literary agents of Steinbeck, Hammett, and Chandler and got them to renew their agreements.

This would create a revolution in the traditional French police novel, since in these imported detective stories the cops were often more corrupt than the murderers they were after. In addition, the stories did not usually present a mystery or puzzle to be solved by the reader along with the detective. There was no moral to be drawn from them; there were violent feelings and passions, love, and lots of action that always contained one indispensable element—a caustic, cynical humor. To be bloody *and* funny, that was the new style of the Série noire, in which translators would play a definite, if not often recognized, role.[17] Duhamel himself translated the first four volumes of the series: Cheyney's *Poison Ivy* and *This Man Is Dangerous*, Chase's *No Orchids for Miss Blandish*, and then, with Sabine Berritz (Mrs. Robert Aron), Horace McCoy's *No Pockets in a Shroud*.

June 7, 1946, was "the great night of the Série noire," when a party that brought together the Saint-Germain-des-Prés elite publicly confirmed the success of the collection. A year later, Duhamel had his own office and secretary at Rue Sébastien-Bottin and was bringing out two titles per month. Printings rarely exceeded 40,000. One exception: *Touchez pas au grisbi* (Hands Off the Loot), by Simonin, which would go over the 250,000 mark, showing how well the Série noire worked with the movies. More than a quarter of the series titles were made into movies, and each movie tripled the sales of its book.

Gaston had every reason to be delighted with the success of the Série noire. The series caught on quickly, confounding some of the purists on his editorial board but bringing in quick and regular profits to the House of Gallimard. More valuable to Duhamel than the catalogue of the collection, or than the high prices paid by some of its fans for rare or out-of-print titles, or even than the boundless gratitude of Gaston, was the compliment paid to him by one of "his own" authors, those he popularized in France for the simple reason that he liked them—Chester Himes. Himes had previously had several books published by various publishers, including Gallimard in his Collection blanche. These were stories of black detectives working in the violent world of the Harlem ghetto. He told an interviewer in 1983:

> Without Marcel, I probably would never have written detective stories. Some of my prison stories and writings did approach the detective genre through their subjects. When I started to write in prison, Dashiell Hammett was probably the one who most impressed me through his example. But I did not dream of imitating him or of making a career of the detective novel. In 1956 Marcel offered me a large amount of money, at least it seemed so to me at the time; it was so large that I accepted. He had already translated my *If He Hollers, Let Him Go* into French in 1948. He had recently started editing the Série noire. I had confidence in him and his judgment. I got started on the story of a couple of poor guys who got taken by some swindlers, the Gold Dust Twins, who claimed they could change gold through a chemical process and make it multiply. That story became *For Love of Imabelle*, which won the Grand Prix de Littérature Policière the following year. Marcel never corrected my manuscripts; he never told me how to write. He had confidence in me, that's all.[18]

As for Gaston, he would more prosaically tell the first translators employed by Duhamel: "If I can afford to publish poets whom nobody understands, it is thanks to the Série noire."[19]

After the war, two publishing houses played a determining role in French literature: Hachette, "a heavy weight on the economic side," and Gallimard, "a shaper of French literary judgment."[20] Without Hachette, there was no distribution; without Gallimard, no criticism.

Even if that is a slight exaggeration and the picture is oversimplified, it was still discouraging for lesser publishers who would have liked to think of themselves as independent. Although Les Editions de Minuit, Julliard, and Le Seuil, with their different characters, had come into prominence, the two old companies remained in the lead. For Gallimard the purge had meant mainly the loss of influence over the juries of the literary prizes. From 1945 to 1949 the firm was made to feel a reaction against the quasi monopoly it had exercised on such prizes—on the Goncourt especially—before the war and during the Occupation. For a while Gallimard had to take a back seat to the small new companies that had earned their prestige during the war, and to Julliard, the most dynamic and energetic of the old-timers.

That did not keep Gaston from redoubling his efforts. He kept three things in mind: his very considerable backlist, his current output, and the future. In the immediate aftermath of the war Gaston already had in his catalogue most of the titles that were to form the battalions of his heavy sellers during the twenty years to come: *Night Flight, The Little Prince, Wind, Sand, and Stars,* and *Southern Mail* by Saint-Exupéry; *Man's Hope* and *Man's Fate* by Malraux; *The Pastoral Symphony* and *The Counterfeiters* by Gide; *Lady Chatterley's Lover* by D. H. Lawrence; *The White Mare* by Aymé; *Swann's Way* by Proust; *L'Equipage (The Pure in Heart)* by Kessel; *Nausea* by Sartre; and *The Stranger* by Camus, soon to be joined by *Les Mains sales (Red Gloves)* and *La Peste (The Plague)*. Not to mention *Gone with the Wind*.[21]

But Gaston still was not satisfied in his quest for durability, for posterity, for the complete oeuvre rather than the one-shot success.

As early as September 1945 he had decided to go after the original of Casanova's *Memoirs,* to publish them in the Pléiade series. Hearing that Maurice Toesca, who was so helpful to him during the Occupation, had been named to the Office of Economic Affairs in the French sector of Occupied Germany at Baden-Baden, he wrote to ask him to visit the firm of Brockhaus in Leipzig and persuade them to let him have the original Casanova text: "But don't mention it to those around you, because I am afraid some of my competitors might then try to make a deal with Brockhaus."[22] In 1945 Paulhan was also using the good services of Toesca: to find out what had happened to his friend Gerhard Heller, whom he had not heard from since the Liberation.[23]

Gaston was persistent: Casanova's *Memoirs* would indeed be included in the Bibliothèque de la Pléiade, but only thirteen years after he contacted Toesca about it.

Meanwhile, back home on Rue Sébastien-Bottin, Camus was as much the fair-haired boy as Sartre. He was not only an author with good sales, a salaried reader-editor, and the model of a Resistance writer, but also general editor of a new collection called Espoir (Hope), in which he was to bring out books by Jean Daniel, Violette Leduc, Simone Weil, René Char, Brice Parain, and Roger Grenier, among others. It would go on for ten years until Gaston, seeing that it was not profitable, decided to drop it. But Camus remained par excellence the writer of the Liberation. The hundreds of thousands of readers of *The Plague*—"It was responsible for more victims than I expected," he was to write ironically[24]—were discovering or rediscovering *The Stranger* and *Cross Purpose*. At Gallimard he was one of the privileged few to have an office with its own balcony, of which he was so proud that he took all his visitors out on it, even in winter. Camus's friends at the office included Michel Gallimard, Jacques Lemarchand, and Jean Grenier.[25] (Paulhan did not much care for Camus, who did not appreciate Paulhan's sense of humor.)

The postwar period was one of transitions and renewals. Georges Simenon left the fold: Sven Nielsen, who had just bought out the Presses de la Cité, had become one of his best friends.[26] Montherlant, on the other hand, joined the fold, having finally freed himself from Grasset. Aragon was editing a collection called Littératures soviétiques (Soviet Literatures), and directing to either Gallimard or the Party's own publishing house all those manuscripts and authors that were being developed in the wake of his *Lettres françaises*. A young Romanian philosopher, Emil Michel Cioran, who had already published three books in his own country, brought Gallimard his first work written in French: *Précis de décomposition* (Précis of Decomposition); it was immediately accepted. But this time the author was the one who rejected the offer: he was not satisfied with his text and wanted to rewrite it. This moralist's book, most unusual and arcane, would appear only in 1949.

A few months after leaving the psychiatric asylum of Rodez, where he said he had been "deported inside France," Antonin Artaud got an agreement from Gaston to publish his complete works (some twenty volumes would appear). Meanwhile Gaston developed an affection for yet another drop-out from society, Jean Genet.

This upper-bourgeois propensity to provoke people by championing the rejected and disinherited was one of Gaston's most praiseworthy qualities. It would sometimes cost him dearly, as when authors did not hesitate to demand disproportionate advances on the royalties that their works were not likely to earn. Or when they made public scenes. Everyone at Rue Sébastien-Bottin would long remember the commotion brought about by the loss of Genet's manuscript of *Pompes funèbres (Funeral Rites)*. Having had words in public with the boss's son, the writer went through the hallways shouting:

"And to top it all, your employees refer to me as the bugger!"

Nor did he leave it at that. He sent a letter full of abuse to Gaston, his protector, who would see to it that the "mislaid"—not lost— manuscript was located. It turned out to be just as scandalous as its author.

More than ever, Gaston tried not to let anything get away. The troubles of some of the other publishers let him recover certain authors and make up for some past mistakes. His 1945 editorial board, with new blood, combined tradition and innovation. It was made up of fourteen men. The old guard were Marcel Arland; Bernard Groethuysen, who was to die of cancer a year later; Brice Parain; Jean Paulhan; and Louis-Daniel Hirsch, who had declined several offers from other publishers since the Liberation, including a very serious, urgent, and better-paying one from Robert Laffont. Sitting beside them were the younger readers who had only a few years with the firm: Jacques Lemarchand, Dionys Mascolo, Raymond Queneau. And finally there were the newcomers. Roger Caillois, thirty-two years old, was a graduate of the Ecole Normale Supérieure and a cofounder of the Collège de Sociologie. He edited the collection La Croix du Sud (The Southern Cross), in which he would bring out the works of some great Latin-American writers (Borges, Asturias). Caillois was also in charge of cultural development at UNESCO, and was himself an essayist, distinguished as much by the classicism of his writing as by his fascination with the mineral world and with poetical and fantastic universes: *L'Homme et le sacré (Man and the Sacred)* in 1939 and *Le Rocher de Sisyphe* (The Rock of Sisyphus) in 1945. Albert Camus, also a newcomer to the board, needs no further introduction.

Finally, alongside Gaston, his son Claude, and his brother Raymond, there was now the son of the latter, Michel Gallimard, who was twenty-seven. Michel was a quiet but attractive figure in the firm. Generous and cultivated, unwilling to exercise the power that he was nevertheless endowed with because of his name and his position, and because of his extraordinary affinity to his uncle, Michel appeared not so much the nephew as the spiritual son of Gaston, which created certain tensions within the company.

All things considered, Gallimard output from the Liberation to the early 1950s struck a good balance between political concessions to the times and literary and commercial considerations. Of course, alongside the important books by Aragon or Raymond Aron, Berl and Bernanos, Eluard and Péguy, there were a few that would never have had a chance with the *NRF* under other circumstances: *Les Clandestins: la vie ardente et secrète de la Résistance* (The Clandestine Ones: The Ardent and Secret Life of the Resistance) by Jean Nocher; *Résistance spirituelle* (Spiritual Resistance) by Paul Petit (containing a poem by Claudel); or even *Mort de l'Etat républicain* (Death of the Republican State) by Michel Debré, later a prime minister. The publication of Caillois's *Circonstancielles 1940–1945* (Circumstantials 1940–1945) and Guéhenno's *Journal des années noires* (Diary of the Dark Years) was looked upon as an act of contrition by Gaston, since the content and philosophy of both works so strongly condemned the attitude he had adopted during the Occupation. But that did not keep him from going back, as early as 1947, to publishing authors who had been officially banned two years before: Jouhandeau and Montherlant. For Drieu La Rochelle it would take longer. At the same time Gaston was republishing writers whom the Germans had banned, such as Kafka (*Amerika* and *The Penal Colony*) and the great Americans, who came back in full force in the wake of the GI's who had carried out the D-Day landings: Faulkner, Hemingway, Steinbeck, Caldwell, and Dos Passos. In very different genres but with a loyalty and regularity that Gaston highly appreciated, Maurice Blanchot, Jacques Audiberti, and Marcel Aymé continued to give him an average of one book a year.

"Search, sniff out, discover—that is the motto of the trade," he often said. In 1949, the year when he renewed his distribution contract with Hachette and when the first Frankfurt Book Fair was held, Gaston came back in full form. Again he dominated, as he had before the war, in the race for literary prizes: he got the Goncourt for Robert Merle's *Week-end à Zuydcoote (Weekend at Dunkirk)*, the Renaudot for Louis Guilloux's *Le Jeu de patience* (The Game of Patience), and in 1950 the Interallié for Georges Auclair's *Un amour allemand* (A German Love), the Femina for Serge Groussard's *La Femme sans passé* (The Woman without a Past), and another Goncourt for Paul Colin's *Les Jeux sauvages* (The Wild Games).

Gallimard rides again! That might have been the ad line, if publishing were a Western. The trade knew it, not only because Gaston was again monopolizing the prizes, but because he was not letting anyone push him around. When the Goncourt Prize was given to Paul Colin for *Wild Games*, a malicious rumor began to circulate in Paris, that the book was not selling. If true, this would mean that the commercial allure of the Goncourt had failed—to the discomfiture and damage of a few privileged characters. Gaston had several court officers check with his printers and collect sworn affidavits attesting to the number of copies printed at each plant. He then published the list of their authenticated figures on a full page in the *Bibliographie de la France*, and on the facing page, in huge type: "122,500 copies, printing certified by official count."[27] That put an end to the rumor.

Gaston was top dog again. René Julliard, well aware of it, wanted to be the new Grasset. He actually did share some of the traits of Mauriac's former publisher, being turbulent, indomitable, somewhat whimsical and somewhat social, easily provoked, available to his authors, ready to commit the best of himself to promote the books he believed in. In the country of publishing, with Gallimard in power, Julliard made a good leader of the loyal opposition—but not the rival he would have liked to be. To become the postwar Grasset, Julliard would have needed the literary context of the 1930s, with its great reservoir of talent. But his Radiguet would be Françoise Sagan, and his *Devil in the Flesh* was *Bonjour tristesse*. And that made all the difference. From the 1950s on, genuine writers were becoming increasingly rare, as radio, television, and advertising extended their hold on the public mind, and the publishers were inclined to encourage this trend by turning to academics, journalists, intellectuals—particularly people with nothing to say but a lot to tell, generally their own life stories.

Julliard and young Robert Laffont were the two publishers who in that period modified the publishing landscape radically. It is no accident that for a time they were associates.

Grasset was by now completely out of the picture, not because of age—he was seventy in 1951—but out of weariness. He had never quite recovered from the ordeal of the purge and his repeated stays in psychiatric hospitals. Suffering from nervous exhaustion, he no longer had the drive to cross swords with his authors' enemies or faith enough to put across the books he felt for strongly.

Interviewed about the crisis in publishing, Grasset, who had been through more and deeper crises, took the opposite view from that of his many competitors: according to him, the crisis was not what most thought it was, a phenomenon caused by the price of paper and the disproportionate rise in production costs. The trouble lay elsewhere, in the lowering of standards and the paucity of writers worthy of their great predecessors:

Being a publisher consists mainly in saying no. Unfortunately, over the last years too many publishers no longer know how to say no. Because of them, the market has been invaded by "valueless stocks." . . . The bookseller is no longer interested in the books sent him, because he knows that publishers are publishing indiscriminately.[28]

Disillusioned, but still lucid about all that concerned his profession, Grasset was bitter mainly about the ingratitude of authors. The case of Montherlant destroyed his last illusions. In 1942 the two men quarreled. Montherlant had just published *Le Solstice de juin* (June Solstice) with Grasset and *La Reine morte* (The Dead Queen) with Gallimard. Angry with Grasset for not having reprinted his books of the preceding twenty years, Montherlant went so far as to suggest that others among the company's authors—Mauriac, Maurois, and Giraudoux, for example—were treated better. Grasset, on the other hand, wanted to renew Montherlant's overall contract without delay, since it was about to expire; he wanted to extend it for another ten years. Each of the parties made light of the other's demands. Montherlant asked for time to think it over whenever Grasset tried to pin him down. Their disagreement ended in the law courts. Eight years after their first falling out, in 1950, the civil court of the Seine decreed the cancellation with prejudice to both parties of all the publishing contracts they had entered into between 1922 and 1944, condemned Grasset to pay a symbolic one franc in damages, and ordered an expert to sort out the accounting between them. Montherlant appealed, asking not only that the contracts be canceled with prejudice to his publisher alone, but that in addition he be granted a million francs in punitive damages, and two million that he claimed were due him under his royalty agreements. Naturally, Grasset also filed an appeal, demanding that the validity of the contracts be upheld, and that he be granted a million francs in damages.

After an awesome string of "whereases," the court overturned the 1950 decision, finding against Grasset. He was ordered to pay 912,213 francs in royalties and 400,000 in damages to Montherlant. As Grasset saw it, this ruling of July 8, 1953, had to be considered historic for the trade, for now "publishing contracts no longer have the force of law" between author and publisher.[29] The long, complex, and arduous Montherlant affair would be the last of Grasset's battles to hold on to an author, and the beginning of Gallimard's offensive to win over his former writers.

Céline was free, available for the asking. Since 1947 he was again owner of all his own rights: his contract with Denoël, signed in 1932, was not valid, because the company was no longer allowed to reprint his books. While the writer was in exile in Denmark, having fled with the Vichy government, Gaston made a first overture. In vain: the painter Jean Dubuffet, whom he had asked to serve as go-between, refused the commission. In 1951 Céline was back in France, and Gaston, worrying that Flammarion might make an offer, contacted him, urged by Jouhandeau, Paulhan, and Malraux. Céline's interests were being represented by Pierre Monnier, a forty-year-old freelance in the trade who was a Célinian to the core. He had set himself up as a publisher under the name of Frédéric Chambriand for the sole purpose of getting Céline's books back into the bookstores.

Jouhandeau having taken the first steps, Monnier came to Gaston's office in July 1951. Greeting him with a long, satisfied smile that lasted a good ten seconds without a word being spoken, Gaston finally said:

"I would be delighted to be able to publish Céline. I have on my list the greatest names in literature: Gide, Claudel, Faulkner, Valéry— all of them. And the only one I missed out on was Céline. Yes, I let Céline get away. That was a mistake, an error. So you can well understand that today I will do whatever is necessary to get him."[30]

Monnier reeled off Céline's demands and conditions: 18 percent royalties (which he had from Denoël), an advance of 5 million francs in cash, retention of subsidiary rights, and republication of all the novels (not including the pamphlets, now banned). Gaston accepted them all, had a contract drawn up, signed it, and appended to it a plane ticket so Monnier could fly to Nice as soon as possible and take the good news in person to Céline, who was staying there.

The interview lasted no more than forty-five minutes. Less than an hour to wipe out a regret that had been eating away at Gaston for nearly twenty years. Between the signature of this contract and the death of Céline, ten years would go by, during which writer and publisher would meet no more than ten or so times. Which would not keep them from carrying on a full and colorful correspondence. Céline was often rough on his publisher: he damned him as a "disastrous grocer" and a "Shylock," denounced his penny-pinching and the poor organization of his company, and treated him as a hopelessly outmoded businessman: "You will always remain desperately 1900! Smiles! Understatement! Black stockings and the lot!" he wrote him in 1955.[31] The letters were sometimes violent, sometimes amusing, and Gaston, who had read worse during his long career, was surprised when Céline went several weeks without writing him.

He was willing to forgive much in this author, who suggested to him in 1955 that he publish his complete works in the Pléiade collection "between Bergson and Cervantes, for example." Indulgent with Céline as he had been with Paul Léautaud when publishing his *Journal littéraire* (Literary Diary), Gaston did not mind including on his list books which contained an unflattering portrait of himself—whether in a transparently disguised form as Achille Brottin in *D'un château l'autre (Castle to Castle)*, or under his real name as in *Entretiens avec le professeur Y (Conversations with Professor Y)*. But Gaston bristled when the author tried to interfere in his publishing strategy. When Céline gave him the manuscript of *Féerie pour une autre fois* (Fairyland for Another Time) with instructions to publish it in June, but send out review copies later, in October, he lost his temper, assured him that the firm's legal expert had checked the manuscript and that there was nothing to worry about, and insisted on making his own commercial decisions. But Céline, fearing libel suits, preferred to let a summer pass between publication and promotion, a lapse of three months to protect him under the statute of limitations.[32] More than once, Gaston called him to task for not being cooperative and not taking into account sales considerations. When Céline complained of the poor distribution of *Normance* and *Féerie pour une autre fois*, it was easy for Gaston to reply:

"You don't do a thing yourself, on such occasions, to attract public attention. To break the conspiracy of silence, we need a bit of a stir, interviews, feature stories. But you don't want to see anybody!"[33]

Gaston was an ideal scapegoat for a writer in need of venting spleen. Used to putting up with the whims of more than one author— Gide, Simenon, Aragon, Genet—he was willing to play this role in the mind and even the work of Céline, realizing that it was his position and not his person that was under attack. Céline had, after all, treated Denoël no better. "If the publisher is a target in Céline's novels, it is because to Céline he is the incarnation of the boss: the one who does no work but lives off the work of others. . . . If a book does not sell, it is because the publisher did not do his job in selling it; if it does sell, he is the one who gets rich by doing nothing, at the expense of the worker."[34]

But Gaston, though happy to have Céline in his catalogue, had to pay the price: the demands of the author, the curses, the consequences of some of his writings,[35] and the hatreds he still stirred among the *NRF* old-timers, such as Claudel, who did not have Gaston's open-mindedness. In 1952, when Gaston published a sequence of Céline books and Sartre's *Saint Genet comédien et martyr* *(Saint Genet, Actor and Martyr)*, Claudel wrote him:

> I would like to think they will earn you a lot of money. Unfortunately, you will not have long to enjoy it and, whether you like the idea or not, there will come a time, soon, when you will have to answer for it. . . . And when these books come into the hands of your grand-children and their descendants, they will find—in large type, on the cover—the name of their grandfather. Unerasable. I send you a saddened salutation.[36]

It would take more than that to intimidate Gaston. In July 1961 he would go to Céline's home in Meudon with a priest and pray over the writer's remains. Pray between Arletty and Rebatet, with their respective pasts.

In 1952 Gaston was determined to revive the *Nouvelle Revue Française*. The time had come. Twice, during the intervening years, he had succeeded in getting exemptions to its proscription, to publish special issues of the magazine as tributes—one to Gide, the other to Alain. If the rule could put up with that many exceptions, it could be dispensed with. The magazine could indeed appear again, he was told; but there was one condition he must observe. The title could not be the same.

Gaston gave it some thought. At the risk of sounding ridiculous, he decided to keep the old title but put another "Nouvelle" over it in small type, making it the *NNRF* or the neo-*NRF*. This did look strange, but he predicted—correctly—that in a few years it would not matter. They would be able to drop the new "Nouvelle" and no one would notice.

Paulhan was naturally the first one whom Gaston approached about editing the magazine. He consented, but conditionally, for he was very busy with his own works on language and writing, as well as his reading for the publishing house. He could edit the new *NRF* only if he shared that burden with someone else, namely, Marcel Arland. Gaston agreed, well aware that the real difficulty would start only when they went after material from authors with opinions and qualities as varied as in the period between the two wars. People's confidence had to be built up; they had to know that the magazine would be its prewar self, faithful to those who were taken to its bosom, and that it would again be able, if necessary, to print the works of new authors no matter how many subscribers canceled, as had happened in the case of the first poems of Henri Michaux.

Gaston was not worried about the first few issues. *Les Cahiers de la Pléiade*, which would cease publication, had enough of a backlog of articles to get the *NNRF* well on its way. But what about later? The criticism, the book reviews and such, posed the fewest problems: instead of calling on the great names of the past such as Gide, C. F.

Ramuz, and Charles-Albert Cingria, they would develop a whole new team of critics who, in the wake of Maurice Blanchot and Jean Starobinski, would avoid fads, analyze writings without regard to reputations, and open the magazine to foreign literature. Though there would be a unified style, the tone and particularities of each member of this young group of critics—Robert Abirached, Philippe Jacottet, Claude-Michel Cluny, Jean Duvignaud, and so on—would be respected.

But what about the front part of the magazine? Would writers like Nimier, Aragon, Malraux, and the rest agree to have extracts of their forthcoming books published alongside one another? Arland got a foretaste of the troubles ahead when Camus told him:

"Marcel, if it weren't for you, I would never contribute to a magazine that published Jouhandeau."[37]

Some signs led Gaston to be optimistic. In February 1952 he succeeded in publishing the thousand-page novel *Les Deux Etendards* (Two Flags) that Lucien Rebatet had written in the prison of Clair-vaux. Despite pressures and threats, Gaston insisted on publishing this manuscript, which one could hardly believe had been written by the author of *Les Décombres*. It was the same pen, but no longer the same ink. The critical support of free minds like Etiemble and Paulhan was helpful to Gaston, for there were many who felt this to be an ill-advised undertaking, however great the qualities of the novel—because its first result was to bring about the release of Rebatet from prison in July. Rebatet had been condemned to death. His pardon came even before his death sentence had been commuted to life imprisonment.[38]

Listening only to his own instincts, but buoyed by the encouragement received, Gaston was delighted with the number of letters urging him to revive the magazine. Some were sincere, others self-serving. It was hard not to think of the many "encouragements" he had also received in the summer of 1940 when he was hesitant about reactivating his company, when some authors, interested in their own royalties more than anything else, urged him to return to his trade. In August 1952 Saint-John Perse congratulated him and assured him of his solidarity in the project. In his eyes, the *NRF* was "a great magazine destined to play a national role in a literary renovation."[39]

January 1, 1953, was the date of the first issue of the *NNRF*. Its lead editorial linked it to the past, to the magazine that had existed between the two wars: "The principles that then gave it its raison d'être also give us ours; the more strongly since they are now more neglected." Naturally there were articles signed by Paulhan, Arland, and their close associate Dominique Aury, but also by Malraux and Saint-John Perse, Fargue and Montherlant, Schlumberger and Blanchot, Supervielle and Henri Thomas, Jouhandeau and Audiberti.

The editors held open office hours on Wednesdays from 5:00 to 7:00 P.M. Tradition socialized with innovation peaceably. But since the Liberation, other magazines had been hoping to take the *NRF*'s place, above all *La Table ronde* (The Round Table), as expressed by Roger Nimier in a letter to Mauriac in 1949: "It would be good if it could replace the old *NRF* with its rancors and hypocrisy."[40] Many fine writers—one could not say of all tendencies, for the magazine's tendency was clear from the names on its masthead—contributed to it regularly. The famous "Bloc-notes" (Notepad) of its editor François Mauriac was rarely disappointing. At the beginning of 1953, Mauriac provoked a scandal by his virulence, and not only in the precincts of Rue Sébastien-Bottin. The famous novelist used the pretext of the *NRF*'s reappearance to square some old scores. The ensuing hostilities came to be called "the magazine war."

I am well aware that old magazines, like old people, tend to be far-rather than near-sighted. You cannot see your most recent history. I would not dream of quarreling with you on this point, if that history were not that of Pierre Drieu La Rochelle. Drieu's fate was a far cry from that of M. Gaston Gallimard. Had history taken the opposite turn, M. Gallimard would still be in good shape. Either way, he was covered. Drieu, for his part, had played double or nothing. He lost, and paid infinitely beyond his debt. On the temporal plane, he has put himself out of reach of men who might harm him, though they can make him die a second time through their silence. You have the right to observe such a silence about the *NRF* of the Occupation, but not about the lad who sat in that chair and corrected proofs at that desk. It is not a different *NRF* which is reappearing today. . . . You were not obliged to revive the magazine, but you did anyway. So you no longer have the option of remaining silent. You have the floor, since Drieu is not available to explain just what went on at . . . Rue Sébastien-Bottin during those four years.[41]

This was but a foretaste of what the polemicist had in store. Point by point, he went over the "Notice to the Reader" concocted by Paulhan and Arland. They promised to maintain their magazine against all fads—laudable—and "against the ridiculous enticements of the prizes." Mauriac could not let that one go by: "Try to figure out the millions that the firm of Gallimard owes to the Goncourt Prize and never again—do you hear?—never again speak of putting young French novelists on their guard against 'the ridiculous enticements of the prizes.' "[42] This pretense infuriated Mauriac. The following month he drew up a list of the literary prizes, large and small, awarded to books published by Gallimard during the preceding months: "When, at the next Gallimard party, young authors see Paulhan coming in on the arm of Arland—purity supporting authenticity—they may find it amusing to rub the noses of those two in the *Calendrier des prix littéraires* [Calendar of Literary Prizes]. Eight prizes in four months! Who can do better? It is the banquet of the *dentuso*."[43]

The *dentuso* as well as the *galano*—dogfish sharks—were none other than Gaston Gallimard. Speaking directly to Paulhan, Mauriac wrote: "You are also, you will agree, I am sure, the indefatigable pilot fish that for years has swum attached to the nicest, the dearest of his friends, the most voracious *dentuso*, the most famished *galano* of all French publishing."

The polemicist concluded with a warning.

I still like the *NRF*. I entertain a bit of tenderness for the dear old lady whose shaved hair took eight years to grow back. It is not enough to say I mean her no harm. . . . As far as the new *NRF* is concerned, which so modestly refuses to look back over its most recent past, we will not let a chance go by to judge her in the light of this past. She will be forced either to recognize it or publicly disown it. In both cases, we will strip her of that purity, purely verbal, which is the refuge of those two innocents, Arland and Paulhan—while their masters, as soon as one publishing house is taken over, start laying siege to another, keeping an eye out for those that are dragging a wing, and attend all the death rattles.[44]

The tone had been set. It was war, or rather "brotherly throat-cutting." Mauriac would one day feel remorse over having gone so far against the house on Rue Sébastien-Bottin, which was to be the publisher of his complete works in the Pléiade collection. He would "forget" these excessive lines as he edited the final version of his "Bloc-notes" to be published in book form.

9

Changes in the Business

1953-1966

Nineteen fifty-three was a watershed year not only for Gallimard but also for the entire industry, for structural reasons. Merchandising, to the surprise of many, was introduced into the publishing business. A book was now looked upon as a product no different from any other, a thing "manufactured" on the basis of market research to fit the tastes and expectations of the public. In addition, a phenomenon appeared which would totally transform publishing in ten years: conglomeration. Grasset, Fayard, and Stock were absorbed by Hachette; Plon and Julliard sought refuge under the wing of the Presses de la Cité; while Gallimard hovered with sympathy and interest over the fate of Denoël, La Table ronde, and Le Mercure de France.

Grown bolder, and encouraged by his son, Gaston developed imperialistic ambitions. So that no writer should succeed or persevere anywhere else but in his catalogue or one of the houses under his control, he would do anything, even buy a 50 percent interest in

Grasset, and he made no bones about it. For once, Céline's remark hit the target: "a dogfish, a great devourer of publishers!"[1]

Gaston began with Denoël. After months of negotiations, early in 1952 ZED Publications, run by Michel Gallimard, bought 90 percent of the shares of the Denoël company. Five years later Roland Laudenbach, the thirty-six-year-old head of La Table ronde, came to terms with Gaston after a brief and courteous talk. The one needed outside capital, the other was ready to invest; the deal was closed, fifty-fifty. And a few months later Gaston bought up the old Mercure de France, the house built by Vallette, his onetime model as a publisher.

At the same time Gaston took glee in raiding from his competitors. Stealing writers, that is. For his editorial board he recruited Grasset's senior editor since the Liberation, Jean Blanzat. The 1942 winner of the French Academy's Grand Prize for the Novel with his *Orage du matin* (Morning Storm) and a founding member of the National Writers' Committee, Blanzat was to become—as almost everyone agreed—the most conscientious reader-editor at Gallimard. He was able to tell the entire plot of the involved manuscripts of Pierre Guyotat and explain his evaluation of them to a doubting editorial board.

That same year, 1953, a few months before Blanzat, Gaston wooed away Robert Kanters, the literary counselor at Julliard. This was at a time when the two companies glared in hatred at each other across Rue de l'Université. The joke was that if a smart author stood in the middle of the street, halfway between no. 17 and no. 30, shouting "What am I offered?" as he waved his manuscript, he would immediately get a hefty advance against royalties. Accepting Gallimard's offer, then, meant going over to the enemy. Kanters thought about it a while. For personal reasons, he was ready for a change. Here was the chance to be a full-fledged *directeur littéraire** at 140,000 francs per month, a big jump over his current salary. So he accepted. Julliard tried to keep him by offering him a big raise (Julliard had

*Literary director, equivalent to editor-in-chief in the United States.—TRANS.

previously taken over one of Gallimard's editors in the same way). In vain. Kanters was made head of the team at Gaston's new Denoël company.

In each house he controlled, Gaston always respected its autonomy. Never a veto, no editorial line to follow. Manuscripts sent over from Rue Sébastien-Bottin were immediately looked at with suspicion, as if they were poisoned gifts.[2] In case of a dispute between Gallimard and La Table ronde, Roger Nimier, who had been published by both and was Gaston's protégé, smoothed it out. All he had to do was go across the street. At Denoël it was Philippe Rossignol who served as liaison. The Denoël literary director did not receive any directives from Gaston either, although the company was totally under Gallimard control. Kanters had absolute freedom of choice, but his backlist was weak: a little Cendrars, some Malaparte. Once in a while Gaston would send a manuscript over to him—only to take it back to publish himself, the minute Kanters evinced enthusiasm for it.[3]

Gaston was eventually to pull out of La Table ronde, the only company he did not own outright. Realizing that he could not be partner in a publishing house with such a pronounced political character, and so offbeat, he bowed out and allowed it to be taken over by Grasset, represented by Bernard Privat and then Jean-Claude Fasquelle.

It was now 1955. Mme. Weissweiler's town house was decked out for a gala—a magnificent reception for Jean Cocteau, just elected to the Academy. In the crowd he noticed Henri Muller coming toward him, his face haggard with grief. Cocteau hastened over to him, both hands lifted, as if to ward off the messenger of evil news.

"I know," he said. "Don't tell me about it. Not today."[4]

The party had to go on. At that very moment, alone in his room at the Hôtel Montalembert, Bernard Grasset was breathing his last. He died while correcting the proofs of his last book, a sort of testament: *L'Evangile de l'édition selon Péguy* (The Gospel of Publishing according to Péguy). To see his company taken over by Hachette had been the last straw. He still clung to a few friends (Christine Garnier, Henri Muller, among them) and to public honors. He wanted to have his complete works published by Gallimard (and Gaston was willing), but only in the Pléiade collection (to which Gaston would not agree).[5] When Grasset turned his firm over to Hachette, Malraux called the shot correctly:

"He strikes me as a weightlifter who can no longer find anything but cardboard weights to lift."[6]

At his death, the tributes were unanimous. He would have loved it had he been alive, being so attached to fame. Cocteau would comment: "While I was entering the Cupola, Bernard Grasset was entering a much higher and more weighty cupola of immortality."[7]* From Mauriac ("I am indebted to him") to Maurois ("He made an art of publishing") and Henri Muller ("His secret was that he was committed to action"), the Grasset catalogue paid tribute to its progenitor. Montherlant's statement was much noticed because of their litigation ("I bow my head before death"), and Gaston's because of it sincerity: "I liked Bernard Grasset for his very faults. They grew out of his passion. His competition was a stimulant. He was the greatest publisher after Alfred Vallette."[8] There could be no finer compliment. It gave eloquent testimony to the strength of the bond between the two men, which underlay their commercial and literary rivalry. Seven years later, at the death of Julliard, Gaston would express more shaded feelings, in a message of circumstance rather than fellow feeling:

> The disappearance of René Julliard creates an indisputable vacuum within French publishing. In a few years he was able, by his personal dynamism and taste for adventure, by an acute sense of current events and what they demand, to invent many new authors and also invent an audience. He did this with elegance and efficiency—thus serving, in a manner

---

*The domed building of the Institut de France, in which the French Academy meets, is commonly referred to as "the Cupola," and members of the Academy are known as "the immortals."—TRANS.

that was his very own, a cause which is common to all of us. His presence, his activity, his loyalty were a ferment beneficial to all of French publishing—and for which it must be grateful to him.[9]

Among those qualities that Gaston pointed out in Julliard, there was one that he himself did not have: a sense of current events. More than once, his quest for durability made him turn down projects for books or collections that struck him as too ephemeral, too tied in with passing fancies, with the moment. To be sure, he had launched collections such as the Documents bleus (Blue Documents), Problèmes et Documents (Problems and Documents), and Sous la Troisième (In the Third Republic). But Julliard had shown that one could successfully turn books into journalism and book publishers into city editors who assigned subjects for reportage or investigation to the big bylines of the Parisian press.

In 1951 Gallimard was to launch the collection called L'Air du temps (Temper of the Times), under the general editorship of a friend of Joseph Kessel and Saint-Exupéry, Pierre Lazareff, who had been editor of the leading evening paper *France-Soir*. Lazareff would turn the collection into one of the most prolific in the catalogue and put some of the spirit of *France-Soir* into the old *NRF*-Gallimard. This unnatural marriage quickly met with public acceptance. Lazareff's far-flung correspondents and great feature writers became the foremost suppliers of the collection. It started with Michel Gordey's *Visa pour Moscou (Visa to Moscow)* and continued with reportage by Kessel—his *La Piste fauve* (The Wild Track), *Avec les alcooliques anonymes (The Road Back: A Report on Alcoholics Anonymous)*, *Hong Kong et Macao*—and Lucien Bodard on China and the Indochina war. The most typical examples were works like August Kubizek's *Adolf Hitler, mein Jugendfreund (Young Hitler: The Story of Our Friendship)* or Josef Wulf's *Martin Bormann, Hitlers Schatten* (Martin Bormann, Hitler's Shadow), and stories by former criminals, survivors of Soviet prison camps, or British spies en route to Moscow.

Launching the Air du temps series a few years after the Série noire was another way for Gaston to remind his people that in order to continue publishing poems and books "that nobody could understand," he also had to publish these 250-page articles that made *France-Soir* "the only daily paper with a circulation of over a million copies." These quick and easy sales made it possible for him to allow true literary works to mature as long as necessary. The large-selling collections underwrote the publication of some fifteen books by Raymond Queneau between his *Le Chiendent (The Bark Tree)*, which sold 744 copies two years after its appearance in 1933, to the successful *Zazie dans le métro (Zazie)*, which sold 315,000 copies in two years after its 1959 publication. The same applied to Violette Leduc: her first novel, *L'Asphyxie* (Asphyxiation), sold 840 copies all told, but *La Bâtarde* had sales of 120,000 when it was published in 1964.[10]

To dare to select and then to know how to wait: such might be the golden rule for any publisher. But that required staying power. Gaston liked to remind listeners that he sold only 600 copies of Ernest Hemingway's *A Farewell to Arms* when he first brought out the French translation, and that it took less daring for a publisher to go with young French novelists than young foreign novelists.[11] But he never forgot that his foreign best-seller *Gone with the Wind* was the work of an American novelist totally unknown in France. In 1958 he took a chance on a Russian writer, whose book and past work did not seem to indicate that he could hit it big in the West. This would lead to the "Pasternak Affair." *Doctor Zhivago* was published under mysterious circumstances never fully explained by those involved, who felt they had to protect the intermediaries.

The book came out at almost the same time in twenty-four languages. The Gallimard French translation appeared in June. It was to have a sale of over 400,000.[12] The campaign against the author in the Soviet Union intensified in proportion to the book's success abroad. When Boris Pasternak accepted the Nobel Prize for Literature in October 1958, he was condemned by Radio Moscow, the Soviet Writers' Union, and the journal *Literaturnaya Gazeta*. Dropped from the ranks of the Writers' Union, the poet was fair game for everyone, subjected to the vilification of the Communist Party, the press, the university. Fearing that he might be exiled from his Russian home, he publicly declined the Nobel Prize and wrote a letter of atonement to *Pravda*. This put an end to the direct attacks upon him and calmed the general anger—an anger hardly understandable, in that very few in the Soviet Union had had a chance to read *Doctor Zhivago*.

The main Gallimard office accommodated four men: the two brothers and their two sons. Raymond, the administrator, opposite his son Michel, a literary type; Gaston, the literary one, opposite his son Claude, an administrator. For a while the two brothers faced each other across their desks, while the two cousins sat back to back. Then the cousins worked face to face, or at least tried to.

This office geography was of extreme importance. Any change in the seating arrangement reflected, in the eyes of the company's staff and associates, a change in management. Wishing to show his independence and to distance himself from decisions he did not always approve of, Claude moved out of the main office in 1957 and set himself up, alone, in what had previously been the library of original editions.

Soon after the war, it became apparent that the two cousins did not hit it off. They were opposites in everything: temperament, tastes, friends, opinions. Even though Claude was involved mainly in the commercial aspects of the publishing house while Michel ran ZED Publications, they both sat on the editorial board and shared in the firm's development. Through his intellectual training and his approach to people and things, Gaston felt an affinity to his nephew, but he was to grow gradually closer to his son when the latter gave him grandchildren (Françoise, Christian, Antoine, Isabelle). Their presence and company brought out an unexpected facet of the shrewd publisher, the lover of women and literature: the affectionate grandfather.

More sentimental, vulnerable, and sensitive than in the past, Gaston was extremely upset in the late 1950s by a crisis that tore his entourage apart and almost shattered the company. Earlier crises he had weathered with equanimity, since politics had always left him indifferent. He abhorred militancy, considering it an intolerable reduction of an individual's intelligence. (In 1947 he had gone to a mass meeting for intellectuals organized by the Gaullist RPF at the Palais de la Mutualité, and sat in the front row of an audience of sympathizers.[13] There as an onlooker, he was curious to see and hear how some of his authors would express themselves on the platform: Malraux, the Gaullist party's propaganda chief, and Raymond Aron.) In 1958 the left-wing weekly *France-Observateur* had twice had its issues seized because of an article by André Philip entitled "Le Suicide de la France" (France Commits Suicide). Algeria was then a taboo subject. The newspaper had started a collection to give financial support to the victims of the government-ordered bombings of an Algerian city. On one of the first weekly lists, the largest individual contribution was 200,000 francs in the name of Les Editions Gallimard.[14] But no conclusion could be drawn from that concerning Gaston's political convictions. He was an opportunist by necessity, and a publisher above all. However, not everyone within his firm shared his detached nineteenth-century spirit, which could conceive of no commitment other than a literary one. In the corridors at the magazine and the publishing house, people were cold-shouldering one another. General de Gaulle's return to political office, the referendum on the new constitution, the "pacification" of Algeria, and the various assassination attempts had radicalized the most moderate positions. At Gallimard two informal cliques took shape, centered around Claude and Michel.

Those gravitating toward Claude could be placed "on the right." One was Michel Mohrt. He had been editing the English-language translations since 1952, after having been a lawyer, the general secretary of a trade association of industrialists during the Occupation, and then a college teacher in the United States. Mohrt had also published essays on Montherlant and on the new American novel. Jean Dutourd, a onetime civil servant and former newspaperman, had been hired in 1950 as a literary adviser, which left him plenty of time to write his novels, *Au bon buerre (The Best Butter)* and *Les Taxis de la marne (The Taxis of the Marne)*, which were to establish his reputation. But the most dominant personality of the clique that united these Gallimard associates by a shared sensibility rather than by specific political positions was undoubtedly Roger Nimier, one of Gaston's brilliant protégés, a young man of promising talent whose first novel, *Les Epées* (The Swords), Gaston had published in 1948, followed by *Le Hussand bleu (The Blue Hussar)* two years later. Active but bashful, often provocative, Nimier proved a formidable polemicist gifted with an instinct for the killing phrase. To general amusement he sent the following telegram to Mauriac upon Gide's death: "THERE IS NO HELL STOP GO AHEAD AND BE DISSOLUTE STOP LET CLAUDEL KNOW (signed) ANDRÉ GIDE." But Nimier provoked more than one of his friends when he declared that France could never be rebuilt with Sartre's shoulders and Camus's lungs. After this shaft, the author of *The Stranger* understandably preferred not to bump into him in the corridors of the *NRF*. Since Nimier had been a literary adviser to the firm since 1956 and in this capacity had an office in the building, the atmosphere was often tense, and it would not have taken much to bring the two into a conflict more than verbal.[15]

The clique on Michel Gallimard's side could be classified as left-oriented, though he himself affected to shun politics: Dionys Mascolo, the most committed of them all; Robert Gallimard, Michel's cousin (the son of Jacques, Gaston's brother), who had joined the firm in 1949, and since 1955 had been Sartre's house editor; and of course Camus. But even here, it was more a matter of intellectual affinities than outright politics.

The escalation of the conflict in Algeria hardened attitudes on either side, making even the most moderate strongly pro French Algeria or pro the National Liberation Front. Michel Gallimard himself, who for a long time had maintained a middle-of-the-road position, was to upset his friend Camus when he expressed sympathy for the Algerian revolutionaries:

"You will have blood on your hands," the writer told him, removing himself from the intrahouse squabble.[16]

The war between the cliques, the corridor sniping disturbed and depressed Gaston. Nothing good could come of it. And the immediate future proved him right. The political split between those around him actually hid a much deeper difference of opinion. Gaston had seldom argued with his brother Raymond, and the differences in their characters never affected their deep friendship and mutual respect, which went beyond the blood relationship and had stood the test of time. But the growing antagonism between their sons now threatened to drive them toward mutual anger and even a parting of the ways.

The crisis came in 1958. Rumors circulated about the hostility developing between the two Gallimards in their shared directorial office, into which no one now dared enter. Jean Schlumberger tried to play peacemaker: after all, next to the Gallimard family itself, he and Mané Couvreux held the largest number of shares in the company, and he was one of the oldest friends of both Gaston and Raymond. In his home on Rue d'Assas, Schlumberger held meetings in turn with the brothers, each of whom pleaded his own case—or, rather, the case of his son. It was not a matter of politics or the war in Algeria, but of overall management; the unhappiness of foreign publishers; the complaints of authors; the well-established reputation for disorganization that for decades had plagued the *NRF*-Gallimard business methods; the new imperialism of the company, concerned with buying up competitors fallen on hard times rather than rebuilding itself from the inside; the ideologies of the house's literary output; and conflicts between individuals from different departments. The brothers seemed to agree about virtually nothing.

By the fall of 1958 they had reached an impasse. The company's activity was seriously impaired. Schlumberger felt that the complaints on both sides were ridiculous when compared to what was at stake; he refused to believe that anyone would risk breaking up such a company for "minor matters of petty pride."[17] For a while there was an attempt to find a vice president who might act as an arbitrator. But even before the search was started, the two cliques were at odds over what his jurisdiction should be and where he would fit into the existing organizational chart. So another solution was seriously considered: a physical separation, with Raymond and his son moving out of Rue Sébastien-Bottin and taking with them the collections under their supervision, the Pléiade especially. But apart from the legal problems inherent in such a fission, it was hard to see how Raymond and his son could continue that prestigious collection by drawing only on the works of writers in the public domain, excluded from using the Gallimard writers: Gide, Saint-Exupéry, Martin du Gard. Thus the Pléiade would become like any other series of reprints, open to imitation on all sides.

Nor could Gaston resign himself to see the edifice he had built so patiently over the decades be divided in this way. The authors whom he had kept in his catalogue through diplomacy and sacrifice could use this rift as a pretext for leaving the firm. And how could the company exist if it were to speak with two different voices? Schlumberger, who knew what the Hachette management was like, was particularly skeptical: they would easily get from one Gallimard whatever the other had refused to give them.

Schlumberger pleaded for reconciliation, asking the four contestants to put their susceptibilities aside and consider above all the interests of the company. To divide it would amount to destroying the old publishing house, at the very moment when the Hachette octopus had devoured Bernard Grasset. He asked Gaston and Raymond to revive their long-standing brotherly relationship by a conciliatory gesture, an affectionate letter in which reason would predominate over passion. To the cousins he recommended a frank discussion of their respective intentions, based on the premise that the future head of the company could be no one but Claude, that the main contacts with authors and the outside world belonged to his domain; whereas Michel would remain in charge of the Pléiade and other collections, while also running the ZED company. Schlumberger's plea was moving, for it was sincere. He could not imagine that Gaston wanted a break:

> [Let us not] give satisfaction to the bystanders who are sick with jealousy over the success of our team. All this, which has demanded so much effort and devotion and taken on so great a significance in literary history, must not disappear in one day—for you know that without you the edifice immediately crumbles. We—and you most of all—have

invested more than money in this venture. The money might be saved in such an upheaval, but the spirit and faith that we have given will suffer an irremediable defeat.[18]

A few months later, things more or less settled back into place. Compromises were made, and a fair dividing up of responsibilities, as wise Schlumberger had foreseen. Claude, the heir apparent, would gradually take his place at the helm through his own skill and tenacity.

In January 1960 there was an automobile accident on a road in the Yonne, near Villeneuve-la-Guyard. In the front seat of the Facel Vega were Albert Camus and Michel Gallimard, and in the back seat the latter's wife Jeanine and their daughter Anne. A tree—a smashup—ambulances. Camus was killed on the spot, and Michel died a few days later from his injuries. Jeanine had only some contusions; Anne was unhurt. The funeral of Michel Gallimard was held in the little cemetery of Sorel-Moussel in the Eure-et-Loir, on a cold, muddy day beneath a leaden sky.

The day before his death, when everyone already knew there was no hope despite several operations, an old employee walked into the management office without knocking: for the first time, he saw Gaston totally overwhelmed, weeping, holding his head in his hands.

In 1960, the same year the new franc and the new ocean liner *France* were launched, Gaston turned sixty-nine.

On August 25, 1960, *L'Auto-Journal*, which regularly devoted a full page to "a man whose fate or success was of an exceptional nature," ran the story of Gaston Gallimard's life, with a headline over its eight-column width: "Shrewd Businessman or Benefactor of Letters?" The article was well informed, specific, and balanced. But what especially struck the reader's eye was the photograph, the portrait of Gaston: the smile, the bow tie, and the nonchalance, distinguished and wily at the same time. Age had taken nothing away from his personality. No one knows at which party that strikingly accurate picture was taken. But those close to him noted that one element was missing: sadness. They were dead, Michel Gallimard and Martin du Gard; dead, Copeau and Dullin; dead, Gide and Camus; dead at the end of the war, so many years ago, Giraudoux and Fernandez, Groethuysen and Saint-Exupéry, and Drieu.

The older you get, the more familiar you become with cemeteries, especially when you have the weakness of being attached to the men and women whose books you publish. Gaston was weary, and deeply hurt by those fratricidal struggles. He liked his profession as much as ever, refused to get out of harness, did not even want to hear the word retirement. Even though he gradually turned the reins of power over to his son, he was still active, still making himself felt. He was often found at the office of the American literary agent Jenny Bradley, in her apartment on the Ile-Saint-Louis where he enjoyed meeting and chatting with his New York colleague Alfred Knopf and the latter's wife Blanche; with Janet Flanner, the correspondent for *The New Yorker* magazine, and Jacques Forel, the son of the actress Réjane; with James Hadley Chase and Erskine Caldwell; with Nathalie Barney and Truman Capote.[19] The company of people before that of ideas and books. He had not changed, and was delighted when Cocteau organized for him and a few privileged *NRF* people a luncheon on Rue d'Anjou at the home of Mme. de Chevigné, who had been one of Proust's models for the Duchesse de Guermantes.[20]

He was unpredictable and contradictory. His art director, Massin, was sometimes unable to interest him in the cover designs of upcoming books, although Gaston could certainly appreciate graphic art, having grown up in the presence of Carrière and Renoir and written his very first articles about art shows.

Louis Guilloux noted that Gaston and Martin du Gard, shortly before the latter's death, would slip off into a corner after dinner to exchange a serene dialogue about death.[21] Yet Gaston bought himself a new Studebaker—not to impress anyone, but just to drive it, and drive it fast, and if possible with a pretty woman beside him.

When young Robert Laffont came to ask advice of the Publishing Elder, Gaston told him:

"You will never be a publisher as long as you talk about sure things. After forty years in this business, I can tell you only this: no one can ever predict how a book will do."[22]

In 1953 the weekly news magazine *L'Express* included Gaston Gallimard and René Julliard on its "list of 100 who prepare the future." Not a directory, not a list of winners, not even a dictionary of famous Frenchmen, it was, instead, an enumeration of "motive forces." These men would determine the future "either by the evolutionary influence they exert within their own professions, or by their power of renewal through creativity." Their strength would lead the youth of the nation toward its destiny. About Gaston the article said: "Perceives the voice of the writers of the future when they are still only babbling. He does not take risks, but knows how to force the reader to take them." And about Julliard: "By his very presence, keeps Gallimard from falling asleep on the job. Gives Sartre the means for publishing *Les Temps modernes*. By being willing to take all risks, forces French publishing to take a few."[23]

People saw Gaston's fantastic self-assurance and thought that his timidity was only an act; they remembered his reputation for wiliness and forgot the mistakes he made. Yet often he was anxious, depressed, disoriented—especially in the early 1950s. Louis Guilloux, who was temporarily living in a room of the Rue de l'Université town house that was the home of both the Michel Gallimards and the Claude Gallimards, was aware of this. In his fits of melancholy, Gaston often said strange things in the presence of this writer who acted as his confidant:

"My life has been a failure . . . from the day I became a businessman, I lost my real friends. We no longer talked about the same things."

Or another time: "You know, I don't sleep. The other night, I wrote a whole book in my mind. But you will think I'm ridiculous. You're lucky, writing is your vocation. Not mine: all I have is money. But having money doesn't really do me any good. After all—you'll think I'm ridiculous—I only like people who are failures. The greatest ones always commit suicide."

And Gaston reeled off the names of Jesus Christ, Napoleon, Joan of Arc, Oscar Wilde, André Citroën, the couturier Poiret.[24]

Yet this was the same Gaston who, when the need arose, could pound on the table, negotiate contracts off the cuff, "borrow" the writers on his competitors' lists and "forget" to return them, and stand intractable over a matter of a few sous or a question of principle. As soon as there was any infringement of rights he called in his lawyer, as for instance when a publisher used several Eluard poems instead of the one for which he had obtained permission, or when another brought out a counterfeit *Lady Chatterley* or a *Pastoral Symphony* "based upon the movie of the same name." Gaston did not like to be taken advantage of.

He had his likes and dislikes, his preferences, his habits. Honors? Decorations? He had always detested them and nothing could change his mind about that. When in 1947 he was told he would be nominated for the Legion of Honor, he politely declined, only adding, "My brother might enjoy that."[25] So, shortly afterward, President Vincent Auriol invited Paulhan, Camus, Jacques Lemarchand, and Michel Gallimard to be present at the Elysée Palace as he pinned the insignia to the lapel of Raymond, while they looked on with interest and amusement. As for Gaston, the last thing he wanted was to be worthy of such an "honor." He was still the "slacker" of 1914–18. In his eyes the height of indecency was a military medal pinned to the folds of a flag draping a coffin. This disgusted him as much as the pomp and circumstance of the French Academy. Yet when Marcel Arland was elected to it in 1969 to fill the chair left vacant by André Maurois, Gaston attended the ceremony. He went two years later as well, when Roger Caillois received his Academician's sword. For them it was allowable, but not for anyone else. In the case of Kessel and Paulhan, he declined to attend. When Kessel told him he was being inducted, Gaston snapped:

"Unless you think it'll look nice on your letterhead, what the hell use is it?"[26]

That retort, from an upper bourgeois to a journalistic adventurer, was not without its irony. From that day on, Kessel remained convinced that Gaston was "the most extraordinary intellectual anarchist I've ever met."[27] Which would not keep Gaston from publishing Kessel's acceptance speech, as he had traditionally done for so many other writers.

But he never forgave Paulhan for going after the Academy's green uniform. This was in 1964. Gaston reminded Paulhan of the oath that bound the old-timers of the *NRF*: never to set foot in that den of iniquity. Hadn't the magazine, as well as the Théâtre du Vieux-Colombier and a not negligible part of the publishing house's output, always been against the "spirit of academicism"? Malraux tried to temper Gaston's wrath by explaining to him that if they did not encourage people like Paulhan to join the Academy, for this very reason it would remain as stodgy and self-serving as they all claimed it was. But Gaston turned a deaf ear. Paulhan's motives were similar to his character: varied and complex. But according to his friend André Dhôtel, vanity was predominant: as Paulhan gladly told newspapermen, he was happy to be finally thus honored after seeing so many of his comrades accepted. It was another way of saying, "Look, I am a writer, too."[28]

That was probably what Gaston most held against him: Paulhan had officially crossed the Rubicon separating the territory of the publisher/editor from that of the writer. Gaston absolutely refused to go to the Hôtel Meurice to the party that Florence Gould gave for the new academician. And Gaston's displeasure would be projected into the future: the complete works of Jean Paulhan, an *NRF* and Gallimard man if ever there was one, would eventually be published not in the Pléiade collection but by another publisher, Claude Tchou.

Despite his age Gaston held to the principles he had always respected, preferring to stay with a bad idea rather than continually switch from one idea to another. But his relations with authors adjusted to the tastes of the day, the needs of the moment. When Jean Genet asked for money so he could put a new motor in the car of his current young man, Gaston refused. They argued for hours. When Genet, out of patience, exclaimed, "You don't even know what a crankshaft is!"—Gaston explained to the writer, in detail and with amazing technical precision, exactly how one worked. And then he gave him the money.

Roger Nimier knew he was Gaston's pet. The publisher often asked him to lunch at the expensive and chic Restaurant Berkeley, spent hours in his office chatting about this and that, and made him the gift of a sports car, which the grateful Nimier quickly baptized his "Gaston-Martin." It must be said that apart from his qualities as a writer and person Nimier appealed to Gaston because of his efficiency: at a moment's notice he could tell authors exactly where their manuscript or book stood, and without making them feel that they were imposing on him. One need only read some of Céline's communications to realize how indispensable Nimier was in his essential though unglamorous position. For his sense of humor, too, Gaston valued the impudent young fellow, one of the few with whom he could banter or plan practical jokes, making fun of people and situations. Since he had an inbred aversion to embarrassing anyone, Gaston pretended to be the janitor one evening when, thinking he was the last to leave, he walked into Nimier's office without knocking and caught him flagrante delicto with a famous actress. Without displaying the slightest surprise, Gaston asked respectfully:

"Am I to turn out the lights in the corridor, Monsieur Nimier, sir?"

Gaston knew how to have a good time as well as how to work. How to drop everything and take a long vacation, how to forsake the office for a lengthy good meal, and duck out on boring businessmen to spend his time with poets. He liked to drop in on people in their offices, make bets on the most farfetched things, or discuss with his associates how they should reply to a letter from the tax collector addressed to "M. Franz Kafka, 5 Rue Sébastien-Bottin." He despised people who were discourteous, vulgar, or gross, complained that manners were no longer what they used to be, but admired nerve, if accompanied by finesse and humor.

One day in 1950 he got a request for an appointment from a thirty-year-old writer. Some time before, Gaston had sent the writer a short encouraging note after the appearance of his essay, *Le Complexe de César* (The Caesar Complex), a note that had really been a form letter: "I was very much interested . . . I would feel honored to publish one of your forthcoming books." After all, one never knew. The author was published by Laffont, but it was better not to thumb one's nose at the future, and he was young and appeared promising. Now the writer was reminding him of that. Gaston received Jean Dutourd, who said to him:

"Four years ago, you wrote me—"

"Indeed I did."

"Well, the thing is, since then I've spent three years in London in the French Service of the BBC, but I got homesick and I've come back. I came across your note again and—well, I'm unemployed, quite penniless. Do you need someone to sweep up the place?"

Gaston smiled and asked for time to think it over. Twenty-four hours later, Dutourd got a letter hiring him as a literary adviser. He stayed on for sixteen years. The salary was not great, but neither was the work onerous. He quickly understood that the "job" of literary adviser was filled mostly by authors in whom the company had an interest, authors whose eventual work the company wanted to have first refusal on. To keep up appearances and try to make use of him in some way, they gave him an office on the third floor, between Camus and Lemarchand. He was asked to write press releases, short descriptions of books for the use of busy or lazy newspaper people. These were often written without reading the book. Dutourd would usually give the book a quick sniff—or, even better, get the author to write his own blurb. For years that would be Dutourd's main activity—aside from translating Hemingway's *Old Man and the Sea*, updating the Littré dictionary, and a brief stint on the editorial board, where he was as bored as he was boring to the others.[29] During this period he produced close to fifteen books; some sold well, some received rave reviews, and some did both. For Gaston, both were what mattered.

When Gaston wooed Roger Vailland away from the Buchet-Chastel house, he did not care that the author was an active member of the Communist Party.

"I am not a Communist but I publish quite a few Communist authors," he told him,[30] knowing that Vailland's novel *Beau Masque* (Fine Face) was creating something of a problem for its rather traditionalist publisher because of the political content. He sent him a large advance check against royalties, in the hope that he would sign the contract submitted. But Vailland returned the check and contract, requesting a separate agreement for each individual book, since he did not wish to tie himself down for his entire future output. Gaston did not like the terms, but accepted them. And he was right: the second Vailland novel, *La Loi (The Law)*, won the Goncourt Prize in 1957.

Gaston never stopped trying. In 1952 he was on the dock, between his competitors Sven Nielsen and Jean Fayard, to welcome—along with thousands of admirers—Georges Simenon, who had been an "American" since the Liberation.[31]

That same year Gaston wrote Cocteau, who had just had his *Journal d'un inconnu (The Hand of a Stranger)* published by Grasset: "You are right to use the word tragedy, because that is what it is for me to see your books published elsewhere. I am indifferent to many things, but I still feel the jealousy of my youth about those I like and by whom I would like to be chosen."[32]

He was furious that his rival Julliard should have had *Bonjour tristesse*, one of the best-selling books of the 1950s, but that did not keep him from being a witness at the marriage of Françoise Sagan to Guy Schoeller in 1958. He was ready to fight tooth and nail to enforce his voracious contract with Jouhandeau, but when the lawyers for both parties suggested a compromise, Gaston finally gave in—largely because of the length of time Jouhandeau had been in his catalogue. Jouhandeau, like Céline, Sartre, Nimier, and so many others, would die owing the firm money. That did not matter: the company still had fifty years of literary ownership, the future, their authors' consecration by inclusion in school textbooks—until the day they too fell into the public domain.

The landmarks for the company were landmarks for the industry as a whole. Examples? The hundredth volume in the Pléiade collection, the complete works of Marcel Proust, in 1954. The law of March 11, 1957, covering literary and artistic property, which permanently established the material and intellectual ownership of the writer over his work. The first broadcast of "Lectures pour Tous" (Reading for Everyone), the first of all TV shows devoted to literature, in 1953. And that same year, Saint-Exupéry's *Night Flight*, one of the first pocket books to be put on the market in France. (The Gallimard backlist would account for a good third of the titles in the Livre de Poche, one of the main paperback trademarks.) The controversy and polemics, in *Le Mercure de France* and *Les Temps modernes* in 1965–66, about this "pocket culture," accused of depreciating literature by dressing it up in cheap clothing. The end of the "Librairie Gallimard" label, which in 1951 became "Les Editions Gallimard," while the *NRF* logo stayed on. The thousandth volume of the Série noire, *1 275 âmes (Pop. 1280)*, by Jim Thompson . . .

10

Without Gaston

1967-1975

It was time for the final balance sheet.

From 37,538,311 francs in 1969, the assets rose to 47,049,964 by 1971. The catalogue had grown in bulk. The quality had improved. As long as Gaston remained in place, he was seen as a guarantee. But what about afterward?

To the old-timers on the editorial board—Marcel Arland, Louis-Daniel Hirsch, Jacques Lemarchand, Brice Parain, Raymond Queneau, Gaston and Claude Gallimard—there had been gradual additions since the war: Dominique Aury (the first woman to sit on it), Jean Blanzat, Roger Caillois, Michel Deguy, Louis-René Des Forêts, Jean Grosjean, Georges Lambrichs, Michel Mohrt, Pierre Nora, Claude Roy, and two new Gallimards—Robert (son of Jacques, Gaston's other brother) and Christian (Claude's son, Gaston's grandson).

At a time when the competition was going in for "books on tape," as told to a professional writer by an eyewitness of events, Gaston could still leaf through his catalogue with pride, read his magazine, converse with the members of his editorial board, and look over his sales figures. In 1967 his collections and their editors were like lookouts posted at strategic points, and guarantees that the lasting qualities of a work would remain the criteria:

COLLECTION	EDITOR
Le Chemin (The Path)	Georges Lambrichs
Littératures soviétiques (Soviet Writings)	Louis Aragon
Le Point du Jour (Daybreak)	René Bertelé
La Pléiade (The Pléiade)	Pierre Bugé
La Croix du Sud (Southern Cross)	Roger Caillois
La Série noire (The Black Series)	Marcel Duhamel
Idées (Ideas)	François Erval
Connaissance de l'Orient (Knowledge of the Orient)	René Etiemble
Livre du jour (Book of the Day)	Roger Grenier
L'Air du temps (Temper of the Times)	Pierre Lazareff
Bibliothèque des sciences humaines (Library of the Humanities)	Pierre Nora
Connaissance de l'inconscient (Knowledge of the Subconscious)	J.-B. Pontalis
Encyclopédie de la Pléiade (Pléiade Encyclopedia)	Raymond Queneau
L'Avenir de la science (The Future of Science)	Jean Rostand
Bibliothèque de philosophie (Philosophical Library)	Jean-Paul Sartre[1]

And they were all selling, and some selling very well, which was all the proof needed that quality and profit could go hand in hand. These unshakable principles, and the "philosophy of the trade" that he drew from them, were transmitted by Gaston to his son as he progressively gave him full power over the house and its operation.

In 1970 Claude, the crown prince, was fifty-six. A secretive and determined man, more at home with account ledgers than books, he had taken thirty years to acquire a given name—the most terrible of ordeals in entrenched dynasties. In order no longer to be merely "Gaston's son" but head of a company with some 200 employees, Claude had to expand his activities, create new collections or imprints, and assert his personality among his fellow publishers—or at least among some of them, hand-picked, upon whom he conferred the honor of not considering them mere businessmen. Claude brought about the merger in 1967 of ZED Publications with Gallimard, which added ZED's customers, its authors' contracts, and its shares in a number of bookstores and publishing companies, as well as a sizable portfolio of investments, to the company. He worked to create an image of quality. Some authors, even a few he had been close to for political or strategic reasons, proved poor public relations agents for him within literary Tout-Paris. One of them, who had worked in the house for fifteen years, having been hired by Gaston but fired by Claude, was to say:

"I entered Gallimard's under Louis the Fourteenth and left it under the presidency of Félix Faure."*

Claude began to give interviews, to show the outside world that the *NRF* heir was not so scornful, distant, or quarrelsome as many claimed. And the "Hachette affair" provided him with the chance to demonstrate that "his" Gallimard company was turning over a new leaf. The exclusive distribution contract Gaston had signed with Hachette in 1932 was renewed in 1949 without too much difficulty. In 1956 it was extended again, but this time the two parties struggled and negotiated every inch of the way for nearly two years before signing the fifty-odd-page document. To Gaston, that was a warning signal. Hachette was gradually eliminating the guarantee that had been Gaston's insurance for so many years, and was taking a

---

*Félix Faure—president of France's Third Republic, during whose troubled term the Dreyfus Affair rocked public opinion.—TRANS.

commission of 48 percent of the retail price. Since Hachette received 50 percent from its ordinary customers, the traditional "bonds of friendship" which until then had governed the relationship of the two great companies began to seem only a memory.

The contract was to be in force until the end of February 1971, but intention of cancellation had to be given by February 28, 1970. This time the negotiating was even tougher. As expected, Hachette made new demands, but now they did not come from an old friend of the Gallimards, Guy Schoeller, but from new men: Ithier de Roquemaurel, who was the company's president and CEO, and especially Bernard de Fallois, head of the Book Division. It was soon apparent that the clash between the companies was in fact a clash between two individuals, each trying to establish his authority in his own company: Claude Gallimard and Bernard de Fallois.

Gallimard began the negotiations by proposing that it take over sales costs and commissions to bookstores, so that Hachette would handle only billing, shipping, and storage, services that Gallimard evaluated at 11 percent of the retail price of the books. They waited for an answer, which was not forthcoming. At Rue Sébastien-Bottin they argued for direct involvement in the sale of new titles, now being poorly handled by Hachette, which continued to concentrate on the backlist.[2] Hachette rejected this reduced role, but at first made no comment and no direct reply. At the same time Hachette let it be privately known that, should Gallimard find itself in financial straits, the Hachette group would be ready to step in and take the company over, as was their habitual strategy. Then it finally presented its counterproposal: the distribution fee would now be over 52 percent.[3]

Claude got the contract extended for an additional year at the old terms. He had twelve months in which to maneuver out of the impasse. Hachette's strategy was obvious: it obeyed the logic of an empire that grows and becomes regenerated through the misfortunes of its clients, and was fueled by the personal psychology of Fallois, who had to justify his position in the firm. At Gallimard the increase in distribution costs was considered excessive and unjustified, whatever the actual costs of warehousing, shipping, and rebates to booksellers, "since the rise in the cost of books had been approximately proportional to that of salaries."[4] Clearly, the special advantages given Gallimard by Hachette in 1932 had been gradually whittled down; almost nothing was left of them. "While Hachette continued to buy outright 75 percent of the printings of new titles up to a press run of 3,000, at the end of the year the unsold copies were being exchanged for reprints of backlist titles with assured sales,"[5] an arrangement that had its advantages for the budding company of the 1930s, but thirty years later did not appeal to the going concern on Rue Sébastien-Bottin.

"Moreover, the deliveries of all kinds made to Hachette were paid for by ninety-day drafts—that is, more slowly than the bookshops paid Hachette itself for their orders. Hachette's largesse toward Gallimard was therefore an old myth that had to be demolished. Through the time difference in the payments, Hachette was actually getting a month's free ride."[6]

Giving in was out of the question. Gaston was impressed by his son's determination and by the support of his grandson Christian, now twenty-nine, who had just come back from a study trip of several months in the United States, during which he had done a stint in the offices of Harcourt Brace Jovanovich. The Gallimards, meeting as a family council if not as the board of the company, tried not to rush things. There was too much at stake. And what was going to happen to the four collections they were copublishing with Hachette: the Série noire, the Livre de Poche, the Encyclopédie de la Pléiade, and the Univers des formes (Universe of Shapes)?

They finally decided on a leap into space. Even though they would have to go into debt and create new infrastructures, Gallimard decided to break with Hachette rather than lose this battle, which would mean losing the war. In six months Gallimard set up its own distribution company, Sodis, and shortly thereafter its own pocket-book collection, Folio. One year before, Gallimard had accounted for 13 percent of all Hachette-Distribution business, and owned the rights to 516 of the 1,500 titles that had appeared in the Livre de Poche catalogue.

Facing this enormous loss, Hachette stated: "This departure creates a breach which we shall have to fill." The economics journalist Michel Tardieu summed up the situation: "Hachette and Gallimard have obtained a divorce. For the professionals of the publishing industry this is the most significant event in half a century. For others it is an incongruous news item in these times when what is fashionable in business is moving closer together, if not merging. . . . Their association seemed perfect: it combined the power and the glory."[7]

For Gallimard it meant starting out on a new venture.

Without Gaston.

By 1975 all his friends were dead. Long dead. In 1968 he lost his wife Jeanne, two years later his brother Raymond. Then Paulhan and Schlumberger, Parain and Hirsch. His address book had nothing but crossed-out entries.

At eighty-four, he was no more than the shadow of his former self. Dying a few years too late—whispered those who loved him, sick at heart at seeing him decline, imprisoned in his body. His hearing had deteriorated; he no longer had keen vision; but his intelligence was unimpaired. He asked for certain manuscripts to be submitted to him, the work of men of real talent, but no one knew whether he actually read them. He was no longer in charge.

To stand up for the literature and poets he loved, he made it a duty still to attend the editorial meetings on Tuesdays at 5:00 P.M. He dressed the same way—bow tie and dark blue suit—but his face was emaciated, his thick lenses hid the twinkle in his eyes, his voice was no longer steady. Sitting quietly, he was an attentive observer who tried to go unnoticed by the board members, engrossed in their reports. Gaston felt himself to be too old to try to temper the enthusiasm of the young, even when he judged—and his instinct was still intact—that a given work did not have "the required qualities" to take it from manuscript to printed page and publication under the

NRF logo. Isolated by his failing hearing, when he saw one of the editors burst out laughing, he would ask his nephew Robert, seated at his right, to translate the joke for him in a loud and intelligible voice.

Gaston remained lucid, and understood his limitations. He never went to the office until the afternoon, when he was dropped off by his chauffeur at a set time: thus he made his best moments available to friends, authors, and associates. He still tried to be part of his century, but he was not succeeding. Newspapers? He could not follow them—not even *Le Figaro*. The more he thought over his life, the more confused he felt. He tried to keep up with the literary magazines, a few new books, and to watch the new literary TV show, "Apostrophes." In vain. Letting go, he fell back on rereading Diderot, who never let him down. What he felt was wrong with his younger contemporaries was their vanity, their insistence on appearing in print when they had nothing to say, their lack of modesty. In the old days, he had had no trouble in getting Paul Valéry to cut a few lines from his *Eupalinos ou l'Architecte* (*Eupalinos, or The Architect*), which seemed too long for the layout. Once set in type, the text was too short. Valéry did not grumble about restoring those few lines. Today such modesty would be exceptional among writers, and that was what upset him so.

His pleasures? The smiles of his grandchildren, his son's success, the memories he could exchange with his nephews, a good meal shared with a writer of the old school, the company of pretty women, and trifles: the volume on Louise de Vilmorin in the Poètes d'aujourd'hui (Poets of Today) collection, searched for for years because it was missing from his set, and which its publisher, Pierre Seghers, now gave him.

Regrets? The same as usual. A few writers—among them, Julien Gracq or François Mauriac—whom he had wanted for his imprint and missed. Not for the triumph, but to make the Gallimard catalogue "complete." That would have made him as happy as "his" authors had been with the medals and decorations bestowed on them: eighteen Nobel Prizes, six of them to Frenchmen, twenty-seven

Goncourts, eighteen Grand Prizes for the Novel of the French Academy, twelve Interalliés, seven Médicis, ten Renaudots, seventeen Feminas, not to mention those awarded to authors of outside firms he now controlled and other less ambitious prizes. But these were as nothing, compared to the absence of a Gracq or a Mauriac.

Regrets as an author? Probably, but not what one might have thought. He would have liked "his" *Judith*—the translation and adaptation of Friedrich Hebbel's play that he and Pierre de Lanux had done at the turn of the century—to have been given on a Parisian stage. The theater lover in him as well as the "author" would have been gratified. His dream almost came true in 1963.

Overwhelmed and entranced by the reading of *Judith,* a dusty old copy of which she had stumbled upon while rummaging through the *NRF* cellars, the actress Sylvia Montfort had told Gaston she wanted to put it on. He was agreeable, in fact enthusiastic, but balked at the prospect of having to become a member of the Société des Auteurs.* "Me? You must be kidding," he replied. "I have always been horrified at the idea of belonging to any kind of organization, and I don't intend to start at my age!" Still, he joined. A small sacrifice for the great happiness of being performed. But a misunderstanding and a series of intrigues spoiled the pleasure for him: another troupe got ahead of them and put the play on without Montfort, and without Gaston's consent. Appalled and disappointed, he did not have the heart to sue these interlopers, which he was perfectly entitled to do, a few days before their dress rehearsal. The harm was done. They had ruined his only authorial pleasure, just as he had been giving interviews to tell the columnists how good "his" play was.[8]

He might have known an even headier pleasure, had he wanted to: writing and publishing his memoirs, savoring while still alive the concert of praise that would certainly be his on the day he died. But despite constant requests, he had always refused to commit his recollections to paper. There were plenty of reasons: a certain laziness; a literary standard he could not hope to meet; his close association

---

*The French counterpart of the Dramatists' Guild.—TRANS.

with the greatest of writers from his earliest days, imposing a humility that became an inhibition; the fear of being judged. For many years he refused to give interviews, answering as had other men of action: one had to choose between living one's life and telling it. Most especially, he knew that he would never be able to tell all: the whole truth would have hurt too many people. He enjoyed telling anecdotes—often spicy ones—to his friends and associates about the great men of literature, but always off the record. His own self-censored and cleaned-up memoirs—in character with him, hence discreet and courteous—would have been filled with omissions and banalities. Yet a great many people were eagerly awaiting such a book. A notice in Bernard Pivot's column in *Le Figaro littéraire* read: "Gaston Gallimard is putting the finishing touches to his *Memoirs,* which will be published next fall by Jean-Jacques Pauvert." Only as an afterthought did readers realize that the date of the paper was April 1, 1968—April Fool's Day.

Too much to tell about too many people.

Researchers could count on being received by Gaston if they had questions about Malraux or Drieu, and they would be warmly welcomed if they came to talk about Fargue or Léautaud. But Gaston avoided newspaper interviewers. He did weaken once—for Madeleine Chapsal, a novelist published by the Mercure de France. Two hours each month for a whole year he sat with her and talked about the past and present into a tape recorder—on condition that this conversation, fascinating from beginning to end, never see print during his lifetime.

While he did not mind talking about the past, Gaston could never bring himself to tell the *whole* story of his company. He picked and chose among people and events. In the fall of 1975 Marcel Arland showed him the proofs of a piece the magazine had commissioned from Gerhard Heller, the Occupation censor to whom the house was deeply indebted: "Bribes d'un journal perdu" (Bits from a Lost Diary). Gaston's name occurred some ten times in the sixteen pages of these recollections of the dark years. That was too much. He strictly forbade the appearance of the piece. For him, the period was taboo, even thirty years later. To learn more about that, one would have to wait for the highly problematical publication of the diary of Jacques Lemarchand, locked away in the company safe on the advice of its legal counsel, and the diary of Raymond Queneau, covering his own life and also containing the minor incidents and the hours of glory of the House of Gallimard and its employees.

Those memories were not to Gaston's taste. He wanted to be associated only with the things that lasted, the bequests to posterity, not the mistakes and mishaps along the way. He had a catalogue like none other in the world. In *Publishers Weekly* for January 15, 1968, Herbert Lottman proclaimed that Gallimard's "name is synonymous with the French literature of our time."

Fall, 1975. As usual, Gaston was finishing his vacation on the Riviera with a stay at his son's place at La Croix-Valmer. Returning to Paris, he did not feel very well. Just tired, it seemed. Three years before, he had had a scare, a high fever followed by pneumonia. He had been hospitalized. This time, to be on the safe side, he was made to stay in his room at the American Hospital in Neuilly. Only his son, his grandchildren, and his nephew Robert were allowed to visit him. Death? He would talk about it only in joking terms, as he had at Parain's funeral, on one of the rare Tuesdays when the editorial committee did not meet. "He was a truly fine person," Gaston had said then. "He never asked me for a raise." Another time, holding a newspaper in his hand, he had hailed one of his associates near his office and remarked, "Look! Stravinsky died!"—as if the death of men of his generation was something to delight in, by the last one to remain.

At the hospital all he would talk about were women and literature, asking one visitor whether a given author should be published, and another how a certain collection was doing.

Suddenly he drew his last breath.

He died a good death, without agony. To the end a sworn enemy of ceremony, he willed that he be buried in the strictest privacy, and that was not just a figure of speech. On the day he was buried in the little cemetery of Pressagny-l'Orgueilleux, where he had bought a house, the only people in attendance were his son Claude, his daughter-in-law, his grandchildren, and his companion of long standing, Mme. D.

In compliance with his wishes, the following day his son informed those who were close to him that Gaston had died and was buried. The press was unanimous in eulogy and dithyramb. The writers who had made the glory of the *NRF* lauded both the publisher and the man, forgetting fallings-out, differences of views, even lawsuits. All rancor disappeared in the words of farewell. Many recounted their whole lives and works in terms of their relationship with Gaston Gallimard. It did not need to be pointed out that, but for him, the literary history of the country would not have been what it was. The sincerest tribute was also the shortest one: an article that appeared in the local paper of Pressagny-l'Orgueilleux, *Le Démocrate vernonnais,* on January 2, 1976.

> The famous Parisian publisher whose publishing house had the greatest influence on French literature died on Christmas Day in Paris. He was ninety-four. He left his mark on the twentieth century by choosing the greatest authors. . . . Old local residents, when speaking of his house, called it "Gaston's house," and old-timers all referred to him as M. Gaston.

Acknowledgments

This book could not have been written without precious help. I must first of all thank Marie-Hélène Dasté and Alain Rivière: their advice, assistance, and files (concerning the lives and works of Jacques Copeau and Jacques Rivière, respectively) are beyond estimation.

Many of those who knew Gaston Gallimard—family members, friends, business contacts, even enemies—agreed to meet with me, on condition that their names not be used. And so it is. My thanks to all of them, as well as to:

Mmes. Sabine Robert-Aron, Lucienne Couvreux-Rouché, Renée Drouelle, Jeanine Gallimard, Catherine Gide, Sara Halperyn, Marie-Louise Heller, Anne Hirsch, Monique Hoffet-Schlumberger, Henriette Jelinek, Laffitte-Larnaudie, Sylvia Montfort, Jacqueline de Proyart, Jean Voilier, Madeleine Wiemer, and

Messrs. Jean Adhémar, Marcel Arland, Claude Aveline, René Barjavel, Marc Bernard, Pierre Boncenne, Father Bruckberger, Maurice Chapelan, François Chapon, Lucien Combelle, Michel Drouin, Jean Dutourd, Jean Favier, Henri Fluchère, Gerhard Heller, René Hilsum, Vidar Jacobsen, Ro-

Acknowledgments

bert Kanters, Stéphane Khémis, Roland Laudenbach, Hervé Le Boterf, Claude Martin, Dionys Mascolo, Pascal Mercier, Pierre Monnier, Marcel Montarron, Maurice Nadeau, Philippe Robrieux, André Schiffrin, Simon Schiffrin, Pierre Seghers, Claude Sicard, Georges Simenon, Philippe Soupault, Henri Thyssens, Maurice Toesca, Vercors.

To them I owe the little merit that people may find in this book, while I alone am responsible for its errors, inevitable in any pioneer biography.

Claude Gallimard and his associates, Jean-Pierre Dauphin and Pascal Fouché, facilitated my access to the press file on Gaston Gallimard, gave me a succinct "historical rundown" of the company and the makeup of the principal editorial boards at different key periods (except that of the Occupation), and replied in writing to some of my questions—which allowed me a glimpse of the tip of the submerged iceberg. May they, nonetheless, accept my thanks.

Finally, I am grateful to my daughter Meryl (one year old) for not having destroyed quite all of my documentation.

Notes

___

1: His Father (1881–1900)

1. Sophie Monneret, *L'Impressionnisme et son époque,* vol. I, 1978.
2. Most of the paintings from the Gallimard collection are today in the museums of Tokyo and Copenhagen and in large private American and Italian collections.
3. Paul Léautand, *Journal* (1936).
4. Louis Guilloux, *Carnets,* vol. II, 1982.
5. R.-P. Bruckberger, *Tu finiras sur l'échafaud,* 1978.
6. Francis Jourdain, *Sans remords ni rancune,* 1953.
7. Gaston Gallimard-Madeleine Chapsal interview, *L'Express,* January 5, 1976.
8. Jourdain, op. cit.
9. Ibid.
10. Article by Gaston Gallimard, *Le Figaro littéraire,* August 30, 1958.
11. Gallimard-Chapsal interview, op. cit.
12. Ibid.
13. Lycée Condorcet archives.

2: A Young Publisher (1900–1914)

1. Guilloux, op. cit.
2. Rivière, op. cit.
3. Ibid.
4. "Gaston Gallimard raconte Marcel Proust" (Gaston Gallimard on Marcel Proust), *Marianne,* May 3, 1939.
5. Ibid. See also Gaston Gallimard, "Première rencontre" (First Meeting), *NRF,* January 1, 1923.
6. Interview with Jean Schlumberger, *France-Observateur,* February 26, 1959.
7. Auguste Anglès, *André Gide et le premier groupe de la Nouvelle Revue Française* (André Gide and the First *NRF* Group), 1978.
8. Jean Schlumberger, *Eveils* (Wakenings), 1950.
9. Michel Drouin, "Jacques Copeau, André Suarès ou les chemins de 'amitié" (Jacques Copeau, André Suarès, or The Paths of Friendship), *Australian Journal of French Studies,* vol. XIX, no. 1, 1982.
10. Anglès, op. cit.
11. Schlumberger, op. cit.
12. Gabriel Boillat, *La Librairie Bernard Grasset et les lettres françaises* (Bernard Grasset Books and French Literature), 1974.
13. *Péguy et les Cahiers: textes concernant la gérance des Cahiers de la Quinzaine* (Péguy and the *Cahiers*: Texts Relative to the Management of the *Cahiers de la Quinzaine*), 1947.
14. Bernard Grasset, *Evangile de l'édition selon Péguy* (The Gospel of Publishing According to Péguy), 1955.
15. Chapsal interview, loc. cit.
16. Auguste Anglès article, *NRF,* March 1, 1969.
17. Letter, January 5, 1911, Bloch papers, Bibliothèque Nationale.
18. Chapsal interview, loc. cit.
19. Ibid.
20. *Lettres inédites de Gustave Flaubert à son éditeur Michel Lévy* (Unpublished Letters from Gustave Flaubert to His Publisher, Michel Lévy), 1965.
21. The grandson of Gide's music teacher, Lanux became Gide's secretary after preparing for the Ecole Polytechnique and then studying literature.
22. Gallimard letter to J.-R. Bloch, March 30, 1911, Bloch papers, Bibliothèque Nationale.

23. Bloch papers, loc. cit.
24. *NRF*, December 1911.
25. *NRF*, February 1912.
26. *NRF*, August 1912.
27. Gallimard letter to Jacques Rivière, September 4, 1912, in the Alain Rivière files.
28. Letter of August 26, 1912, Alain Rivière files.
29. Letter of August 30, 1912, Alain Rivière files.
30. Gallimard letter to Jacques Copeau, December 15, 1912, M.-H. Dasté files.
31. Alain Rivière files.
32. Letter of November 5, 1912, *Correspondance de Marcel Proust*, vol. XI, 1984.
33. Letter of November 6, 1912, ibid.
34. Ibid.
35. Proust letter to Copeau, October 24, 1912, ibid.
36. According to the George Painter biography of Proust.
37. Chapsal interview, loc. cit.
38. Léon Pierre-Quint, *Proust et la stratégie littéraire* (Proust and Literary Strategy), 1954.
39. Chapsal interview, loc. cit.
40. *Correspondance Gide-Valéry 1890–1942*, 1955.
41. Gallimard letter to Rivière, April 29, 1913, Alain Rivière files.
42. Boillat, op. cit.
43. "Souvenirs autobiographiques et littéraires" (Autobiographical and Literary Memoirs), Roger Martin du Gard papers, Bibliothèque Nationale.
44. Martin du Gard papers, loc. cit.
45. Telegram of July 2, 1913, Martin du Gard papers.
46. Letter of July 5, 1913, Martin du Gard papers.
47. Martin du Gard papers, loc. cit.
48. Martin du Gard letter to Gaston Gallimard, July 14, 1913, *Correspondance générale*, vol. I.
49. Martin du Gard papers, loc. cit.
50. Draft letter and letter from Martin du Gard to Gallimard, November 28, 1913, Martin du Gard papers, loc. cit.
51. Letter of November 29, 1913, Martin du Gard papers, loc. cit.
52. Draft and letter from Martin du Gard to Gallimard, November 30, 1913, Martin du Gard papers, loc. cit.

53. Jacques Copeau, *Souvenirs du Vieux-Colombier* (Memories of the Vieux-Colombier), 1931.

54. *Bulletin des amis de Rivière et Fournier,* no. 27.

55. Jacques Copeau, *Les Registres du Vieux-Colombier III* (Records of the Vieux-Colombier, III), 1979.

56. Souvenirs autobiographiques et littéraires, Martin du Gard papers, op. cit.

57. *Registres du Vieux-Colombier,* op. cit.

58. Roger Martin du Gard and Jacques Copeau, *Correspondance.*

59. Auguste Anglès article, *Bulletin des amis d'André Gide,* no. 61, January 1984.

60. Gide letter to Gallimard, March 27, 1914, Jacques Doucet Library.

3: World War I (1914–1918)

1. Guilloux, op. cit.

2. Léautaud, op. cit.

3. Guilloux, op. cit.

4. Ibid.

5. Darius Milhaud, *Notes sans musique* (*Notes without Music*), 1949.

6. Jacques Rivière, *Carnets 1914–1917* (Notebooks 1914–1917), 1974.

7. Letter of March 30, 1915, *Correspondance,* op. cit.

8. Martin du Gard-Copeau correspondence, op. cit.

9. Rivière, *Carnets,* op. cit.

10. *Registres du Vieux-Colombier,* op. cit.

11. Ibid.

12. Letter to Jacques Rivière, August 30, 1915, Alain Rivière files.

13. Roger Martin du Gard, *Correspondance générale,* 1980.

14. Gallimard letter to Jacques Rouché, November 20, 1915, Rouché files, Bibliothèque Nationale.

15. Gallimard letter to Copeau, December 27, 1915, Dasté files.

16. Fargue-Larbaud, *Correspondance,* 1971.

17. Martin du Gard letter of January 20, 1916, *Correspondance générale,* op. cit.

18. Henri Ghéon letter to Gide, June 12, 1916, *Correspondance,* 1976.

19. Martin du Gard letter to Gallimard, July 22, 1916, *Correspondance,* op. cit.

20. Letters of September 2 and October 19, 1916, Bloch papers, loc. cit.
21. Guilloux, op. cit.; Martin du Gard–Copeau *Correspondance,* op. cit.
22. Letter of April 4, 1917, op. cit.
23. Letter of June 24, 1917, Alain Rivière files.
24. Martin du Gard letter to Gallimard, July 22, 1917, *Correspondance,* op. cit.
25. Martin du Gard papers, loc. cit.
26. Pierre Andreu and Frédéric Grover, *Drieu La Rochelle,* 1979.
27. Gallimard letters to Valéry, March 7 and 26, 1917, in de luxe edition of *La Jeune Parque,* 1957.
28. Gide letter to Valéry, November 1, 1917, *Correspondance Gide-Valéry,* 1955.
29. Gallimard letter to Bloch, May 21, 1917, Bloch papers, loc. cit.
30. Boillat, op. cit.
31. Ibid.
32. Chapsal interview, loc. cit.
33. *Le Figaro littéraire,* February 10, 1962.
34. Edith Mora interview of Gaston Gallimard, *Bibliographie de la France,* no. 9, 1954.
35. Gallimard letter to Copeau, May 30, 1918, M.-H. Dasté files.
36. Guilloux, op. cit.
37. Maria van Rysselberghe, *Les Cahiers de la petite dame* (The Little Lady's Notebooks) (1937–1945), 1973.
38. Robert Aron, *Fragments d'une vie* (Fragments of a Life), 1981.
39. Letter of September 22, 1918, *Bulletin des amis de Rivière et Fournier,* no. 29.

4: The Firm (1919–1936)

1. Lina Morino, *La NRF dans l'histoire des lettres,* 1939.
2. Jean-Alexis Néret, *Histoire illustrée de la librairie et du livre français,* 1953.
3. *Bulletin des amis de Rivière et Fournier,* No. 29.
4. Ibid.
5. Ibid.
6. M.-H. Dasté files.
7. Private sources.
8. Ibid.

9. André Beucler, *La Fleur qui chante,* 1939.

10. Gallimard letter to Rivière, August 3, 1919, Alain Rivière files.

11. Alain Rivière statement to the author.

12. Gallimard letter to Rivière, August 12, 1919, Rivière files.

13. Painter, op. cit. (France had written the preface to Proust's first book of essays.—TRANS.)

14. Céleste Albaret, *Monsieur Proust: A Memoir,* translated by Barbara Bray, 1976, pp. 302–3.

15. *Les Nouvelles littéraires,* September 29, 1923.

16. Aron, op. cit.

17. This dialogue is taken from Robert Aron, op. cit. He witnessed it as Gaston Gallimard's secretary.

18. Emmanuel Berl, *Interrogatoire par Patrick Modiano,* 1976.

19. Imprimerie Nationale (National Printing Office), 1912.

20. Sansot, 1917.

21. Proust was very fond of what had been a popular parlor game at the turn of the century, which he remembered from his youth: having one's friends fill out questionnaires about their favorite colors, flowers, animals, authors, painters, sayings, etc. He managed to get answers to the questionnaire from a number of his celebrated contemporaries.—TRANS.

22. *Biblio,* August-September 1963.

23. Marcel Jouhandeau article, *Biblio,* August-September 1963.

24. *Jean Paulhan, le souterrain,* Colloque de Cerisy, 10/18 ed., 1976.

25. A. Eustis, *Trois critiques de la NRF,* Nouvelles Éditions Debresse, 1961.

26. Jean Paulhan, *Mort de Groethuysen à Luxembourg,* Fata Morgana, 1977.

27. Brice Parain, *Entretiens avec Bernard Pingaud,* Gallimard, 1966.

28. Berl, op. cit.

29. Jacques Rivière and Ramon Fernandez, *Moralisme et littérature,* Corrêa, 1932.

30. Aron, op. cit.

31. Ibid.

32. Sabine Robert-Aron letter to the author.

33. Aron, op. cit.

34. P.-V. Stock, *Mémorandum d'un éditeur,* 1935.

35. Aron, op. cit.

36. Martin du Gard–Copeau, *Correspondance,* op. cit.

37. Marcel Arland statement to the author.

38. By way of contrast, Maurice Bedel, the Goncourt winner for 1927, supplied a standard-length novel practically every year to Gallimard until 1937.
39. Marcel Arland statement to the author.
40. Mme. L.-D. Hirsch statement to the author.
41. Ibid.
42. Chapsal article, loc. cit.
43. Cocteau interview with Mathieu Galey, *L'Express*, September 30, 1983.
44. Maurice Martin du Gard, *Les Mémorables I*, 1957.
45. Bernard Grasset article, *Candide*, March 28, 1929.
46. Maurice Martin du Gard, op. cit.
47. Bernard Pivot, *Les Critiques littéraires*, 1968.
48. Françoise Werner article, *L'Histoire*, no. 28, November 1980.
49. Georges Duhamel, *Le Livre de l'amertume*, 1984.
50. *Les Nouvelles littéraires*, October 31, 1931.
51. *Les Nouvelles littéraires*, November 14, 1931.
52. *Gringoire*, November 20, 1931.
53. Bernard Grasset, *Evangile de l'édition selon Péguy*, 1955.
54. Jean Ajalbert, *Les Mystères de l'Académie Goncourt*, 1929.
55. Gabriel Boillat article, *Revue d'histoire littéraire de la France*, September–December 1983.
56. Georges Charensol, *D'une rive à l'autre*, 1973.
57. Edouard Bourdet, *Théâtre II*, 1954.
58. Henry Muller, *Trois pas en arrière*, 1952.
59. Bernard Grasset, *La Chose littéraire*, 1938.
60. A photograph of Bernard Grasset, appearing on the front page of *Comoedia* during the war (January 10, 1942), astounded more than one reader.
61. Grasset letter to La Varende, May 21, 1941, French National Archives.
62. Grasset, *Evangile*, op. cit.
63. Boillat article, loc. cit.
64. Maurice Chapelan, *Rien n'est jamais fini*, 1977.
65. Ibid.
66. Ibid.
67. Henri Muller, *Retour de mémoire*, 1979.
68. *Paris-Presse L'Intransigeant*, August 6, 1951.
69. *Journal spécial des sociétés françaises par actions*, August 5, 1930.
70. Muller, *Trois pas*, op. cit.

71. Marcel Jouhandeau article, *La Table ronde,* no. 102, June 1956.
72. Jacques Chardonne's *Claire* (1931), for example.
73. *Les Nouvelles littéraires,* November 14, 1931.
74. Jean Lacouture, *André Malraux,* New York, 1975, p. 136.
75. Grasset, *Evangile,* op. cit.
76. *Bibliographie de la France,* February 21, 1930.
77. Paul Morand article, *Arts,* November 2, 1955.
78. Grasset interview, *Paris-Presse,* August 9, 1951.
79. Giraudoux interview, *Les Nouvelles littéraires,* February 20, 1926.
80. Georges Duhamel, *Chronique des saisons amères,* 1944.
81. *Renaissance politique, littéraire, artistique,* 1924.
82. *Paris-Presse,* August 6, 1951.
83. March 21, 1922, letter in Boillat, op. cit.
84. Aron, op. cit.
85. *Correspondance Lévy-Flaubert,* op. cit.
86. Léautaud, op. cit.
87. Jean-Paul Sartre, *Situations II,* 1948.
88. Duhamel, *Le Livre de l'amertume,* op. cit.
89. July 26, 1920, letter, Alain Rivière files.
90. Jean Galtier-Boissière, *Mémoires d'un Parisien III,* 1963.
91. Martin du Gard, *Journal,* loc. cit.
92. Charensol, op. cit.
93. Berl, *Modiano,* op. cit.
94. Curtis Cate, *Antoine de Saint-Exupéry,* 1970.
95. Maurice-Edgar Coindreau, *Mémoires d'un traducteur,* 1974.
96. Simon Schiffrin statement to the author.
97. Gide, *Journal,* op. cit.
98. Jean-Michel Belle, *Les Folles Années de Maurice Sachs,* 1979.
99. Jean Cocteau, *The Hand of a Stranger,* 1956.
100. André David article, *La Revue des Deux Mondes,* July 1975.
101. Jean Lacouture, *André Malraux,* op. cit.
102. Albert Cohen interview, *Le Magazine littéraire,* no. 147, April 1979.
103. *Les Nouvelles littéraires,* January 24, 1925.
104. Cohen interview, loc. cit.
105. Fenton Bresler, *The Mystery of Georges Simenon: A Biography,* 1983, p. 109. These passages are largely verbatim transcripts of Bresler's interview with Simenon.
106. Ibid.

107. Georges Simenon letter to the author.
108. Ramon Fernandez, *Itinéraire français*, 1943.
109. Letter of September 10, 1919, Bloch papers.
110. Letters of September 15 and December 17, 1919, Bloch papers.
111. Robert Mallet article, *Bulletin de la Société Paul Claudel*, no. 65, 1977.
112. Interview in *Arts*, November 14, 1956.
113. Chapsal article, loc. cit.
114. *Marianne*, May 3, 1939.
115. Mallet article, loc. cit.
116. All the contracts and correspondence quoted in these pages have been consulted in the Morand papers at the Institut de France.
117. James Harding, *Lost Illusions: Paul Léautaud and His World*, 1974.
118. Harding, op. cit.; Ginette Guitard-Auviste, *Paul Morand*, 1981.
119. Letter of June 24, 1924.
120. Letter of July 1, 1924.
121. Letter of July 28, 1924.
122. Letter of December 1, 1924.
123. Letter of April 20, 1928.
124. Pierre Citron article, *Bulletin de l'Association des Amis de Jean Giono*, no. 12.
125. Letter of July 10, 1920, Alain Rivière files.
126. Pierre Daix, *Aragon, une vie à changer*, 1975.
127. Jacques Brenner article, *Lire*, no. 94, June 1983.
128. Léautaud, *Journal* (November 25, 1927), op. cit.
129. René Barjavel statement to the author.
130. "Denoël raconte Céline," *Marianne*, May 10, 1939.
131. François Gibault, *Céline I*, 1977.
132. André Calas article, *Lectures pour tous*, November 1961.
133. Gibault, op. cit.
134. Robert Poulet, *Mon ami Bardamu*, 1971.
135. *Marianne*, May 10, 1939.
136. Ibid.
137. René Hilsum statement to the author.
138. José Corti, *Souvenirs désordonnés*, 1983.
139. Letter of August 20, 1919, Alain Rivière files.
140. Statement of Jean-Gabriel Sérusier (photographer at the paper) to the author.

141. Léautaud, November 1931 entry, op. cit.
142. Chapsal article, loc. cit.
143. Florent Fels, *Voilà*, 1957.
144. *Le Magazine littéraire*, no. 206, April 1984.
145. André Beucler, *Plaisirs de mémoires*, 1982.
146. Jacques Paget article, *Presse-Océan*, January 8, 1976.
147. *Le Figaro littéraire*, June 7, 1952.
148. Edith Mora interview with Gaston Gallimard, *Bibliographie de la France*, no. 9, 1954.
149. André Beucler, *De Saint-Pétersbourg à Saint-Germain-des-Prés*, 1980.
150. Gallimard letter to Martin du Gard, September 6, 1955, loc. cit.
151. Beucler, op. cit.
152. Béraud and Massis were very conservative writers. Jean Galtier-Boissière, an offbeat journalist and World War I veteran, edited *Le Crapouillot*. Lucien Dubech, a royalist journalist and fervent follower of Charles Maurras, was drama critic for *L'Action française* and *La Revue universelle*.
153. Beucler, op. cit.
154. Maurice Martin du Gard, III, op. cit.
155. Beucler, op. cit.
156. Ibid.
157. Léautaud, 1934, op. cit.
158. Roger Nimier, *L'Elève d'Aristote*, 1981.
159. *France-Soir*, December 30, 1975.
160. Céline, *Entretiens avec le professeur Y*, 1955.
161. Madeleine Chapsal interview of Céline, *L'Express*, June 14, 1957.
162. Gibault, op. cit.
163. *La Table ronde*, February 1953.
164. Guilloux, II, op. cit.
165. Fels, op. cit.
166. Max Favalelli article, *Ici Paris*, November 10, 1952.
167. Aron, op. cit.
168. Ibid.
169. *Cahiers du cinéma*, no. 78, December 1957.
170. *Gringoire*, January 19, 1934.
171. Aron, op. cit.
172. Private sources.

5: Taking Sides (1936–1939)

1. *La Chose littéraire*, op. cit.
2. *Journal officiel*, June 2, 1939.
3. *Journal officiel*, June 3, 1939.
4. Grasset article, *Paris-Presse*, October 5, 1951.
5. French National Archives.
6. *Pavés de Paris*, November 18, 1938.
7. Gallimard letter to Rivière, September 22, 1919, Alain Rivière files.
8. Ibid.
9. According to a letter from Jean Paulhan to Marcel Jouhandeau, *Cahiers de l'énergumène*, no. 3, 1983.
10. Marc Bernard letter to the author.
11. Boudot-Lamotte letter to Paul Morand, January 8, 1938, in Morand papers at the Institut de France. The book was published only three years later.
12. Denise Tual, *Le Temps dévoré*, 1980.
13. Bruckberger, op. cit.
14. Gallimard letter to Bloch, February 15, 1937, in Bloch papers, loc. cit.
15. Andreu and Grover, op. cit.
16. Barjavel statement to the author.
17. *NRF*, February 1, 1939.
18. *Je suis partout*, January 14, 1938.
19. Charensol, op. cit.
20. Letter to Michel Déon, in *Ce que je voulais vous dire aujourd'hui*, 1969.
21. Muller, *Trois pas en arrière*, op. cit.
22. Mme. Hirsch statement to the author.
23. Anne Edwards, *The Road to Tara: The Life of Margaret Mitchell*, 1983.
24. *Je suis partout* went on raving about *Gone with the Wind* almost every week, as if carrying on a campaign for it, even after the German Occupation started.

6: Collaborate or Resist? (1939–1944)

1. *Bibliographie de la France*, September 15 and November 10, 1939.
2. André Gide, *Journal*, op. cit.

3. Pierre Seghers statement to the author.

4. Léautaud, *Journal,* op. cit.

5. Bruckberger, op. cit.

6. Ibid.

7. Barjavel statement to the author.

8. Claude Aveline letter to the author.

9. Otto Abetz, *Histoire d'une politique franco-allemande,* 1953.

10. Gérard Loiseaux, "Collaboration littéraire au service de l'Europe nouvelle," *Lendemains,* Berlin, no. 19, 1983.

11. Grasset letter to Sieburg published in *L'Affaire Grasset* by the Comité d'action de la Résistance, 1949.

12. Grasset letter of August 4, 1940, to Hamonic, in *L'Affaire Grasset,* op. cit.

13. French National Archives.

14. Archives of the CDJC, or Centre de Documentation Juive Contemporaine.

15. French National Archives.

16. Pseudonym of Jean Mamy, onetime actor for Dullin and onetime film director, in *Au pilori,* October 10, 1940.

17. Gerhard Heller statement to the author.

18. Propaganda Division letter to Gaston Gallimard, November 28, 1940. In French National Archives.

19. Gerhard Heller, *Un Allemand à Paris,* 1981.

20. Gerhard Heller, "Bribes d'un journal perdu," unpublished article.

21. Léautaud, op. cit.

22. Maria Van Rysselberghe, *Les Cahiers de la petite dame,* op. cit.

23. French National Archives.

24. *L'Affaire Grasset,* op. cit.

25. André Lang, *Pierre Brisson, le journaliste, l'écrivain, l'homme,* 1967.

26. *Bibliographie de la France,* February 28, 1941.

27. Loiseaux article, loc. cit.

28. Karl Rauch article, *Cahiers franco-allemands,* July–August 1941.

29. Loiseaux article, loc. cit.

30. Georges Blond article, *Deutschland-Frankreich,* no. 6, 1943.

31. Answer to circular no. 298 of April 1, 1943, French National Archives.

32. *Le Magazine littéraire,* no. 130, November 1977.

33. Ibid., no. 21, September 1968.

34. Survey by Hubert Forestier, *Cahiers du livre*, second installment, 1941.
35. Quoted by Jean Galtier-Boissière, *Mon journal pendant l'Occupation*, 1944.
36. Letter of June 5, 1941, French National Archives.
37. Letter of June 17, 1941, French National Archives.
38. French National Archives.
39. Pierre-Marie Dioudonnat, *L'Argent nazi à la conquête de la presse française, 1940–1944*, 1981.
40. Bertrand de Jouvenel, *Un voyageur dans le siècle*, 1979.
41. Correspondence exchanged in May 1933, quoted in Gottfried Benn, *Double vie*, 1954.
42. Thomas Mann, *Les Exigences du jour*, 1976.
43. September 1945 letter, quoted in Jacques Brenner, *Tableau de la vie littéraire en France*, 1982.
44. Berl-Modiano, op. cit.
45. Roger Caillois, *Circonstancielles*, 1945.
46. Daix, op. cit.
47. Heller, op. cit.
48. Michel Contat and Michel Rybalka, *Les Ecrits de Sartre*, 1970.
49. James Wilkinson, *The Intellectual Resistance in Europe*, 1981.
50. Heller statement to the author.
51. Jean Guéhenno, *Journal des années noires*, 1947.
52. Vercors statement to the author.
53. Vercors, *La Bataille du silence*, 1967.
54. Henri Michel, *Paris allemand*, 1981.
55. Ibid.
56. Ibid.
57. Guillevic, *Vivre en poésie*, 1980.
58. According to Jünger in Daniel Rondeau, *Trans Europ Express*, 1984.
59. *Le Magazine littéraire*, no. 130, November 1977.
60. Interview by Frédéric de Towarnicki, *Le Magazine littéraire*, loc. cit.
61. Pascal Ory, *Les Collaborateurs*, 1976.
62. Lucien Rebatet, *Mémoires d'un fasciste*, II, 1976.
63. Henry de Montherlant, *Mémoire*, 1976.
64. Simone de Beauvoir, *The Prime of Life* (translated by Peter Green), 1962, p. 385.
65. Ibid., p. 398.
66. *Comoedia*, October 16, 1943.

67. Louis Guilloux, *Carnets I,* 1978.
68. Heller, op. cit.
69. Gallimard letter to Morand, October 21, 1941, Morand papers, loc. cit.
70. Report of September 8, 1941, French National Archives.
71. Jünger, op. cit.
72. André Thérive, *L'Envers du décor,* 1948.
73. Marcel Jouhandeau, *Journal sous l'Occupation,* 1980.
74. Jünger, op. cit.
75. Galtier-Boissière, op. cit.
76. Maurice Toesca, *Cinq ans de patience,* 1975.
77. Loiseaux article, loc. cit.
78. Rebatet, *Mémoires II,* op. cit.
79. Following a second increase in capital in 1943, Andermann was to hold 1,480 shares out of 3,000, so that Denoël was still in control.
80. *Bibliographie de la France,* October 23, 1942.
81. *Signal,* no. 2, January 1942.
82. Grover-Andreu, op. cit.
83. Dionys Mascolo statement to the author.
84. Patrick McCarthy, *Camus,* 1982.
85. Herbert Lottman, *Camus,* 1978.
86. Antoine de Saint-Exupéry, *Flight to Arras,* translated by Lewis Galantière (New York: Reynal & Hitchcock, 1942), p. 26.
87. *Le Cri du peuple,* January 31, 1943.
88. *Je suis partout,* January 8 and 15, 1943.
89. Catalogue no. 17, Le Tour du Monde bookstore, autumn 1983.
90. *L'Alerte,* no. 72, January 31, 1942.
91. Circular no. 224, March 7, 1942, in French National Archives.
92. Consulted at the Bibliothèque Nationale.
93. Quoted in Louis Parrot, *L'Intelligence en guerre,* 1945. [In French the lines rhyme.—TRANS.]
94. *Gesämtliste des fördernswerten Schrifttums,* to December 31, 1942, in CDJC Archives.
95. Loiseaux article, loc. cit. See also Loiseaux's contribution to the international colloquium "La Littérature française sous l'Occupation," held at Rheims in September 1981.
96. The first full French translation of this book is contained in Gérard Loiseaux, *La Littérature de la défaite et de la collaboration,* 1984.

97. *L'Affair Céline,* Comité d'action de la Résistance, 1949.
98. Renée Drouelle statement to the author.
99. French National Archives.
100. Archives of the CDJC.
101. Questioned by the author, the Gallimard firm said it had "no recollection of this offer" (letter to the author, April 9, 1984).
102. Georges Charensol interview in *Les Nouvelles littéraires,* January 1, 1923.
103. French National Archives.
104. Ibid.
105. Heller, op. cit.
106. Ibid.
107. *Je suis partout,* February 19, 1943.
108. *L'Union française,* June 5, 1943.
109. Letters reproduced in Pierre Citron article, loc. cit.
110. Toesca, op. cit.
111. Toesca statement to the author.
112. Daniel Rondeau, *Trans Europ Express,* 1984.
113. *Je suis partout,* July 16, 1943.
114. Mascolo statement to the author.
115. *Comoedia,* May 15, 1943.
116. Tual, op. cit.
117. *Comoedia,* May 22, 1943.
118. Gide, *Journal,* entry of March 16, 1943.
119. Jacques Isorni, *Le Procès de Robert Brasillach,* 1946.
120. Lottmann, op. cit.
121. *Comoedia,* August 7, 1943.
122. *Le Pays libre,* October 30, 1943.
123. *Réagir,* September 9, 1943.
124. *Je suis partout,* August 27, 1943.
125. Simone de Beauvoir, *The Prime of Life,* p. 442.
126. "At the CNE [Comité national des écrivains, or National Writers' Committee.—TRANS.] we took the liberty of saying a great many things between committee members, just like that." (Vercors statement to the author.)
127. *Comoedia,* April 24, 1943.
128. Lucien Combelle statement to the author. M. Combelle was editor of the weekly *Révolution nationale.*

129. Laffont-Bompiani, *Dictionnaire des oeuvres,* 1983.

130. Combelle statement to the author.

131. Hervé Le Boterf, *La Vie parisienne sous l'Occupation,* 1975.

132. Letters of March 15, March 24, and April 26, 1944, to the cabinet secretary of the general commissioner for Jewish Questions, in Archives of the CDJC. [The information concerning Elsa Triolet is almost entirely false: it was her sister Lily who was the wife or companion of the poet Vladimir Mayakovski. The *Columbia Encyclopedia* gives Triolet's maiden name as Elsa Blick, while other sources spell it Brik. Triolet was not a pseudonym but the name of a Frenchman she married in order to be allowed to leave the U.S.S.R. She was indeed Jewish.— TRANS.]

133. André Roussin, *Rideau gris et habit vert,* 1983.

134. Jean Galtier-Boissière, *Mémoires d'un Parisien III,* 1963.

135. Lottmann, op. cit.

136. Toesca, op. cit.

137. Heller, op. cit.

7: Settling Accounts (1944–1945)

1. Quoted by Le Boterf, op. cit.

2. Galtier-Boissière, *Mémoires d'un Parisien,* op. cit.

3. Jean Guéhenno, *Journal des années noires,* op. cit.

4. Pierre Arnoult, *Les Finances de la France et l'Occupation allemande,* 1951.

5. Interview in *L'Express,* June 14, 1957.

6. Lionel Richard article in *Revue d'histoire de la Seconde Geurre mondiale,* no. 97, January 1975.

7. *Les Lettres françaises,* September 9, 1944.

8. *France libre,* September 22, 1944.

9. *Les Lettres françaises,* September 30, 1944.

10. Pierre Seghers statement to the author.

11. *Les Lettres françaises,* September 16, 1944.

12. Vercors statement to the author.

13. Ibid.

14. Ibid.

15. Ibid.

16. The Illicit Profits Committee of the Seine condemned one company,

for example, to pay a fine of 1.5% of the value of the business it had done with the Germans, and nothing more.

17. Simone de Beauvoir, *Force of Circumstance* (translated by Richard Howard), 1965, pp. 21–22.
18. *Bibliographie de la France*, July 6–13, 1945.
19. Isorni, op. cit.
20. Seghers statement to the author.
21. Ibid.
22. Letter of February 9, 1945, quoted in Michel Winock, *Histoire politique de la revue Esprit 1930–1950*, 1975.
23. Letter of September 14, 1944, in Paul Léautaud, *Correspondance générale*, 1972.
24. Pierre de Boisdeffre, *Une histoire vivante de la littérature contemporaine 1939–1960*, 1960.
25. French National Archives.
26. Report of March 18, 1948, French National Archives.
27. French National Archives.
28. *L'Affaire Grasset*, op. cit.
29. French National Archives.
30. *France-Soir*, June 17, 1948.
31. Grasset, *Evangile*, op. cit.
32. *L'Affaire Grasset*, op. cit.
33. *France-Dimanche*, January 23, 1949.
34. Henri Muller article, *Carrefour*, January 8, 1976.
35. Galtier-Boissière, *Mémoires d'un Parisien*, op. cit.
36. Voilier statement to the author.
37. Ibid.
38. Ibid.
39. Barjavel statement to the author.
40. French National Archives.

8: New Blood (1946–1952)

1. Peter Novick, *The Resistance versus Vichy: The Purge of Collaborators in Liberated France*, 1968.
2. Ibid.

3. Marcel Montarron statement to the author.
4. Simone de Beauvoir, *Force of Circumstance*.
5. *Les Temps modernes*, no. 4, January 1, 1946.
6. *The New York Times*, March 9, 1948, quoted in de Beauvoir, op. cit., p. 168.
7. *Les Temps modernes*, no. 34, July 1948.
8. Raymond Aron, *Mémoires*, 1983.
9. Beauvoir, *Force of Circumstance*, op. cit., p. 169.
10. Bruckberger, op. cit.
11. Ibid.
12. Father Bruckberger letter to the author.
13. Ibid.
14. Dominique Aury article, *Le Monde*, September 2, 1977.
15. Marcel Duhamel, *Raconte pas ta vie*, 1972.
16. Ibid.
17. Boileau-Narcejac, *Le Roman policier*, 1975.
18. Interview with Jean-Paul Kaufmann, *Le Matin*, October 27, 1983.
19. *Encyclopedia universalis*.
20. Robert Laffont, *Editeur*, 1974.
21. List drawn up by *L'Express*, December 14, 1958.
22. Toesca statement to the author.
23. Ibid.
24. Letter to Michel and Jeanine Gallimard, published in *Le Point*, no. 16, January 1984.
25. McCarthy, op. cit.
26. Simenon letter to the author, loc. cit.
27. *Bibliographie de la France*, February 9, 1951.
28. Grasset interview, *Paris-Presse*, August 9, 1951.
29. Grasset, *Evangile*, op. cit.
30. Pierre Monnier statement to the author. See his book *Ferdinand Furieux*, 1979, as well as *Le Lérot rêveur*, no. 33, February 1982 (article on the Frédéric Chambriand company).
31. Henri Godard, "Céline et ses éditeurs," in the Pléiade edition of Céline's novels, 1974.
32. Gibault, op. cit.
33. Poulet, op. cit.
34. Godard, op. cit.

35. A German court was to condemn Gallimard to pay damages to the Scherz family, with whom Céline had been friendly during 1944–45, and who felt they had been libelously caricatured in *Nord*.
36. Paul Claudel, *Journal*, II, 1969.
37. Marcel Arland statement to the author.
38. Pol Vandromme, *Lucien Rebatet*, 1968.
39. *NRF*, no. 278, February 1976.
40. Quoted in Jean Lacouture, *François Mauriac*, 1980.
41. François Mauriac, "Bloc-notes" (January 2, 1953), *La Table ronde*, no. 62, February 1953.
42. Ibid.
43. *La Table ronde*, no. 63, March 1953.
44. Mauriac article, *La Table ronde*, no. 62, op. cit.

9: Changes in the Business (1953–1966)

1. Céline, *Entretiens avec le professeur Y*, 1955.
2. Roland Laudenbach statement to the author.
3. Robert Kanters statement to the author.
4. Henri Muller, *Retour de mémoire*, 1979.
5. Guilloux, II, op. cit.
6. Chapelan, op. cit.
7. *Arts*, October 26, 1955.
8. *Combat*, October 22, 1955.
9. *Le Figaro littéraire*, July 7, 1962.
10. Figures stated by Claude Gallimard in his report to the National Convention of Booksellers reported in *France-Soir*, June 5, 1965.
11. Interview in *Le Figaro littéraire*, September 27, 1958.
12. According to Brice Parain in *Lectures pour tous*, November 1961.
13. Raymond Aron, *Mémoires*, 1983.
14. *France-Observateur*, March 20, 1958.
15. McCarthy, op. cit.
16. Ibid.
17. Drafts and minutes of a letter from Jean Schlumberger to Raymond Gallimard, October 21, 1958, in the Jacques Doucet Library.
18. Schlumberger letter of November 13, 1958, loc. cit.
19. Thomas Quinn Curtis article, *International Herald Tribune*, July 22, 1983.

20. Jean Cocteau, *Le Passé défini*, I, 1983.
21. Guilloux, II, op. cit.
22. Robert Laffont, *Editeur*, 1974.
23. *L'Express*, November 7, 1953.
24. Guilloux, II, op. cit.
25. Marcel Duhamel, op. cit.
26. *Le Magazine littéraire*, no. 32, September 1969.
27. Ibid.
28. *Les Lettres françaises*, November 22, 1968.
29. Jean Dutourd statement to the author.
30. Elisabeth Vailland, *Drôle de vie*, 1984.
31. Fenton Bresler, op. cit., p. 182. See Georges Simenon, *Intimate Memoirs* (translated by Harold J. Salemson), 1984, p. 343.
32. Cocteau, *Le Passé défini*, op. cit.

10: Without Gaston (1967–1975)

1. List drawn up by *Le Nouvel Observateur*, May 31, 1967.
2. Claude Gallimard interview, *Le Monde*, May 30, 1970.
3. Claude Gallimard interview, *La Croix*, June 2, 1970.
4. Claude Gallimard interview, *Le Monde*, loc. cit.
5. Ibid.
6. Ibid.
7. *L'Express*, May 18, 1970.
8. Sylvia Montfort statement to the author.

Bibliography

Abetz, Otto. *Histoire d'une politique franco-allemande.* Paris: Fayard, 1953.

Ajalbert, Jean. *Les Mystères de l'Académie Goncourt.* Paris: Ferenczi, 1929.

Albaret, Céleste. *Monsieur Proust.* Paris: Robert Laffont, 1973. *Monsieur Proust: A Memoir,* edited by Georges Belmont, translated by Barbara Bray. New York: McGraw-Hill, 1976.

Amouroux, Henri. *Les Beaux Jours des collabos, juin 1941–juin 1942.* Paris: Laffont, 1973.

Andreu, Pierre. *Le Rouge et le noir 1928–1944.* Paris: La Table ronde, 1977.

——— & Grover, Frédéric. *Drieu La Rochelle.* Paris: Hachette, 1979.

Anglès, Auguste. *André Gide et le premier groupe de la Nouvelle Revue française: la formation du groupe et les années d'apprentissage 1890–1910.* Paris: Gallimard, 1978.

Aragon, Louis. *Traité du style.* Paris: Gallimard, 1928.

Arland, Marcel. *Proche du silence.* Paris: Gallimard, 1973.

———. *Avons-nous vécu?* Paris: Gallimard, 1977.

———. *Ce fut ainsi.* Paris: Gallimard, 1979.

Arnoult, Pierre. *Les Finances de la France et l'occupation allemande.* Paris: Presses Universitaires de France, 1951.

Aron, Raymond. *Mémoires.* Paris: Julliard, 1983.

Aron, Robert. *Histoire de l'épuration 1944–1953,* book 3, vol. II. Paris: Fayard, 1975.

———. *Fragments d'une vie.* Paris: Plon, 1981.

Audiat, Pierre. *Paris pendant la guerre.* Paris: Hachette, 1946.

Baldensperger, Fernand. *La Littérature française entre les deux guerres.* Paris: Le Sagittaire, 1943.

Bardèche, Maurice. *Lettres à François Mauriac.* Paris: La Pensée libre, 1947.

Bartillat, Christan de; Gourcuff, Alain de; and Prigent, Marc. *Stock 1708– 1981, trois siècles d'invention. Une approche historique.* Published by the authors, 1981.

Beach, Sylvia. *Shakespeare and Company.* New York: Harcourt Brace Jovanovich, 1959.

Beauvoir, Simone de. *La Force de l'âge.* Paris: Gallimard, 1960. *The Prime of Life,* translated by Peter Green. Cleveland & New York: World, 1962.

———. *La Force des choses.* Paris: Gallimard, 1963. *Force of Circumstance,* translated by Richard Howard. New York: Putnam, 1965.

Belle, Jean-Michel. *Les Folles Années de Maurice Sachs.* Paris: Grasset, 1979.

Benn, Gottfried. *Double Vie.* Paris: Editions de Minuit, 1954.

Béraud, Henri. *La Croisade des longues figures.* Paris: Editions du Siècle, 1924.

Berl, Emmanuel. *Interrogatoire par Patrick Modiano.* Paris: Gallimard, 1976.

Bernanos, Georges. *Lettres retrouvées: Correspondence inédite 1904–1948.* Paris: Plon, 1983.

Beucler, André. *La Fleur qui chante.* Paris: Gallimard, 1939.

———. *Dimanche avec Léon-Paul Fargue.* Paris: Point du jour, 1947.

———. *Les Instants de Giraudoux.* Geneva, 1948.

———. *De Saint-Pétersbourg à Saint-Germain-des-Prés.* Paris: Gallimard, 1980.

———. *Plaisirs de mémoire.* Paris: Gallimard, 1982.

Billy, André. *Histoire de la vie littéraire: L'Epoque contemporaine.* Paris: Taillandier, 1956.

Blondin, Antoine. *Ma vie entre les lignes.* Paris: La Table ronde, 1982.

Blumenson, Martin. *Le Réseau du Musée de l'Homme.* Paris: Le Seuil, 1979.

Boileau, Narcejac. *Le Roman policier*. Paris: Presses Universitaires de France, 1975.

Boillat, Gabriel. *La Librairie Bernard Grasset et les lettres françaises: les Chemins de l'édition 1907–1914*. Paris: Honoré Champion, 1974.

Bourdet, Edouard. "Vient de paraître," *Théâtre*. Paris: Stock, 1954.

Brasillach, Robert. *Notre avant-guerre*. Paris: Plon, 1941.

Bréal, Auguste. *Philippe Berthelot*. Paris: Gallimard, 1937.

Brenner, Jacques. *Tableau de la vie littéraire en France d'avant-guerre à nos jours*. Paris: Luneau-Ascot, 1982.

Bresler, Fenton. *The Mystery of Georges Simenon: A Biography*. New York: Beaufort Books, 1983.

Bruckberger, R.-P. *Tu finiras sur l'échafaud*. Paris: Flammarion, 1978.

Buchet, Edmond. *Les Auteurs de ma vie*. Paris: Buchet-Chastel, 1969.

Butin, Jean. *Henri Béraud*. Roanne: Horvath, 1979.

Cahiers Céline II. *Céline et l'actualité littéraire 1957–1961*. Paris: Gallimard, 1976.

Cahiers de l'Herne. *Drieu*. Paris, 1982.

———. *Thomas Mann*. Paris, 1973.

Caillois, Roger. *Circonstancielles 1940–1945*. Paris: Gallimard, 1945.

Canne, G. *Messieurs les best-sellers*. Paris: Perrin, 1966.

Cate, Curtis. *Antoine de Saint-Exupéry*. New York: Putnam, 1970.

Céline, Louis-Ferdinand. *Entretiens avec le professeur Y*. Paris: Gallimard, 1955. *Conversations with Professor Y,* Bilingual edition, translated by Stanford Luce. Hanover, N.H.: Brandeis University/University Press of New England, 1986.

———. *Romans,* vol. II. Paris: La Pléiade/Gallimard, 1974.

Chapelan, Maurice. *Rien n'est jamais fini*. Paris: Grasset, 1977.

Chapon, François. *Mystère et splendeurs de Jacques Doucet 1853–1929*. Paris: Lattès, 1984.

Chardonne, Jacques. *Ce que je voulais vous dire aujourd'hui*. Paris: Grasset, 1969.

——— and Nimier, Roger. *Correspondance 1950–1962*. Paris: Gallimard, 1984.

Charensol, Georges. *D'une rive à l'autre*. Paris: Mercure de France, 1973.

Charlereine (General Odic). *Le Maréchal Défaite*. Paris: Gallimard, 1945.

Claudel, Paul. *Journal*. Paris: La Pléiade/Gallimard, 1969.

Cocteau, Jean. *Journal d'un inconnu*. Paris: Grasset, 1953. *The Hand of a Stranger*, translated by Alec Brown. London: Elek Books, 1956.

———. *Le Passé défini I*. Paris: Gallimard, 1983. *Past Tense*, Volume I, Diaries. Introduction by Ned Rorem, annotations by Pierre Chanel, translated by Richard Howard. New York: Harcourt Brace Jovanovich, 1987.

Coindreau, Maurice-Edgar. *Mémoires d'un traducteur*. Paris: Gallimard, 1974.

Colloque de Cerisy (July 1973). *Jean Paulhan, le souterrain*. Paris: 10/18, 1976.

Comité d'action de la Résistance. *L'Affaire Céline*. Paris, 1949.

———. *L'Affaire Grasset*. Paris, 1949.

Combelle, Lucien. *Je dois à André Gide*. Paris: Chambriand, 1951.

———. *Prisons de l'espérance*. Paris: ETL, 1952.

———. *Péché d'orgueil*. Paris: Orban, 1978.

———. *Liberté à huis clos*. Paris: La Butte aux Cailles, 1983.

Compagnon, Antoine. *La Troisième République des Lettres*. Paris: Le Seuil, 1983.

Contat, Michel, and Rybalka, Michel. *Les Ecrits de Sartre*. Paris: Gallimard, 1970.

Copeau, Jacques. *Souvenirs du Vieux-Colombier*. Paris: Nouvelles Editions Latines, 1931.

———. *Les Registres du Vieux-Colombier*. Paris: Gallimard, 1979.

Corti, José. *Souvenirs désordonnés*. Paris: Corti, 1983.

Coston, Henri. *Dictionnaire de la politique française*. Paris: published by the author, 1967.

Dabit, Eugène. *Journal 1928–1936*. Paris: Gallimard, 1939.

Daix, Pierre. *Aragon, une vie à changer*. Paris: Le Seuil, 1975.

Debû-Bridel, Jacques. *La Résistance intellectuelle*. Paris: Julliard, 1970.

Delay, Claude. *Chanel solitaire*. Paris: Gallimard, 1983.

Descaves, Pierre. *Mes Goncourt*. Marseilles: Laffont, 1944.

Deschodt, Eric. *Saint-Exupéry*. Paris: Lattès, 1980.

Desert, Gabriel. *La Vie quotidienne sur les plages normandes du Second Empire aux années folles*. Paris: Hachette, 1983.

Dinar, André. *Fortune des livres*. Paris: Mercure de France, 1938.

Dioudonnat, Pierre-Marie. *Je suis partout 1930–1944: les maurrassiens devant la tentation fasciste*. Paris: La Table ronde. 1973.

————. *L'Argent nazi à la conquête de la presse française 1940–1944*. Paris: Picollec, 1981.

Drieu La Rochelle, Pierre. *Fragments de mémoires 1940–1941*. Paris: Gallimard, 1982.

————. *Sur les écrivains*. Paris: Gallimard, 1982.

Duhamel, Georges. *Chronique des années amères 1940–1943*. Paul Hartmann, 1944.

————. *Le Livre de l'amertume*. Paris: Mercure de France, 1983.

Duhamel, Marcel. *Raconte pas ta vie*. Paris: Mercure de France, 1972.

Dumas, Charles. *La France trahie et livrée*. Paris: Gallimard, 1945.

Edwards, Anne. *The Road to Tara: The Life of Margaret Mitchell*. New Haven, Conn.: Ticknor & Fields; London: Hodder, 1983.

Epting, Karl. *Frankreich im Widersprach*. Hamburg, 1943.

————. *Réflexions d'un vaincu*. Bourg, 1953.

Epting-Kullmann, Alice. *Zwischen Paris und Fluorn*. Hunenburg Verlag, 1958.

Escarra, Jean; Rault, Jean; and Hepp, François. *La Doctrine française du droit d'auteur*. Paris: Grasset, 1937.

Eustis, A. *Marcel Arland, Benjamin Crémieux, Ramon Fernandez: Trois critiques de la Nouvelle Revue Française*. Paris: Nouvelles Editions Debresse, 1961.

Ezine, Jean-Louis. *Les Ecrivains sur la sellette*. Paris: Le Seuil, 1981.

Fabre-Luce, Alfred. *Journal de la France I*. JEP, 1940.

————. *Journal de la France II*. JEP, 1942.

Fargue. Léon-Paul. *Le Piéton de Paris*. Paris: Gallimard, 1932.

———— and Larbaud, Valery. *Correspondance 1910–1946*. Paris: Gallimard, 1971.

Fels, Florent. *Voilà*. Paris: Fayard, 1957.

Fernandez, Ramon. *Itinéraire français*. Editions du Pavois, 1943.

Ferrat, André. *La République à refaire*. Paris: Gallimard, 1945.

Flaubert, Gustave. *Lettres inédites de Flaubert à son éditeur Michel Lévy*. Paris: Calmann-Lévy, 1965.

————. *Correspondance I*. Paris: Pléiade/Gallimard, 1973.

Fouché, Pascal. *Au sans pareil*. Paris: Université de Paris-Jussieu, 1983.

————. *La Sirène*. Paris: Université de Paris-Jussieu, 1984.

Frank, Bernard. *Le Dernier des Mohicans*. Paris: Fasquelle, 1956.

————. *La Panoplie littéraire*. Paris: Julliard, 1958.

————. *Un siècle débordé*. Paris: Grasset, 1970.

Gallimard, Paul. *Les Etreintes du passé*. Paris: Gallimard, 1928.

Galtier-Boissière, Jean. *Mon journal pendant l'occupation*. Garas: La Jeune Parque, 1944.

————. *Mon journal dans la drôle de paix*. La Jeune Parque, 1947.

————. *Mémoires d'un Parisien III*. Paris: La Table ronde, 1963.

Gibault, François. *Céline I*. Paris: Mercure de France, 1977.

————. *Céline III*. Paris: Mercure de France, 1981.

Gide, André. *Journal I, II*. Paris: Pléiade/Gallimard, 1951, 1954. *Journals,* translated, with an introduction and notes, by Justin O'Brien. London: Secker & Warburg, 1948–1955.

———— & Ghéon, Henri. *Correspondance*. Paris: Gallimard, 1976.

———— & Valéry, Paul. *Correspondance*. Paris: Gallimard, 1955.

Giraudoux, Jean. *Pleins Pouvoirs*. Paris: Gallimard, 1939.

Goncourt, Edmond and Jules de. *Journal des Goncourt: Mémoires de la vie littéraire,* edited by Robert Ricatte. Monaco: Les Editions de l'Imprimerie Nationale de Monaco, 22 vols., 1956–59.

Gracq, Julien. *Préférences*. Paris: Corti, 1961.

————. *En lisant, en écrivant*. Paris: Corti, 1981.

Grasset, Bernard. *La Chose littéraire*. Paris: Gallimard, 1929.

————. *A la recherche de la France*. Paris: Grasset, 1940.

————. *Evangile de l'édition selon Péguy*. Paris: Bonne, 1955.

Grover, Frédéric. *Drieu La Rochelle*. Paris: Gallimard, 1962.

————. *Six entretiens avec Malraux sur les écrivains de son temps (1959–1975)*. Paris: Gallimard, 1978.

Guéhenno, Jean. *Journal des années noires*. Paris: Gallimard, 1947.

Guerre, Pierre. *René Char*. Paris: Seghers, 1981.

Guillevic. *Vivre en poésie*. Paris: Stock, 1980.

Guilloux, Louis. *Carnets I, II*. Paris: Gallimard, 1978, 1982.

Guitard-Auviste, Ginette. *Paul Morand*. Paris: Hachette, 1981.

————. *Jacques Chardonne*. Paris: Orban, 1984.

Haedens, Kléber. *Une histoire de la littérature française*. Paris: Gallimard, 1954.

Halévy, Daniel. *Péguy et les Cahiers de la Quinzaine*. Paris: Grasset, 1941.

Harding, James. *Lost Illusions: Léautaud and His World*. Madison, N.J.: Fairleigh Dickinson University Press, 1974.

Hebbel, Friedrich. *Judith*. Translated by Gaston Gallimard and Pierre de Lanux. Paris: Gallimard, 1911.

Heller, Gerhard. *Un Allemand à Paris 1940–1944*. Paris: Le Seuil, 1981.

Huret, Jules. *Enquête sur l'évolution littéraire (1891)*. Vanves: Thot, 1982.

Isorni, Jacques. *Le Procès de Robert Brasillach*. Paris: Flammarion, 1946.

Jouhandeau, Marcel. *Journal sous l'occupation*. Paris: Gallimard, 1980.

Jourdain, Francis. *Né en 76*. Paris: Pavillons, 1951.

———. *Sans remords ni rancune*. Paris: Corrêa, 1953.

———. *Jours d'alarme*. Paris: Corrêa, 1954.

Jouvenel, Bertrand de. *Un voyageur dans le siècle*. Paris: Laffont, 1979.

Jünger, Ernst. *Journal*. 3 vols. Paris: Christian Bourgois, 1979–80.

Kanters, Robert. *A perte de vue*. Paris: Le Seuil, 1981.

Kessel, Joseph. *Les Enfants de la chance*. Paris: Gallimard, 1934.

Lacouture, Jean. *André Malraux, une vie dans le siècle*. Paris: Le Seuil, 1983. *Andre Malraux*, translated by Alan Sheridan. New York: Pantheon, 1975.

———. *Léon Blum*. Paris: Le Seuil, 1977.

———. *François Mauriac*. Paris: Le Seuil, 1980.

Laffont, Robert. *Editeur*. Paris: Laffont, 1974.

Lamy, Jean-Claude. *Pierre Lazareff à la une*. Paris: Stock, 1975.

Lang, André. *Pierre Brisson, le journaliste, l'écrivain, l'homme*. Paris: Calmann-Lévy, 1967.

Lannes, Roger. *Jean Cocteau*. Paris: Seghers, 1945.

Larbaud, Valery. *Journal 1912–1935*. Paris: Gallimard, 1955.

Laurent, Jacques. *Histoire égoïste*. Paris: La Table Ronde, 1976.

Léautaud, Paul. *Lettres à Marie Dormoy*. Paris: Albin Michel, 1966.

———. *Correspondance générale*. Paris: Flammarion, 1972.

———. *Journal littéraire*. 19 vols. Paris: Mercure de France, 1954–66.

Le Boterf, Hervé. *La Vie parisienne sous l'occupation*. Paris: France-Empire, 1975.

Lefèvre, Frédéric. *Une heure avec . . .* Paris: Gallimard, 1924, 1925, 1927, 1930.

Loiseaux, Gérard. *La Littérature de la défaite et de la collaboration*. Paris: Publications de la Sorbonne, 1984.

Lommel, Hermann. *Les Anciens Aryens*. Paris: Gallimard, 1943.

Lottman, Herbert R. *Albert Camus*. Paris: Le Seuil, 1978. *Camus* (in English). New York: Braziller, 1981.

————. *La Rive gauche*. Paris: Le Seuil, 1981, *The Left Bank: Writers, Artists and Politics from the Popular Front to the Cold War*. Boston: Houghton Mifflin, 1982.

McCarthy, Patrick. *Camus*. New York: Random House, 1982.

————. "Aspects de Pierre MacOrlan, 1882–1970." *Cahiers du C.E.R.C.L.E.*, no. 1. Paris: Université de Paris XII, 1984.

Mallac, Guy de. *Boris Pasternak, His Life and Art*. London: Souvenir Press, 1983.

Mann, Thomas. *Les Exigences du jour*. Paris: Grasset, 1976.

Martin, Claude. *La Nouvelle Revue Française 1919–1943*. Lyons: Université de Lyon II, 1975–77.

Martin du Gard, Maurice. *Les Mémorables I, II*. Paris: Flammarion, 1957, 1960.

————. *Les Libéraux de Renan à Chardonne*. Paris: Plon, 1967.

————. *La Chronique de Vichy 1940–1944*. Paris: Flammarion, 1975.

————. *Les Mémorables III*. Paris: Grasset, 1978.

Martin du Gard, Roger, & Copeau, Jacques. *Correspondance 1913–1949*. Paris: Gallimard, 1972.

Maurois, André. *Mémoires I, II*. New York: La Maison française, 1942.

Michel, Henri. *Paris allemand*. Paris: Albin Michel, 1981.

Milhaud, Darius. *Notes sans musique*. Paris: Julliard, 1949. *Notes without Music*. New York: Da Capo Press, 1970 (reprint of 1953 edition).

Monnier, Adrienne. *Les Gazettes d'Adrienne Monnier*. Paris: Julliard, 1953.

————. *Rue de l'Odéon*. Paris: Albin Michel, 1960.

Monnier, Pierre. *Ferdinand furieux*. Lausanne: L'Age d'Homme, 1979.

Montherlant, Henry de. *Textes sous une occupation 1940–1944*. Paris: Gallimard, 1953.

————. *L'Equinoxe de septembre, Le Solstice de juin, Mémoire*. Paris: Gallimard, 1976.

Morand, Paul. *Souvenirs de notre jeunesse*. Geneva, 1948.

————. *Journal d'un attaché d'ambassade 1916–1917*. Paris: Gallimard, 1963.

————. *Lettres à des amis et à quelques autres*. Paris: La Table ronde, 1978.

Morino, Lina. *La NRF dans l'histoire des lettres*. Paris: Gallimard, 1939.

Muller, Henry. *Trois pas en arrière*. Paris: La Table ronde, 1952.

————. *Six pas en arrière*. Paris: La Table ronde, 1954.

————. *Retours de mémoire*. Paris: Grasset, 1979.

Néret, Jean-Alexis. *Histoire illustrée de la librairie et du livre français*. Paris: Lamarre, 1953.

Nimier, Roger. *L'Elève d'Aristote*. Paris: Gallimard, 1981.

Novick, Peter. *The Resistance versus Vichy: The Purge of the Collaborators in Liberated France*. New York: Columbia University Press, 1968.

Ory, Pascal. *Les Collaborateurs 1940–1945*. Paris: Le Seuil, 1976.

Painter, George D. *Marcel Proust: A Biography*. 2 vols. New York: Random House, 1978.

Parain, Brice. *De fil en aiguille*. Paris: Gallimard, 1960.

————. *Entretiens avec Bernard Pingaud*. Paris: Gallimard, 1966.

Paris 1940–1944: la vie artistique . . . Dossiers du Clan, no. 2. Paris, May 1967.

Parrot, Louis. *L'Intelligence en guerre*. La Jeune Parque, 1945.

Paulhan, Jean. *Les Fleurs de Tarbes ou la Terreur dans les Lettres*. Paris: Gallimard, 1941.

————. *Mort de Groethuysen à Luxembourg*. Scholies-Fata Morgana, 1977.

———— and Aury, Dominique. *La patrie se fait tous les jours*. 1947.

Paxton, Robert O. *Vichy France: Old Guard and New Order, 1940–1944*. New York: Columbia University Press, 1982.

Pierre-Quint, Léon. *Proust et la stratégie littéraire*. Paris: Corrêa, 1954.

————. "Raymond Queneau." *Europe*, no. 650–51, June 1983.

Pivot, Bernard. *Les Critiques littéraires*. Paris: Flammarion, 1968.

Poulet, Robert. *Mon ami Bardamu*. Paris: Plon, 1971.

Proust, Marcel. *Correspondance, tome XI, 1912*. Paris: Plon, 1984.

Quéval, Jean. *Première page, cinquième colonne*. Paris: Fayard, 1945.

Rambures, Jean-Louis de. *Comment travaillent les écrivains*. Paris: Flammarion, 1978.

Rebatet, Lucien. *Les Décombres*. Paris: Denoël, 1942.

————. *Les Mémoires d'un fasciste II, 1941–1947*. Paris: Pauvert, 1976.

Riese, L. *Les Salons littéraires parisiens du Second Empire à nos jours*. Privat, 1962.

Rivière, Jacques. *Aimée*. Paris: Gallimard, 1923.

———. *Carnets 1914–1917*. Paris: Fayard, 1974.

——— and Fernandez, Ramon. *Moralisme et littérature*. Paris: Corrêa, 1932.

Robert, Louis de. *Comment débuta Marcel Proust*. Paris: Gallimard, 1969.

Rondeau, Daniel. *Trans Europ Express*. Paris: Le Seuil, 1984.

Roussin, André. *Rideau gris et habit vert*. Paris: Albin Michel, 1983.

Roy, Claude. *Moi je*. Paris: Gallimard, 1969.

———. *Nous*. Paris: Gallimard, 1972.

———. *Somme toute*. Paris: Gallimard, 1976.

Rypko Schub, Louise. *Léon-Paul Fargue*. Geneva: Droz, 1973.

Sachs, Maurice. *Au temps du Boeuf sur le toit*. Paris: Nouvelle Revue Critique, 1939.

———. *La Décade de l'illusion*. Paris: Gallimard, 1950.

———. *Le Sabbat*. Paris: Gallimard, 1950. *Witches' Sabbath*. Translated by Richard Howard. New York: Stein & Day, 1982.

Sadoul, Georges. *Aragon*. Paris: Seghers, 1967.

Saint-Exupéry, Antoine de. *Œuvres*. Paris: Pléiade/Gallimard, 1953.

Saint-Paulien. *Histoire de la collaboration*. Paris: L'Esprit nouveau, 1964.

Sairigné, Guillemette de. *L'Aventure du Livre de Poche*. Paris: Le Livre de Poche, 1983.

Salacrou, Armand. *La Salle des pas perdus I, II*. Paris: Gallimard, 1974, 1976.

Salmon, André. *Souvenirs sans fin II*. Paris: Gallimard, 1956.

Sartre, Jean-Paul. *Situations II: Qu'est-ce que la littérature?* Paris: Gallimard, 1948. *What Is Literature?* Translated by Bernard Frechtman, introduction by Wallace Fowlie. New York: Harper & Row, 1965; Magnolia, Mass.: Peter Smith, 1978.

———. *Lettres au Castor et à quelques autres 1940–1963*. Paris: Gallimard, 1983.

Schlumberger, Jean. *Eveils*. Paris: Gallimard, 1950.

Seghers, Pierre. *La Résistance et ses poètes 1940–1945*. Paris: Seghers, 1974.

Sérant, Paul. *Les Vaincus de la Libération*. Paris: Laffont, 1964.

Soupault, Philippe. *Mémoires de l'oubli 1914–1923*. Paris: Lachenal & Ritter, 1981.

Spiriot, Pierre. *Montherlant sans masque I*. Paris: Laffont, 1982.

Stéphane, Roger. *Toutes choses ont leurs saisons*. Paris: Fayard, 1979.

Sternhell, Zeev. *La Droite révolutionnaire 1885–1914 (Les Origines françaises du fascisme)*. Paris: Le Seuil, 1978.

————. *Ni droite ni gauche (l'idéologie fasciste en France)*. Paris: Le Seuil, 1983.

Stock, Pierre-Victor. *Mémorandum d'un éditeur*. 3 vols. Paris: Stock, Delamain & Boutelleau, 1935, 1936, 1938.

Thérive, André. *L'Envers du décor*. Paris: La Clé d'Or, 1948.

Thibaudet, Albert. *Panurge à la guerre*. Paris: Gallimard, 1940.

Toesca, Maurice. *Cinq ans de patience 1939–1945*. Paris: Emile-Paul frères, 1975.

Tual, Denise. *Le Temps dévoré*. Paris: Fayard, 1980.

Vailland, Elisabeth. *Drôle de vie*. Paris: Lattès, 1984.

Vandegans, André. *La Jeunesse littéraire d'André Malraux*. Paris: Pauvert, 1964.

Vandromme, Pol. *Lucien Rebatet*. Paris: Editions Universitaires, 1968.

van Rysselberghe, Maria. *Les Cahiers de la petite dame I–IV*. Paris: Gallimard, 1973–77.

Varillon, Pierre, and Rambaud, Henri. *Enquête sur les maîtres de la jeune littérature*. Paris: Bloud & Gay, 1923.

Vercors. *La Bataille du silence*. Paris: Presses de la Cité, 1967. *The Battle of Silence*. Translated by Rita Barisse. New York: Holt, 1969.

Vialatte, Alexandre. *Dernières Nouvelles de l'homme*. Paris: Julliard, 1978.

————. *Et c'est ainsi qu'Allah est grand*. Paris: Julliard, 1979.

Wilkinson, James D. *The Intellectual Resistance in Europe*. Cambridge, Mass., & London: Harvard University Press, 1981.

Winock, Michel. *Histoire politique de la revue Esprit 1930–1950*. Paris: Le Seuil, 1975.

Wiser, William. *The Crazy Years: Paris in the Twenties*. New York: Atheneum; London: Thames & Hudson, 1983.

Zeldin, Theodore. *France 1848–1945*. 5 vols. Oxford & New York: Oxford University Press, 1973–80.

Throughout the preparation of this volume, I have made constant use of the following references: vols. 10–16 of *Nouvelle Histoire de la France contemporaine (1871–1952)* (Paris: Le Seuil, 1973–1983); the Laffont-Bompiani *Dictionnaires des oeuvres et des auteurs* in the Collection Bouquins;

Who's Who; and the many bulletins published, for the delight of researchers, by the associations of friends of various writers, namely, Rivière and Fournier, Claudel, Gide, Giono, and Nimier.

I have also partly or wholly referred to the back issues of various publications:

Dailies: *France-Soir, Le Monde, La France libre, La Croix, Le Journal officiel, Le Figaro, Paris-Presse, L'Intransigeant, Combat, International Herald Tribune, Le Matin de Paris, The New York Times;*

Weeklies: *Le Magazine littéraire, Les Lettres françaises, Carrefour, Notre Combat, L'Union française, Le Pays libre, Réagir, L'Alerte, Le Cri du peuple, Le Nouvel Observateur, France-Observateur, The New York Times Book Review, The (London) Times Literary Supplement, L'Express, Le Point, Marianne, Candide, Gringoire, Comoedia, Je suis partout, Au pilori, Les Nouvelles littéraires, La Bibliographie de la France;*

Periodicals: *L'Histoire, Lire, La Nouvelle Revue Française, Cahiers franco-allemands, Revue d'histoire littéraire de la France, Le Lérot rêveur, La Revue des Deux Mondes, Arts, Les Cahiers du livre, La Revue musicale, La Revue juive, Les Cahiers de la Pléiade, Revue de la Table ronde, Lectures pour tous, La Quinzaine littéraire, Pavés de Paris, Les Cahiers du cinéma, Publisher's Weekly, L'Auto-journal, Les Temps modernes, Revue d'histoire de la Seconde Guerre mondiale, Europe, Les Cahiers de l'Energumène.*

Archives consulted: Bibliothèque Jacques Doucet, Bibliothèque nationale, Archives de Paris, Archives du Centre de Documentation juive contemporaine (CDJC), Greffe du tribunal de commerce, Lycée Condorcet, Archives de l'Institut de France, Archives nationales (files of the Propaganda Division, files of the Comité national interprofessionnel d'épuration), Institut d'Histoire du Temps Présent, Centre de Formation et de Perfectionnement des Journalistes, morgues of *France-Soir* and *L'Express,* Ministère des Relations extérieures.

Index

Index